CLASS TALK

CLASS TALK

COMMUNICATIONS UNBOUND

HELEN DAVITT

Peter Lang
Oxford • Bern • Berlin • Bruxelles • New York • Wien

Bibliographic information published by Die Deutsche Nationalbibliothek
Die Deutsche Nationalbibliothek lists this publication in the Deutsche
Nationalbibliografie; detailed bibliographic data is available on the Internet at
http://dnb.d-nb.de.

A catalogue record for this book is available from the British Library.

A CIP catalog record for this book has been applied for at the Library of Congress.

ISBN 978-1-78997-590-1 (print) • ISBN 978-1-78997-591-8 (ePDF)
ISBN 978-1-78997-592-5 (ePub) • ISBN 978-1-78997-593-2 (mobi)

Cover design by Helen Davitt for Peter Lang Ltd.
Cover photography by Helen Davitt
© Peter Lang Group AG 2020

Published by Peter Lang Ltd, International Academic Publishers,
52 St Giles, Oxford, OX1 3LU, United Kingdom
oxford@peterlang.com, www.peterlang.com

Helen Davitt has asserted her right under the Copyright, Designs and Patent Act,
1988, to be identified as Author of this Work.

All rights reserved.
All parts of this publication are protected by copyright.
Any utilisation outside the strict limits of the copyright law, without the permission
of the publisher, is forbidden and liable to prosecution.
This applies in particular to reproductions, translations, microfilming, and storage
and processing in electronic retrieval systems.

This publication has been peer reviewed.

Dedication

To those outstanding landmarks in the inner landscape, the memory of my ever compassionate, amazing mother, Bella; Hazel, compelling and sympathetic presence to family, friends, strangers; Josie, lodestar of empathy; Irmgard, holocaust refugee, miracle of benevolence.

To my cherished sister, Isabel, soul of fortitude and kindness, her beloved husband, Douglas, and their children, my precious niece and nephew, Miriam and Robin.

To life-long friends, David, Desrine, Jean, Marina, Morag, Nick, Rita, Rou, Val,

To stalwart friends who both challenge and sustain - they know who they are.

Helen H. J. Davitt
Hove, East Sussex

Contents

Acknowledgments   xi

Preface   xiii

CHAPTER 1
Power, Force and Social Class   1

CHAPTER 2
Competitive Production, Exploitation and Profiteering   9

CHAPTER 3
Usurious Banking and the Great Depression   15

CHAPTER 4
WWI, Fascism, WWII, the Cold War   27

CHAPTER 5
Post-WWII Western Economic Growth, Offshoring, Privatisation, Deregulation of Banking and Finance   35

CHAPTER 6
Twenty-first-century Resource Wars   41

CHAPTER 7
Bank Racketeering   55

CHAPTER 8
Big Technology, Agri-business, Big Pharma, Medical
Profiteering, Blockchain ... 67

CHAPTER 9
Trading Blocs ... 87

CHAPTER 10
Battles for Justice, Quest for Peace ... 91

CHAPTER 11
Propaganda ... 101

CHAPTER 12
The Socio-biological Nature of Language Acquisition ... 105

CHAPTER 13
The Socio-cultural Nature of Literacy Development ... 109

CHAPTER 14
Sociopathy of Defective Hypotheses ... 121

CHAPTER 15
Politics of Ego and Entitlement ... 143

CHAPTER 16
Housing in the UK ... 153

CHAPTER 17
Grenfell ... 159

Contents

CHAPTER 18
Charities and Foreign Aid — 167

CHAPTER 19
Educational Apartheid — 175

CHAPTER 20
English National Curriculum and Key Stage Testing — 191

CHAPTER 21
Pre-privatisation of State Schools — 201

CHAPTER 22
Parliamentary Monitoring of State Education — 209

CHAPTER 23
Educational Technology — 211

CHAPTER 24
Office for Standards in Education — 217

CHAPTER 25
Battle for Critical, Political and Multi-functional Literacy — 223

CHAPTER 26
Workplace Democracy — 229

CHAPTER 27
Democratisation of Mass Media — 235

CHAPTER 28
Education for Democratic Socialism … 247

CHAPTER 29
Into the Future … 261

CHAPTER 30
Signposts … 269

CHAPTER 31
Pandemic Politics … 291

Notes … 325

Bibliography … 331

Subject Index … 349

Acknowledgments

I am most grateful to Anthony Mason, Commissioning Editor at Peter Lang, and to the anonymous peer review reader who cut to the core of the mega –wordy first draft and recommended publication. Thanks to Michael Garvey, copy editor, to the ever polite and patient Production Manager, Jonathan Smith, and to new Production Manager, Sasireka Sakthi. Very many thanks also to the typographers and administrative staff, whose names I do not know.

Preface

Class Talk – Communications Unbound concurs with the Marxist analyses that under capitalist economic conditions, the dominating 'ideas of the ruling class are in every epoch the ruling ideas'. Many of today's books and media directed at the problems of the capitalist political economy sideline the central facts of that economy: the social-class division between the 99% majority and the 1% elite; that capitalism creates an exploited working-class majority; the majority is eventually left with no choice but to become the grave-diggers of capitalism.

In a nutshell, the mechanisms of the social class–based capitalist political economy dictate that in a 40-hour week, for example, a worker labours for 10 hours of those hours, let's say, to earn the necessities of life and pay for the material outlay of the capitalist owners of the means of production, finance and communications. The worker's remaining 30 hours of productive labour, codified by Marx as 'surplus value', is syphoned off by the bosses as profit for their company shareholders and directors. To reduce labour costs, capitalist competitors introduce machinery, and in chasing cheaper labour will also move production abroad. Capitalist corporations lobby politicians to get governments to deregulate banking and finance and decimate laws on health, safety and duties of care. To protect their profiteering, capitalist trading blocs, backed up by national governments, will also hike tariffs on imported goods, and, so long as price-fixing protects their overall profits, will also lower the prices of exported goods.

Marx thought trade unionism wasn't capable of mounting much more than local action to increase local wages. And it can be true that trade union success in one sector often leads capitalists to cut wages and jobs in another. According to Marx, the contentious social relations amongst workers, unionised or not, are generated by the inbuilt divisiveness of the capitalist means of production, finance and communications. Marx thought that those alienating relations also arose from the estrangements of workers from the natural environment.

According to Marx, the internationally united working class, the proletariat, finally analysing the exploitation of the whole of the working class across national boundaries, eventually organises itself as the greater political, economic and socio-cultural force. The organised working class then demands socialist economics and culture, inclusive of replacement of private property with public ownership, which is paid for and maintained by the now egalitarian proletariat-controlled means of production, finance and communications. In communist economics, production and consumption are geared to meeting people's needs, automation becoming the means by which people, freed from the burdens of work, can develop all their talents:

> In communist society, where nobody has one exclusive sphere of activity, but each can become accomplished in any branch he wishes, society regulates the general production and thus makes it possible for me to do one thing today and another tomorrow, to hunt in the morning, fish in the afternoon, rear cattle in the evening, criticise after dinner, just as I have a mind, without ever becoming hunter, fisherman, herdsman or critic. (Marx, *German Ideology*, 1845)

Italian Marxist political activist, Antonio Gramsci (1891–1937), imprisoned for his communist activism, wrote 30 densely packed notebooks about Italian and world history and culture in relation to Marxist theory, later published as *The Prison Notebooks*. Antonio Gramsci demonstrated that through ruling-class education systems, organised religion, belief in 'magic', folklore and the machinations of mass media, populations are coerced into consenting to the bogus separation of the interlocking hard and soft powers of the dominating capitalist political economy, militarism and war. Gramsci identified this interwoven propagandistic coercion as the capitalist hegemony. An essential tool for getting out from under the mystifications of that coercive hegemony is, according to Gramsci, autonomous education:

> The history of education shows that every class which has sought to take power has prepared itself for power by an autonomous education ... The problem of education is the most important class problem. (Cited in Davidson's (1977) *Antonio Gramsci: Towards an Intellectual Biography*. London: Merlin Press, p. 77. See 'Antonio Gramsci', Wikiquote)

Preface

Autonomous education doesn't mean studying without assistance. It also involves in-depth explorations of the subject being studied – cookery, politics or medicine, for instance. Autonomous, or self-emancipatory, education must also examine information that is both for and against whatever the proposition. It must also cross the borders of the routinely separated studies of the humanities, sciences, arts. Those principles of borderless consideration also hold for the development and applications of the sciences, humanities, arts, etc.

A crucial difference between autonomous education and academic learning is that in the study of history, for instance, the autonomous learner is obliged to acquire knowledge of a particular time and place *and* to cross the boundaries of the conventions of historical study. History can no longer be merely framed by the likes of timelines of major events that omit the overriding contexts of ruling-class force, power and domination. Further, since the answers discovered by the autonomous learner beg the next set of questions, there can, in any case, be no such thing as history divorced from the study of slavery, colonialism, neo-colonialism, sexism, racism *and* the persistent struggles of the poor and working-class majority against the powers and forces of domination.

Autonomous education inevitably counters the conventionally separated subjects of formal curricula and the orthodoxies of capitalist 'debate', both of which regularly treat the inter-related structures of the capitalist political economy as though they were separable phenomena. Homelessness and the housing crises are treated as though disconnected from the debt-based interest-bearing banking system; terrorism is divorced from foreign policy; crime is viewed as though the vast majority of those imprisoned had not been subjected to maleducation, impoverishments and the systemic boom and bust of capitalism's cycles of employment and unemployment, and so on.

Class Talk – Communications Unbound attempts to serve as a mini-sourcebook on the historical roots and prevailing contemporary features of the capitalist political economy. It also outlines the alternative of an economically viable, politically robust and socio-culturally inclusive democratic socialism fit for the twenty-first century and beyond.

In reviewing the matters under discussion, while some chapters go into more detail than others, the list of chapters in *Class Talk – Communications Unbound* is crucially indicative of the institutionally interwoven nature of the capitalist political economy, and, consequently, of the cross-curricular nature of the book. The inter-related approach attempts to both replicate how people tend to develop their knowledge and understanding of the wider world. That inter-related approach also links the conceptual, material, psychological and socio-cultural connections between subjects. For instance, Chapter 3 examines 'Usurious Banking and the Great Depression'; Chapter 12, 'The Socio-biological Nature of Language Acquisition'; Chapter 15, 'Politics of Ego and Entitlement'; Chapter 28, 'Education for Democratic Socialism'.

The title of the book refers to the poor and working-class majority's struggles for class consciousness against false consciousness. It signposts the discussions, debates, solidarity and organisational activism in which the poor and working-class majority must engage if societies are to be built and maintained for the common good. The *Class Talk* of the title also refers to the dominating talk and behaviours of those in temporary command and control, that is, the 1% politico-economic elite and the 20% of the middle class who also act as the capitalist managers and disciplinarians of the poor and working-class majority.

Twenty-first-century democratic socialism does not promote violent revolution, but depends instead on autonomously well-informed populations acting in solidarity to establish the democratic socialist political economy based on the principles of reverence for life, equal human rights and responsibilities, and the involvement of all citizens in devising the governing structures and maintaining their stewardship of the world they inhabit.

That's a tall order. Nevertheless, despite the brutalising efforts of the powers that be, exploitation, oppression and domination have always been inherently opposed in some manner or another. In this particular historical moment, though the outcomes are as yet far more murky than clear, and potentially very alarming, there are also signs of that resistance to power and domination is becoming more widespread, is more organised and is spreading.

For instance, in April 2019, the governors of Western central banks reinforced the message of the Extinction Rebellion campaign that unless governments act within the next 12 years to re-engineer the fossil fuel-based, capitalist political economy, the planet will enter a state of irretrievable decay.

Extinction Rebellion has three demands: that government tells the truth about the climate emergency; act to reduce greenhouse gas emissions to net-zero by 2025; and the establishment of a Citizens' Assembly to lead government's response to climate breakdown. Extinction Rebellion's direct action on London's bridges and main thoroughfares in April 2019, intended to focus public attention on climate breakdown and lead to meetings with government ministers, appears to have pushed the UK government to become the first government to officially declare a climate emergency on 1 May 2019 – though with a target of net-zero emissions by 2050. The co-founder of Extinction Rebellion, Rupert Read, plans to get 20,000 to 30,000 people on the streets over a longer period to press the government into stronger action (Ian Sinclair, 'We could get 20,000 or 30,000 people willing to take direct action on the streets', *Morning Star*, 25 June 2019).

From November 2018, the French Yellow Vest Movement of workers, an amalgam of socialists, anti-immigrant, anarchists and anti-EU protestors, have mounted weekly protests against the French government's privileging of the wealthy at the expense of the working-class majority.

Posing no immediate obstacle to capitalist production or social class relations, Extinction Rebellion's laudable attempts at strategic non-violence in their intermittent mass protests could result in outsourcing police brutality against those who conclude that the exploitative capitalist state must, ultimately, be also physically confronted. Extinction Rebellion gets an easier ride in the capitalist media than the Yellow Vest Movement, which disrupts business by blocking roads, roundabouts and oil depots and demands increased wages and pensions, taxes on the wealthy, government-funded public services, etc. ('The Yellow Vest Movement: Special documentary on France's "gilets jaunes" movement,' YouTube, euronews (in English), 17 December 2018; and 'Vanessa Beeley Interview – Yellow Vests, Police Violence and The Suppression of A Global Movement,' YouTube, 28 January 2019). How far the Yellow Vest Movement will go remains in question. Will the French government succeed in suppressing it? Will the Yellow Vests run out of steam? Or, after possibly acquiring a share of the capitalist pie, will the movement die and government revert to the 'yellow socialism' of the centrist politics that support the capitalist political economy ('Yellow Socialism', Wikipedia, 2019)?

Despite their considerable differences, Extinction Rebellion and the French Yellow Vests Movement have demands in common, for example, educational reform, a ban on the planned obsolescence of goods, on plastic bottles, on GM foods, carcinogenic pesticides and mass-mono-crop agriculture.

Raising what was for Marx the vexed question of the 'lumpenproletariat,' the usual labelling of the jobless as a 'feckless' underclass; or the likes of the UK convicts exported to Australia and known there as the 'intractables'; or referring to the US 2016 presidential election campaign dissenters as a 'basket of deplorables', and so on, this book defers to the inevitable cry of every human being for economically just and politically fair treatment, basic human rights that, through rational inference, must apply to all. Consequently, the qualities of democratic socialism this book supports means that *Class Talk – Communications Unbound* must inevitably opt for the building of a politico-economic democratic socialist home for all, one that requires citizens to engage in autonomous education and participate, as a matter of course, in the maintenance and development of that inclusive politico-economically, socio-culturally modern democratic socialist accommodation, the house rules of which are reverence for life, equal human rights and responsibilities for all.

Academic language seeks to usefully compress the complexities of already known concepts, but it can also butcher understanding. *Class Talk – Communications Unbound*, though unable to avoid all academic language, inclines instead towards more conversational language and tone.

So that readers can confirm and access additional information as they go along, or easily spot in-text references to look up later, quick fact-checking references are supplied in the body of the text. The endnotes refer to longer or more seminal works. The bibliography includes the endnote references and any necessary additional bibliographical details on in-text references.

Preface

Some of the quotes used have been in the public domain for over a century; many come from today's progressive activists.

The political, financial and corporate players currently in command and control are seldom mentioned by name. The aim is to highlight their politico-economic functions instead. Readers who want the full monty can check out the in-text references and endnotes for names.

As autonomous learners, readers must inevitably challenge the point of view presented in the book; take some responsibility for filling in the blanks in the evidence provided; and they are also obliged to examine the processes through which the writer, the authors of the referenced materials and they, the readers themselves, come to their political judgements and conclusions.

Autonomous learners are also obliged to reveal to themselves and others the existential realities of their politico-economic and socio-cultural circumstances, locally, nationally and globally, and to make transparent the principles upon which their worldview may – or may not – be founded.

CHAPTER 1

Power, Force and Social Class

Politico-economic and socio-cultural dominations of the populations are not relegated simply to military force but are daily exercised through the economic and political powers of the wealthy 1% elite (shorthand for around 0.7%) over the poor and working-class majority, the 99% – about 20% of whom align themselves with the powers and State institutions controlled by the 1% elite.

Besides profiteering from the conventional capitalist political economy, the wealthy elite transacts much of its business in tax-evading secret tax havens, known by some as Britain's Second Empire, where the wealth handlers, the accountants, bankers, financiers, lawyers, largely recruited from the UK's upper-class, private school old-boy network, charge huge fees for their services managing and investing around $21 trillion a year of the world's wealth. Tax haven activities involve market rigging; illegal arms trading; the setting-up of shell companies; illegal donations to political parties; fraudulent invoicing; contracts, kickbacks, bribery, money laundering, etc. The wealth handlers become very well-off ('The Spider's Web: Britain's Second Empire (Documentary)', YouTube, 4 September 2018).

The individuals using tax havens typically have $30 million in assets to play with, and the relationship between the wealthy and their wealth managers can be 40 years long, continuing into the next generation. Wealth handlers set up tax-avoiding 'legitimate' business across the globe for their clients, buy and sell assets, real estate, yachts, luxury goods, art, etc. (Brooke Harrington, 'How to hide it: inside the secret world of wealth managers', *The Guardian*, 21 September 2016).

Bearing no loyalty to nationality, race or religion, users of tax haven secrecy include the wealthiest families of poor countries who extract their country's wealth to invest their ill-gotten gains across the globe. In a process known as 'capital flight', they leave their impoverished populations without funds to develop the country's economy.

The International Consortium of Investigative Journalists' *Panama Papers* report exposed the global activities of one secret tax haven firm among thousands. An anonymous whistleblower leaked 11.5 million documents referring to 214,488 secret offshore business operations to the tune of billions of dollars, inclusive of the involvement of 12 current and former world leaders and 128 other public officials, politicians, celebrities, businessmen and wealthy individuals in over 200 countries intent on tax avoidance to the detriment of populations worldwide ('Panama Papers 2016', Wikipedia 2019). A second such leak resulted in the ICIJ's November 2017 *Paradise Papers* report. The ICIJ reports appeared simultaneously in newspapers across the globe. This news round-up of the financial jiggery-pokery of politicians and the rich and famous also revealed the goings-on of the Queen's Duchy of Lancaster investment arm that provides the monarch with around £20 million a year in unearned income. That unearned income is inclusive of the Queen's offshore tax haven investment in a chain of UK high-street furniture rental shops extracting high charges from poor people for the hire purchase of their living-room furniture. Prince Charles, through his Duchy of Cornwall investment arm, also uses tax havens to invest millions on which he receives unearned income. Watch *The Paradise Papers Investigation. The True Story Behind the Secret 9-Month Paradise Papers Investigation* (HBO, 13 November 2017). The father of the UK prime minister who stepped down from politics after losing the referendum to stay in the EU, and who had avoided testifying to the FAC about the debacle of the UK's involvement in the Libyan conflict under his watch, had millions in investments in offshore tax havens. The ex-prime minister's father declared UK assets worth around £2.5 million but had another £6.5 million in secret assets hidden in tax havens on which no death duty taxes would be levied either, meaning more inheritance for the already wealthy ex-prime minister and his already wealthy family.

Secret tax haven scams result in losses of $200 billion a year in tax revenue. The result for populations across the globe is job losses, cuts in funding for social welfare, State school systems, serious underfunding of healthcare, the withdrawal of child and elderly care, etc.

Thanks to whistleblowers and the ICIJ, the machinations of the secret tax havens can now be conveyed in a few irrefutable paragraphs. Nevertheless, in the jurisdictions where tax haven secrecy is practised, it's legal, and there is no effective UK legislation to prevent tax haven wealth being laundered into the UK economy. For millions, the phrase 'tax havens' can itself be obfuscatory in that it doesn't spell out the mafiosi-like economics involved, that people don't have the time or inclination to read the details, and newspapers don't come with headlines like 'How to Stop Greedy Secret Tax Profiteering Bastards Robbing People Blind'. Such an unlikely media event would, in any case, be ephemeral, here today, gone tomorrow, and having fewer total column inches than the three-day reportage of a royal birth in May 2019, and, before that, the screeds devoted to the engagement and marriage of the couple who then had that baby.

Western voters have the 'democratic' right to vote for a candidate about whom the voter is presumed to have the necessary information that deems the candidate fit for public office. An uninformed vote impinges on all citizens who stand to be negatively affected by the future actions of the candidate thus elected to office. How many UK citizens who voted for the MP who then became the current UK Secretary of State for Work and Pensions knew that they were voting for a member of parliament, who – briefly – had also been secretary of State for Energy and Climate Change; was also – briefly – Secretary of State for the Home Office, to which was added Secretary for Women and Equalities, a post from which the secretary had to resign over the *Windrush* scandal, that is, the gross inequality of the denial of National Health Service Care, passports, and employment for UK citizens of Caribbean origin? How many voters knew that this same privately educated secretary of State, father a stockbroker, was formerly a mainstream investment banker who then subsequently worked for a firm based in a secret offshore tax haven? In the political campaign materials used to persuade citizens to vote for this politician to be a member of parliament, the candidate's tax haven employment history was not divulged. It was revealed instead in leaked data related to around 175,00 offshore companies, one of which was registered in the Bahamas (Dave Pegg and Holly Watt, 'Leaks reveal Amber Rudd's involvement in Bahamas offshore firms,' *The Guardian*, 21 September 2016). In the swing-seat constituency to which the Secretary of State was elected, though the Green Party honourably stood down in favour of Labour, this prospective MP and future minister, backed by the wealthy, attained 46.9% of the vote in a 70% turnout, winning by a slim majority of 346 votes.

Where is the election legislation that requires transparency of the constituency candidate's work history? If there was UK legislation requiring all citizens to vote, and if the missing 30% of eligible voters in that constituency had turned out to vote, would that minister have won a parliamentary seat? How democratically 'fair' is it that this minister is currently in charge of the 'welfare' system that sees hundreds of thousands of poor people unable to pay their rent and buy food? This same minister is also charged with 'repairing' the bodged Universal Credit System that sees impoverished and disabled citizens having to wait intolerable weeks for the money to pay rent and buy the necessities of life. The minister, seen by many as a future leader of the Conservative Party, is likely to stand in a safer parliamentary constituency next time. Or, in this Age of Information, has this minister been so found out that this politician will opt for a less onerous, more lucrative, career?

For ordinary people caught up In the inevitable helter-skelter of holding onto a job; paying the bills; looking after families and loved ones, such crucial political and economic facts underpinning their daily lived experiences can slip easily from view; become deliberately distorted; remain as though hidden in plain sight – something to be looked into later when there's more time.

Millions of ordinary people are also likely to be swayed by the upper and middle-class tenets of individualism and the notion that the upper and middle-classes are best equipped to manage the economic and political life of the nation. Populations are thus left in states false consciousness, uncertainties and false certainties that, according to Gramsci, leads to the morbidity of political crisis:

> The crisis consists precisely in the fact that the old is dying and the new cannot be born; in this interregnum, a great variety of morbid symptoms appear. (Gilbert Achcar, 'Morbid Symptoms – What did Gramsci mean and how does it relate to our time?', *International Socialist Review*, May 2019)

Gramsci believed all human beings are innately intellectual; that the political, economic and socio-cultural understandings of the working class exceed that of the other capitalist classes; that traditional bourgeoise intellectuals don't know about those connections in the same way; nor do they grasp the intrinsic intellectual nature of all human beings. According to Gramsci, democratic socialism requires leadership by professional revolutionary intellectuals 'organically' related to and arising from the working-class majority. Though his concept of 'organic' intellectual revolutionary leaders is qualitatively somewhat different from that of apparatchiks working for a revolutionary political vanguard, the question remains as to how the actions of professional revolutionary intellectuals differ in practice from the political vanguardism that declares that a revolutionary elite must lead the majority?

Here's the good news: despite the divide-and-conquer machinations of mass media, the failure of State education to render youngsters politically and economically literate, millions more people in this Age of Information can now gain access to the realities behind the dominating narratives of the global government–corporate–banking–educational–communications complex.

That complex works to portray socio-political phenomena as the 'hard facts' of an inescapable and unchangeable 'human nature'. One such 'hard fact' is that tens of thousands of UK pupils continue to leave State schools each year without the levels of literacy to enable them to fully understand the instructions on a packet of aspirins. It is not a 'fact', however, as is implied by the government-media complex, that compared to their more literate and numerate European cousins, UK children are cognitively deficient, intellectually lazy and deliberately feckless. Instead of resigning themselves to the 'blame the victim' opinions of government and media pundits, people can now discover for themselves the reasons why 16% of the UK population, 5.2 million people, the great majority of whom have had the 'benefit' of 11 years of State schooling, suffer from the educational neglect that leads to them leaving school functionally illiterate and innumerate. (For more details, see Chapters 12 and 13 on the sociobiological of language acquisition and the socio-cultural nature of the development of literacy.)

The propaganda of modern mainstream media works less through crude brainwashing and more through the sophistry of partially informing while diverting media consumers from fundamental politico-economic realities. The following paragraphs are offered as an example of how that 'informative diversion' works.

Recent UK media reports on the wildfires in faraway Borneo reported that those fires killed 19 people, caused respiratory problems in over 500,000, and are likely to lead to the early deaths of 100,000 people. Newspaper reports attributed those wildfires to the El Niño weather effect and dry peaty soil conditions. Some reports also reported that some fires had also been deliberately set to burn the remaining undergrowth from huge swathes of natural forest being cleared for the planting of acres of palm oil trees.

Providing a patchwork of different information, most reporting focused on the tragedy of the fires, with little said about the politico-economic causes of those fires. 85% of palm tree oil comes from plantations mainly owned and operated by agri-corporations; some from plantations owned and operated by small landowners, and from a few plantations nationalised by the Malaysian government.

A locally milled export commodity of the poor Global South, palm tree oil is exported to the wealthy Global North to be used as an ingredient in an enormous amount of consumer goods from chocolate to instant noodles, lipstick to plastics to detergent, etc.

The IMF has extended loans for the production of palm tree oil for export. Land for plantations has also been grabbed from indigenous groups, and palm oil tree plantations are dependent on immigrant forced labour (Jason Mollagh, 'Palm oil for the West, Exploitation for Young Workers in Malaysia', *The Atlantic*, 9 April 2013).

The UK 2003 Communications Act and the Broadcasting Code for Advertising Practice (BCAP) prohibits ads and paid-for newspaper content on issues of public concern that are judged 'political'. The 18 August 2018 weekend magazine supplement of a UK newspaper with a middle-class readership of around 681,000 included a four-page spread of text and photographs on Borneo, an 'infomercial' paid for by a non-governmental environmental campaigning agency that operates in 55 countries. That paid-for content revealed the deforestation caused by agri-businesses engaging in the 'dirty' and 'lucrative' palm oil tree agri-business that causes 'loss of habitat' for orangutans in particular. Readers are entreated to sign a petition asking big companies to stop using 'dirty palm oil' as an ingredient in their products.

That paid-for newspaper content didn't mention that palm tree oil has for decades been used as a substitute for the trans fats that are more harmful to human health; that the Malaysian economy is highly dependent on palm tree oil production; that palm tree oil is not good for the heart; and that it's a common ingredient in the calorie-rich foods that help cause the Western obesity epidemic – and not once do the words 'capitalism' and 'profiteering' appear in that paid-for newspaper content. Nor is there a word about agri-forestry, i.e the combining of agriculture and tree planting on farms that produces healthier soil and higher yields and supports bio-diversity.

Greenpeace International also produced an animated short video, 'Ran-tan: the story of dirty palm oil', with viewers again invited to sign a petition against the production of palm oil. The Iceland supermarket chain wanted to use this video as its Christmas advertising because 'It would have blown the John Lewis ad out of the window. It was so emotional'. Iceland was prevented from doing so because as an ad the video was judged as being political.

The above is an example of how the mass-media and advertising industry selects what facts it will pass on, withhold and distort. UK consumers are left in the position of not being able to easily acquire the comprehensive information that might enable them to say yes or no to products containing palm oil; no to the intents of the eugenicist perspective that works to 'save nature' at the expense of populations; no to environmentalism and green politics that diverts attention away from the transitory relief, and overarching harm, that capitalism brings to billions of people.

The environmental crises caused by palm tree oil production, a complicated phenomenon, is never so complex that it could not be resolved by the national and international upholding of land and labour rights and fair trade agreements that slash the profiteering of the wealthy middlemen of the Global North and South.

This chapter has briefly tried to show there's more to power, dominance and force than out-and-out militarisms, and how, for example, the government–corporate–media complex and State education systems can constitute force by another name.

This chapter also intimates that, despite positives in a leadership of organic intellectuals, all citizens have a civic duty to put their innate human intelligence at the service of the good of the majority, that is, the poor and working classes at home and abroad.

CHAPTER 2

Competitive Production, Exploitation and Profiteering

No political economy comes into being on the whim of any supernatural power, or by the diktats of a purportedly unalterable 'human nature'. Political economies are created by people acting within, and contributing to, specific economic and political conditions.

The essential characteristic of capitalism is its integral competitiveness whereby the owners and operators of businesses must crush their competitors, leading in turn to factory automation, robotisation, mass agri-business monoculture, the digitisation of information and communications, and the uses of artificial intelligence. No matter the sophistication of that artificial intelligence, no one should be persuaded that it ever could or should replace humanity. Nor should anyone for one moment ever forget there's no such thing as a human robot.

Historically, the aristocracy paid for private tutors to educate their offspring, subsequently paying for the schooling of the many clever but poorer boys needed to be administrators in the growing capitalist political economy. That 'public' school system morphed into the private day and boarding schools to which the wealthy then sent their male offspring, bursaries offered to those other poor but clever boys. Thus were the children of the elite educated to be the managers of the capitalist political economy, its industries, the church, the navy, the military, the legal system, etc.

The reality behind such phrases as 'the industrial revolution' was that hundreds of thousands of miners working in life-threatening conditions in the privately owned coal mines hewed out by hand the millions of tonnes of coal required to fuel the privately owned capitalist factories, railways, etc. Poor women and boys and girls as young as 9 years old hauled the coal wagons from the coal face to the surface for a pittance.

Capitalism's owners of the means of production, finance and communications set wages as low as ordinary workers can bear, with skilled workers paid more for the skill value they add to capitalist production. The price of goods and services are set as high as buyers will pay, or at the rate that keeps the capitalist owners of the means of production in profit and control. Wages allow the millions of low-paid workers to buy the necessities of life, with some left over for whatever makes workers' lives bearable, booze, tobacco, sport, etc. The managers and administrators are paid enough to enable them to buy the more the costly consumer goods of their choice.

Early capitalist production of the vastly increasing variety of new goods and services needed skilled and unskilled labourers, factory hands, construction workers, carpenters, plumbers, glaziers, teachers, scientists, designers, architects, technicians; travelling salesmen, delivery drivers, warehousemen, entertainers, etc. Capitalists also needed inventors, financiers and stockbrokers. The burgeoning numbers of hotels, restaurants, coffee shops, pubs, etc., needed chambermaids, cooks, waiters, bar staff, and so on. To the millions of workers who previously had no choice but to live in rural or urban poverty, new opportunities to make a living in the burgeoning capitalist employment market opened up previously unimagined possibilities.

Many people at home and abroad were able to set up new businesses and partnerships. The cities of the UK, built to receive raw materials from colonies abroad and to ship products made from those raw materials, became the bustling metropolises of capitalism.

Later, State school systems would educate the millions who were needed as capitalism's middle managers and would train ordinary workers and the reserve army of the unemployed to the level the capitalists required. Social identity was no longer related to occupation, for example, blacksmith, farmer, cook but was defined instead by the divisions of social class: the aristocratic ruling class, the upper capitalist mercantile class, the middle class, the working classes, the unemployed.

Western colonisers used unpaid or slave-waged indigenous labourers to develop the ports and build the roads and railways required to get the raw materials from the interior of the colonised countries onto the ships bound for the West. In the Indian subcontinent, the British colonisers, few compared to the population of a huge country, trained an indigenous civil service to administer the colony and exert control over the rest of the population.

To produce the raw materials coveted by the capitalists, from gold to iron ore, minerals, hides, silks, spices, etc., capitalist businesses used the people of the South as even cheaper labour than their Northern cousins. In the factories of the North, the raw materials were turned into manufactured goods to be sold to other countries, including the countries of the impoverished South.

Living conditions in the Global North rose considerably, while to this day, the fragile neo-colonial economies of the Global South continue to be exploited, suppressed and impoverished. The Third World 'out of sight, out of mind' impoverishment is too seldom revealed, except in TV advertisements asking the public for donations to help Third World populations living in rural impoverishment where there's no money to pay for water utility systems to provide children with clean water to drink.

In the West meanwhile, via taxation and profitable investment by private capitalist companies, governments organised the building of roads, canals, sewerage, waterworks, railways, shipping, etc., with immense profits made from charging millions of paying customers for such services. Later, many also bought their household goods, indeed their clothes, on the never-never from the rentier-owned warehouses selling goods on hire purchase.

With a finger in every profiteering pie, from manufacturing to insurance, etc., the largest businesses became the massive conglomerate corporations that in conjunction with that 1% of the interconnected global elite and their military forces now rule today's world.

From the end of WWII until the mid-1970s, the managerial middle-class and working class in the Western democracies had steady employment and the safety net of public services. During those 35 years, living standards for those who flourished under capitalism went sky high. In the UK, working-class wages were substantial enough for people to buy expensive goods and cars, sometimes their homes, though the majority of the working classes continued to occupy private rented accommodation and social housing. Those boom times for the West lasted until the colonised countries began to assert themselves. At the same time, the banking and corporate world looked to banking and finance deregulation to enable them to expand their profiteering operations at home and abroad. In the Global South, living conditions also improved markedly for many. For most people in most Third World countries, however, impoverishment was still the name of the game.

From the early 1800s, it was known that modern mass mono-crop agriculture reduced biodiversity, altered natural water courses, and affected climates. From the mid-1800s, it was also known that the burning of fossil fuels trapped pollution and gasses in the atmosphere and created the greenhouse effect of affecting the earth's climate. After decades of obfuscation, it's only within the last 40 years or so that it has become more commonly known that mass monocultural agri-business and the excessive burning of fossil fuels in the Western countries in particular endangered plant, animal and human life across the globe.

Today, unable to make a living in drought-torn countries and caught up in capitalist resource wars, populations in the Global South flee those countries, some 50 million people migrating across the globe in search of a living. The United Nations High Commission for Refugees 2015 Report states that:

> We are witnessing a paradigm change, an unchecked slide into an era in which the scale of global forced displacement as well as the response required is now clearly dwarfing anything seen before. (UNHCR, 18 June 2015)

In the Central American client states of US corporate rule, where governments are weak and corrupt, there is mass unemployment, crime, drug dealing, the breakdown of law and order; in Honduras, for instance, there are up 50 murders a day. This state of affairs and the climate change that caused two years of drought in a row, making it impossible for farmers to grow food, led to hundreds of thousands of people fleeing Central Amerian countries. In October 2018, 7,000 individuals and families with children, walking together in caravan for safety, left Guatemala, El Salvador and Hondorus, heading for Mexico and the US border. The majority of the migrants in that particular caravan – there were, and are, many others – were expected to end up living in Mexico, with about 1,400 reaching the US border where they intended to claim asylum legally, as per US law.

The two major US political parties, both funded by the wealthy, have at various times supported the building of a wall on the Southern borders to prevent migrants from crossing into the US. In the run-up to the US November mid-term elections, the chauvinist, racist billionaire US president, about to face charges over decades of corrupt business practices and income tax fraud, hyped up the anti-immigrant fears of his political base, declaring that this particular caravan, which he named an 'invasion' of drug addicts, criminals and terrorists, would be prevented by armed US troops from crossing the border. Should those migrants as much as throw a stone in retaliation against inhuman treatment, such as the practice of separating the migrants from their children, they could expect bullets in return. The same president is also an anti-establishment politician who has in the past threatened to expose the shadow government of Deep State operatives he believes, as do millions of other US citizens, engineered the US 9/11 destruction of the World Trade Centre buildings and Building 7 as a false flag inside job.

A white working-class woman, herself a descendant of immigrants, as is the president, when interviewed at one of the president's political rallies declared that she supported the president, his political party and his stance against immigrants, because 'He's a smart businessman', was doing 'great things' for the country, and she didn't see why the US authorities should let anybody into the country without a passport. Believing she was doing her civic duty by attending that circus of a rally, and doubtless kind to family, friends and neighbours, it did not appear to occur to her that should some hapless US soldier shoot one of those desperate migrants, the bullet also has her name on it.

In response to the furore caused by his remarks about using armed forces against unarmed immigrants, the president declared his 'Make America Great Again' policy of reducing taxes for corporations and the wealthy meant the US economy was booming. The president appeared not to understand the instability behind that temporary spike in economic growth in some areas of the US, the devastation and poverty in other parts of the US. He claimed the US population of 322 million had 'never had it so good'. He further declared that although the US now needed more immigrants to support the supposedly growing economy, they must come into the country legally.

This chapter has briefly signposted the prevailing tenets of the capitalist political economy through which exploitative profiteering created great wealth for the few; syphoned up profits into the pockets of the owners of the means of production and their shareholders; created a growing middle class, leaving ordinary workers dependent on the trickling-down of the wages allowing them to purchase the necessities of life.

This chapter also intimates that the division of populations into social classes also severely affects social psychology and social relationships between people, as established by the founder of the academic discipline of sociology, Émile Durkheim (1857–1917), who by extrapolating verifiable 'social facts' from statistical data showed, for example, that crime and suicide were related to states of alienation and anomie, and that those states arose largely from the capitalist political hegemony.

If the good news is that governments, banks and corporations are now possibly beginning to attempt to legislate to avert the atrocity of ecocide and bring a fair and just political economy into being, the next question must be why billions of human beings across the generations have been forced to suffer exploitation, poverty, ill health, early death, the tragedy and awful pity of needless capitalist wars?

CHAPTER 3

Usurious Banking and the Great Depression

Endemic to capitalist corporatist and banking competitiveness are its inbuilt cycles of unstable economic 'boom and bust'. Booms, or the good times, occur when businesses increase employment to produce an abundance of saleable goods and services and pay workers sufficient wages to buy those goods and services. Busts can occur when businesses overproduce and set prices too high for people to pay, leading to a decline in prices and profits, the firing of workers, the ripple effect causing local recessions or an economic depression throughout the global economy. The capitalist speculators and shareholders hoard their wealth, cash in their shares and put their money into safer investments, for example, in property, gold, art, etc.

Commerce, as the fair exchange of goods and services, is essential to life. So too is the entrepreneurship of joint venturers seeking reasonable profit and taking the risk of possible loss – which is in contrast with usury and the accumulation of money through the prior ownership of surplus money lent out at interest to acquire unearned income.

Though the Bible forbids the lending of money at interest to family and fellow religionists, it permits extending credit at interest to strangers. Today's Islam still forbids usury – and also looks for ways of allowing usury by another name.

When a business fails under the principles of 'free-market' capitalism, the government does not normally intervene to prop up the enterprise with taxpayers' money. The business falls, and another entrepreneur enters the market instead in hopes of more successfully producing goods and services.

If morality means people exercising the ethical responsibility to look after and assist one another in support of the survival and thriving of individuals and the human collective, then since it's based on usury, exploitation and profiteering at the expense of the survival and thriving of others, 'free-market' capitalism can't be said to be moral.

A quick tour of banking history tells us that from around 2000 BC, bankers from Assyria and Greece to India and China were in the business of creating interest-bearing debt. The rise of the global capitalist banking system is attributed to fourteenth-century bankers in the prosperous Italian cities of Florence, Venice and Genoa, who are credited with inventing the fractional reserve banking system that continues to be used by today's central government banks and the related private banking empires.

For a fee, the medieval bankers offered to store in their vaults for safekeeping the jewellery, precious objects and surplus gold owned by the wealthy. The bankers issued promissory notes that guaranteed that the wealthy could get their gold back any time they wanted, just by surrendering the promissory note. Bankers and financiers also lent notes out at interest to entrepreneurs who came up with a profitable business plan and pledged property as loan collateral. Since the owners of the gold didn't all want their precious metal back at the same time, the bankers took to lending out more promissory notes than they had gold in their banks, or pledged collateral, to cover the value of those promissory bank notes. The worth of the bank notes, money, was thus guaranteed partly by the gold held in 'fractional' reserve by the bankers; partly by the bankers' promises to pay on demand; and by people's agreement that the notes were a trustworthy means of exchange in the trading of goods and services.

A rare metal, difficult to get at and accumulate, gold is valued because there is a limited amount of it, and because people agree on its worth. The banknotes issued against the gold became fungible common currency, that is, the notes were issued in varying values, for example, £20, £10, £5, £1, the coins representing a portion of the £1 banknote, which meant that instead of the problems of exchanging material goods and services, money, as notes and coins, could be used as a means of exchange for a whole variety of goods and services, large and small. The seller decided on the selling price; the buyer decided whether the goods and services represented enough value for him/her to hand over the money.

The early bankers, financiers and investors, using their unearned shareholder income for which they had no immediate use, also created the stock markets. The value of the stock share certificates was initially aligned with the stock, that is, the commodities, being traded, for example, coal, wool, mineral ores, slaves, etc. The new market in shares offered investors greater flexibility and shorter-term profits than does the running of a business or factory, for instance, or the purchase, upkeep and rental of real estate property. The stock market also enables investors to avoid the risks taken by the owners of the companies that traded whatever the stock was. If one company in the investor's portfolio of shares fails, the dividends from the shares in the other companies more or less guarantee that the shareholder will be in profit from the unearned income received through the ownership of the other stocks and shares. In essence, the investors, including the banks and royalty, profiteered off the backs of the workers who did the extracting, transporting, refining, manufacturing and physical trading of whatever the stock was. Nowadays those processes are done less by physical labour, more by machines, though it is often forgotten that those machines have been produced, purchased, are, and will be used, at the expense of the labour of millions of people, past and present and future.

Over time, most companies were no longer owned by families or business partners producing and trading goods, but by the corporate shareholders, with the corporations themselves often owned by huge conglomerates consisting of a number of other corporations, linked not necessarily by a particular industry but by financial ownership of diverse businesses.

'Blue-chip' stocks are the most valued shares of the most well-tried and powerful corporations that have global markets for their brand of goods and are expected not to fail. Government bonds issued by the UK government, for instance, are known as 'gilts', are not as valuable as blue-chip stocks, but since governments have the option of raising taxes to cover any losses, government bonds are regarded as a safe bet. At the maturity date of the bond, the government pays the bondholder the initial face value of the bond. In the interim, the total amount of the dividend cheques sent out quarterly to bondholders is ginormous. Government and corporate bonds can also be traded on the stock market, their stock market valuation going up or down.

Though stock market shares also represent the value of the actual stock, commodity or services produced, the share value is more related to fluctuating prices of the shares as gambled on the stock market, the shares gaining and losing value. The shareholder aims to earn considerable amounts of money in quarterly, six-monthly, yearly dividends and to sell the shares at a higher price than the purchase price. Even though share prices are inflated compared to the worth of the commodities and services being traded and though only around 5% of people own stock market shares, stock markets reveal how the affluent are choosing to invest their wealth, so investors and countries keep a close eye on the stock market share prices.

In 1971 the US government legislated to forbid the US Federal Reserve bank from exchanging bank notes for gold. Thus the dollar was 'freed' from the value of the gold allegedly backing it. The value of the US dollar is tied to the Gross Domestic Product of the US, that is, to the value of the goods and services that all its industries and services produce. The US Federal Reserve, an independent entity from the US government, though with rules and regulations that make it also accountable to government, continues to issue the most valued promissory note in the world, the US dollar, which is also backed up by the enormous military reach of the US which acts to also control economies and markets. As long as the industrial world's most essential commodity, oil, continues to be traded in US dollars, the US dollar is likely to continue to be the world's reserve currency. The Federal Reserve, and all banks, continue to operate a fractional reserve system, that is, the money in bank deposits, assets in shares, property, etc., held by the bank is a fraction, usually around 10%, of the assets needed to cover the debt-based, interest-bearing contracts executed by the bankers. Much of banks' ledger-based assets create money from nothing, that is, by the banks creating a bank ledger entry onto its accounting system.

Modern money, created as legal tender by the banking-government complex, and issued without corresponding value in assets is called 'fiat' money, printed and issued by government and based on whatever bankers decide is its value. In charging interest on fiat money, plus a fee for advancing a bank loan, plus an administration charge to cover the costs of drawing up the contract that legally enables the banker to take possession of the goods and property signed over as collateral if the debtor fails to pay back the loan, the bankers are onto a sure winner.

Today, bank assets purportedly supporting the financial capabilities of banks to lend money are likely to be government bonds, stock market investments; real estate mortgages; whatever collateral backing up other bank loans; customers' current and savings accounts, and, most of all, billions in interest-bearing debt in such as car loans, student loans, and massive credit card debt. The greatest assets of the banks are indebted companies, small businesses, and tens of millions of indebted citizens.

Since companies, businesses and corporations operate under laws of limited public liability, when these businesses fail, banks included, they have limited legal responsibility towards employees, shareholders and bank depositors. There is also a lucrative market in the selling of public liability insurance, allowing companies to safeguard their risks even against the low levels of public liability.

Shaped by interest-bearing indebtedness, fuelled by competitive profiteering and the adversarial trade and foreign policies that go along with profiteering, in order to capture and dominate markets, capitalist banks, businesses and corporations must continue to outperform and crush their competitors. When trade 'agreements' and backscratching diplomatic negotiations don't work, the outcome is war – not least because war is a massive business opportunity for transnational banks, corporations and investors. Financiers seek war profits by lending money to opposing nations to conduct those wars. Feeble laws against 'trading with the enemy' notwithstanding, the corporations rush to manufacture and sell war goods to all and sundry. The purpose of lending to opposing sides is firstly to increase the lenders' war profiteering, secondly to ensure that should the outcome of war not go as expected by the various banker–government alliances, the financiers have a foot in the door of both the winning and losing economies.

Towards the end of WWII, US war economy spending was at $908 billion. In peace, by 1947, it had reduced to £141 billion (Andrew Feinstein, *Shadow World, Inside the Global Arms Trade*, London: Penguin, 2011, p. 238). Global war spending was ratcheted up again by the US–Russian armaments race and by capitalist and communist sponsorship of the 'cold war'.

Awarded top military honours, US Major General Smedley Butler (1881–1940) said that after a lifetime of taking and giving orders, in retirement, when he began to think for himself, he discovered the secretive and massive enterprise of profiteering from war and only then did he understand that all of his working life he'd functioned as an armed racketeer for international capitalism – a racket being:

something that is not what it seems to the majority of people. Only a small inside group knows what it is about. It is conducted for the benefit of the very few at the expense of the masses. ('Smedley Butler (1881–1940)', Speech 1933, Wikiquote, 2019)

The apex of today's private global banking system was, and remains, the Bank for International Settlements (BIS) in Basel, Switzerland. Established in the 1930s by US and European private central bankers, the aim of the BIS was, and is, to coordinate the mechanisms of the world's 60 main national central banks. The ties of the central banks to governments notwithstanding, they are private banks owned by shareholders. The BIS aims to promote global capitalist economic growth and operate as a bulwark against the development of a communist political economy.[1]

To fund the Nazis, the BIS facilitated arrangements between US, UK and European banks, financiers and the transnational corporations.[2] The BIS private banking cartel also funnelled money to the Russian Bolsheviks to assist them in the removal of the Russian Tsarist government, the aim being for the global private banking–corporate matrix to replace the Russian State-controlled banking system with a private central bank, enabling greater control of the country's wealth, raw materials, and population.

The relationship between the central banks, the other banks, the control of money, debt, and profiteering from war has a long history. Here is what some of history's movers and shakers have to say about that relationship.[3]

> When a government is dependent upon bankers for money, they and not the leaders of the government control the situation, since the hand that gives is above the hand that takes ... Money has no motherland; financiers are without patriotism and without decency; their sole object is gain. (Napoleon Bonaparte, 1769–1821. Previously a fellow traveller of the international bankers, Bonaparte turned against them in the last years of his rule)

> Bankers own the earth; take it away from them but leave them with the power to create credit; and, with a flick of a pen, they will create enough money to buy it back again ... If you want to be slaves of bankers and pay the cost of your own slavery, then let the bankers control money and control credit. (Sir Josiah Stamp, Director, Bank of England, 1940)

Usurious Banking and the Great Depression

> It is well enough that people of the nation do not understand our banking and money system, for if they did, I believe there would be a revolution before tomorrow morning. (Henry Ford, Ford Motor Company)

In the 1920s, the robber barons and corporatists clawing their way to the top of the US capitalist economic pile promulgated the unregulated roaring twenties economic boom that pre-dated the Wall Street Crash and Great Depression of the 1930s that was, in turn, the precursor to WWII. Sparked by the minimally regulated economic activities of private bankers, by commercial and agricultural mismanagement and overproduction and unsustainable financial and stock market speculation, the Great Depression was exacerbated by a government lacking the national will and political structures required to conduct comprehensive economic analyses and apply effective interventions.

Instead, there was massive lending by private banks to stock market speculators, many of whom were ordinary middle-class people with very little in the way of assets who believed the 'dead cert' way to wealth was through short-term ownership of shares they could sell at a profit. In extending interest-bearing debt/credit for stock market speculation, the banks created an unsustainable stock market bubble. Prices rose well beyond the value of the businesses the shares were supposed to represent. When speculators could no longer afford to buy the shares, and share prices began to drop, the banks attempted to call in the loans they'd made to the speculators. The speculators rushed to sell their shares, lowering the share prices even more. People with savings deposits queued to get their money out of the now heavily indebted banks, causing many banks that had lent out far more than the worth of the assets they held to go bust and close their doors. The banks that managed to survive cut back on lending, which put existing companies out of business and cut the investments needed to start new businesses.

When the other private banks don't have enough funds to lend to each other, the private US Federal Reserve Bank is the lender of last resort to the other banks. Instead of expanding the money supply to shore up the banking system during the world banking crisis of 1929–39, the Fed contracted the money supply, thus contributing significantly to the 1930s banking crash and the terrible impoverishments of the global Great Depression that followed.

> The Federal Reserve definitely caused the Great Depression by contracting Americas' money supply by one third between 1929 and 1933. (Milton Friedman, Nobel Prize-winning economist, Stanford University)

Employment plummeted, people couldn't pay the rent, were evicted, and had no money to obtain the necessities of life. Around 2 million people ended up living in tent cities or eked out a living by begging and getting their food from the soup kitchens run by churches, charities and volunteers, and later by the federal government.[4]

Intertwined globally with other banks, other stock markets, and other economies, the US financial crash was global. Millions of people around the world lost their savings, their houses, jobs and any means of earning a livelihood. The wealthy and the surviving private bankers then bought up the stocks and shares at the lower prices, later selling them at a profit when prices rose.

In 1966, the 1964 Nobel Peace laureate Martin Luther King confided to his staff:

> this means that we are treading in difficult water, because it really means that we are saying that something is wrong with capitalism. There must be a better distribution of wealth, and maybe America must move toward a democratic socialism. ('Martin Luther King Was A Democratic Socialist', *Huffington Post*, 2017)

Coming early or late to the logic of democratic socialism, those prominent individuals brave enough to call for socialist unity have come up against the viciousness of capitalist dominance and force. In the Berlin of 1919, Socialist activists Rosa Luxemburg and Karl Leibknecht were murdered; in 1968 Memphis, Tennessee, Martin Luther King was assassinated.

***

Nowadays, corporate chief executives are paid partly by company shares, the aim being to incentivise executives to boost long-term company performance and profits. However, there being no legislation to stop CEOs from selling their shares back to the corporations, CEOs have been doing just that and, incentivised by government cuts in taxes, they pay less tax on capital gains on income from the selling of shares. The sell-off of shares can also signal a lack of confidence in the company, causing a temporary dip in the share price. When speculators then buy up the shares and raise the share prices of the stock market overall, they don't necessarily raise the productive value of the companies whose stocks they buy.

Besides reducing wages, firing workers, raising prices, corporations also seek to maintain their profits and expand business by selling corporate bonds, incurring bond debt to be repaid on the maturity date of the bond, meantime paying the interest payments on the bond as unearned income to the bondholders.

Banks are currently attempting to raise interest rates, which will result in the corporations becoming further indebted. The global slowdown in economic activity and the 2018 corporate debt level of $13 trillion now poses a serious threat to the global economy, with some analysts predicting that the next big financial bust will be caused by massive corporate debt (Richard Partington, 'Rising level of corporate debt poses threat to global economy – OECD', *The Guardian*, 26 February 2019).

***

Playing a crucial, though now largely forgotten part in the economic disaster of the 1929–34 Great Depression, was the catastrophe of US dust bowl economics across the grassy prairie lands of the US once known as the Great American Desert because of the prairie's lack of trees, its droughts, strong winds and only 10 inches rainfall per year. Once home to the American Indians, who depended on the bison for their food and standards of living, the prairie lands had previously teemed with millions of bison. White adventurers arrived to profit from hunting the bison almost to extinction, the decimated Indian tribes ending up on poor land in reservations where they could barely make a living. The US government, keen to turn the prairie lands into a going agricultural concern, incentivised its city people and immigrants to take landholdings. Many of the new farmers were teachers accountants, doctors and lawyers, who knew little about farming and next to nothing about ecology. To buy the mechanised ploughs and combine harvesters needed to work the landholdings that otherwise needed more farm labour, the new farmers indebted themselves to the banks and agricultural machinery businesses. The machinery dug into the roots of the grasses that absorbed the scarce rains, degrading the soil and causing dust particles to rise to the surface. Within a comparatively few years, huge swathes of the prairie lands were engulfed in the dust storms that also reached towns and major US cities. Much of the prairie lands became deserted barren dustbowls. Indebted and impoverished small-scale farmers, tenant farmers, labourers and their families, 2.5 million people, migrated from the dustbowl prairie lands to California and other states.

The US government of the 1930s, its malinformed farmers, and a maleducated population did not understand how the combination of unfettered environmental exploitation and debt-based, interest-bearing capitalist banking practices would lead to both the dust bowl environmental catastrophe and economic disaster, which a few years later would contribute to the banking and finance system collapse and the Great Depression.

Only the persistent opposition of a well-informed, unified, economically and politically literate, democratised and engaged populace could have prevented the likes of the Great Depression. The US was no such society. Established only 150 years before that Great Depression, the country was founded on the slaughter of the indigenous population, the enslavement of millions of African slaves and mass immigration from Europe.

Seriously threatened with opposition from the executive officers and the worker members of the American Federation of Labor and Congress of Industrial Organisations (AFL-CIO), the government of the day came up fast with the American New Deal, an economic and socio-cultural programme designed to get the country out of the economic Depression and away from thoughts of socialism. The New Deal created employment through government-funded schemes, which included the setting-up of soil protection and environmental agencies to teach farmers better farming methods.

Using irrigation systems with water from the underground aquifers, the US prairie lands then became the breadbasket of the US, creating massive surpluses that could be sold abroad. Some of that surplus went to feed destitute people in the counties around the globe that had been devastated firstly by the Great Depression and secondly by what it led to, WWII. Another consequence of that surplus was, however, the underdevelopment of Third World agriculture. In the US, with the aquifer water depleting fast, farming in the US prairies is today in severe decline, exacerbated by landowners selling off the remaining aquifer water to Californian cities short of water. The past half-century of the prairie-land farming boom will soon go bust, and when there's no aquifer water left to sell to water-scarce California, millions of people in the prairie States and in water-hungry California will suffer serious hardships.

Fresh surface water is only 3% of the world's water, and with hundreds of thousands of boreholes and irrigation systems using aquifer water to support mass agri-businesses, the depletion of aquifer water is a global phenomenon resulting in dried up wells, boreholes and functionless irrigation systems.

Instead of water being a privatised commodity that pits town-dwellers against farmers, traditional small farmers against agri-business, instead of unbridled use and pollution of fresh water, water must become a protected resource managed by collectively agreed legislation that caps agricultural profiteering. Legislation would include regulations for water pricing and for farming that requires less water.

Imagine a US federal democratic socialist government intent on managing the country's water supply effectively and that ensured water levees were properly engineered and kept in repair, thus preventing the devastations caused by the likes of Hurricane Katrina in 2005. Imagine a UK government that legislated for a land management policy of rewilding treeless barren uplands, and prevented rich landowners burning grouse moors in preparation for the UK shooting season, the land then unable to hold winter rains, causing flooding in nearby towns, the taxpayer charged for the rebuilding of flood defences. Meanwhile, the wealthy landowners pocket the EU Common Agricultural Policy grants paid for by the taxpayers (George Monbiot, 'This flood was not only foretold – it was publically subsidised', *The Guardian*, 29 December 2015).

Initially a UK colony, then a nominally democratic republic, the US continues to be politico-economically and socio-culturally rooted in the historical habits of its sexist, racist, white male ruling class elite past. Its history has also been one of a gun-owning militia in place of the expense of an army. The legacy of racism, guns and the socio-cultural battles between the 'liberal' Northern industrial States and the slave-owning States of the South continues. Via the US civil rights and feminist movements, considerable progress has also been made.

The US relies on a Constitution and Bill of Rights that attempts to balance State powers between the House of Congress representatives elected by voters in the voting districts, the upper Senate of State governors and the Supreme Court that hands down judgements purportedly based on legal interpretations of the Constitution and Bill of Rights – except that those founding documents were drawn up by the country's male, slave-owning bourgeois elite.

Most countries now have written constitutions – notable exceptions are Israel, New Zealand and the UK – but few constitutions are drawn up through democratic participation of all sectors of society.

Here's some good news: using aeroponic and hydroponic methods, urban farming in disused factories is currently being developed. For domestic water use, houses are being fitted with corrugated roofs, rainwater gathering gutters, pipes and collection tanks. The YouTube videos available on these developments are worth watching though the jury is still out on whether such methods can provide the staple food crops like rice and cereals in the amounts needed, or whether water conservation and desalination plants can provide water on the scale needed for survival. It's also good news that rewilding projects across the globe are bringing back biodiversity, restoring watercourses and improving local climates. However, to the millions of people caught up on in today's global water shortage, droughts, crop failures and rising sea levels, such developments are little more than words on a page.

The above paragraphs focus on the US and the West, but they are also relevant to the other capitalist 'democracies' and also to the 'communism' of China's State capitalism.

Though systematic odds arrayed against today's socialist movements are clear, also becoming clearer by the day is that the inbuilt human resistance to political, economic and socio-cultural oppression doesn't stop either.

CHAPTER 4

WWI, Fascism, WWII, the Cold War

Propagandised as the War to End All Wars, accurate statistics of those who died in the four years and three months of WWI (1914–18) are not easy to come by. Amongst those killed were men sent from the British Empire to fight on the side of the British. The general estimate for military deaths overall is 16 million men, with two out of three soldiers killed in combat, the others from infections and diseases, and with 21 million civilian deaths caused by war-related events, atrocities, war-induced displacements, increased epidemics and starvation.

WWI is characterised by industrialised slaughter through the use of tanks, bombs, mines, poison gas, the machine guns that mowed down soldiers the second the emerged from the trenches and by the deadly stalemate of trench warfare. The causes of WWI are commonly said to have been the battles for geopolitical domination by the alliance of the German–Austrian–Hungarian empire and Italy against the alliance of the colonialist powers of Britain and France, joined by a Russia that feared attack by a powerfully industrialised Germany. These military alliances are said to have been spiked also by the nationalism of each ruling elite intent on pursuing its interests. What seldom gets a mention is the overarching class warfare nature of military pursuits. Backgrounded at best is the underlying intent of the elites to preserve their position and expand their control over land, people, industry and raw resources.

After the decimations of the four years of WWI, Germany signed the 1918 armistice, the Treaty of Versailles, which ended the war. Often noted is the fact that 5% more of the UK officer class were killed than the percentage of working-class enlisted men, that statistical quote taking pride of place over the reality that very many more enlisted men than officers were sacrificed, many more civilians than soldiers. All war deaths are to be mourned, and there now needs to be greater remembrance of those millions of civilians killed and better knowledge about the sociopathy and narcissistic psychopathy of those in power who promulgate war.

In the UK, the loss of loved ones to the horrors of WWI drove the struggle for greater democracy, breaking the stranglehold of the UK political establishment, leading to the 1924 election of the first Labour government. Four years later in 1928, UK citizens over the age of 21 won the vote.

During WWII (1939–45), propagandised this time around as a 'Just War', the lives of 60–70 million people were sacrificed, with contingents again sent from the countries of the British Empire, including the West Indies, to assist the British war efforts.

Thanks to the millions of men and women of Europe, Russia and later of the US who fought against fascism, Western capitalist democracies do not have totalitarian fascist governments. Without exception, they have ruling class elites and capitalist governments enticing, pushing, pulling the UK working-class majority into wars not incidentally promulgated to protect and expand the wealth of the ruling class elite at home and abroad.

Newsreels and documentaries depicting WWI and WWII commonly focus on the spectacle of ground and air combat; the battle strategies; the victories; the setbacks, and so forth. Fictions in print and film highlight the heroic acts, the fears and trauma of war, the camaraderie of the servicemen, the bravery of ordinary citizens. Generally omitted, sidelined, backgrounded, decontextualised from all those factual and fictional accounts of war is the overarching structures of the capitalist war economies that used soldiers across the globe as 'cannon fodder', the civilians as 'collateral damage'.

In Europe, Mussolini, Hitler and Franco, the demagogic frontmen for the capitalist political economy, propounded fascism as the cure-all for their countries' politico-economic ills. As well as suffering the economic devastations of WWI, countries were also in the sloughs of the 1930s global financial disaster that led to the Great Economic Depression of 1939, the precursor to WWII. Declaring war, Germany, the largest economic power in Europe, quickly invaded and crushed its continental European neighbours.

Hitler, an avid reader of the social pseudo-sciences of those times, imbued by Darwin's survival-of-the-fittest racism, also used Le Bon's hypothesis of crowd psychology to popularise the mythology that Germans came from a superior Nordic Aryan race. Hitler's 1925 autobiographical political manifesto, *Mein Kampf* [My Struggle], a propagandistic rant of grievance, myth and hatred, sold in the millions and was given free to millions more, newly-weds, for instance. It reflected the psychopathic narcissism of the aggrieved lower-middle-class men who saw no place for themselves in what was also becoming outmoded German imperialism. In the age of industrialisation and trade union struggles for a better slice of the pie, Marxist egalitarianism held no appeal either for the ingroup/outgroup lower-middle-class men of those times. Redolent with thoughts of personal and national persecution, Hitler's public propaganda rants fed the fascist ideology of a 'survival-of-the-fittest total war' against purportedly 'inferior' Jews and Marxists who had tricked Germany into signing the WWI Armistice. The National Socialist German Workers' Party vowed to fight against what they perceived as a grave injustice, promising a 'thousand-year rule' for the hard-done-by German people instead (Callum Macdonald, *The Assassination of Reinhard Heydrich*, Edinburgh: Birlinn, 2007, Chapters 1 and 2).

Though Darwinism made God a theoretical irrelevancy, organised religion held considerable socio-cultural power, and the Nazi's were resolute in their bid to control the power of Roman Catholicism in particular, which they believed owed more allegiance to Rome than to the Nazi vision of an Aryan German fatherland.

From 1933, the German government was systematically killing those they considered unfit to be German citizens. Doctors selected the disabled, those designated mentally ill, and so on, to be killed by nurses, whether by lethal injection, starvation, or leaving patients to die of cold and pneumonia. People were also transported to gas chambers built – before the war – for eugenicist purposes, with doctors, nurses, clerks, cleaners, porters, drivers and gravediggers implementing government policy to kill civilians regarded by the Nazi government as 'useless eaters'. Working for the Nazi Children's Euthanasia Programme, Austrian paediatrician Dr Hans Asperger selected autistic children, including those with Asperger's syndrome, who were to be sent to the Am Spiegelgrund clinic in Vienna to be killed.

The Nazi totalitarian dictatorship propagandised the notion that women who dedicated their lives to 'Kinder, Kuch and Kirche', children, kitchen and the rules of religious chauvinism were to be honoured. The Nazis introduced laws to prevent women from working, to stay at home and have children to increase the Aryan birthrate. (See the documentary about daily life for women under Nazi rule: 'Women in Nazi Germany', History Documentary Films, YouTube, 18 October 2015.)[5]

The Nazis regarded workers' rights, trade unionism and well-informed democratic participation as obstacles to their politico-economic ambitions and the ideology of anti-trade unionism, sexism, racial supremacy and treating other races and outsider groups such as Slavs, gypsies, Jehovah's Witnesses, and homosexuals was ardently proselytised by the purportedly well-educated German elite.

Hitler appointed Joseph Goebbels, a university graduate with a degree in philosophy, as Head of the National Socialist German Workers' Party, Ministry of Enlightenment and Propaganda. Goebbels quickly brought the communications and broadcasting systems, education, youth and sports movements and the arts under the control of the Nazi Party. Goebbels, whose strategy was secrecy, deceit, manipulation and outright lies, infamously declared, 'If you tell a lie, tell a big one'. Goebbels was an admirer of the founder of the US public relations industry, Edward Bernays, and Bernays' use of crowd psychology techniques to manipulate the public mind. In 1933, the Nazi government paid $6,000 a month to a US public relations firm to portray Nazi Germany in a positive light (Ronn Torossian, 'Hitler's Nazi Germany Used an American PR Agency', *The Observer*, 22 December 2014).

Nazi racist scapegoating focused on the Jewish population of Europe, the government ordering soldiers to round up and shoot Jewish people and bury the bodies in mass graves. Deemed too inefficient to fulfil the German government's secret intentions to wipe out the Jews of Europe, those early methods were replaced by the rounding up of Jewish men, women and children, transporting them to gas chambers in concentration camps built for the specific purposes of genocide. Millions of Jewish men, women, children were gassed to death, only those fit to work as slave labourers for the German war economy temporarily spared. In the labour and concentration camps located within Germany and across the countries occupied by the German State, Poland, Serbia, Ukraine, Netherlands, Latvia, Hungary,

Belarus, Austria, Estonia, 11 million people were starved, shot, gassed, and worked to death. Of that 11 million, 6 million Jewish people, 64.5% of Europe's Jewish population, were murdered. At the end of the war, the Western media reported on the existence of only a handful of those camps, so it was not – and is still not – understood how many Nazi concentration camps there were. The Nazi dictatorship had:

> established about 42,500 camps and ghettoes ... [this] includes 30,000 slave labor camps; 1,150 Jewish ghettoes, 980 concentration camps. Berlin alone had nearly 3,000 camps. (Jewish Virtual Library, 'Concentration Camps: How Many Camps? (1933–1945)')

Another of Hitler's henchmen, Martin Bormann, a poorly educated school dropout and ruthless political infighter admired for his punctilious carrying-out of Hitler's orders, was appointed by Hitler to head up the Nazi Chancellery. With fingers on the financial pulse of the Nazi Party, Bormann had immense power. He was also up to his neck in the Nazi programme to imprison communists, the mentally disabled, etc., and in the genocidal plot to exterminate Jewish people.

Bormann declared:

> Education is dangerous ... every educated person is a future enemy.

German schools, universities and mass-media propagandised the population into fervent belief that the superior race of Aryan Germans had been tricked by the inferior Jews, Marxists and corrupt victors of WWI into signing the Treaty of Versailles that prevented the renewal and development of German industry and forced the German government to hand over unpayable amounts of compensation to those victorious nations.

Dismantling democratic rights and promising fantasised futures, the fascist, capitalist dictatorships of Europe, Germany, Italy and Spain dragged their populations into the hellhole of fascism. In the UK, members of the UK royal family were amongst the enthusiasts for fascist governance. In the US, many fascist organisations recruited thousands of members, with US businesses enjoying the support of racist societies like the Ku Klux Klan.

The UK declared war on Germany after the UK government's attempts to work with the belligerent German government through the policy of appeasement failed. The United States entered the war after German submarines attacked the US ships filled with cargos of war goods bound for Europe. When Germany attacked Russia, Soviet Russia, the UK and the US joined forces to defeat the Nazis.

Initially, the UK soldiers of WWI were volunteers until their numbers proved insufficient and government legislated to conscript men into the armed forces. The existential choices of those times were unemployment or becoming a soldier and attempting to defend family, friends, neighbours and country against ruthless aggression and totalitarian governance. Few could hold out against the tsunami of abuse aimed at those who refused to take up arms. Of those conscripted into WWI, 16,000 men refused to serve in the UK armed forces and were called to attend local Military Service Tribunals. The majority of these conscientious objectors, 'conchies', were sent to the war fronts to serve as medics and ambulance drivers. In WWII, the number of conscientious objectors rose to 60,000 men. The absolutists amongst them, refusing on political, religious and humanitarian grounds to have anything to do with war, also refused to serve as ambulance drivers, and many of those absolutists ended up in prison.[6] Small in number, significant in portent, the stories of the conchies are seldom told.

Amongst the British working class, there were also many who understood the sudden wealth raised to conduct WWI and WWII was the other side of the coin that had for decades kept the poor and working-class majority living in poverty, squalor, and, in many cases, malnutrition.

***

The period from the end of WWII in 1945 up to the fall of the USSR in 1991 is called the Cold War, not because there were no hot wars but because the capitalist and communist powers did not engage each other directly in those proxy wars. During that period, many countries in the Global South ended up as proxy dictatorships controlled by alliances of the nations of the capitalist West or by West's adversaries, the Soviet Russian and Communist China.

Better to examine the roots and types of dictatorships arising during the post-WWII colonialist movements and the Cold War from Tanzania to North Korea than to come down on the side of the media-based judgements about those countries. Consider, for instance, the US preventing its citizens from visiting communist Cuba, and that during the Korean War the US carried out a bombing campaign that wiped out 85% of North Korea's towns and cities, which is one reason why North Korea, repressively ruled by a family dynasty, subsequently obtained and maintains a nuclear arsenal to this day.

CHAPTER 5

Post-WWII Western Economic Growth, Offshoring, Privatisation, Deregulation of Banking and Finance

The post-WWII US European Recovery Plan, 1948 to 1952, known as the Marshall Plan, granted £100 billion in today's money to rebuild the war-exhausted capitalist European industrial economies and ward off communism in Europe. The UK received the largest share of aid to Europe, around 26% ('Marshall Plan', Wikipedia). The US also extended aid to Canada and Asia.

Socialist Soviet Republics had lost 27 million people to the war. The capitalist politics of the USA and the West opposed the interests of communist USSR. Perceiving the offer of US aid as a means of Western capitalist infiltration of the USSR and its Eastern European satellite countries, the USSR refused US aid, setting up the Molotov Plan instead, a system of economic alliances and bilateral trade agreements between the communist countries of the Eastern communist bloc.

From the end of WWII until the 1970s, the UK experienced the stability of the 'long economic boom', a steady rise in manufacturing and employment in a regenerated UK economy based on private businesses, nationalised industries and government-financed public services. The UK government had nationalised the major industries of rail, aerospace, energy, etc.; established the British Welfare State and National Health Service; instituted the 1944 Education Act that made secondary education free for all; supported a programme of private house–building for those with the salaries to buy their homes; embarked on a course of building social housing for those who could not. Poverty was significantly reduced, and upward socio-economic mobility for millions became possible.

Lasting until around the mid-1970s, as the UK became less able to compete with other countries, for example, Germany and Japan, from the mid-1970s, UK businesses began transferring industries to the low-labour-cost countries of the Third World. In the Western democracies, wages fell, jobs disappeared, unemployment rose – and the income of the financial elites increased.

From around 1980, Western governments also bowed to pressure from the transnational corporations, bankers, and financiers to allow the free flow of capital around the globe, enabling the global corporate–banking matrix to exert more control over both the so-called 'mature' economies and also those of the developing nations.

The UK government also began to divest itself of responsibility for the upkeep of the public services. Divestment is also a condition imposed by the International Monetary Fund and the World Bank for loans to governments, part of the loan contracts being Structural Adjustment Programmes that forced the sell-off of public services to private investors, usually at less than the value of the services. Over the next several decades, government funding for local authority public services was incrementally slashed, the remaining services cut back, disappearing entirely or being taken over by 'private providers'. Rolled out from the 1980s, the sell-off of the public services through public-private finance initiatives (PPFI) was touted as providing money to fund infrastructure projects and to build much needed new hospitals and schools.[7] Those PPFI contracts locked hospitals and local authorities into privateer loans with years of interest-bearing payments. The new owners and managers of the privately run services cut jobs, wages, and the necessary maintenance and investment costs of the service sometimes to the point that the government, via the taxpayers, had to step in to save the services from collapse.

The rentier privateers now own most of the previously publicly owned services, the railways, telecommunications, bus and transport services, the water, gas and electric utilities, and large chunks of the NHS and State school services.

In 1986, the regulations under which the London Stock Exchange operated were also substantially changed in what became known as the 'big bang' of financial deregulation. Combined with the advent of new information technologies, deregulation allowed enormous amounts of money to be transferred speedily around the globe. Stock market deals could be conducted at the click of a button; shares could be bought and sold by pre-set algorithmic calculations. Mega-investor speculations on national currencies could also undermine the entire economy of another country overnight.

In 1988, the government also denationalised the Bank of England, which then became an independent organisation answering only to the Treasury. The Bank of England was now able to set monetary policy, and government could no longer be blamed for the raising or lowering of bank interest rates.

Government media and corporate banking propaganda reinforced the narrative that 'free-market' capitalism 'raises all boats', that those who save and provide for their futures prosper, while those who can't have only themselves to blame. Deprived of funds, local government must 'tighten their belts', and populations must learn to 'live within the country's means'. Such media-hyped divide-and-rule tactics also praised private sector workers as 'productive', and labelled public sector workers 'pampered'.

The consequence for Western democracies, the US included, of the slashing of central government grants to the local authorities and stripping them of local democratic powers and duties is that local governments don't have the funds to carry out their statutory duties, for example, to house the homeless, look after the disabled and elderly, fund early-years childcare and State school systems and so on. In the UK the local authorities' statutory duties have been reduced to the likes of approving planning applications for the building of unaffordable housing; providing the licences for the betting shops that now line UK high streets; signing off on corporate outsourcing contracts over which, once signed, local government has no control.[8]

It took 40 years for the public to fully understand what was going on, inclusive of privateers outsourcing the work to giant debt-laden Ponzi scheme corporations that failed, the government then using more taxpayers' money to rescue the deal. Eventually, public fury over the outrageous costs of the PPFI deals reached such a pitch that governing politicians concluded that to stay in power they would have to ban new PPFI contracts, which they did in the government's October 2018 Budget Statement.

It is no coincidence that Britain is now one of the most unequal capitalist societies in the industrialised world; that richest five families own more wealth than the bottom 20% of the population, 12.6 million people.[9] In the UK 16 million people have less than £100 in their bank account; of the 14 million UK citizens living in poverty, half are in in-work poverty; with low-income families needing taxpayer-funded tax credits to get by. The UK government has accused the UN rapporteur's reporting of such facts as a fiction.

Third World countries, unable to afford the safety net of social security for their impoverished populations, must instead foot the bill of perpetual interest on loans from the World Bank and International Monetary Fund, the conditions of which are the rentier privatisation of utilities, water, communications, gas, electricity, etc. (see Chapter 18, 'Charities and Foreign Aid').

Here's some good news: increasing numbers of people in Western democracies now know that the media–corporate–government–populist phenomena of 'silo' reporting, as though each issue of public concern had very little connection with another, and the scapegoating of people because, for example, of their religions, ethnicities, race, gender, serves as a cover for the global elite's perpetuation of the gross economic and political inequalities arising from the elites' command and control of the capitalist political economy.

More people than ever also now understand that essential as single-issue battles against racism, sexism, evictions, student debt, fracking, the armaments trade, the closure of a library, etc., that, the separation of those protests one from the other is right up the street of the overarching divide-and-conquer ecology of the dominating forces of the capitalist powers.

This chapter has provided a thumbnail sketch of post-WWII economic recovery in Europe, aided by US grants to rebuild capitalist Europe and ward off communism, with the UK government establishing a mixed economy of private business, nationalised industries and publicly funded public services such as the NHS and State schooling for all.

That economic consensus lasted until the mid-1970s. Corporatism and the transfer of UK industries to Third World countries, the sell-off of public services, and deregulation of the banking and finance system led to exponential increases of wealth for the elite, wage reductions and job losses for millions.

As autonomous learners, more people are now retrieving the details of that history. The further good news is that political movements like the People's Assembly, Extinction Rebellion, and PositiveMoney.org are showing how the current capitalist government's politically chosen imposition of austerity policies on the majority are unnecessary and untenable, are demanding the re-engineering of the capitalist banking and finance system – and are also beginning to show how that might be done.

Despite all the odds the powers that be have stacked in their favour, the consequences of the innate human drive for freedom, fair treatment, justice and equality is that capitalist politicians can't ever get it all their own way.

CHAPTER 6

Twenty-first-century Resource Wars

For the corporations and the armaments producing countries of the affluent West, War means big business. Few UK citizens know, for instance, that bankers in Switzerland, Germany, Britain and the US bankrolled both the Nazis and the Bolsheviks (History International, *Banking with Hitler* (1988), Top Documentary Films; also, 'Wall Street Funded the Bolshevik Revolution – Interview with Professor Anthony Sutton (1925–2002)', YouTube, 10 October 2011; see also 'Chomsky on Lenin, Trotsky, Socialism and the Soviet Union', YouTube, undated).

Governments hand over taxpayers' money to private contractors for the supply of war goods and services, from boots to bullets; uniforms to jet fighters; cooks to lorry drivers, etc. Governments also hire mercenary companies, some of whose fighters are also known to be involved in illegal arms sales, sex trafficking and drug running. The costs of government-sparked wars against populations in poor oil-rich countries add to government debt and increases in government austerity policies.

Recent wars in the Middle East were not, as propagandised, 'humanitarian' wars to protect populations against rogue dictators. Nor were they interventions designed to protect the citizens of Western countries against terrorist attacks. They were long-planned military operations intended to commandeer oil and gas resources and support geopolitical and global financial control by the transnational corporations and the Western elites.

The Project for the New American Century, the US foreign policy document of 2000, provides chapter and verse of the intentions of the USA to use economic and military dominance to control the global economy ('The Project for the New American Century', Wikipedia, 2019).

The account of a US General about his visit to the US Pentagon in November 2001 reveals the Iraq War had been pre-planned as one of a series of wars to be undertaken in support of Western vested interests.

As I went back through the Pentagon in November 2001, one of the senior military staff officers had time for a chat. Yes, we were still on track for going against Iraq, he said. But there was more. This was being discussed as part of a five-year campaign plan, he said, and there were a total of seven countries, beginning with Iraq, then Syria, Lebanon, Libya, Iran, Somalia and Sudan ... He said it with reproach – with disbelief, almost – at the breadth of the vision. I moved the conversation away, for this was not something I wanted to hear. In addition, it was not something I wanted to see moving forward, either. ... I left the Pentagon that afternoon deeply concerned.[10]

Afghanistan

The US/coalition war against Afghanistan (2001–14) was started on the premise that Afghanistan was sheltering the leader of Al-Qaeda, accused by the US of being responsible for the supposed commercial airliners crashing into the New York World Trade Center skyscrapers on 11 September 2001. That premise is now believed by a majority of US citizens to have been a 'false flag' operation conducted by a powerful group of US neoconservatives (see 'The New American Century (Complete)', YouTube, 7 November 2013).

Tens of thousands of soldiers and civilians have been killed in Afghanistan. Taxpayers' money has been and is being extracted in the billions from the citizens of the countries prosecuting the wars in Afghanistan and elsewhere. In the UK, taxpayers have paid out £37 billion, £2,000 for every taxpaying household. Keeping British forces in Helmand Province cost £15 million a day. That's £25,000 for each of the 1.5 million inhabitants of Helmand, more money per head than most of them will ever earn in their lifetimes.[11]

Though combat ended in 2014, UK forces still maintain a presence of around 1,000 armed personnel. The UK government and its alliances, with an eye on the country's many raw materials, remain in command and control of much of Afghanistan's economy.

Amongst the generally unreported reasons for the war in Afghanistan is that it's an existing and potential route for oil and natural gas pipelines from the ex-soviet Caspian States that sit on enormous reserves of natural gas and oil. Europe depends on Russia for 40% of gas for heating, cooking and other needs; Russian wants to protect its natural gas exporting pipelines; the US and EU want the EU to get its gas supplies from elsewhere, reducing its economic and political ties to Russia. Add to that volatile mix that US corporations want to sell natural gas from their fracking operations onto the world market – and that Iran, backed by Russia, is also a player in the pipeline politics of the Middle East (European Parliament Briefing, *TAPI natural gas pipeline project: Boosting trade and remedying instability?*, 26 November 2016). The Middle Eastern oil-based economies also seek to privilege their global oil exports against their competitors. In the Byzantine mix of the geopolitics of those with an interest in Afghanistan's strategic position, and exploitation of its many natural resources, are those groups who seek to protect Afghanistan's poppy farming agriculture that supplies 93% of the illegal global heroin trade (Alfred McCoy, 'How the heroin trade explains the US–UK failure in Afghanistan', *The Guardian*, 9 January 2018).

The first casualty in war is said to be the truth. Adding to misinformation in the depictions of the wars in the Middle East is that of the war in Syria being simply a tale of a despotic dictator waging war on his own people. Still being debated in the press a year after the bombing of an apartment block in Douma that killed 70 people is whether or not it was caused by a chemical weapons attack by the Syrian army. Add also to that media mix that the motivation of Western-backed, super-rich Saudi Arabia's for bombing and wrecking of the economy of one of the poorest countries in the world, Yemen, is that Saudi Arabia is simply bombing terrorist targets.

In Nigeria, South Sudan, Somalia, and Yemen, the lives of 20 million people are currently at risk from starvation, drought and military conflicts. The £3.5 billion needed to save the lives of those 20 million people, and the funds required to boost the economies of poor countries so that millions don't have to risk their very lives to migrate across the world in search of a living is a drop in the bucket compared to the wealth hoarded by the world's billionaires.

The Iraq War (2003–2011)

If a neighbour intends to harm you and your family, you have a right to take measures to protect yourself from that harm and look at ways of improving relationships with your neighbour. Intelligence agencies are designed to inform governments of possible harm so that appropriate actions to prevent harm and improve future relationships can be taken. It may indeed be the case that the situation is so urgent that immediate action, minus parliamentary debate, may have to be taken. That must be the exception that proves the rule.

Protests against the West's threat of war in Iraq began in September 2002, culminating on 15 February 2003 in the greatest mobilisation against war in world history when in over 750 cities in around 80 countries across the globe, 15–30 million people from all walks of life marched in protest against the aims of an alliance of Western nations to go to war against oil-rich Iraq.[12] People working in peace organisations, trade unionists, left-leaning political parties, and ordinary citizens all helped to organise those marches (Ian Sinclair, 'The march that shook Blair', *Peace News*, London 2013). Typical campaign slogans were 'No Blood for Oil' and 'Not in My Name'.

There is truth in the argument that since the protests did not include the withdrawal of labour as in a general strike, those marches across the globe, posing no threat to capitalist profiteering, were bound to be ineffectual.

The prior role of the Western Nations in helping to establish the Iraqi dictatorship in the first place, their subsequent relationship with the Iraqi government they now sought to destroy is documented in 'Saddam – The Truth (Documentary)', published on YouTube, 10 January 2017. That the Iraqi leader was a thuggish dictator is not untrue. Also true is that as long as it suited their geopolitical interests, UK politicians, businessmen and British royalty maintained political and commercial connections with the Iraqi dictatorship.

Three days after the 15 February 2003 march, UK MPs went ahead on 18 February 2003 and voted 412 to 149 for the war anyway. The UK Attorney General knowingly wrote the legal opinion based on fake intelligence that was then used to underwrite the UK's commitment to going to war against Iraq. Many MPs later claimed their vote for war was based on the false intelligence presented to them by the PM and politicians in the higher echelons of government. The Iraq War killed approximately 1.5 million people, mainly civilians; destroyed much of Iraq's physical infrastructure, economy, and civil institutions; and sparked burgeoning acts of terror that continue to plague the West and the rest of the world.

Eventually pressured into holding an inquiry into the government's role in promulgating the Iraq War, that inquiry began in 2009 and was not completed until seven years later, in 2016. In 2003, the proportion of the population who believed that going to war was wrong was 49%. Well before the publication of the Chilcot Report, that figure rose to 79%. The chair of the inquiry, Sir John Chilcot, stated that a key element in the UK parliament's decision to go to war was the then prime minister's 'sheer psychological dominance'. The decision to commit the country to war was made 'without reference to Cabinet', while in parliament overall there was a 'failure to exert and exercise sufficient collective responsibility for a very big decision'. The government had for two years also resisted the request brought under the Freedom of Information Act for the Cabinet Office to disclose the documents showing how the frames of reference of the Chilcot Inquiry had been designed. Only after the Chilcot Inquiry Report had already been presented to the Commons Liaison Committee were those documents released, revealing that inquiry had been framed to prevent 'individuals being held accountable', the declared focus being instead on 'lessons to be learned'.[13]

Libya

Rich in oil, sovereign wealth and gold reserves, Libya was attacked in March 2011 by a coalition of Western nations under a UN resolution sanctioning air strikes, a euphemistic phrase for deadly bombardments. Billed as a 'humanitarian' intervention purportedly to protect the Libyan people from attacks by the Libyan dictator, UK MPs voted 557 to 13 for those air strikes. The death toll from those initial air bombardments was around 25,000. Libya was left leaderless, fragmented and broken.[14]

In his 26 October 2011 article for *The Guardian*, 'If the Libyan war was about saving lives, it was a catastrophic failure', Seamus Milne provides the information about the mass murders committed before the war by rebels funded by Britain, France and the UK to foment civil war to get rid of a dictator who was not obeying the West's instructions. The ultimate aim was for the West to get control of Libya's oil wealth.[15]

When the secularist pan-Arabian Libyan Gaddafi government sought to introduce a pan-Arabian currency based on Middle East oil wealth, Libya was bombed by US forces. Later also invaded by Britain, France and NATO, Libya is now an economic wreck. The suicide bomber who killed himself and 22 young people attending a concert in Manchester on 22 May 2017 was a member of the Manchester-based extremist Libyan Islamic Fighting Group, cultivated by UK intelligence services for over 20 years and encouraged to stir up opposition in Libya and Syria. The suicide bomber was on the UK's terrorist watch list, and three months before the attack, the US FBI warned the UK that the LIFG was looking for a terrorist target in Britain. These facts undermine the UK media story that the bomber acted as a 'lone wolf' (John Pilger, 'Terror in Britain: What Did the Prime Minister Know?', counterpunch.org, 31 May 2017).

The West's interventions in Libya helped to consolidate support for the Islamic State, and other armed groups funded by oil and armaments corporations seeking to promote their geopolitical interests in the region.[16]

Five years after UK intervention in Libya, the 14 September 2016 UK parliamentary Foreign Affairs Committee Report notes the UK's faulty prior 'intelligence' on Libya, and that, as with Afghanistan and Iraq, derisory post-war planning led to the political and economic chaos in Libya. The report concluded that the then prime minister, who had told the FAC he was too busy to attend its hearings, was 'ultimately responsible for the failure to develop a coherent Libya strategy'.[17]

The capitalist commercialisation of exploitable resources causes what economists call the 'Dutch disease'. The discovery of exploitable raw resources, for example, Holland's 1970s massive oil deposits in the North

Sea, means global capital investment flows in to support the new industry and its domestic supply chain. This causes a spike in the value of the country's currency, raises the price of exports, resulting in businesses exporting fewer goods, job lay-offs and failures in the general economy. Profits from the single raw resource go into the pockets of the owners of whatever the means of production who enjoy a luxurious import-based lifestyle, with little money going to develop the productive economy, resulting in unemployment and lower standards of living for the rest of the population. In good times, other productive industries were not developed. Consequently, the moment the raw resource price drops, the whole economy falls into general decline. The Dutch disease affects counties as diverse as Saudi Arabia and Venezuela. Saudi Arabia's reaction has been to extend its capitalist structures, forcibly sequestering funds from its economic elite to do so (Martin Chulov, 'How the Saudi Elite became five-star prisoners in the Riyadh Ritz Carlton', *The Guardian*, 6 November 2017). Venezuela used its oil wealth to fund social housing, free education, healthcare, etc. In attempting to build diversifying industries, such industries as there are remain in the hands of the country's economic elite.

Whilst anti-war protesters mounted campaigns against Western militarism in the Middle East, right-wing politicians campaigned against the EU's influence over UK domestic policy, blaming UK unemployment and lower standards of living on both non-European immigration and the right of free movement of people into the UK from the EU countries – while saying next to nothing about the banking and finance system's free movement of capital around the globe.

Employing cheaper immigrant labour, businesses put the squeeze on wages. Without immigrant labour for the knowledge-based industries, agriculture, construction, heavy industry and elderly care, many UK industries and the National Health Service would grind to a halt.

As people grow too old to work, and they take their pensions, to maintain the tax base and make contributions to the pension funds, the working population must increase, and 2.1 births per woman are needed to do so. In the UK the birth rate is 1.80, immigrant birth rates boosting it by another 0.06. Though in parts of the country it may not seem to be the case, the main driver of low wages and the reduction in public services are businesses and government austerity policies, not immigrants. With populist right-wing politicians leaching support away from the government, the prime minister promulgated the 2016 referendum on the UK staying in the European Union or leaving it – expecting the vote to be in favour of remaining. On 23 June 2016 with a 72.2% turnout of eligible voters, 33 million people, 51.9% of the voters opted to leave the EU, 48.1% to remain. Approximately 400 out of 650 constituencies voted to leave, younger people 18–34 tending to vote to remain. Over 50% of the other age groups voted to leave ('EU referendum: the results in maps and charts', *BBC News*, 4 June 2016).

Having lost the vote, the prime minister stood down, said he would keep his parliamentary seat until 2020, but chose instead to resign his seat two days before the publication of the FAC report criticising his role in the Libyan debacle.

In August 2013, UK Members of parliament voted 285 to 272 against intervention in the Syrian Civil War. Two years later in December 2015, that vote was overturned by 397 to 223 in favour of the UK taking part in air strikes on Syria, ostensibly against the Islamic State extremists.

The question is, to what extent did MPs know of the covert Western, Middle Eastern, Iranian, Kurdish, Russian and other groups involved in the Syrian war, in which combatants from around 70 countries were also involved? Before voting for air strikes against Syria, had UK MPs informed themselves of all of those complexities?

Poor countries are often patriarchal, classist, racist, sexist, with women in perpetual economic, political, economic and social subjugation to men. The 'backwardness' of these countries can be used as legitimation for military interventions by the 'progressive' West. Such countries also often lack strong civil institutions, and such legal infrastructure as they do have is generally disregarded by the occupying powers. Organised religions are also deeply ingrained as are ethnic and tribal behaviours, all helping to shape ingroup/outgroup economic, political and socio-psychological judgements and behaviours, such behaviours also being hijacked by internal and external forces aiming to stir up strife to their own advantage.

In their otherwise inferior arsenals, terrorism is the weapon of terrorist groups. Some terrorist groups will also raise funds through people-smuggling, sex-trafficking, and will also use the most brutal aspects of religious texts to underwrite enslavement, beheadings, mutilations, murder, kidnapping, rape and the selling of 'enemy' women.

Media soundbites will also posit that Third World insurgents are not so much fighting against internal and external exploitation, impoverishments, landlessness, the effects of climate change, the deaths of loved ones, and the loss of their futures, but that they fight, kill and torture because it is their cultural DNA to do so.

Western democracies will often depict Western military interventions around the world as 'humanitarian' interventions against corrupt dictatorships. It is not untrue that most dictatorships are ruthlessly corrupt. It is also the case that the dictatorship was likely to have been installed with the collusion of the West, and is no longer compliant with Western intentions. 'Democratic' governments and corporations also legislate in support of selling billions worth of armaments, jets, tanks, guns and bombs, etc., to despotic regimes.

The unbearable question is this: locked into the capitalist profiteering network of corporations, shareholders, governments, and politicians intent on supporting that system, is what crucial differences are there between terrorist aggressions and the acquiescence of workers and trade unionists in the capitalist armaments factories who, should they down tools in the name of humanity and against the political economy under which they labour, must also consign themselves to lives of unemployment and poverty?

The prevailing reason for today's wars is the determination of the wealthy global elite, oligarchic-compliant governments and the transnational banking, finance and corporate system to exert economic and political supremacy over people's intrinsic desire to be free from internal and external exploitation and domination. That determination by the economic elite remains paramount even in the most extreme circumstances. For instance, while Palestinians attempt daily to oppose the repression of the Israeli State, the US Strategic Advisory Board for Genie Energy plans the exploitation of the massive oil reserves in the Golan Heights, land captured from Syria by Israel in the 1967 Arab–Israeli Six-Day War between Israel, Egypt, Jordan and Syria. Amongst the motives for that war were the survival of the Israeli Jewish people against the threat of extermination; the battle by the West and its Middle Eastern allies for geopolitical for control in the region, and the West's control of the world's oil reserves. The Strategic Advisory Board of Genie Energy is composed of a former US vice president; a global media mogul; a former director of the CIA; a former head of the US Treasury; a former US State governor; a former US ambassador to the UN; an ex-US Energy Secretary; a former US State Senator, a US hedge fund manager; and a British mega-investor, a member of the global Rothschild banking family ('Genie Energy', Wikipedia).

The task of the world's 6,545 think tanks, funded by governments, universities, corporate-funded associations, etc., is to research and evaluate the information that governments and corporations and other organisations require to assist them in devising foreign policy and trade agreements; to decide which science and technology research and developments to fund; what climate and environmental policy to follow; how State education systems should be structured; how public opinion can be shaped, and so on.

North America and Europe have 3,707 think tanks, 1,198 are in Asia, and there are 1,640 in the rest of the world (<http://newint.org/blog/2017/02/10/who-funds-the-think-tanks>). Who funds which think tanks for what purposes is routinely made deliberately opaque.

It can fairly safely be said that, though there are also think tanks that serve the progressive left, the aim of the majority of influential Western think tanks is to help shape the desire of citizens in the Western democracies to being amongst capitalism's winners, and to get the populations of the poorer countries to believe capitalism is their best possible means of escaping impoverishments. In the dog-eat-dog capitalist world, many sectors of First and Third World populations oppose capitalist exploitations. Many others, think tank–influenced or otherwise, see in capitalism their best possible means of survival.

In the UK, the public appeared to be initially swayed by the new PM chosen by the governing party to replace the outgoing PM who had promulgated the EU referendum. The new PM had voted for the wars in Afghanistan and Iraq; for a no-fly zone in Libya; for air strikes in Syria. The new PM self-characterised as a no-nonsense politician who just got on with the job and promised a 'strong and stable' government. The shine wore off, and the upshot was that in 2017 election, called by the governing party to try to increase its slim majority of 331 seats, only five above the required 326 seats for a majority, won only 318 seats, eight seats less than a majority. To stay in power, the party had to go into coalition with the Irish Democratic Unionist Party.

The PM has also given a political welcome to uber-wealthy Saudi Arabia. Besides armaments, Saudi Arabia buys UK telecom surveillance equipment to police their citizens, 37 of whom it publically executed in April 2019. Six months earlier, in the offices of the Saudi embassy in Turkey, Saudi government operatives assassinated a once favoured wealthy Saudi who had become a mildly critical Saudi journalist, his views intolerable to the governing royal family. In the international spotlight, arrests over that murder were made, with no blame laid on the Saudi government. Execution, hanging, beheading, mutilation and eye gouging remain legal punishments on the Saudi Arabian lawbooks.

The PM welcoming the Head of the Saudi government had a previous career in the banking sector as a financial consultant at the Bank of England as its Head of European Affairs, then as Senior Advisor on International Affairs for the Association for Payment Clearing Services. The PM has made speeches that ticked off the Bank of England for setting interest rates low after the 2008 banking crash, resulting in low mortgage rates which sent property prices rocketing. The PM also slapped the wrists of the Bank of England for making ordinary people poorer through its quantitative easing that favoured the wealthy. The PM then congratulated the Bank of England for the progress it had made in establishing new procedures that rendered the unstable banking system more stable. It's one thing to say a few obvious words about the bank's fiscal policies, another to risk the ire of the government's capitalist backers in legislating against the banking activities that damage the productive economy.

In the snap June 2017 general election the government berated the opposition party for its manifesto pledging to take some UK public services back into government control; abolish university tuition fees; provide more funding for State schools, the NHS, and so on. The PM categorised the opposition party's manifesto a mere wish list, declaring there was no such thing as a magic money tree to pay for such promises. The PM's riposte sounded to many voters as though during that career in banking the PM had acted less as banking's monitor, more as its dutiful bookkeeper – and if the banking world's money tree shakedown of interest-bearing mortgage debt, commercial loans, and the interest-loaded debt of millions of credit card holders didn't much concern the PM, what else didn't register?

Nonetheless, despite its increasingly obvious instabilities, capitalism was – and continues to be – championed by a government-corporate-banking-media elite that 'knows best', defines capitalism as the 'best system possible' and declares that to foolishly abandon it for socialism would make everyone poorer and lead to communist totalitarianism.

In the UK, after almost three years of the PM and government's failed attempts to negotiate the terms of Britain leaving the European Union, the content of those terms largely unknown to the British public, no longer having the confidence of the governing party, the PM resigned from office.

The above brief overview of recent wars over resources and geopolitical influence doesn't cover the other conflicts going on in Africa, India, Pakistan, Kashmir, Ukraine, Crimea and elsewhere, or the looming threat of conflict in the China seas as the US and China battle for control of the region. Nor does it cover the issue of a nuclear standoff between the US and North Korea and between the US and Iran, nor the fact that the US and NATO are increasing their military presence around the world at a rate not seen since WWII. With nine of the world's nations possessing thousands of nuclear weapons between them, Einstein's remarks seem all too portentous:

> I know not with what weapons World War III will be fought, but World War IV will be fought with sticks and stones.

This chapter has briefly outlined some of the prevailing causes of recent wars over oil, natural gas, other resources and the profiteering drive of those in political and economic command to control governments and populations.

Positive news seems scarce, but it's good news that more people than ever at least now know there's far more to the government–corporate–media complex than populations are led to believe. Today's new economic, political and socio-cultural understandings are due in part to the work of some of today's journalists and documentary makers in providing analyses of the geopolitical positioning and profiteering behind the wars over oil and gas and other highly exploitable resources. See, for example, 'The

Secret of the Seven Sisters, 4 of 4; A Time for Lies', *Al Jazeera*, 26 April 2013, YouTube, 7 November 2017. See also Jimmy Dore's satirical 'Why Are We In Syria? Shocking Facts Media Doesn't Tell You', YouTube, 26 October 2016.

Economist Professor Richard Werner's *Princes of Yen* shows how the economy of one of the losing nations of WWII, Japan, was re-engineered by the US. Part of that re-engineering was to set up worker-owned cooperatives to try to prevent the Japanese industrialists regaining wealth and power. Demonstrating the role of the central banks in controlling both the national economies and the global capitalist system, the *Princes of Yen* documentary makers also produced the 2012 documentary, *97% Owned*, which gives chapter and verse by the organisation positivemoney.org on how the banks create money and control economies.

Economist Mariana Mazzucato demonstrates how the private sector often 'only finds the courage to invest after an entrepreneurial state has made high-risk investments' in publicly funded innovations and also reveals how taxes are used to rescue private enterprises in danger of bankruptcy. According to Mazzucato, the State, too often seen as an external bureaucratic leviathan, has very often previously been, and must again be, an innovative force from within, with the State and the public properly awarded their fair share of the profits (Mariana Mazzucato, *The Entrepreneurial State*, London: Anthem Press, 2015; see also Mariana Mazzucato's June 2013 TED talk, 'Government – investor, risk-taker, innovator').

In highly fragmented and volatile political times, the good news is that today's politicians, technocrats, and financiers know that people everywhere, though slowly, are beginning to get it that there's no alternative to coming together in solidarity to build the organisations and political institutions that say no to the profiteering idiocies of war, nuclear destruction, and ecocide.

The next chapter will review how the 2008 global financial crash and governments' subsequent austerity policies to cut social welfare, school and hospital budgets, and so on, led millions to oppose the status quo, some attracted to right-wing populism, many others towards socialist progressivism.

CHAPTER 7

Bank Racketeering

Only 3% of money is in actual banknotes and coins. 97% of money is created by banks writing a loan entry onto its books. That ledger entry is turned into a contract between the bank and a mortgagee, let's say to 'lend' £100,000, let's say, at an interest rate of 3.65% compounded over a 25-year term. At the end of that term, the debtor-mortgagee will have paid the bank £151.644 from her/his salary. That's a banking money-tree shakedown of more than one and a half times the debt created from nothing ('How Banks Create Money', positivemoney.org).

The beginnings of the 2008 global financial crash can be traced to the 1986–95 US Savings and Loan disaster when, to reduce inflation, the US Federal Reserve raised the interest rates from 9.5 to 12%, which included rates on bank loans needed by Savings and Loan companies (S&Ls) to top up their mortgage lending from customer deposits. The S&Ls had already issued long-term low-interest rate mortgages and savers' deposit accounts at high interest rates. In the financial deregulations of 1997, the S&Ls took to investing in high-risk speculative ventures to find the money needed to finance their mortgage lending. Many of those ventures failed, the upshot being the closure of around a third of US S&L companies to the tune of around $407 billion.

That switchover in banking regulations that allowed savings and loan companies to engage in high-risk commercial banking operations was a crucial element in the 2008 global financial crash.

Modern banking is a globally linked phenomenon, and though all banks were affected by the 2008 crash, banks in the Global South were less affected than those in the Global North.

The subsequent origins of the 2008 global financial crash can be traced to the US banks granting mortgages to poor people who couldn't afford the mortgage payments. Bundling up dud mortgages with other saleable debt assets, banks called the bundles 'Collateralised Debt Obligations' and offloaded the bundles to 'investment' speculators, other banks and finance houses seeking unearned income from purportedly collectable interest-bearing debt packages. The rating agencies, paid by the banks to grade investment risks, gave the CDOs top ratings, thus allowing the financial insurance companies to attempt to insure the CDO buyers against loss.

Discovering the fraud of massive amounts of uncollectable debts, the investors rushed to sell the CDOs. Many banks, now unable to borrow against their remaining dodgy assets, had no way of lending, went bust and closed their doors. While foreclosing on the mortgages 94 million US 'homeowners', the US bankers and financiers continued to pay themselves bonuses.

Economist Alan Greenspan, chairman of the private US Federal Reserve Bank from 1987 to 2006, adviser to the political elite, was named by *Time* magazine as one of the '25 People to Blame for the Financial Crisis'. In October 2008, Alan Greenspan was called to testify before the US Congress about the causes of the global financial crash. In his testimony, he admitted to being 'partially' wrong in opposing regulation of the banking system.

> Those of us who have looked to the self-interest of lending institutions to protect Shareholders' equity – myself especially – are in a state of shocked disbelief.

In the capitalist theory of the self-interested 'free market' that would work inevitably to protect investors and consumers, Alan Greenspan said he'd found a 'flaw':

> I don't know how significant or permanent it is. But I have been very distressed by that fact.

A congressman summarised: 'In other words, you found that your view of the world, your ideology, was not right, it was not working.'

Greenspan replied:

> Absolutely, precisely. You know, that's precisely the reason I was shocked because I have been going for 40 years or more with very considerable evidence that it was working exceptionally well.

In the UK, Northern Rock, previously a savings and loan company, became instead a private bank listed on the London Stock Exchange. Northern Rock could now borrow huge amounts of money from the bigger banks, using this borrowed money to fund its mortgages.

In classic paradigm, with insufficient assets to cover loans, and unable to borrow more money from the big commercial banks, which, stung by the CDO scam, had stopped lending, by autumn of 2007 US and UK banks, inclusive of Northern Rock, were on the brink of collapse.

In the UK, there are around 5.7 million UK Small and Medium Enterprises, making up 99% of all businesses. Unable to access bank loans to maintain and extend their businesses, many SMEs had to fire workers or close down, creating unemployment, which reduced the tax base, which in turn limited the government's ability to pay for public services through taxation alone. Governments chose not to regulate profiteering but to introduce instead government policies of 'austerity', that is, cutbacks in government funding of social welfare and public services.

At the height of the crisis, taxpayers' money and government funds were pumped into banks, but it wasn't enough, so the big fix was 'Quantitative Easing', that is, creating billions of QE money from nothing and syphoning up those billions onto the balance sheets of the private commercial banks (Polly Curtis, 'Reality check: how much did the banking crisis cost taxpayers', *The Guardian*, 12 September 2011).

Named as 'the greatest experiment in banking history', in the eyes of some modern economists and the minds of the few savvy citizens clued up on the world of banking and finance, QE was instead the biggest confidence trick in banking history that led to the greatest transfer of wealth from the poor to the rich since colonial times.

In the UK, the Bank of England created £375 billion worth of QE money, more than six months' worth of government spending, amounting to £6,000 for every man, woman and child, £24,000 for a family of four. QE money was intended to be used by the banks to buy up the likes of government treasury bonds, the safest bet, and corporate bonds, a safe bet. However, the government didn't bother to regulate to ensure the banks went along with that assumption behind QE. Banks chose instead to buy up high-return stockmarket assets, sending the value of the stock market up by

20%. Since only 5% of the population owns 40% of stocks, the result of QE was that wealthy shareholders got richer by around £128,000 per investor.

For every £1 of QE money, only 8p was spent into the productive economy. With the tax base shrinking, and with a government austerity policy of simultaneously reducing State borrowing, the government cancelled the likes of the project to construct 715 schools and fix 1000 flood defences. Those schools could have been built for £1 billion, 375 times *less* than the money the wealthy put into buying up the stocks and shares. Hundreds of thousands of people were put out of work, including tens of thousands of construction workers (positivemoney.org, 'How to Waste £375 Billion', YouTube, June 2014).

The developing countries of Brazil, India, China and South Africa criticised QE as gaming the global banking system in favour of the Western nations. What QE did do was inject enough liquidity into the Western banks to keep them open.

Without QE, the automated bank teller machines would have stopped working. People wouldn't have been able to get cash from the ATMs to purchase the daily necessities of life. Depositors wouldn't have been able to access their chequing and savings accounts and cheques to pay bills and purchase goods wouldn't have been honoured. What often goes unmentioned about QE is that without it, the business world would have been unable to collect payment from the consumers of its products.

That the US bankers and financiers didn't have a clue about the outcomes of their dud mortgage selling spree, is hardly believable. That Northern Rock and the other UK banks didn't comprehend that banks must keep assets in reserve if they are to be considered bona fide lenders, is implausible. That the capitalist central bankers, economists and government ministers responsible for QE had no intimation about the likely outcome of a bankers' QE, isn't credible.

Government rescue of the 'too big to fail' banks run by the 'too big to jail' bankers means that bankers could now also be confident that should their sleight-of-hand, deregulated short-term profiteering cause another crash, they can almost certainly count on being bailed out by taxpayers' money and another tranche of bankers' QE.

The 2010 award-winning documentary written and directed by Charles Ferguson, *Inside Job*, shows the steps taken – and not taken – by the bankers, politicians and regulators which then led to the 2008 global financial disaster, leading in turn to 'austerity' policies by capitalist governments. With the example of the bankers' QE there for all to see, there is every good reason for trade unionists, economic and political activists to demand a comprehensively thought out People's Quantitative Easing in support of the manufacturing and service industries, the funding of the public services, and the setting-up of well-planned and viable worker-owned enterprises that can provide reliable and steady employment locally and nationally.

The one affected country not to go down the banker bailout route was Iceland, a country of less than half a million people (359,000) that had its own currency and central bank. The government of Iceland allowed commercial banking operations to go bust, and managed to get a swift loan of $5.1 million from the IMF to enable the government to guarantee depositors' savings and checking accounts. The government also introduced retrospective financial regulation under which it arrested bankers and sent 70 of them to jail.

After the 2008 crash, banks set interest rates at near zero, which fuelled another public and private debt mountain. The debt mountain, which also includes corporate debt, means that the raising of interest rates, ostensibly to ward off inflation; along with trade wars, and currency wars as countries try to escape the dollar domination of world currencies; a slowdown in the Chinese economy that would ripple across the globe, could, singly or in combination, spark off another global crash, the next one worse than the last.

In 2000 there were seven countries whose banking system did not come under the umbrella of the Western private banking system: Afghanistan, Iraq, Sudan, Libya, Cuba, North Korea, and Iran. After the wars in Afghanistan, Iraq, Libya, Sudan, the remaining economies not controlled by the globalist capitalist banking system are Iran, Cuba, and North Korea.

Amongst the economic realities brought to the surface by today's progressive economists is that a March 2014 Bank of England poll of 100 MPs revealed that only one in 10 MPs understood how money is created. This extrapolates to only 65 of the UK's 650 MPs knowing how the banking system works ('Poll Results: Only 1 Out of 10 MPs Understand That Banks Create Money', positivemoney.org. 19 August 2014). Three years later, positivemoney.org reported that only another 5% of MPs had brought themselves up to scratch on the workings of the banking and finance system, meaning that 85% of UK MPs still did not understand the basics – and not least because the banking and finance sector would rather the majority of politicians, and the public, remained without that essential knowledge. Usually ignored is the fact that a currency-issuing government can't run out of money, so that, if it wants to, it can always afford to pay for healthcare and welfare.

Moreover, to control inflation, governments could also legislate put a cap on prices. However, the wealthy are disincentivised to change the political economy since that wealth depends upon the exploitation of labour within the productive economy and the debt-based, interest-bearing banking and finance and the rentier services churned out by the wealthy. The incentive for change belongs to the majority. The onus on an organised majority is to devise devise a fair and equitable politico-economic and socio-culturally responsible society where the questions to be pursued are how to best live the economically viable, most interesting, insightful life that is based on mutual respect for each other's humanity.

The MPs also believed that 50% of bank loans went to businesses when only 10% did. Most lending goes instead on real estate mortgages, credit card debt, corporate and government debt. If MPs attempting to sort out the UK's housing crisis don't understand the role of bankers and real estate developers in helping to create that crisis in the first place, the solutions they come up with are going to be inadequate to the task ('Why Are House Prices So High', positivemoney.org, 2014).

In classic capitalist manner, one of the UK's largest housebuilding corporations slashes its competition by buying up other building companies; pays its chief executives millions in bonuses; makes £66,000 profit on every home it sells; with many of those homes shoddily built. Much of that profit comes from the government's 'right-to-buy' mortgage scheme for first-time buyers. Independent property expert, Henry Pryor, states that 'Help-to-buy has been the crack cocaine of the housing industry' (Rupert

Neate, 'Outrage as help-to-buy boosts Persimmons profits to £10bn', *The Guardian*, 26 February 2019).

Many MPs, not knowing their sums and skiving off doing their homework, or setting their own, can become embroiled in such matters as Brexit at the exclusion of too much else. They will champion such as the planting of an ecologically resuscitative forest across the north of England while pressing for extra Heathrow airport capacity and the construction of 400 miles of environmentally damaging new roads.

Occasionally reported in the interim is the fact that in many cities across the globe, including in the UK, the air is seriously polluted and unfit to breathe. We now know that seas are full of plastic debris, but don't know so much about the thousands of bits of space junk orbiting the earth at thousands of miles per hour that are dangerous to the hundreds more satellites launched each year – to the point that private companies are now lobbying government for the business of clearing the rubbish from outer space.

Meanwhile, Europe inundates Africa with EU subsidised farming produce, which in turn debases African agriculture and businesses, depriving African countries of earning the surplus required to build infrastructure, reducing standards of living and causing an exodus of millions of people migrating the world in search of a living.

The government continues to make much of the fact that it's paying down the national deficit, that is, the difference between tax receipts and government spending calculated over a short period, resulting in either a credit or deficit. Temporary deficit reductions don't reduce the government's long-term national debt of £1.7 trillion on which £52 million in interest payments must be paid each year.

In the 1950s, the government debt of around £640 billion was 250% of GDP, and much of that debt went to fund the establishment of the welfare state. In 2018, government debt stood at approximately £1.7 trillion was around 87% of total GDP – and the National Health Service is on its knees.

As to who owns today's massive interest-bearing government debt, 28% is owned by insurance and pension funds; 27% is in the hands of overseas investors; the Bank of England holds 23%; other banks and financial institutions hold 17%; wealthy individuals hold 5% (Tejvan Pettinger, 'Who owns government debt', *Economics Help*, 1 November 2017).

***

In possession of that socio-cultural passport to parliamentary power, an Oxford University degree in Philosophy, Politics and Economics, a recent UK Secretary of State for Work and Pensions described government's cutting of social welfare benefits for 88,000 of Britain's poor families by £2,000 a year as a 'real success' (Heather Stewart and Sarah Butler, 'Damian Green says government's benefit cap is a "real success"', *The Guardian*, 7 November 2016). While previously serving as an MP, that same government minister continued to work as an associate director of a water company, pocketing £16 million for his 112 hours of advice to the water company. During his tenure as associate director, the water company also paid out £18 billion in dividends to shareholders. Neither of those facts was considered by those in charge of parliamentary ethics to conflict with parliamentary rules of representation. This politician had also been a Home Office Minister of State for Immigration; Secretary of state for Police and Criminal Justice; Secretary of State for Work and Pensions; and had latterly been promoted by the PM to First Secretary of State and Minister for the Cabinet Office.

On a TV discussion programme, this politician was accused by the opposition party's shadow chancellor of profiteering from his position as associate director of the water company. The minister's rebuttal was that the shadow chancellor didn't understand capitalism. Instead of pursuing what for the home audience would have been a 'useful line of enquiry', the TV host hurriedly intervened to tell his two TV guests, 'Calm down both of you', quickly going on to ask the minister whether the government intended to increase taxes to pay for its manifesto pledges, conveniently allowing the minister to repeat the government meme that a growing economy would pay for the governing party's meagre manifesto pledges ('Damian Green and John McDonnell on costing manifestos', *The Andrew Marr Show*, BBC, 21 May 2017, YouTube video, at 28:47 minutes).

The prime minister had to sack this minister from his post as First Secretary of State and Minister to the Cabinet because he lied to parliament and police by denying that in between writing government emails he regularly watched internet pornography on his parliamentary computer. UK democratic deficits are such, however, that this politician is allowed to keep his parliamentary seat to continue as an 'honourable' member of parliament. It is surely no coincidence that a privileged white male politician ideologically obsessed with slashing meagre welfare benefits to the point of causing poor people to commit suicide, and seemingly narcissistically unable to relate to people in ordinary human relationships is a habitual user of pornography.

During the last few decades, acquisitions and mergers of accountancy firms have led to the monopolising of the auditing and 'management consultancy' business. Instead of honestly auditing their clients' books, these accountancy 'consultancy' firms charge enormous fees for acting as the 'consultants' whose main aim is to cook the client's books to make it appear as though the firm is worth more than it is, which in turn raises the firm's corporate profile and share price. For a comprehensive account of how the accountancy giants have also colluded and shaped fraudulent banking and corporate practices, see Richard Brooks, *Bean Counters: The Triumph of the Accountants and How They Broke Capitalism* (London: Atlantic Books, 2018).

Dismissing the science of greenhouse gas damage to the planet, the Royal Bank of Scotland promoted itself as the oil-, gas- and coal-financing bank. A significant part of its business was to lend to companies building coal-fired power stations and opening coal mines across the globe. In classic capitalist fashion, RBS also sought to increase its global competitiveness by acquiring other banks in the US and UK, and by entering into consortium, or cartel, with other banks, such as Banco Santander, and also became a not insignificant shareholder in the Bank of China.

Before the global banking crash of 2008, having overextending itself by billions more than the value of its assets, RBS had set up its Global Restructuring Group (GRG), the aim of which was the asset-stripping of Small and Medium Enterprises. On loans made to supposedly help the SMEs, RBS charged huge administration fees and high interest, and also regularly altered the terms and conditions of the loans to take more money and assets from the 'looked-after' SMEs. The RBS GRG scheme is global, with operations in the US, the Netherlands, Italy and Ireland.

Along with the other UK banks on the verge of collapse in 2008, RBS was bailed out by the UK government to the tune of £36 billion, the equivalent of £167 for every UK citizen, the government taking around 84% ownership of RBS. In March 2009 RBS announced plans to cut 3700 jobs, in addition to the 16,000 job cuts already planned. Meanwhile, the RBS board threatened to resign unless the government permitted it to pay £1.5 billion in bonuses to its investment executives.

After the government bailout, RBS continued with its Global Restructuring Group operations of asset stripping the non-corporate small and medium businesses. A former senior RBS executive was heard on tape saying that RBS had 1000 backroom staff engaged in 'data cleanup and reconciliation', that is, the falsification of loan documents that made it almost impossible for RBS to be sued for fraud ('White Collar Crime: Mind the Gap', *Renegade Inc.*, Russia Today TV, presented by Ross Ashcroft, 4 December 2017). An owner of one of the SMEs also discovered that 800 GRG employees had been trained in how to asset strip the SMEs while GRG executives skimmed profits off the top of the GRG deals to pay themselves big remunerations. When these SME businesses failed, as through RBS's GRG operations they were bound to do, RBS took them over and profited further by selling the businesses on. Of the businesses 'looked after' by RBS' GRG, 90% of them have been ruined at the cost of thousands of jobs. Of the thousands of businesses affected, some of the owners of SME businesses have committed suicide.

It was also discovered that the majority of UK MPs had RBS complaints cases on their desks. The response of MPs across the parties appears to have been one of collective amnesia, and a covert agreement to downplay what is likely to turn out to be more corrupt than the billions in corporate-banking-government kick-backs made to Saudi Arabia over armaments sales. On receiving a leaked investigatory report, the opposition party's shadow Treasury MP went so far as to say that RBS GRG asset stripping was 'the largest theft anywhere, ever' ('RBS squeezed struggling businesses to boost profits, leak reveals', *Newsnight*, BBC, 10 October 2016, documentary by Andy Verity and Jake Morris; see also 'Bailing Out RBS', Ann Pettifor on Russia Today's *Renegade Inc.*, 2017, and 'The Hillsborough of British Business', Neil Mitchell on *Renegade Inc.*, April 2018).

In assigning responsibility for making banks accountable for their fraudulent practices, the Financial Conduct Authority pointed to the Information Commissioner's Office (ICO), the police pointed to the FCA and the ICO. The FCA eventually came up with the classic fudge that though 'We feel strongly that those companies that have suffered losses as result of how they were treated while in GRG must be compensated ... we have concluded that our power to discipline for misconduct does not apply and that any action in relation to senior management for lack of fitness and propriety would not have reasonable prospects of success' (James Moore, 'RBS to face no action over GRG small business lending scandal as the banks get away with it again', *The Independent*, 31 July 2018).

Hardly aware of RBS's GRG operations, generally also unknown to the public is that RBS had a history of financing corporations that make cluster bombs – despite the International Convention on Cluster Munitions. Though RBS changed its policy on financing cluster bomb manufacturing after pressure from campaign groups, RBS is one of many banks and finance businesses that invest in the nuclear weapons industry.

Though the prospect of Mutually Assured Destruction (MAD) has, over the last 74 years, appeared to have prevented psychopathic men in overweening charge of governments from pushing the nuclear button, there are those amongst them who believe it's possible to use the nuclear option selectively and win. The perception that wiser heads may rule may be wishful thinking. The 2018 report of the Christian PAX organisation, *Don't Bank on the Bomb: A Global Report on the Financing of Nuclear Weapons Production*, reveals that the intention of the manufacturers involved deliberately blur the line between conventional and nuclear weapons. Most of the financial institutions investing in nuclear arms manufacturing are in the USA. They are also in China, India, the UK and elsewhere. The banks investing in nuclear arms production include Royal Bank of Scotland, Lloyds, Barclays, Santander, HSBC, and Bank of Ireland.

Corruption in Third World countries means payoffs to corrupt officials handling contracts for goods and services supplied by the West. In Western countries, kickbacks and corruption and banking investment strategies are such as those described above.

The facts mentioned above are only some of the details now beginning to inform people's understanding that the entire rejigging of the profiteering bedrock of usurious capitalist global banking and finance and its asymmetrical trade 'agreement' system is deeply connected to urgently doing all that can be done ward off genocidal climate change.

Here's some good news: in this Age of Information, the corruptions of the banking and trading system are being revealed at an unprecedented rate. Abraham Lincoln's astute political observation that you can fool some of the people some of the time but can't fool all of the people all of the time might echo across the decades to mean that fewer people are now being fooled less of the time. For these times of ecocide, the more prescient conclusion might be Robert Louis Stevenson's 'Sooner or later, everyone sits down to a banquet of consequences' – except not with an unrepresentative and toothless parliament and the likes of the FCA presiding. Opposition to the exploitation that has led us to this particular juncture of history is also inexorable – whether it's people bringing court cases against those who sexually abused them; plaintiffs opposing the pesticide manufacturers like Monsanto who must pay billions in compensation to the victims who contracted cancer from using the pesticides manufactured by the agribusiness, to countries clawing back money in lost taxes from businesses operating tax free from tax havens, to millions of people marching against war and government 'austerity' policies against the poor, while providing tax cuts for the rich.

To swig back the whiskey, swallow a pill, or take a holiday is no antidote for the depressing activity of unravelling the venal activities that lie at the heart of the capitalist political economy. Nor can its bedrock, the corrupt banking system, be altered by a tweak here, a reversible 'reform' there. Only when enough people can manage to get themselves out from under the propaganda systems and get themselves organised enough to commandeer the political clout to say to no to the psychopathology of the likes of bank racketeering will the system be changed.

CHAPTER 8

Big Technology, Agri-business, Big Pharma, Medical Profiteering, Blockchain

Collectively and as individuals, human beings are inventive, from making needles from animal bone to designing the wheel, concocting medicines, systems of writing, art and agriculture, inventing metal ploughs to spinning jennies, toilet paper to smartphones, televisions to vaccines, etc.

Governments and the wealthy owners of the means of production finance and communications, usurping, or paying for the inventions of others, also ordered technological inventions to suit their purpose. For instance, small businesses in the UK Midlands manufactured slave chains and farm implements, the workers paid a pittance.

The world of technology is often perceived as though beyond the ken of individual human beings – as, indeed, its specific technicalities often are, but no one is incapable of perceiving the dangers of the unbridled application of technology, from the production of the nuclear bomb to carcinogenic pesticides manufactured by the mass agri-businesses.

In the 1940s, the US, concerned that Nazi scientists would produce the atomic bomb, organised its government–military–industrial complex to fund the research, development and production of atomic bombs designed to kill hundreds of thousands per bomb – and intended to fetter the minds of millions more.

Nowadays, approximately 31 countries have around 440 nuclear plants for the production of electricity, with the construction of plants also underway in 16 countries. The countries with nuclear plants also have the know-how to make weapons-grade plutonium for nuclear warheads. Today, nine countries have a joint inventory of roughly 27,000 nuclear warheads, most of them in the US and Russia ('Nuclear weapons – the facts', *New Internationalist*, 2 June 2008). Though many countries have signed the Nuclear Non-Proliferation Treaty, there is no guarantee this will stop a country from launching a pre-emptive nuclear strike, using nuclear bombs as though they were conventional weapons with a restricted kill centre.

Though right-wing politicians and their followers are swift to blame today's threat of nuclear terror on rogue 'regimes', it was the supposedly 'non-rogue' US that dropped the nuclear bomb on civilians in Hiroshima and Nagasaki.

Using nuclear technology to generate electricity, nuclear plant disasters have caused hundreds of thousands of death by radiation and cancers, rendered land uninhabitable, affected neighbouring countries, and in the case of the Fukushima disaster, caused radiation to pollute the ocean. Once touted as the cleanest possible source of energy, nuclear plant disasters prove it to be one of the deadliest sources of energy on earth.

Natural disasters are those that humankind can do nothing about. Man-made atrocities occur when those employing science and technology allow their efforts to take precedence over human wellbeing. Historian Serhii Plokhy's 2018 book, *Chernobyl, History of a Tragedy* (London: Allen Lane), traces the unaccountable bureaucracy and unwarranted confidence of the scientists and politicians that led to the Chernobyl disaster. Radiation caused the sickness and deaths of those working at the plant and amongst those involved in trying to contain the fire and close down the reactor. Atmospheric radiation affected neighbouring Eastern and Western countries, causing radiation sickness and death in the human and animal population throughout several States of the Soviet Union. Through imminent damage to the earth's river and water table systems, Chernobyl verged on polluting the whole world with radiation. Emergency responder workers and those few politicians who understood the consequences also knew that they were sacrificing their lives to prevent that global atrocity. In the Soviet States most affected, Belarus and Ukraine, the Chernobyl atrocity led to the eco-nationalism that contributed in turn to the breakup of the Soviet Union. See the US–UK-produced docu-drama series *Chernobyl* for a blow-by-dramatic-blow account of the April 1986 nuclear plant atrocity.

Mass pollutions from coal, oil and gas and grave dangers of nuclear energy have driven technology towards renewable solar and wind power. However, there is also likely to be a reckoning between extensive use of land for solar and wind energy and the hyper-consumptive profiteering of the capitalist political economy. The bottom line is that runaway economic growth and mass consumption will have to be reduced, and reduced fairly.

Competing enterprises continually having to cut jobs and prices means that profits end up in fewer hands, with, for instance, five or six supermarket chains now monopolising the UK food industry. Today's high streets all look alike, same banks, newsagents, retail outlets, pubs, restaurant chains, etc. Globally, it's estimated that 147 capitalist corporate conglomerates control all industries of all types ('The 147 Companies that Control Everything', *Forbes*, 22 October 2011).

With renewable green technologies now believed to be the least dangerous and most feasible means of producing the energy needed to run industries, homes and transport, the 'Green New Deal' now being pursued by industrial countries promises new 'green' jobs. There is not much discussion on whether new 'green' wealth also means the offshoring of green jobs, the eventual cutting of green jobs and the syphoning up of 'green' profits into the pockets of the wealthy.

Six corporations now dominate the world market for petrochemical products. Petroleum and petrochemical products range from fuel to pesticides and plastic, to the resins used in medicines and cosmetics, shampoos, detergents, wax, to mulch, fertiliser, herbicides, pesticides, fungicides, to synthetic rubber, carpeting, etc.[18] In part to replace profiteering from the supply of gasoline to governments to power the vehicles of war, tanks, aeroplanes, ships, landing craft, jeeps, lorries, etc., petroleum and petrochemical corporations created new post-WWII markets that also fed the West's post-WWII long economic boom.

Half a century ago, in her 1962 book, *Silent Spring*, US marine biologist Rachel Carson documented how the use of chemical herbicides, fungicides and pesticides severely affected biodiversity, killing off insects, birds, wildlife, poisoning soil, contaminating rivers and seas, with a serious impact also on human health. The silent spring of Carson's book refers to the dearth of birdsong as the birds in the affected areas died off.

Chlorpyrifos is a petrochemical-based pesticide first developed as a nerve gas in WWII, then manufactured by petrochemical corporations as a pesticide. Its usage is linked to respiratory problems, infertility, miscarriages, birth defects, brain damage, Attention Deficit Hyperactivity Disorder and other neurological and developmental problems in children ('Chlorpyrifos – Toxic Pesticide Harming Our Environment and Children', Earthjustice, 2019).

In 1964 a US chemical company, Stauffer Chemical, patented petroleum-derived glysophate, a chemical chelator herbicide that binds and removes minerals from the weeds, causing the weeds to die, the actual crops also genetically designed to resist the pesticides, herbicides, fungicides.

The widespread use of glysophate-containing sprays causes soil degradation which leads deficiencies of up to 30% in the protein, vitamin and mineral content of the crops, for example, calcium, magnesium, manganese, copper, and zinc. The result is nutrient malnourishment, even when bellies are full ('Glysophate', Wikipedia).

Glysophate, a probable carcinogen, was found in the urine of the 48 Members of the European parliament who volunteered to take the urine test. The usual term of licence for agri-chemical manufacturers is 15 years. Industrialised farming is so dependent on glysophate containing agri-chemicals it will take years to find alternatives. The EU parliament's compromise was to reduce the usual 15-year production licence to seven years. The recommendation is that these products should only be used by those who know how to take precautions and shouldn't be used in public locations like parks and playgrounds. Though some retailers have pulled glysophate containing weedkiller off their shelves, it's still available in other retail outlets, and consumers, none the wiser, use those products in their gardens where their children play.

In August 2018, Monsanto, the giant agri-business producing products containing glysophate, was found guilty of having caused the cancer suffered by a worker who had to use the product up to 30 times a year, the claimant awarded $289 million in damages. In May 2019, a California judge ordered Monsanto to pay £2 billion in compensation and legal costs to a couple who got cancer from using Roundup weedkiller. The prosecution lawyers argued that 'Instead of investing in sound science they [Monsanto] invested millions in attacking science that threatened their business agenda.' There are now 13,000 such cases against Monsanto/Bayer. The giant German chemical corporation, Bayer, now owns Monsanto.

Glysophate is not the only compound used in these agri-products, and may even be the least rather than the most damaging ingredient ('Toxicity of formulants and heavy metals in glysophate-based herbicides and other pesticides', *Science*, <http://www.sciencemag.org>).

Glysophate and the other ingredients can result in alterations to human enzymes; are thought to decrease male fertility; be a cause of the global spike in celiac disease, asthma, other diseases and health conditions, inclusive of congenital deformities and brain damage in newborn children (Arjun Walia, 'It's Not the Zika Virus – Doctors link Monsanto Pesticides to Birth Defects', Prepare for Change Network, 16 February 2016).

Crops are now also becoming resistant to the herbicides, with new species of weeds growing up to 12 foot tall and taking up soil nutrients. The combination of contaminants in food and drink and the lowered nutritional value of foods are now being linked to the increases in diabetes, Parkinson's, disease, kidney failure, liver disease, respiratory diseases, cancers and dementia. Dr Paul Winchester, medical director of the neonatal intensive care unit of the Franciscan St Francis Health Network, Indianapolis, USA, states:

> People think global warming is the biggest threat, but it's not. This is. (Carey Gillam, *Whitewash, The Story of a Weed Killer – Cancer and the Corruption of Science*, Washington, DC: Island Press, 2017, Chapter 11, 'Under the Influence', p. 234)

Though public officials have long known of the environmental dangers of agri-chemically dependent mass agri-business, that vital information remains next to invisible in, for instance, the school curriculum for science, food technology, geography, history, and English.

Agri-businesses claim it is their right to reap increased profits from what they assert are their superior seeds, many of those seeds genetically modified, including some seeds modified to be 'terminator' seeds that don't reproduce seeds for the next crop. Where the agri-business crop does produce seeds, farmers must sign a contract that they will not harvest seeds from the post-harvest plants. Either way, farmers are forced to buy their next seed-crop from the agri-businesses instead.

In 2007, the production of patented seeds became one of the most lucrative industries in the world, accounting for 82% of the commercial seed market worldwide, the top 10 seed corporations controlling of 67% the global market ('Who Owns Nature? Corporate Power and The Final Frontier in the Commodification of Life', ETC Group, November 2008; ETC is an international organisation dedicated to conservation, sustainable development and human rights).

From 1950 to 1980, enormous swathes of land in the countries of the Global South were cleared for the planting of mono-crops, resulting in grain exports increasing by 295% during the 1960s and 1970s. In this 'green' revolution, the fast-growing crops from hybrid seeds used in the production of grains, soy, etc., were also modified to resist the negative effects of the agri-chemicals used in the repeated sprayings of crops. Supposed to need less water, these seeds required more.

Research by investigative journalist, Mark Dowie, revealed the role and motivation of the US Ford and Rockefeller Foundations in funding the agri-science that promoted the mono-cultural, corporate agri-business–based 'green revolution':

> The primary objective of the program was geopolitical: to provide food for the populace in undeveloped countries and so bring social stability and weaken the fomenting of communist insurgency.
>
> There is significant evidence that the Green Revolution weakened socialist movements in many nations. In countries such as India, Mexico, and the Philippines, *technological solutions* were sought as an alternative to expanding *agrarian reform* initiatives, the latter of which were often linked to socialist politics. ('The Green Revolution', Wikipedia)

Though poor yields of water-deprived 'green revolution' crops from these hybrid seeds in Third World countries cause impoverished farmers to fail, these seeds continue to be sold in areas of water scarcity. Many tenant farmers and owners of smallholdings, indebted to the agri-businesses and money lenders, no longer able to feed their families, have, and are, committing suicide. Across India, there are 45 farmer suicides a day, a third in men under 30. Those families who owned their land have little choice but to sell up to pay the debts incurred to buy the seeds and herbicides.[19]

Much of the grain exported from Third World countries is used in the West for animal feed, leading to an increase in Western animal husbandry.

Globally, the methane gases produced by cattle, sheep, goats, pigs now contribute approximately 15% of the emissions of carbon dioxide that alters the balance of the earth's ecosystem.

It takes 15,415 litres of water to produce a kilo of beef; 8,763 litres of water per kilo for sheep and goat; 5,988 litres for pork; 4,250 for chicken. By contrast, it takes only 962 litres of water to produce a kilo of fruit; 9,063 litres per kilo for nuts; 322 litres of water per kilo for vegetables.

Soybean crops have shallow root systems and need lots of watering. During a recent rainstorm in Argentina, a hidden underground river created by years of watering the soy crops burst through the topsoil, this new river splitting the enormous soy farms in two.

Through pollination, genetically modified seeds can affect non-GM crops. GM foods have been implicated as dangerous to human health, though to what extent hasn't yet been made clear. Some countries ban the use of GM seeds; others do not. The separate countries of the EU are free to set their GM crop policy. For marketing reasons, it's the policy of some EU countries not to grow GM crops because millions of people don't want to eat GM foods. Except on an experimental basis, GM crops aren't grown in the UK, but the UK imports tons of GM crops for animal feed.

No regulations require imported food to be labelled as GM or non-GM, and there is no legislation in place that would allow consumers to know whether cereals, for instance, come from GM crops or whether vegetables, nuts and fruit have been treated with agri-chemicals containing glysophate and other harmful chemicals. Consequently, it's almost impossible for supermarket customers to gauge the safety of most of the foods they consume.

That the widespread use of agri-chemicals threatens flora and fauna, and the health and well-being of millions of people is now undeniable. Just who is responsible, and how do we develop the institutions that would disseminate vital information and enable citizens to participate in decisionmaking about the permissible uses of agri-technology?

In response to *The Guardian*'s long 12 March 2018 article, 'What is biodiversity and why does it matter to us?', the Beyond Extinction Economics response was published in the 15 March 2018 *Guardian* article, 'Awkward questions about diversity'. Beyond Extinction Economics aims to identify the economic, political, and socio-cultural drivers of extinction economics.

> First, to say 'we' or 'human activity' is responsible for biodiversity loss sidesteps the more serious challenge of identifying the specific socio-cultural, and, more centrally, economic drivers of destruction. Second, to slip easily from population rises to industrial development, housing and farming as the causes of the destruction of wild areas evades critical questions about what sort of industry, producing what sort of consumer goods and what kind of farming and food distribution system – let alone questions as to who has the power to decide and who gets to consume and who doesn't. Drastic declines in biodiversity not only compete with climate change for importance, but are intertwined with it and other processes of environmental degradation which together constitute multi-dimensional crises in the relationship between our global economy and society and the earth that sustains us. Popular pressure and inter-governmental cooperation to restrain these forces are urgently needed. In the longer term, only deep economic and social transformations give us any hope of a livable and sustainable world. (Signed: Prof. Pritam Singh, Oxford Brookes University; Jenneth Parker, Schumacher Institute; Ted Benton, Prof. Emeritus, University of Essex, and Red-Green Study Group, and seven others)

Besides the 1.25 million people a year killed in traffic accidents, it is now real beyond doubt that exhaust fumes from millions of fossil fuel–burning vehicles make the air in cities unfit to breathe. In 2012, indoor and external pollution caused an estimated 6.5 million deaths across the globe (World Health Organisation Report, 'Almost half of all deaths now have a recorded cause, WHO data show', WHO 2017).

The argument that natural forces cause the climate emergency has all too little to say about the atrocious planetary damages of man-made pollutions. Further, the US National Aeronautic and Space Administration (NASA) understood from 1975 that man-made greenhouse gas was having severe effects on the earth's climate. In 1988, the UN set up the Intergovernmental Panel for Climate Change to assess climate science and help shape policy. The IPCC findings on climate change were unwelcome news to the business world, which then put great efforts into manufacturing doubt about the science of climate change.

In 2012 before he was elected president of the USA, businessman Donald Trump claimed that global warming was a hoax concocted by China to make the US economy non-competitive. In blunderbluss them and us fashion, he said in November 2018 that it was countries like China that had to reduce carbon emissions, not the USA – as if it were not a fact that the West has for decades offshored its carbon emissions to Third World factories, including China, and continues to do so.

In October 2017, the former UK politician who served, briefly, as a UK Chancellor, before serving, briefly, as Secretary of State for Energy, and who now sits in the unelected UK House of Lords as a Tory politician, was heard on BBC Radio Four pronouncing in tones of broadcast authority false facts about climate change, the programme producers failing to challenge those false pronouncements.

Communications gigolos like press secretaries use academic phrases such as 'sustainable development' to push meaning into no-exit roundabouts of the social class apartheid. For the establishment and maintenance of economic justice within countries and between the wealthy northwest and the Global South nothing less is required than the total rejigging of the profiteering political economy that fills ruling class lives with luxury and stuffs ordinary consumers with flim flam they don't need – along with the short-term habits of mind that come with all that stuff.

The point of presenting all this gloomy information isn't to say that humanity could or should return to being hunter-gatherers. It is to say that amongst the reasons for the atrocity of planetary decay is that, unwillingly coerced and unwittingly colluding with politicians, corporations, scientists and technologists, we have permitted the discounting of the primacy of the socio-biological imperatives of nurture and care of the plant, animal and human world, allowing the government–corporate–banking world to put profiteering above the invention of the politico-economic and socio-culturally superior political economy of democratic socialism and the production of technologies required to meet people's need instead of the psychopathy of greed.

***

In 1984, the world's biggest non-nuclear industrial disaster in Bhopal, India was caused by the massive leak of tonnes of toxic gases from the negligently maintained chemical plant that manufactured pesticides, a technological disaster that killed 3,500 people immediately and exposed a million more to danger. Nobel Peace Prize–winner Mother Theresa arrived on a flight from New Delhi and, on an eight-hour propaganda initiative by government and organised religion, visited hospitals and the homes of survivors, handing out aluminium medallions of the Virgin Mary, urging people to forgive the atrocity: 'Forgiveness offers us a clean heart and people will be a hundred times better after it.' The Pope later reiterated those sentiments (Sanjoy Hazarika, 'Mother Theresa Carries Her Message to Bhopal', *New York Times*, 12 December 1984).

Union Carbide Corporation and its subsidiary Union Carbide India Limited, denying legal liability for the accident, paid what was essentially a nominal sum settle the case of negligence against it. Dow Chemical then became the owner of Union Carbide. With an annual income of around $10 billion dollars, Dow isn't short of the means to provide compensation for the lives lost; for medical treatment for poisoned survivors, and for the care of the brain-damaged children that were born thereafter. The Bhopal campaigners make an irrefutable case that it is untenable that corporations be allowed to purchase the wealth of an enterprise while divesting themselves of liability for the prior criminal negligence of the businesses they take over.

Dow Chemical is a global chemical conglomerate selling herbicides and pesticides, through its subsidiary Dow AgroSciences. The US Environmental Protection Agency is now warning that research shows that Dow pesticides may also be linked to increases in autism, ADHD, and learning difficulties in children.

Dow is also the world's largest producer of silicone, the material used by another subsidiary, Dow Corning, to manufacture breast implants. Even after Dow Corning knew their breast implant product was unsafe, causing thousands of women systemic health problems, and although the implant business accounted for only 1% of Dow Chemical's profits, fearing the dangers to its reputation by admitting liability, the corporation continued to produce and sell the implants.

Some of the women affected embarked on and won class action lawsuits. For the 2 million plus women who have undergone the implant operations, problems and anxieties continue. According to the Corporate

Conduct Quarterly, *Ethikos*, Dow Corning's action amounts to 'a 30-year medical experiment on women who were uninformed as to the risks'.[20]

What Dow Chemical did pay for was to become a corporate sponsor of the 2012 London Olympics. Few of the athletes competing, or the crowds cheering them on, were likely to know of the Bhopal disaster; of chemical pesticides altering the internal workings of the human brain; the breast implant scandal; of Dow's persistent avoidance of responsibility for its corporate wrongdoing.

Greenwashing its corporate image, Dow, manufacturer also of Napalm and Agent Orange, has instead set aside £64 million dollars to be an Olympic Games' sponsor for the next 10 years. Dow will also profit considerably from the infrastructure required by the world Olympic Games, for example, from the urethane foam for the running tracks to the materials used in the manufacture of the lighting used in some of the Olympic events.

During the run-up to the 2012 London Olympics, the UK prime minister at the time, plus the Secretary of State for Culture and minister in charge of the Olympics, plus the Chair of the London Olympics organising committee, the former athlete and MP for Falmouth and now a Life Peer, had no problem with Dow being a corporate sponsor. Their response to protesters against Dow's sponsorship was to declare that Dow had complied with all the legislation relevant to the Bhopal atrocity.[21]

Dow has now become part of DuPont, the world's largest chemical corporation in terms of sales, which, along with 3M, is responsible for the carcinogenetic toxins disseminated worldwide through Teflon-based products ('Poisoning America: The Devil We Know', BBC Four, *Storyville*, November 2018).

The point being made here is that populations cannot continue to allow corporations to ignore what must be their first duty, that of care for their workers, for the people of the surrounding community, and for their customers.

***

At over a trillion dollars, the pharmaceutical industry, is one of the biggest industries in the world, with 10 pharmaceutical corporations cornering nearly 50% of the world market. Big pharma also produces copies of patent-expired generic drugs. Generic drugs are also produced in poorer Third World Countries. Big pharma spends more on advertising than on research. Many of big pharma's drugs are based on natural medicines, but the natural remedy market demands more consumer knowledge of the product than slick advertising can provide.

The majority of the Nazi scientists and doctors who had ordered, and performed, horrifying medical experiments on concentration camp prisoners escaped prosecution after the end of WWII, and some of them ended up working for German pharmaceutical companies. One of them was Dr Heinrich Mückter:

> Mückter and his team were working on the development of a typhus vaccine, which was repeatedly tested on concentration camp inmates in Buchenwald and other places. The death figures of those inmates showed Mückter how well his vaccine was working.

Working for a German pharmaceutical company, Grünenthal, Müchkter invented Thalidomide, which was marketed globally to pregnant women as a cure for morning sickness. Thalidomide caused many children to be born with limb deformities or no limbs. The company made billions, and Mückter became a millionaire (*Heinrich Muckter – No Limits*).

The majority of people in the UK have good reasons to be thankful for the medical treatment and care provided by UK doctors and nurses. That treatment also includes the writing of 65 million prescriptions a year for anti-psychotic and anti-depressant drugs by UK doctors, an increase of 109% since 2009. Nearly all prescriptions are for poor and working-class people, 40% more of them for women than for men, some for children as young as 6 years old. Diagnosis of mental illness correlates with areas of high unemployment and government austerity measures. Add to that the conditions imposed on General Practitioners, the 10-minute consultations with patients, the doctors' 10-hour days, and the fact that when GPs retire, surgeries close down because physicians no longer want to become GPs.

The good news is that some mental health practitioners are joining forces with patient groups in support of the right of patients to have 'no decision made about me without me'.

Of the NHS contracts put out to tender during 2016–17, private firms got nearly 70% of those contracts, 267 out of 386. Virgin Care, part of

Richard Branson's Virgin Corporate empire paid no taxes for two years, despite having been awarded NHS contracts worth £2 billion over five years (Hilary Osborne, 'Virgin awarded almost £2bn of NHS contracts in past five years', *The Guardian*, 5 August 2018).

> Virgin Care has been able to avoid tax payments as it has some 13 holding companies between itself and its parent company Virgin GroupHoldings, some of which are registered offshore in the British Virgin Islands and citing Branson as sole shareholder. ('Branson's health service avoids UK corporation tax while racking up millions in NHS profits', 9 January 2018, <http://www.rt.com/uk/415364-branson-virgin-nhs-tax/>)

Private companies, Virgin Care included, now run much of the NHS mental health services for young people. In 2017, after it lost a contract to an in-house NHS and social enterprise consortium to provide health visitors, school nurses, speech and occupational therapy, Virgin Care sued the NHS, forcing the NHS to settle the case for millions of pounds, money that ought to have gone instead to the underfunded NHS.

In his February 2019 capitalist publicity stunt, UK billionaire businessman Richard Branson held a 'benefit' concert in Columbia just over the border from Venezuela, purportedly to raise money for 'humanitarian aid' for Venezuela. Were that his true interest, he could have donated many times the money raised by his 'benefit' concert. Richard Branson's tax-dodging Virgin Group of companies brings him enormous income. He then uses philanthrocapitalism to whitewash his profiteering. He also uses Virgin's profits to fund his commercial space tourism projects. In 2014, Branson said he envisions a colony on Mars and the commercial mining of asteroids and plans to build a space hotel. In the alien world of a tax-dodging investor in space technologies and his admirers, on a planet where a billion people are forced to live on less than a dollar a day, offering flights into space for rich individuals to rocket off for a spot of galactic tourism is considered normal rather than psychopathic behaviour. These psychopathic ambitions flout the plain-as-the-nose-on-your-face medical realities that any long-term experience of the zero-gravity of space causes loss of bone mass density in human beings and, life threatening reverse blood flow and clotting.

***

Domineering cultures of force and power have a negative effect on relations between people, inclusive of their sexual relations Though the one in 10 UK men from all social classes who use prostitutes are not all abusive and violent, many are:

> Since 1990, there have been 153 murders of prostitutes in the UK. ... Rates of post-traumatic stress disorder among women who have been in the sex industry are comparable to those of soldiers returning from a tour of duty; studies suggest two thirds of prostitution survivors are emotionally numb and tortured by recurrent nightmares and flashbacks. (Jo Bartosch, 'It isn't the stigma that is killing sex workers', *The Morning Star*, 6 September 2017)

Many of those women in the sex 'industry' are on anti-depressants or have a drug habit. Leftist politicians should not delude themselves and others into conveniently concluding that 'decriminalising' prostitution is the answer since to do so means the sexual exploitation of women becomes legalised by the state.

As well as an economy and laws that free women and girls from sexual exploitation and men and boys from a distorted view of male sexuality, all people have the human right to knowledge and understanding of the politico-economic and psychosocial circumstances in which societies disallow certain natural male and female biological and psychological characteristics. That not being the case, plus the fact that many men and women cannot be who they know themselves to be because of socio-culturally imposed gender performance roles, it should come as no surprise that sizeable numbers of men and women choose to separately identify themselves as be lesbian, gay or bisexual, or that a small percentage of bisexuals, gay men and lesbians seek to escape psycho-socially imposed pain, gender dysphoria, by embarking on a regime of hormonal drugs and the surgical means of medicalised transsexualism to change the appearance of their bodies, and – they hope – the configurations of their consciousness. The irony is that people choosing to hormonally transgender and surgically transsexualise their bodies are likely to be exchanging one socio-culturally constrained gender role for another.

It should go without saying that LGB, transgender and transsexual people should never be discriminated against on the bases of their choice of gender roles outwith heterosexuality. Nor should anyone be put on the medico-pharma transgender conveyor belt and be left thereafter to get on as best they might. Those seeking hormonal transgenderism and medicalised transsexualism have the medical right to the highest-quality counselling – and outwith the reach of the gender reassignment clinics, whether private or NHS. Such counselling must necessarily include the right to be informed about and consider the mental health problems, regrets and suicides of those who have chosen pharmacology and surgical transsexualism.

People of any chosen gender identity don't have the right to silence discussion of the rights and considered opinions of other gender identities. Nor should anyone have a monopoly on the discussion of transsexualism. Those with concerns about surgical transsexualism, as attested by some of those who have undergone the surgery, should not be denigrated as transphobic. Working together does not mean denying differences; it should mean making room instead for the pursuit of the larger goal of politico-economic equality for all.

For a rare account of the connections between the transgender lobby and the medical-pharma-industrial complex, rival to the military-industrial complex, its reach into government, universities, law, media and popular culture, a must-read is Jennifer Bilek's 20 February 2018 article in *The Federalist*, 'Who are the Rich, White Men Institutionalizing Transgender Ideology?':

> Exceedingly rich, white men (and women) who invest in biomedical companies are funding myriad transgender organizations whose agenda will make them gobs of money. (<http://www.thefederalist.com/2018/02/20/rich-white-men-institutionalizing-transgender-ideology>)

Since the core purpose of militarism is to control and kill, the claims of LGBTQ+ people to equal rights to serve in the military should they choose to do so must not go without comment any more than should the choice of heterosexuals to serve in the military people go unchallenged – keeping in mind that in a world beset by inequality at every turn, 'choice' has little meaning.

Gender activists of any sexual persuasion need to do their best not to permit themselves to be diverted from building political solidarity with the anti-sexist feminist and anti-racist civil rights movements. The good news is that Lesbians and Gays Support the Migrants activists mount protests against the sexual abuse of women by the guards employed by the privatised company running the governments Immigrant Removal Centre at Yarls Wood ('Activist group dumps rotten food in support of Yarls Wood hunger strikers', *CommonSpace*, 2 March 2018).

***

The technological invention of cryptocurrencies operating outside the capitalist banking system, and of the blockchain technology on which cryptocurrencies are based, allow computer-based peer-to-peer validated commercial relationships, a technological development heralded as the silver bullet of monetary reform and a harbinger of socialism. In an atmosphere of almost religious fervour over the sudden appearance of cryptocurrencies, so far most transactions have been conducted by mainly male, tech-savvy users and speculative dealers. Some countries and businesses use cryptocurrencies for specific transactions, while some nations ban them. Facebook is considering issuing a Facebook cryptocurrency for use amongst Facebook users.

Should there be any grievances about the goods and services exchanged through cryptocurrency computer-networked distribution ledgers, there is no route of appeal to external mediators or higher authorities, as there is in the conventional banking system. Unlike with lost or stolen debit cards, lose your private cryptocurrency code, say goodbye to your money.

Though anonymous computer technologists purportedly invented internet cryptocurrency as the antidote to the corrupt banking system that caused the 2008 crash, the invention of cryptocurrencies was not and is not a democratically arrived at fiscal, economic and political solution to the problems of the corruption, mistrust and inefficiencies of the global banking system.

Since the anonymity intrinsic to cryptocurrencies makes it impossible to prevent their harmful uses, cryptocurrencies have been used to buy and sell armaments; fund terrorism; produce pornography, etc. In the 2017 NHS hack-attack blocking of access to patients' computer-stored records, hospitals had to pay up in cryptocurrencies to get the records unblocked.

Internet start-up businesses see opportunities for using blockchain technology to transform transactions in other sectors of the economy, the aim being to provide lower cost, error-free contracts services, for example, peer-to-peer selling of real estate property via blockchain smart contracts that cut out the real estate agents, lawyers, accountants, clerks, etc. Smart contracts necessarily depend on one-size-fits-all parameters of what the contract can include and exclude. Offering a quick fix, blockchain contracts are also inflexible in other aspects. Before clicking the 'Agree' box, users must know precisely what they're getting – and not getting – in that smart contract. With no recourse to contract lawyers or any other authority, there is no room whatsoever for after-sales regrets.

There are also financial and social cost issues in the excessive amounts of electricity required to run the computerised blockchain technology. Users must also provide incentives to the blockchain technology entrepreneurs to operate the systems of the different cryptocurrencies available, which raises the user/entrepreneur trust issue of value-for-money about those incentives. These financial and social cost cryptocurrency trust issues and value-for-money incentives bring us back to somewhere not all that from life before blockchain. Furthermore, how are profits derived from anonymous transactions to be taxed?

Those who understandably seek to escape the control of the corrupt banking and finance system through the sideways move towards cryptocurrency are obliged to accumulate that particular form of currency in the first place – and in ways not dissimilar from any other capitalist accumulative and speculative activity. What cryptocurrencies and blockchain-based technology smart contracts cannot negate are the exploitative commercial relations inherent in the capitalist political economy.

Blockchain cryptocurrencies are used only by those with the money to do so. Nonetheless, many people cite blockchain as heralding socialist economics. In deciding whether people are deserving – or not – of particular goods and services, Western and Chinese surveillance capitalism rank debtors according to their credit/social scores. The consequences of the combined use of mass surveillance and anonymous blockchain economics are that both become integral to the worst totalitarian nightmare imaginable.

Like any other currency, money can be made and lost through the use of cryptocurrencies. Based on the extreme anonymity of mutual distrust, crypto technology capitalism is in no way compatible with what lies at the heart of democratic socialism: behaviours and systems of social, economic and political trust and solidarity. For a select few, cryptocurrencies are their answer to the corruptions of the capitalist. For the majority, it isn't and can't be.

Providing many useful and not so socially useful rentier services to millions of people everywhere, new applications of digital technology appear all the time. The Global Positioning System allows people to get immediate directions to wherever they want to go; smartphones have instant internet connection to front door cameraphones that enable customers to see from hundreds of miles away who is ringing their doorbell, and so on. Some digital technology services are nominally free, such as Google maps, but you still need an internet connection and a gadget to get them. Those gadgets and internet contracts mean that transnational corporations such as Google also become the material technological structures of surveillance capitalism.

What is the social value of the digital rentier service that, for a fee, enables the buyer to purchase clothes that sellers would once have donated to charity? What about the digital application that enables homeowners to post photos of the houses, apartments, rooms they've decided to rent out as short-term lets to holidaymakers? What about commercial lettings agencies getting on the digital bandwagon by renting properties from landlords then subletting them as higher short-term rentals? The knock-on effect is rising rents and real estate prices; job losses in the hotel and restaurant sector; and a diminishing of the sense of neighbourhood. What about the digitalised taxi services that bypass the regulated taxi services, reducing wages and putting qualified, safer taxi drivers out of a job? So unequal is that particular battle that the most competitive of those taxi companies have been listed on the stock exchange, a source of for shareholder income for those who need never take a taxi themselves.

The rentierism that flows from digital technology is evocative of the racketeers making the 'offer that can't be refused'. The fact is, however, that some cities have banned Uber taxi services and Airbnb lettings.

The hidden footnote of the digitalised economy is its environmental impact, from its extraction of raw materials, gadget transportation costs, and its use of electricity. Cryptocurrency 'mining' requires immense computer power. The energy used for cryptocurrency exchanges is now thought to cost as much per year as Switzerland's annual electricity bill.

The old claim that the loss of one sort of job to robotisation is compensated for by the creation of another type of work has long been untenable. The most that can be said is that one country may be a bit better at creating, scarce, high-skilled, well-paid employment for the highly educated, low-waged, part-time and temporary jobs, or no jobs, for the majority.

The 'end of history' concept of a great technology-based revolution, detached from historical and contemporary realities, denigrates people's ongoing battles for economic justice, freedom, equal human rights and responsibilities.

The good news is that more people than ever now understand that millions more jobs have been lost to capitalism's inbuilt competitiveness, automation, robotisation, digitalisation and artificial intelligence than were ever taken by immigrants.

In an increasingly interconnected world, populations will, ultimately, not allow themselves to be discarded and dismissed. At home and abroad, today's activists take it upon themselves to monitor who is in control of what technology, in what ways, and with what effects on which sectors of the populations. That, for instance, 76% of medical genetic technologies are taken up by the Caucasian world and the rich, can't be allowed to continue to be the case.

Though the Big T, modern technology, provides fabulously useful tools, no technology can ever take the place of the intrinsic socio-biological need of all human beings for human connection and understanding of the world into which they are born, live and will die. For all its wonders, modern information technology can never be a stand-in for the fundamental human task of separating the wheat from the chaff in all areas of knowledge, all communication systems, all forms of governance.

The good news is that today's tech-savvy activists keep constant watch, and their whistleblowing on tech giants results in demands for legislation to ensure non-surveillance, non-censorship and non-manipulation of social media and that the giant corporations such as Google, Facebook, Apple, Amazon are turned into public utilities answerable to democratic control.

The further good news is that today's analysts and activists provide increasing amounts of information about the workings, overt and covert, of the capitalist world. Progressive organisations add daily to knowledge and understanding of how to go about changing the competitive capitalist system. The UK's major opposition party now declares that should it gain power it will ensure, for instance, that all employees will have the right to the minimum wage; it will legislate to ban zero-hours contracts; establish regional banks in support of the productive economy; take public services back into government control; improve education, and harness renewable technologies to reduce pollution and deal with the climate emergency.

In the US, the belly of the capitalist beast, a senator declaring himself socialist garnered over 13 million votes in the run-up to the US 2016 presidential elections, and in the 2018 US mid-term Congressional and Senate elections, the Democrats won back the US House of Congress, with many more women and people of colour elected.

The question always asked of democratic socialists is where is the money to come from. The money to fund democratic socialism will come in large part from where wealth always comes from: the surplus value created by the labour and technologies produced by human beings, past, present and future. It will also come from the legislation that decrees that corporations and the wealthy are liable to fair taxation and that the wealthy can no longer hide, launder and invest their wealth via secret tax havens.

CHAPTER 9

Trading Blocs

The hard fight for legislation for a minimum wage is a laudable achievement, and such fights must and will go on. Where is the legislation that sets a maximum cap on the pay of chief executives? On the unearned income of shareholders? On water utility companies that focus more on profit than the upkeep of utility infrastructure, using the cheap technology of microbeads in their water treatment plants, the beads expelled into the sea, polluting the marine environment, ending up on beaches, the wind blowing microbeads onto farmland? Some water companies leak untreated sewage into the ocean because the penalties issued by government watchdog organisations are less costly than carrying out the work necessary to protect public health. Where is the legislation to prevent banks and shareholders from investing in private prisons, so that even incarceration of the least educated and most neglected becomes a source of profit?

As for the promotion of a Universal Basic Income and Job Guarantee Schemes, small price to pay for the continuance of capitalist licence, a bargain for the elite, UBI and JGS won't be long tolerated by the poor and working-class majority.

Today's capitalist trade agreement legislation carves up the global economy into exploitative and protectionist trading blocs through which most of the transnational economy is regulated Those trade 'agreements' are hammered out by corporatists, government officials and lobbyists behind closed doors. Trade agreements also have labour protection clauses written into them, without which the agreements wouldn't be passed. Notable by their absence are clauses on compliance with labour protection laws, such as they are. Though government-corporate-media propaganda campaigns herald today's 'free trade agreements' as promoting a new age of greater economic freedoms and increased prosperity, those asymmetrical trade agreements can adversely affect people's everyday lives, diminish democratic rights, weaken the sovereignty of nations and constrain international relations.

Written into today's trade agreements are the International Centre for the Settlement of Investment Disputes clauses. If governments decide to enact policies that have the effect of reducing corporate profits, ICSID clauses legally allow corporations to sue those governments. Uruguay, Norway, and Australia are amongst those countries that have been sued under ICSID legislation. There are now many ICSID courts worldwide, and ICSID court cases have themselves become big business:

> The number of suits filed against countries at the ICSID is now around 500 – and that figure is growing at an average rate of one case a week. The sums awarded in damages are so vast that investment funds have taken notice: corporations' claims against States are now seen as assets that can be invested in or used as leverage to secure multimillion-dollar loans. (Clare Provost and Matt Kennon, 'The obscure legal system that lets corporations sue countries', *The Guardian*, 10 June 2015)

These disputes are less about honest disagreements amongst equals and more about the powers of the minority elite over the majority.

Here's some good news: political activists are nowadays wrenching back the curtain of trade agreement secrecy, malinformation and manipulation at such a rate that millions of ordinary citizens worldwide, including in the USA and the EU, are now mounting campaigns against what they judge to be the real aim of today's push for new trade agreements: corporate profiteering; job losses; slashing of food safety standards; the demise of health and safety regulations.

Meantime, business 'leaders' and governments commonly use the divide-and-rule argy-bargy over world trade 'agreements' to promote one country as the enemy of the other, a call too often taken up by workers and voters. Much needed are robust transnational worker-consumer organisations that keep their eye on the ball and demand trade agreements be drafted in the interests of fairness for consumers, workers and traders.

A very great deal is at stake, as evidenced, for instance, by the tortuous battles between the EU trading bloc and the British government over the terms of Britain's exit from the EU. At issue is whether the UK and EU politicians are aiming for agreements that favour the wealthy, or if there is sufficient political pressure by a well-informed UK electorate and the opposition party to force government to push for exit terms in support of the UK's now exponentially poorer and working-class majority and its increasingly squeezed middle classes.

***

The last several decades of burgeoning Chinese economic expansion has allowed China to lift 800 million of its people out of poverty. In a vast country with a population of 1.4 billion, a great deal of poverty remains.

The 2008 global financial crash meant the millions of unemployed in the affluent West didn't have the money to buy Chinese goods, which put Chinese factory workers out of work, which unleashed unrest and protests against the Chinese government, the Chinese stock market also going into decline.

As of 2017, there were 35,652 wholly foreign-owned businesses and joint/foreign-owned ventures in China. Those foreign investments and the transfer of manufacturing technology from abroad produced immense profits, better standards of living for many, provided unearned income for battalions of shareholders at home and abroad – and created the new Chinese billionaires.

Through trade, investment and the building of significant road and rail transport systems, China's 'one belt, one road' strategy aims to develop State capitalist economic relations with the rest of Asia, Africa and Europe.

China, home to some of the most polluted cities on earth, is beginning to address air pollution by constructing carbon dioxide absorbing towers and banning diesel – but more cars than ever are on the road. China is also reforesting the Gobi desert, but factories go on spewing pollution into the atmosphere.

China is also deeply engaged in the development of surveillance and data technology capitalism, awarding a 'social credit' trustworthiness score to all citizens. Depending on their score, 'good' citizens can jump the queue to get access to scarce goods and services. 'Bad' citizens may never get to join the queue in the first place.

In the Xinjiang Autonomous Region of the People's Republic of China, the Turkic ethnic Muslim population, low-waged compared to the Han

Chinese who in the Mao era were encouraged to migrate to Xinjiang, there are increased arrests of Muslims, a million of whom are incarcerated in Chinese 're-education camps', with Muslim countries around the world protesting against the treatment of Chinese Muslims.

The dire treatment of the decreasing numbers of Chinese political activists and the lack of anything resembling sustained political opposition, international economic political and military tensions all mean that Chinese State capitalism 'with Chinese with characteristics,' holds no 'get out of jail' card from viciously competitive global capitalism, global instability and planetary unsustainability.

An intensely patriarchal society run by its Central Politburo of 25 men, few women have ever served on the Politburo, nor are there any women in its powerful seven-member Standing Committee. In March 2018, the Chinese government also removed the restriction on the number of terms the Chinese premier can serve.

China has the largest standing army in the world. A source of employment for otherwise workless young men it has over 2 million servicemen and spends two thirds less on its military forces than the USA. Through its one-party system, China has enormous political and economic power to invest in technological research, development and production. Not yet equal to the USA in military technology, China is well on its way to being so.

This chapter has briefly outlined the prevailing state of play with regard to the ongoing fight for progressive legislation; today's adversarial capitalist trade 'agreements'; and need to build inclusive national and international worker-consumer organisations to enable populations to better monitor and steward the world's resources and promote egalitarian distribution of those goods instead of permitting the battalions of global shareholders to hoard unearned income from the world's resources in common.

The next chapter provides a brief outline of people's historical and ongoing struggles against the forces of power and domination. Though specifically referencing the UK, struggles for justice, equality and peace are ongoing in countries across the globe.

CHAPTER 10

Battles for Justice, Quest for Peace

Today's generations are often unaware of how much they benefit from people's persistent historical and contemporary oppositions against the forces of power and dominance. This chapter offers some brief examples of those oppositions and people's struggles for peace.

In 1888, impoverished women and girls working in a London match factory went on strike against cancer-inducing working conditions and slave wages. Appalled at the factory conditions, the activists of the day championed the case, which helped the match girls win their strike for better conditions and pay.[22]

The conservative-minded upper- and middle-class suffragists, more concerned that women weren't allowed to study at university, favoured the reformist parliamentary route to change. That strike of those working-class women and girls, however, also had some influence the 1890s battles of the militant suffragettes who took more radical direct action to gain the vote for women, drawing more working-class women to join this sector of the movement (Sarah Jackson, 'The suffragettes weren't just white middle-class women throwing stones', *The Guardian*, 12 October 2015).

The 1950s protests by UK Caribbean immigrants against racial discrimination in housing and employment led to race riots that led in turn to the Race Relations Acts of 1965, 1968, 1976, 2000 against racial discrimination in a public place, in housing and employment, in State schools and colleges, in the provision of goods and services. Each point on that legislative continuum was fought for and won by groups of people building on each of the prior hard-won gains.

UK Caribbean parent organisations also challenged prejudicial attitudes towards black pupils in UK State schools, campaigning against the high exclusion rates of disaffected black pupils in State schools. Pressures from the black and Asian communities, notwithstanding the tensions between those two communities, also contributed to government's move away from their preferred racial assimilationist policies to UK multi-culturalism. Along with the feminist and the US civil rights movements, multiculturalism contributed to the 1960s–80s campaigns for equal education opportunities in UK State schools. Today, the debate also focuses on the rights of ethnic minorities to be acknowledged in terms of both their religious and secular identities. [23]

In the UK up until the late 1960s, homosexuality was a punishable crime for which gay men could be charged, tried and sent to jail. Campaigns against the criminalisation of homosexuality, and for equal legal rights for gay people, led firstly to the Sexual Offences Act of 1967 which decriminalised homosexual acts in private between two men over the age of 21. Subsequent and persistent campaigning by activists eventually led to the 2014 legal right of gay couples, male or female, to marry.[24]

In 1968 the women workers at the Dagenham car factory went on strike for equal pay. Their actions led to the Equal Pay Act of 1970, followed by the Sex Discrimination Act of 1975. The 2010 film based on their struggle, *Made in Dagenham*, is well worth watching.

Lucas Aerospace, a UK engineering firm, made half of its profits through publicly funded government contracts, much of it for the supply of military goods to the UK government. In the 1970s, the firm became less able to compete in the world market and faced job losses. In 1976, the Lucas Combined Shop Stewards representing the workers in the different craft unions and across the different sites of the company submitted their Alternative Corporate Plan for Lucas Aerospace to convert manufacturing of military products into the production of socially useful goods.

The plan also contributed to the movement for democracy in the workplace:

> The movement that emerged challenged establishment claims that technology progressed autonomously of society, and that people inevitably had to adapt to the tools offered up by science. Activists argued knowledge and technology was shaped by social choices over its development, and those choices needed to become more democratic.[25]

The plan got next to no backing from the Trades Union Congress and none from the government. The Lucas Plan won the Nobel Prize for Peace. It continues to be a prototype of how corporations can be turned into industries that support peace and prosperity.

In 1976, a small workforce of Asian women workers at the Grunwick film processing works went on strike for improved pay and conditions. The workforce got no support from the UK labour unions. Famously known as the 'strikers in saris', the UK media appeared to regard the women strikers more as a curiosity than as a workforce with legitimate claims to decent pay and conditions. Continuing for two years before it failed, the strike created enough of a stir for future workers at the plant to win improved pay and conditions. The socio-cultural effects of the women's strike were almost as significant as the strike itself in that Asian women would no longer be regarded as docile workers to be exploited at will.[26]

One of the longest strikes in UK trade union history was the 1984–5 year-long strike miners' strike. Government energy policy was shifting from coal to the use of oil, natural gas and nuclear energy. Determined to beat the striking miners, the government resorted to the likes of intimidating miners and their families by sending hundreds of policemen to small mining villages; withholding social security benefits from miners' families. Government also used classic carrot-and-stick, divide-and-rule tactics to split the miners, leading the Nottinghamshire miners to believe, for example, that their mines would remain open. Government also planted double agents in the National Union of Mineworkers.

The government–corporate–media complex lodged false stories of covert Russian and East German government interventions in support of UK miners. In tones of melodramatic insincerity, the prime minister played her part by demonising the miners as 'The Enemy Within'.[27] The great majority of miners were already on strike, but the government and mass media chose to hype the secret ballot as the bellwether of democracy, relentlessly criticising the leader of the NUM for disregarding the calls of the punditry to hold a national strike ballot.

The government won the battle; the war continues. The unintended consequences for the powers that be were revelations about the lengths to which a supposedly modern democratic government would go in opposing workers' rights. Consequently, the 1984–5 miners' strike politicised millions more people than ever clapped eyes on a coal mine.

In defeating the miners, the government also quashed potential strikes by any other sizeable UK workforce, which allowed government free rein to embed its preferred technocratically financialised 'free-market' global economy, helping to lead us to where we are now.[28]

In the judgement of many, the attitude of the police during the strike of being above the law and following orders helped breed the negligence of the Yorkshire Police Force in their crowd management duties four years later at the 1989 Hillsborough football stadium event in Sheffield which led to the deaths of 96 football fans.[29] Cover-ups of police incompetence by police and government deflected blame for those 96 deaths onto the football fans, and for more than a quarter of a century most of UK media sided with the false witness statements concocted by the Yorkshire Police Force. In April 2016, the coroner ruled that the fans were not responsible for the disaster, the coroner then ruling that the jury's verdict meant the police force managing the event was to blame. In the November 2019 trial against the police match commander on duty on the day the fans were killed, the jury was unable to reach a verdict. The judge ruled the commander not guilty of the crimes of gross negligence deaths. If the case proved the legal system incapable of reaching a guilty verdict, in this case of unlawful deaths, it also proved beyond doubt the immense resilience of the families who fought a 27-year battle to clear the names of their loved ones, then struggled on for another three years for justice denied.

To many, Hillsborough is an example of the collusive intent of the UK's police forces and government to quash investigations into police negligence and crimes, including those against black people. In 1993, as a result of excessive use of force by the police during the arrest of a 40-year-old mother for deportation to Jamaica, Joy Gardner died.[30] Police also botched the 1993 investigation into the Steven Lawrence case, the unprovoked attack and murder of a black schoolboy by a group of racist young white men.[31] Over the past 24 years, there have been no convictions and no admission of wrongdoing regarding the approximately 500 deaths of black and Asian people while in police custody.[32] During the policing of the City of London 2009 delegates' meeting of the 20 wealthiest nations in the world, the G-20 Summit, an elderly newspaper vendor on his way home was attacked by a policeman wielding a baton, the vendor later dying from his injuries. It was on the evidence not of fellow police officers but of bystanders that the guilty policeman was identified and faced charges, during which it was revealed that though he'd had nine disciplinary charges brought against him, he'd been allowed to continue to work as a policeman ('Death of Ian Tomlinson', Wikipedia).

The majority of policemen and woman daily put their safety on the line doing arduous and stressful work to the best of their ability. Those who don't, act safely in the knowledge that should they commit wrongful acts they are unlikely to be prosecuted.

The persistent resistance to oppression is also seen in the revelations of the abused against paedophilic priests, clergy, football coaches, politicians, celebrities, and in cases of sexual abuse against women, against powerful film producers, famous actors, politicians, and charity workers.

Here's the good news: the persistent unveiling of the physical, emotional, psychological socio-cultural and politico-economic harm done by sexist, racist, classist abuse reveals that people everywhere will do all in their power to oppose that toxic ecology.

War on Want, established in 1951, works with other movements and groups to raise awareness that the causes of poverty are the capitalist system's inbuilt democratic deficits, its economic injustices and inequalities.

The US atomic bombing of the Japanese cities of Nagasaki and Hiroshima instantly killed 200,000 people. The UK-based Campaign for Nuclear Disarmament was set up in 1957 to campaign against nuclear weapons.

The modern peace movement took deeper global root from around 1965 when millions of people worldwide began campaigning against the US war in Vietnam.

In 1974 the Campaign Against the Arms Trade was founded by a coalition of UK peace groups.

In 1981 the Women's Peace Camp at the Greenham Common Royal Air Force Base, England was set up to protest the UK government's decision that the US use the base as the site for intercontinental cruise missiles with nuclear warheads.

The female-only nature of the peace camps also allowed women to assert their own dominance in a political arena often reserved for men. The women of Greenham integrated themselves into these male-dominated political spaces not through violence but through their mere presence at a 'male' location such as the military base RAF Greenham Common. ('Greenham Common Women's Peace Camp', Wikipedia)

In September 2001, a coalition of peace organisations, socialist politicians and grassroots activist founded the Stop the War Coalition to try to prevent what they knew would be the coming wars perpetrated by the West after the 11 September 2001 attacks on US World Trade Centre and the US Pentagon, a fourth aeroplane crashing into a field in Pennsylvania. On the morning the planes crashed into the WTC, a nearby building, untouched by aeroplanes or any falling debris, was razed to the ground in what had all the hallmarks of controlled demolition. This and much other evidence contradicted the officially curated government–media narrative that the 9/11 catastrophe that killed 2,753 innocent civilians was a sophisticated terrorist attack. The subsequent 9/11 Truth.Org movement presents credible evidence of the attacks being false flag operations organised by the US 'Deep State' and its allies amongst the global elite. Amongst the suspected motives for those attacks was to completely destroy without trace massive amounts of documented evidence of gross corruption, and to ignite a government war on 'global terrorism'. After the collapse of the Soviet Union, there could be no more 'reds under the beds' scares about communism. It was to be the new bogeyman of the 'War on Terror' that would provide the rationale for the withdrawal of civil liberties in the Western democracies – in the name of protecting the borders of the Western homelands. It would also provide fake validation for the State terror of waging resource wars on poor countries.

The US Occupy Wall Street movement was set up in 2011 to campaign against the increasing inequalities of the capitalist system, sparking similar Occupy movements in other countries. Police forces removed the campaigners from public spaces, but there was no removing the words of the Occupy Movement, 'We are the 99%'. That defining slogan enabled millions to delineate their real politico-economic identities and aspirations as the polar opposite to that of the elite 1% (more like the 0.1%) who own the vast majority of the world's wealth, and whose power is sustained by the likes of surveillance capitalism, one of the biggest democratic deficits of all.

Edward Snowden is a young man of right-wing persuasions, a member of the US National Rifle Association who believed that traitors revealing secrets and betraying the United States of America should, in his own words, 'be shot in the balls'. Formerly employed as an information technology consultant by the Dell corporation, the USA Central Intelligence Agency and as a spy for the US National Security Agency, Snowden turned out to be the citizen whistleblower who leaked NSA documents revealing that the USA conducted mass surveillance on its population.

Knowing that the US government would arrest him for espionage and that he faced imprisonment, or worse, Snowden made his escape from US territory, ending up in Russia where he currently lives and works. Edward Snowden has stated that having been trapped in the mass surveillance culture that created deep-seated suspicion and distrust amongst the general population, secrecy and deceit amongst those with whom he worked meant he'd had no intellectual and psychological choice but to work out for himself the values of life he could believe in: honesty, integrity, transparency and accountability. Asked if he didn't fear retribution by the US government, his response is that those values now bring him an inner peace that goes beyond the dread of what tomorrow might bring.

Snowden was lucky to have the support of others who helped him escape from the US and gain sanctuary elsewhere, including Julian Assange. Unlike Snowden, Julian Assange had always been a rebel against corrupt governance. Founder of Wikileaks, he is wanted by the USA for leaking videos of US war crimes. The videos of American servicemen in helicopters shooting innocent civilians, the shooters gloating as if they had won a computer game, went viral and shocked the world. Those videos were amongst all the information leaked to Assange by Chelsea/Bradley Manning, a US serviceman pardoned after seven years by the outgoing President Obama after Manning had received a 35-year sentence for revealing those US war crimes. In May 2019, Manning was again imprisoned by the US government for refusing to testify against Assange. Manning states that no prison in the world could imprison her mind to the extent that she would testify against the investigative journalism of Assange.

The UN had declared that Assange had no case to answer against the rape charges brought against him in Sweden. Having spent seven years holed up in the Ecuadorian Embassy where he had been given sanctuary against arrest, a new Ecuadorian leader in hock to US government withdrew asylum and in April 2019 British police entered the embassy and arrested Assange who was charged with having skipped bail to enter the Ecuadorian Embassy. He was sent to Belmarsh Prison. The US wants to extradite him from the UK to stand trial for revealing classified information on US war crimes. The BBC reported on 31 May 2019 that after examining the case, the UN rapporteur on torture concluded that Julian Assange had suffered psychological torture – at the hands of the democratic governments of the UK, US and Swedish governments.

Various US politicians and pundits have called for whistleblowers Edward Snowden and Julian Assange to be shot.

Streamed live from Auckland Town Hall, New Zealand, 'The Moment of Truth' video (YouTube), 15 September 2014 (starts at 22 minutes in), is approximately two hours long. It features Assange, Snowden, lawyer Robert Amsterdam and investigative journalist Glenn Greenwald. The video provides probably the most comprehensively succinct evidence of the workings of the global mass surveillance system.

Despite all the powers arrayed against truth teller whistleblowers, whether a low-paid worker revealing evidence of wrongdoing in a care home; the abused identifying their abusers; tech-savvy whistleblowers exposing State secrets; a policeman revealing the exploitation of vulnerable young people in children's homes; an investigative journalists in pursuit of the truth, what the truth tellers have in common is that there comes the point when the obvious risks to livelihood and safety is chosen over the collusions of silence.

The current leader and the shadow chancellor of the UK's socialist-leaning opposition party are amongst the few UK politicians who consistently voted against war. The party's leaders, despite opposition from its reactionary MPs, have helped shift opinion away from war and right-wing austerity politics – and away from the party's previous stance as a liberal mediator for the capitalist status quo.

The first question always asked of any potential democratic socialist government, is where is the money to come from? As previously indicated, it will come from where wealth always comes from, the surplus value produced by all the labour of all the generations past, present and future.

It must also come from a thoroughly re-engineered legal, finance and banking system that controls the creation and uses of interest-bearing debt; provides credit for the productive economy; ceases the syphoning up of wealth up into the pockets of those to whom it doesn't belong; uses the wealth produced to maintain and expand health services, education, welfare, social care for the elderly, decent housing and child-care, etc.

CHAPTER 11

Propaganda

Public communication systems broadcasting information in the public interest is the opposite of corporate propaganda that seeks to manipulate the public mind for the sake of profit. A crucial element in education for democratic socialism, this chapter will briefly review the basics of how modern propaganda systems work.

Sigmund Freud (1856–1939), the founder of psychoanalysis, famous for his work on individual psychotherapy, was the uncle of Edward Bernays who, influenced by the new field of psychology, was more interested in the theory of crowd psychology as hypothesised by French polymath, psychologist, misogynist, eugenicist, anti-Marxist Gustave Le Bon (1841–1931), who in 1895 wrote *The Crowd: A Study of The Popular Mind*. Le Bon believed that:

> Even in the most intelligent races there are a large number of women whose brains are closer in size to those of gorillas than to the most developed male brains. This inferiority is so obvious that no one can contest it for a moment; only its degree is worth discussion. Women represent the most inferior forms of human evolution and are closer to children and savages than to an adult, civilized man. They excel in fickleness, inconsistency, absence of thought and logic, and incapacity to reason. Without a doubt there exists some distinguished women, but they are as exceptional as the birth of any monstrosity, as for example, of a gorilla with two heads; consequently, we may neglect them entirely. (Gould, quoted in Jerry Bergman, *Darwin's Teaching of Women's Inferiority*, Dallas, TX: Institute for Creation Research, 1 March 1994)

Le Bon's rant about the assumed superior characteristics of men compared to women was highly influential amongst those who believed that democracy, though politically inevitable, was a dangerous concept that must be managed by men with the power to propel society in the directions they regarded as desirable.

Bernays, founder of the public relations 'industry', in his 1928 book *Propaganda* details crowd psychology techniques based on a comprehensive analysis of how government, corporations, the sciences, arts, education systems and the media can be used in a complex of manipulative subterfuges to co-opt people's minds and behaviours. Bernays termed this deliberate coercion of the public mind as the 'engineering of consent'.

Crowd psychology techniques assume a stance of expertise; accentuate a dominating point of view; dictate to the emotions; keep the message simple, sloganistic and repetitive; don't tolerate discussion or debate, and connect attention-grabbing scenarios and spectacle to the selling point of whatever is being promoted – from soap powders to political worldviews and ideologies.

The cigarette-making machine was invented in 1881, and cigarette advertising was directed at men, the male smokers depicted as handsome, macho, ruggedly confident. The male cigarette smoking market reached saturation point, and tobacco company bosses hired Edward Bernays to devise ways of convincing the other half of the population, women, to smoke.

Bernays paid a social psychologist $125 dollars for advice on how to deal with the socio-cultural obstacle that the few women who did smoke were regarded as low-class, vulgar and uncouth. Bernays was advised that the way to change that perception was to portray cigarettes as a symbol of female freedom, the subliminal message being that cigarettes represented the male penis and that women could achieve male power by smoking.

During the 1929 New York Easter parade, alerting newspaper journalists and photographers to attend, Bernays organised the spectacle of a lineup of well-dressed, good-looking, middle-class women doing the unthinkable, smoking cigarettes. The next day, newspapers were full of photos of these 'liberated' women smoking their 'Torches of Freedom'. Feminist leaders got in on the act, calling on women to take up smoking and 'Fight another sex Taboo!' Hollywood produced films portraying beautiful, intriguing, purportedly independent, cigarette smoking women as the height of glamour and sophistication.

Though the medical profession already knew cigarette smoking was seriously harmful to human health, it would be decades before those facts become public knowledge. Bernays, well aware of the dangers of smoking, would break his wife's cigarettes in half and flushed them down the toilet. Jewish, Bernays was later shocked to learn of the Nazi governments use crowd psychology techniques in stirring up of racial hatred against the Jews.

Tobacco corporations knew that to keep the profits rolling in, besides manufacturing trillions of cigarettes, they would also have to manufacture doubt about the truth about the connection between cigarette smoking, respiratory ill health, lung cancer and death. For decades the tobacco CEOs paid for 'medical experts' to declare that smoking posed no threat to human health' (Oreskes and Conway, *Merchants of Doubt – How a Handful of Scientists Obscured the Truth on Issues from Tobacco Smoking to Global Warming*, London: Bloomsbury, 2011).

If you happen to eat bacon and eggs for breakfast, you are likely to be unaware how that choice is might well have been influenced by Bernays' public relations campaigns on behalf of farmers seeking to expand the market for pork and bacon.

Government and corporate lobbyists also hired Bernays to run the 1950s US destabilisation campaign against the newly democratically elected Guatemalan government which had legislated to safeguard its economy from exploitation by US corporatists and politicians, legislation that could set a precedent for other Latin American countries to follow.

Bernays spread a media-hyped rumour that the Guatemalan president was a communist; US Central Intelligence Agency operatives stirred up government opposition groups within Guatemala; funded a Guatemalan right-wing group in exile to invade the country and oust the elected president. The coup leader was installed as the US proxy president-dictator who proceeded to revoke the politico-economically progressive legislation, thus handing back economic and political control to the US government-corporate nexus ('Edward Bernays: Selling War', YouTube, November 2012).

Here's the good news: this Age of information also supports the development of autonomous education, with corporations, governments and politicians beginning to twig to the fact that populations everywhere are getting themselves out from under the propaganda cosh, and how self-emancipatory education leads to there being fewer places for the profiteers and their media moguls to hide.

In ancient Greece, Plato discovered that an uneducated slave, when asked a series of questions about geometry, showed an understanding of geometric principles. Since even by trying to dig into the physical human brain can't reveal the origins of human intelligence, Plato's unprovable surmise became known as Plato's problem. No doubt the slave had other problems on his mind.

Human intelligence is such an immense resource that the forces of dominance do all they can to co-opt, coerce, corrupt and degrade that intelligence for their own ends, famously by integrating organised religions into their power structure. Organised religions are related to, but not the same as, people's religious sense of connection to nature and the universe.

Every human being doing their best to withstand the coercion of propaganda systems ought firstly to be congratulated. The next step is to try to unite with others to resist socio-psychological abuses, and form the progressive activist groups needed to oppose politico-economic and socio-cultural dominations.

The next chapter looks at how, without being directly taught, children use their inborn intelligence to acquire the language of their community by the time they are around three years of age. By age 5, they will have acquired the everyday vocabulary and sentence structure of the average adult.

CHAPTER 12

The Socio-biological Nature of Language Acquisition

Notwithstanding the myriad of speculations, the origin of human speech, the phenomenon that sets humans apart, is as unknowable as the origins of consciousness. Linguists must garner their understandings about the connections between the innateness of human intelligence and the acquisition of language from the empirical evidence available to them.[33] Though some of the brain's generalised operations can be detected by modern technology, the brain and its sources of consciousness are so enormously complex that such technology is about as revealing as trying to detect nails in a skyscraper.

Born with the senses of touch, smell, taste, hearing and sight, the ability to think and act, children are also born with innate ability to analyse and decipher the linguistic and grammatical structure of whatever their community language happens to be. Before they utter a word, children are constantly assessing and categorising the grammatical properties of nouns, verb tenses, conjunctions, prepositions, adjectives, adverbs, etc., and figuring out for themselves how those universals of human grammar are organised in the syntax of their particular language. Bilingual and trilingual children are simultaneously operating these same processes for each different language.

Babies in their babbling phase are already using the nuances of speech intonation, and by about 11–14 months are speaking words and compound phrases. By approximately two and a half years of age, children are uttering phrases and sentences they've never heard spoken. They also know the difference between ordinary speech and song; understand what rhyme is; what a joke is; and what cursing and bad language are.

Children process their thoughts through their internal i-language and express their thoughts, observations and desires in their i-dialect, a mixture of the community dialect, accent, personal phrasing, social speech usage and the standard forms of their language.

Human beings use language to express and help construct their complexities of thought. An estimated 80% of thought and internal language is never expressed out loud. Sensory, emotional, and intellectual awareness of their own and other observable wider states of understanding leads children to ask those endless questions through which they confirm and develop their own understandings.

Through the universal phenomenon of play, children imitate, fantasise, hypothesise, analyse, pursue real and imagined desires. Children play both physical jokes and verbal jokes, understand the difference between rudeness and politeness and will negotiate, lie, shout and bawl their way out of what they don't want to do, or what they know is behaviour likely to get them in trouble. Children also know when someone is speaking grammatical gibberish, and will also catch on, eventually, to when people are telling fibs and lies.

Through the socio-biological imperatives of the interaction between children, parents, family members, carers and others, children are socialised into the world and make their mark on that world while developing their emotions, sense of self, awareness of the agency of others and of what's fair and what isn't. They also learn to stand up for themselves, regulate their feelings, and be empathetic towards others. A fabulous quality all human beings have in common is that each is a unique personality. What the vast majority of children also have in common is that however unique, and whatever levels of the language they experience at home, children are already experienced thinkers, analysers, and users of language before they reach the school gates.

The job of schools is not to demand knowledge, understanding and levels of linguistic competence that is alien to children's experiences. First and foremost, the job of schools is to acknowledge the child's inborn intelligence, help build on what the child already knows and can do, and to then help develop the child's knowledge and understanding to the benefit of the child and for the good of his/her society.

Should proof be needed of innate human intelligence incessantly in operation, the 2015 BBC One three-part documentary, *Poor Kids*, shows a few of the 3.5 million UK children who live in poverty profoundly conveying in their own words the effects of impoverishment on their young lives.

The Socio-biological Nature of Language Acquisition

The likes of the 2015/16 BBC Four documentary series *The Secret Lives of 4 and 5 Year Olds* reveals the richly interwoven aspects of children's social, emotional, psychological, intellectual, and linguistic development, the ego, empathy, competitiveness, cooperation, sense of rule-bound fairness, mischievousness, disagreement, and peace-making skills, all are ceaselessly at work.

In almost all documentaries of this type, the children are from working-class backgrounds, either higher, middle or lower working-class; classroom and play area are richly resourced, and the pupil-teacher ratio is usually one teacher to around six children. On the assertion that competition makes learning more engaging, the teachers commonly introduce competitive tasks and prizes. Disturbing to watch is the induced sense of dominance in the 'winners', the heartache and tears of the 'losers'. Cooperative games and learning tasks are likely to have been more appealing to the children and would have provided the audience with equally if not more interesting TV.

The 2017 BBC Two documentary, *No More Boys and Girls: Can Our Kids Go Gender Free*, presented by Médicins Sans Frontiéres Doctor Javid Abdelmoneim, tackles the institutional sexism amongst children and staff in today's primary schools. The project treats a class of 7-year-old boys and girls as though they were each other's equals, which physically they are until they reach puberty. The project lasts some weeks, and the parents are also given 'homework' designed to deal with the effects of gender stereotyping in the home. Parents are asked not to dress their children in gender-based garments and remove the likes of Cinderella and Spiderman duvet covers; to note and change their gendered language and attitudes towards their children, treating their sons and daughters as equals. In place of gendered toys, the children were given gender-neutral activity packs to play with, and in the classroom, the children are presented with a series of activities designed to get them to consider the effects of gender stereotyping,

One of the outcomes of the project was that children's affable, kind and fatherly class teacher, previously unaware he'd been promoting gender stereotyping, stopped addressing the girls as 'love', 'sweetie' and the boys as 'fella', 'mate'.

By the end of the experiment, the girls became more confident in saying what they thought; the boys, previously more likely to express disagreement, dominance, annoyance and anger, became more empathetic, quickly understanding that it's 'better to talk than strop'. Attitudes and understanding between boys and girls improved. The parents, seeing their children benefit from gender-neutral language and practices in the home, markedly changed their attitudes and behaviours towards their children.

The project questionnaires completed before and after the experiment indicated that, rather than being a here-today-gone-tomorrow phenomenon, the previously stereotypically gendered attitudes and behaviours appeared to have been substantially altered. The school management team and teachers had believed that in publishing their equal opportunities policies, they'd already created an anti-sexist school ethos. The project showed that until policy intentions are integrated into classroom practices, policies are more cosmetic than real.

Though children have already proved – big time – that they are autonomous learners, limitations on the right to go on being autonomous learners are placed on nearly all children, and not least on those 4.1 million UK children who live in poverty, nine in a classroom of 30.

Perennially bemoaning State school failures, government responds to the public exam success of State school children by labelling it 'grade inflation. Ministers pressure the examinations boards to alter the exam grading systems; replace course-work with end-of-school, do-or-die school examinations; introduce less accessible syllabi, such as reducing the number of female political thinkers to be studied got A-level history to one;[34] and to designing the less than truthful history syllabus that teaches children British Imperialism-lite.

The good news is that very many poor and working-class youngsters do succeed in UK State schools, testament to their inborn intelligence, their will to engage and thrive – and to the continual efforts of parents and teachers doing all in their power to support them.

CHAPTER 13

The Socio-cultural Nature of Literacy Development

Based on his meticulous classroom research, Russian pedagogical cognitive psychologist Lev Vygotsky (1896–1934) authenticated the socio-cultural nature of teaching and learning, his theory and practice refuting the top-down theories of transmission teaching and learning. The basics of Lev Vygotsky's theory and practice are that the role of the parent, teacher, fellow pupil, or student, the More Knowledgeable Person, MKP, is to ascertain the learner's level of skill and understanding as it exists at point A. The MKP then assesses how to help the pupil move on from what he/she already knows and can do for him/herself at point A to the next stage of learning, point (B). Vygotsky described the psychological, emotional, intellectual, educational distance from A to B as the learners Zone of Proximal Development, ZPD – and showed that the journey from A to B will be different for each learner. To be able to devise the cognitive scaffold of inter-related tasks that will lead the pupil from point A to the next stage of skill and understanding, B, the teacher must necessarily engage in discursive, socio-cultural interaction with the individual.[35]

Nothing short of revolutionary to the world of traditional transmission teaching, Stalin banned Vygotsky's theory and practice as the work of a 'bourgeois idealist'.[36] Stalin died in 1953, but Vygotsky's work didn't see the light of day in the West until his *Thought and Language* was published in 1962, *Mind and Society* in 1978.

The behavioural stereotyping of the Wendy House and Sand Pit notwithstanding, UK primary schools attempt to be socio-culturally welcoming places. In the teaching of literacy, however, the severing of the socio-cognitive connections between children's language, lived experiences, observations, aspirations and the books they are given to learn to read on has become so 'normalised' as to go almost unnoticed.

Rather than offering young children books with illustrations depicting recognisable people going about their lives in the identifiable world, children are presented instead with a plethora of illustrated fictions dislocated from their everyday experiences, observations, knowledge, understandings. The main protagonists in children's early-years literature are far more likely to be talking animals, witches, ghosts, monsters, wizards, giants, with kings, queens, prince and princesses abounding. *Cinderella* portrays the handsome prince rescuing the beautiful commoner from a life of drudgery, exploitation and impoverishment. In *Little Red Riding Hood*, along comes the heroic woodsman with an axe, ready, willing and able to save the disobedient young girl from getting eaten alive by the big bad wolf. And so on. Still published in industrial proportions, whatever else such books do, they do nothing for sexual and racial equality, even less for the quest for politico-economic justice.

To generate meanings from whatever the communication being offered, the recipient listener, observer, reader, the viewer must bring her/his lived experiences, observations, language and understandings to whatever the narratives and images being presented. The recipient makes connections with whatever is both present and absent in that communication; with what is denoted and connoted; obvious and nuanced; overt and covert. The recipient's initial response is to sort out how the intellectual, psychological, emotional and socio-cultural impact of the communication fits and doesn't fit with whatever the recipient's experiences, language and understandings are. Given the innate human reflex of curiosity, of deciding on attention span, on whether to engage in openness, trust, mistrust, and in problem-solving, the recipient's responses, conscious and subconscious, can range from emotional, psychological and intellectual identification with the narrative content; partial identification; submission to the enthrallments of all or a part of whatever the 'story' being told; to resistance and rejection of all or part of it. The recipient can also be persuaded to permit the narrative to impose its communicative goals – or may reject those aims; may be less than convinced by all or parts of the authorial intents; can acquiesce, resist or downright disbelieve whatever the persuasions of whatever the medium of communication. In modern mass-media culture, however, what can't be underestimated is the cultural predisposition to allow the narratives of the publishing and broadcasting world to influence lived experience. Moreover, the power of media manipulation is such that audiences can all too easily become doubtful about their own perceptions, knowledge, understandings, judgements and conclusions.

In the past, folk, fairy and symbolic tales warning of external physical dangers and perilous inner desires were told face-to-face by a local storyteller to a community audience of adults and youngsters. In the unfolding of the tale, the psychological, moral and behavioural denouements were declared or implied in such a way that the audience was likely to duly consider those warnings and resolutions. Few people were likely to say bollocks to all that guff, you're having me on.

Upon the invention of the printing press, besides publishing those traditional fairy tales, fables and myths, the new tales also produced were directed less at a community audience, more at the reader who could afford to buy those new narratives now based on the perceptions, attitudes and behaviours of the contemporary adult literate world. Sophisticated adults wrote these more attenuated stories for other adults. Also published and popularised were the new books written by adults for children, the settings, characterisations, themes and denouements reflecting adult middle-class notions on how children ought to behave.[37]

Books for 4-year-olds on transgenderism says a good deal about the power of the transgender lobby and publishers bandwaggoning on today's cultural wars ('Kool-Aid for Kiddies – teaching little ones about the gender fairy', lilymaynard.com blog, 29 June 2019).

The majority of today's primary school books are produced via publishers' age-related reading schemes, purportedly designed to move children on from being able to read allegedly simple texts to those that are more complex in structure, vocabulary and concepts.

As children become more adept at decoding text, they are likely to be presented with abridged versions of age-old myths and legends produced for adults in other socio-cultural times. Though all literature depends to a greater or lesser extent on universal archetypes, such tales cannot reflect the experiences and imports of contemporary circumstances. Whatever else those myths and legends do, they are not designed to mediate the circumstances, politico-economic and socio-cultural understandings of children living in today's world.

Modern fictional fare for primary school children does also portray children's everyday acts in common, for example, brushing their teeth, eating their vegetables, learning to share, being kind to others, etc. School-age fictions will also incorporate a modern phantasmagoria of exotic adventures, for example, families rocketing off to other planets named Topia. Fantastical and exotic adventure stories that grab attention and pass the time may provide the reader with a useful inkling or insight or two – or may not.

Today's secondary school fictions will also include stories about the milestone moments experienced by most youngsters, for example, the forming of special friendships, teenage relationships, dealing with difficult problems, family troubles, with choosing moral pathways, and so on.

Whether in those primary school books portraying children's everyday acts in common or in those secondary school fictions based on teenagers' milestone moments, largely omitted are the politico-socio-economic contexts in which children's experiences, choices, problems and concerns are also likely to be rooted.

Parents, carers, teachers are seldom consciously aware of the separation of the realities of children's actual lived experiences from the books children are given to learn to read on. Parents, teachers and the children themselves are keen to get on with the business of the children becoming 'good' readers. Where reading to children signifies closeness and care between child and carer above all else, the oddness of the textual diet becomes a pragmatically acceptable phenomenon.

Parting company with the publisher's reading scheme adherents are those who call for school fictions to be more reflective of children's actual environments. However, such 'real books' as there are tend to reflect the perceptions, values, attitudes and behaviours of middle-class parents for their children. These real books also depict recognisable contemporary settings and characters, so that when such 'real' books are introduced to poor readers from economically impoverished backgrounds, their literacy improves.[38]

Children are influenced by many more things than the media they encounter, and most children are also very resilient, so to what extent do their encounters with a socio-economically and socio-culturally decontextualised children's literature, and multifarious other media manipulations, matter?

The aim of the authors and producers of the media-constructed products for public consumption is to stimulate consumer curiosity and, as far as books for youngsters are concerned, to entertain and influence the audience of children, parents, schools in such a way as to get them to buy the books and the commercial goods sold off the back of those books. Since it also matters to the consumers whether they'll be coming back for more or not, how the publisher handles the content matters a very great deal to both publisher and audience. The publishing world is much geared to making the social class nature of society more covert than overt. Consequently the content of books for the poor and working-class majority of children matters a great deal. In November 2017, the chief executive of the UK's biggest publisher, Penguin Random House, stated in an episode of the *Seriously* BBC Radio Four programme, 'Where Are All the Working-Class Writers', that he was 'sick in my stomach when I realised books and publishing don't reflect the world we live in.'

Nowadays, getting in on the 'cultural diversity' market, the big publishers will publish books on gender and race, but, except for the highly profitable misery memoirs, they publish little that reflects the lives and socio-economic concerns of the poor and working-class majority. The mainstream publishers make hardnosed commercial decisions on what they will and won't publish, avoiding works that could well be outside the publishers' world view and the comfort zones of the readers. Publishers also have their eye on their backlist assets. Introducing books depicting the dramatically convoluted realities of class-based social relations is likely to reduce profits from reprinted editions of their backlists of published books – in the same way that the realities depicted in today's documentary broadcasting render much of the old TV programming unwatchable.

The socio-biological imperatives of nurture and care are essential to all children. Whatever the nature of that care, children could not survive without it. The socio-cultural conditioning that comes with those socio-biological imperatives will also become part of children's consciousness. Their sense of self may also lead them to resist that conditioning. Add to that dynamic the socio-cultural biases in the books children are given to learn to read on, and the likely consequences are that the majority of girls will believe themselves less capable than boys and boys believing it's best for their masculine image if they don't display too many feelings of a caring kind.

In very young children, socio-cultural biases regarding their perceptions of people of a different gender, race and social class tend to take second place to their natural gravitation towards human beings who show a generosity of spirit. Race, gender and social class unfamiliarity tend, however, to connect with the wider socio-cultural prejudices to become the dominating factors.

Though some modern fictions do attempt to address the socio-culturally induced prejudices of sexism and racism, many do not. A University of Florida study of gender stereotypes in children's books found that in a range of children's books published between 1900 and 2000, all books had at 'least one male character, while 25% had no female characters whatsoever, and that 37% had no female characters who spoke.' Another study examining gender stereotypes in the media found that 'only 18.5% of cartoons have female characters who have a job or professional ambition, compared with 80% for male characters' (Francesca Cavallo and Elena Favilli, 'Sexist stories keep girls down. A new kind of heroine can set them free', *The Guardian*, Friday, 13 April 2007).

Fictional portrayals in books, TV and films can affect both the realistic and unrealistic aspirations of children: ballet dancer for the girls, aeroplane pilot for the boys; hairdresser for the working-class girl, teacher for the middle-class young man; carpenter for the working-class lad; scientist for the middle-class university graduate, etc.

The Centre for Literacy in Primary Education (CLPE) reports that 12% of the children's books published in 2017 featured animals as characters. Only 4% of books featured children from Black, Asian and Minority Ethnic backgrounds who make up 32% of the school population. Consequently, young readers had less chance of seeing ethnic minority characters in books, and 'more chance of encountering a rabbit' instead.

In adult BAME books, the point is to expose the overriding racism of society at large and to show that the underlying norms of BAME culture are equal to that of the mainstream culture. Portrayals of the classism, sexism, racism that are also involved BAME hierarchies are not usually a focus of attention.

Popular UK children's authors, for instance, Enid Blyton, Roald Dahl, J. K. Rowling, their books selling in the millions, are criticised for their omission of non-white characters; their discriminatory attitudes towards working-class people; and Roald Dahl also for his misogyny. Enid Blyton's books have been translated into 90 languages; J. K. Rowling's into 80 languages; Roald Dahl's into 59 languages.

To all of the above identifiable factors, add the knowing and unwitting working-class stereotypes in the books given to young children to learn to read on, and there isn't much doubt that the content of the books children encounter matters a good deal.

Animated cartoon films, packing an eye-candy technicoloured punch, routinely reflect racism, sexism, ageism and social class prejudices. Child viewers, often isolated spectators and absorbers of such fare, are left with little chance for psychological and intellectual manoeuvre.[39]

Today's contemporary fictions for older primary and secondary school pupils do also depict some of the issues faced by many of today's youngsters: divorced parents, step-siblings, homelessness, struggles over sexual identity, drug addiction, etc. Some fictions also depict dystopian futures where dictatorial elites are in totalitarian command and control. To the extent that they allow readers to reflect upon some of the personal emotional and psychological aspects of contemporary life, and to consider some of the broader socio-political issues, both types of books may be useful – or not. Such fictions, whether employing the domestic or socio-political palette, feature strong plotting; constrained thematic structure; portrayals of mini-dimensional, and largely classless, young protagonists tasked with negotiating his/her way around single-issue difficulties authorially detached from the realpolitik of the politico-economic and socio-cultural ecology in which such difficulties are rooted.

The conventional rationale for such fare, often propounded as literary theory, is that as with primary school stories of giants and monsters, single-issue teenage fictions provide youngsters with opportunities to deal with troubling and fear-provoking topics at a safe psychological distance, though few teenagers are in reality likely to find comfort in such rationales.

Children are also presented with many more fictions than with factually explanatory books, and a significant problem in getting working-class teenagers interested in reading, boys in particular, is that they are averse to the superficial treatment of their real concerns. The fictions on offer don't provide young readers with convincing portrayals and credible solutions to the problems youngsters encounter in the societies they inhabit. The fictions available are instead likely to contribute to uncertainty, doubt, and unnecessarily delayed understandings. Adults too are turned off by books based on less than recognisable scenarios, peopled by characters who think and speak in less than recognisable tones.

Children's actual observations, contemplations, questions and concerns are also communicated in the colloquial language of their place and time. Projecting a type of 'street credibility', modern fictions do manage to capture that colloquial language – though not for the purposes of revealing plausible solutions to real problems.

The essential question here about the books available to young people is not the extent to which the mainly middle-class authors may, or may not, be capable of representing the lived experiences of others; nor is it whether or not writers are indulging in the conventions of self-censorship; nor is it a question of whether children understand the structures of storytelling – whether fairy, folk, symbolic tales, myths, and legends, or those of more contemporary fictions. Children can and do perceive the themes and archetypes of storytelling; are capable of making some sense of whatever the story happens to be; of rejecting narratives in which they don't find authentic to their understandings of the world they inhabit. What is far more at issue here is the largely unexamined effects that the plethora of politico-economically and socio-culturally decontextualised fictions can have on children's knowledge, perceptions, and understandings.

Thin on the ground are depictions of the activism of those young people who do speak up about injustice and inequality, who do get involved in real-life protests and campaigns. The good news is that young people are becoming increasingly involved in today's activism. A rare account of teenage activism can be found in a non-fictional narrative about, and interviews with, school-aged youngsters who protested against the Iraq War, see Red Marriott's 'Schoolkids against the Iraqi War' (libcom, 8 March 2009).

Hardly covered in the mainstream media, the history of those protests against the Iraq war by UK school kids would be lost if it weren't for the work of these contemporary history bloggers.

The unexamined validation for the mono-diet of more or less status quo themes, language and attitudes in children's books is that it enables learners to access the higher levels of socio-cultural meanings and values. Seldom mentioned is the fact that the curtailing of children's everyday language can impede thought, perception, understanding and the development of language and literacy.

The next question is what part does the routine decontextualisation of analytical, political and economic understandings in the literature published for children and young adults play in inhibiting their development of their critical, political, multi-functional literacy? Indeed, minus that multi-functional literacy, exactly what sort of literacy is it that is being transmitted?

Teachers favouring traditional transmission methods are also more likely to prefer the fictions from the traditional canon than a more socio-culturally contextualised children's literature that must be treated differently from the books in the traditional canon.

In some State schools it's also not an uncommon postulation that poor and working-class children don't want to talk or read about their lives anyway, the presumption being that it could only depress them. Another postulation, sometimes propounded as educational theory, is that the act of reading develops children's imaginations and intellect; that it allows poor children in particular to transcend the problems encountered in their daily lived experiences; that it also allows them to reach higher levels of intellect. The underlying assumptions here are that people's imaginations are separable from their experiences and circumstances and that people's thoughts are only ever about their daily circumstances. Unacknowledged in such presumptions is that human beings inherently engage in dreams, flights of fancy, and in intellectual and philosophical contemplation. The fact is that common 'educational' suppositions about what the act of reading contributes, or doesn't, to human imaginative agility also rest on the illogical conjecture that for textless millennia human beings lived their lives disconnected from the intrinsic human intelligence, imagination and ingenuity that enabled people across the globe to invent languages, technologies, economies, politics, arts, cultures and the societies and civilisations of their time and place – vital human inventions and developments without which this modern era would not exist.

In today's highly literate societies that oblige populations to acquire the skills of decoding and encoding of text, it's a common surmise that as long as the children are developing those essential skills, the textual content is of little consequence. If some broken threads of temporary truth run through some of these presumptions, they are wholly inadequate descriptors of people's innate intelligence and the phenomenal intricacies of human consciousness.

Whether fictions or school textbooks written in the more academic language of the Standard English dialect, the content of both factual books and fictions are discussed and written about in the Standard English dialect, a practice that sidelines children's idiomatic thought and speech. The often unexamined consequence is that this can then have the effect of putting a stop on the ability of youngsters to construct the two-way bridges of the colloquial-standard forms of the language they need to get to and from the linguistic registers of school subjects like physics, mathematics, chemistry, biology, etc. For an analysis of the roles that standard and idiomatic language play in education, see 'Literacy with an Attitude' (Wikipedia).

Decontextualisation is also routine in the likes of glossified geography texts that present, for instance, accounts of Third World agriculture, for example, how pineapples, bananas, or cocoa beans are grown, with no mention of made of the land-grabs, the dangerous usage of herbicides and pesticides, the exploitation of workers, the use of child labour in the harvesting of cacao.

The good news is that beyond the messages constrained in whatever the communication being promulgated, and despite the efforts of the powers that be to manipulate the communicative world, billions of people everywhere, children included, are also capable of coming to their own judgements about what they will and won't accept as tenable propositions. That innate human ability to resist and refute malinformation drives the powers that be to go to extraordinary lengths to try to suppress people's intrinsic intellectual abilities and to do all they can to assimilate people's intelligence for their own ends.

What must surely become a crucial focus of attention for parents, teachers and pupils is what they will do about the fact that the great majority of both fictional and factional books published annually for young people so persistently fails to contextualise the politico-economic, socio-cultural factors and socio-political relations that govern so much of the youngsters' daily lives.

CHAPTER 14

Sociopathy of Defective Hypotheses

The pseudo-scientific 'free-market' and 'survival of the fittest' tropes authored by the eighteenth- and nineteenth-century gentlemen scholars have much to answer for.

Scottish political economist and philosopher Adam Smith (1720–90) hypothesised that the pursuit of wealth suppresses men's interests and passions for heroism, soldiery, war, honour, reputation. He also presumed that the positive moral sentiments of people in business would prevail against the worst excesses of economic exploitation, that this was an inbuilt 'natural' economic law that would hold the overall laissez-faire, free-market political economy in more or less benign equilibrium.

Adam Smith also believed that government had a role to play in protecting the nation by military force when necessary and that the State should also enact laws to protect individuals from injustice and oppression by other members of society. The State should also support public institutions and services for public welfare that would otherwise be unlikely to be supported by wealthy individuals alone, though the provision of such services should not interfere with the incentive to work.

Adam Smith hypothesised that the individual accumulation of wealth contributed to the common good because even the most glutinous man of wealth inevitably created gainful employment by commanding that others meet all his commercial and individual requirements. Adam Smith was opposed to commercial decisions being taken in the interests of others, choosing to believe instead in 'trickle-down' economics.

> By pursuing his own interest he frequently promotes that of the society more effectually than when he really intends to promote it. I have never known much good done by those who affected to trade for the public good. It is an affectation, indeed, not very common among merchants, and very few words need be employed in dissuading

them from it. (Adam Smith, *An Inquiry into the Nature and Causes of the Wealth of Nations*, para IV.2.9, 1776. See Wiktionary, Citations: *Invisible Hand*, 2019)

Hypothesising that self-interest translates into the natural law of an 'invisible hand' that drives the economy, Adam Smith famously wrote, 'It is not from the benevolence of the butcher the brewer or the baker that we expect our dinner, but from their regard to their own interest.'

The British East India Company, the corporate conglomerate giant of the day, with its private army twice the size of the British army, used its dominance to enforce the BEIC's monopolised mercantilism on the rest of the world. Adam Smith believed, nevertheless, that:

> Without any intervention of law, therefore, the private interests and passions of men naturally lead them to divide and distribute the stock of every society, among all the different employment carried out in it, as nearly as possible in the proportion which is most agreeable to the interests of the whole society. (Adam Smith, *Wealth of Nations*, 1776, pp 594–595, as quoted in Albert Hirschman, *The Passions and the Interests, Political Arguments for Capitalism before its Triumph*, Princeton, NJ: Princeton University Press, 1977)

Adam Smith's 'free-market' hypothesis left him theoretically reduced to denouncing the BEIC as being merely uselessly rapacious. Adam Smith's brand of economics also led him to denounce slavery on purely economic grounds, in that badly treated dying slaves had to be replaced at greater eventual cost than the profits from slavery.

With corporatism and slavery explained as an unfortunate glitch in otherwise sound economic hypothesising, like many a 'scholar' of his time and place, and in the interests of the capitalist class of his day, Adam Smith did not envision that what was actually going on instead of 'trickle down' economics was the exponential 'syphoning up' of wealth into the pockets of the already wealthy – and of those who aspired to join them.

Adam Smith, a seemingly sympathetic, liberal-minded, middle-class, university man, along with the other 'gentlemen scholars' of his day, was intellectually ill-equipped to fathom how mercantile capitalism created few winners and millions of losers at home and across the globe.

Adam Smith never married, had no children, his mother looking after him for most of his life, a fairly sure bet as to why women are next to invisible in his theorising. In Adam Smith's view of the world, women of wealth are criticised for having fewer children, thus leaving the job of replenishing the population to those less fit for the job, impoverished women. Getting short shrift in his defective economic hypothesis is the fact that poor and working-class men and women had to work incessantly for survival wages. Nor does he seem to have noticed that while the butcher, the brewer, the baker worked hard to put food on the table for their families, their mothers, wives, sisters aunties were slaving away cooking the meals, looking after the children, cleaning the house, doing the laundry, etc. (Katrine Marcal, 'Paid or not, women have always contributed to the wealth of nations', *The Guardian*, 11 October 2015).

In Adam Smith's 'free-market' hypothesising there is no place for the voices of those who well knew there was no such thing as the 'free' market, and no imagined natural economic law operating as if it were some protective economic 'invisible hand'.

Adam Smith's contemporaries portray him as a kindly man with a benign smile who talked to himself, smiled at imaginary friends, and cannily refrained from speaking about his 'free-market' hypothesis in company, for the self-interested reason that the in-crowd of his day would not then need to attend his lectures or purchase his writings.

Adam Smith doubled his earnings by giving up his university professorship to become the private tutor, travelling companion and economic advisor to the wealthy young Duke of Buccleuch, showing the duke how to manage his extensive estates and invest his considerable disposable income.

Adam Smith was then able to retire in comfort to pursue his own interest and passion for thinking and writing about economics, producing his 1776 magnum opus, *The Wealth of Nations* and unpublished works on jurisprudence (Kirti Shailer, 'Biography of Adam Smith (With His Theories)', *Economist*, online student's blog. <http://www.economicsdiscussion.net/economists/biography-of-adam-smith-with-his-theories-economist/20999>).

The defective hypothesis of non-existent natural laws acting as an imaginary protective 'invisible hand' is experienced by millions at home and abroad as all too real daily politico-economic punches to the gut. Adam Smith's 'free-market' meme remains the socio-economic mantra for today's sociopathic capitalist elites and their beneficiaries.

In the next century, an upper-class gentleman scholar, Charles Darwin (1809–82), would step onto the socio-cultural stage to proselytise his patriarchal, pseudo-scientific evolutionary hypothesis of survival of the fittest.

Though by no means immune to Charles Darwin's pseudo-scientific hypothesising, Karl Marx (1818–83) managed instead to analyse the capitalist political economy more scrupulously than anyone before him ever had. Marx revealed capitalism to be the inexorable pursuit of economic competitiveness backed up by political power, force and dominance, militarism, and the uses of religion as a means of subduing and controlling populations.

> The proletarians have nothing to lose but their chains. They have a world to win. Workingmen of all countries unite! (Marx and Engels, *The Communist Manifesto*, 1848)

Published 160 years ago, Charles Darwin's 1859 *On the Origin of the Species by Means of Natural Selection, or the Preservation of Favoured Races in the Struggle for Life* continues to capture the minds of people living in the right here and now – not least because Darwin's hypothesis continues to be taught in schools and universities across the globe.

Darwin posited that all life is descended from a common ancestor and believed that procreating pairs were driven to mate based on imaginary laws of 'natural selection' that would best ensure the survival of offspring. Offspring that were too unfit to live, died. Darwin also believed that his imaginary 'natural selection' amongst the fittest also caused imaginary random mutations that enhanced the next generation's chances of survival.

Darwin's metaphor for his thought experiment was that of a 'tree of life' through which all biological life evolved in evolutionary stages, with humans being the most evolved amongst the species.

Though Darwin well knew that the fossil record did not support his imaginings, he continued to build his mental algorithm on the presumption that those transitional forms from one species to the next that had to exist for his version of the origins and subsequent evolution of life to be valid would doubtless one day be unearthed somewhere on the planet by somebody else.

Despite the subsequent one and half centuries plus of the digging up of all sorts, no such unequivocal inter-species forms have ever put in an appearance – an irrefutable reality that in no way deters nonstop media musings and hype to the contrary.

The words 'evolution' and 'adaptation' are very frequently wrongly used as though they were interchangeable – which they are not. Evidence abounds for environmental adaptations within each separate species. Also common within species is the intentional hybridisation of plant and animal breeding processes. There is also an abundance of modern scientific proof that all human, animal and plant life forms have a remarkably high number of genetic features in common. There is, however, no evidence of one species ever being in the process of turning into another, no such thing, therefore, of irrefutable proof of inter-species evolution.

In Darwin's day, the custom and practice of the times was for well-heeled and well-connected patriarchal men of scholarly leisure to enhance their reputations by busily adding to the pseudo-scientific postulations of the day. Darwin's half-cousin, Francis Galton (1822–1911), authored a treatise on eugenics that promulgated the breeding of human beings for desired characteristics – and the elimination of those who didn't have them:

> The question was then forced upon me. Could not the race of men be similarly improved? Could not the undesirables be got rid of and the desirables multiplied? (Galton, Victoria Brignel, 'The eugenics movement Britain wants to forget', *New Statesman*, December 2010)

Darwin was also strongly influenced by the theorising of one of the prior generation's 'gentleman' scholars, political economist Thomas Malthus (1766–1834). Though Malthus's calculations were later proved false, he hypothesised that populations would grow to exceed the food supply, leading to misery, want and poverty, and thus to the curtailment of the progress of society as a whole. Malthus also postulated what he abstractly labelled *positive* and *preventative* checks on population. Though reportedly not personally without feelings of compassion, Malthus was philosophically and politically against any organised provision of aid to the poor. He believed that hunger, disease, war, all of which he thought to be ordained by God, and all of which raise the death rate, were the *positive* checks on population growth. *Preventative* checks were that the birth rate should be lowered by celibacy and the postponement of marriage.

The theories of Malthus also fitted in with the desirability of the capitalists of the day to use populations as a source of expendable military manpower (*Malthusianism: Theories of Poverty and Aid*, The Borgen Project Radikha Singh, <http://www.borgenproject.org.malthusianism-theories-poverty-aid/>).

Philosophising about the existence of mechanistic 'laws' of nature also conveniently absolved the dominating powers of any responsibility for caring for a country's population of workers, soldiers and their families. Coming upon the writings of Malthus, Darwin eagerly assimilated the Malthusian postulations into his imaginings

> In October 1838, that is fifteen months after I had begun my systematic enquiry, I happened to read for amusement Malthus on *Population,* and being well prepared to appreciate the struggle for existence which everywhere goes on from long-continued observation of the habits of animals and plants, it at once struck me that under these circumstances favourable variations would tend to be preserved, and unfavourable ones to be destroyed. The result of this would be the formation of a new species. Here, then, I had at last got a theory by which to work by which to work. (*The Autobiography of Charles Darwin*, 1876, pp. 119–121, <http://www.pbs.org/wgbh/evolution/educators/course/session2/explain_c.html>)

Apologists for Darwin claim that the phrase 'survival of the fittest' is attributable to political theorist Herbert Spencer who first coined the phrase after reading *Origin of the Species*. That Darwin thought fit to use the phrase in his subsequent writings is amongst the reasons invalidating such apologetics.

To Malthus, Galton and others of like pseudo-scientific bent, it doesn't appear to have occurred to them to embark on any robust intellectual enquiry as to how and why they came to generate such anti-social hypotheses. Even as a passing thought experiment, such men don't appear to have been intellectually capable of considering how their hierarchical and chauvinistic attitudes and behaviours could be rebutted. Nor did the fifth-century BC Hippocratic Oath of 'First, do no harm,' seem to have crossed their minds.

Darwin's hypothesising repudiates the sanctities held in common across the diverse major world religions on the human obligation to extend care for their fellow human beings. Darwin's unproven and unprovable hypothesising also disregards the socio-biological imperatives and moralities that predate and postdate religious belief: parental compulsions for the survival of their children, the obligations to wider kith and kin, and to the impoverished.

Belonging to the leisured and socially liberal wing of the upper-middle-class capitalist hierarchy of the day, the Darwins abhorred the concept of human slavery. Such socio-cultural liberalism did not affect what was also central to Darwin's hypothesising, that of the parasitic symbiosis of one species serving another. Nor did his liberalism hinder Darwin from fitting in with the racist chauvinism of the era. In his later 1871 book, *Descent of Man*, Darwin declared that:

> At some future period, not very distant as measured by centuries, the civilised races/varieties of man will almost certainly exterminate, and replace, the savage races/varieties throughout the world.

In the run-up to WWI, Charles Darwin's son, Major Leonard Darwin, promoted his father's Darwinian hypothesis by advocating that squads of scientists should travel around the country identifying the 'unfit', who would then be put into colonies and sterilised (Victoria Brignell, 'The eugenics movement Britain wants to forget', *New Statesman*, 9 December 2010).

If compared to the socio-culturally narrow-minded conventions of the times, Charles Darwin was broadly socially liberal, his ideological worldview was also rooted in the sexist chauvinism of his times:

> The chief distinction in the intellectual powers of the two sexes is shewn by man attaining to a higher eminence, in whatever he takes up, than woman can attain – whether requiring deep thought, reason, or imagination, or merely the use of the senses and hands. If two lists were made of the most eminent men and women in poetry, painting, sculpture, music, – comprising composition and performance, history, science, and philosophy, with half-a-dozen names under each subject, the two lists would not bear comparison. We may also infer, from the law of the deviation of averages, so well illustrated by Mr. Galton, in his work on 'Hereditary Genius,' that if men are capable of decided eminence over women in many subjects, the average standard of mental power in man must be above that of woman. Thus man has ultimately become superior to woman. (Darwin, *The Descent of Man*, 1871)

Well connected as Charles Darwin was, he was only moderately well-off. Though he would have had no difficulty gaining well-remunerated employment suited to a gentleman scholar, Darwin wrote that having to earn a living and having to take family responsibilities if he married and fathered children, would consign him to a life not much better than that of a negro slave.

In deciding whether to marry, Darwin drew up a list of the pros and cons, an excerpt of which is below:

> Constant companion, (& friend in old age) who will feel interested in one – object to be beloved & played with – better than a dog anyhow. Home, & someone to take care of house. Charms of music & female chit-chat. These things good for one's health. – but terrible loss of time. (*Darwin's Correspondence Project*, Cambridge University, <https://www.darwinproject.ac.uk/tags/about-darwin/family-life/darwin-marriage>.)

What Darwin wanted was to acquire a large country house with extensive grounds where he could continue unhindered with his zoological studies. To realise these ambitions, Darwin would have to marry into a family of greater wealth than his own.

Darwin opted to marry his cousin, Emma Wedgewood, daughter of the English pottery magnate. Having known each other since childhood, Charles and Emma had affection for one another and thought themselves well enough suited. Throughout their marriage, Darwin continued to work so assiduously at his studies, that Emma Darwin called him 'own dear Nigger'.

Emma Darwin took on the role of being a mother figure to her husband. Indeed, whenever Emma Darwin was absent, Charles Darwin often became nervous to the point of tears. Emma Darwin would bear 10 children, three of whom would die at an early age. Nevertheless, Charles Darwin regarded his wife as being in charge of what he deemed were small matters of household rules and etiquette.

The Darwins employed 12 servants to serve their domestic needs and manage their large house set in 20 acres of land, for example, maids, butler-valet, cook, nursemaid, childminders, tutors, coachmen, gardeners. The economic practice of the times was that servants worked in exchange for room and board and a small stipend, with most servants staying on for years. The Darwin's wage bill for their servants was around £100 a year – less than half of their butcher's bill. Darwin kept a keen eye on his money, on his wife's accounts, on his investments in government bonds, and on the money earned from publishing his books. At his death, Darwin's estate was worth around £13 million in today's money.

One of the ways Emma Darwin submitted to the male chauvinism of their marriage was to comply with Darwin's instructions not to upset his routine or interrupt him in his studies, not that with having 10 children – even with a childminder or two – she'd have had much time to do so.

Close family apart, Darwin avoided company, and there was even a timetable for family meeting times. For much of his life, Darwin suffered debilitating bouts of ill health, heart palpitations, stomach troubles, vomiting, gas, night-time flatulence, muscle spasms, insomnia, tinnitus, hysterical crying, headaches, panic attacks, dizziness, agoraphobia. Medical treatments for his physical ailments were mostly unsuccessful, though he did have periods of relief when he took his physicians' advice to take a rest from his studies. Driven by his passion for zoology and theorising, Darwin claimed that his studies kept his mind off his poor health ('Health of Charles Darwin', Wikipedia).

Though Emma Darwin appears to have had some idea of the concept of psychosomatic illness, Charles Darwin seems not to have known much about the neurobiological inseparability of brain and body upon which modern psychoneuroimmunology is founded. Today's psychologists speculate that Darwin's ability to hyperfocus on his studies despite his many illnesses may indicate that he could have had Asperger's Syndrome.

Emma Darwin, an upper-middle-class, religious and liberal woman of her times, didn't agree with her husband's theory of human biological evolution. Since Charles was not minded to listen much to his wife, Emma resorted to writing him a four-page letter setting out her reasons for thinking he'd taken the wrong track, ending her missive by dutifully apologising for breaking her promise not to bother him.

> I dare say you have often thought of them before, but I will write down what has been in my head, knowing that my own dearest will indulge me. Your mind & time are full of the most interesting subjects & thoughts of the most absorbing kind, viz following up yr own discoveries – but which make it very difficult for you to avoid casting out as interruptions other sorts of thoughts which have no relation to what you are pursuing or to make it possible for to be able to give your whole attention

to both sides of the question ... May not the habit in scientific pursuits of believing nothing till it is proved, influence your mind too much in other things which cannot be proved in the same way, & which if true are likely to be above our comprehension ... I am rather afraid my own dear Nigger will think I have forgotten my promise not to bother him, but I am sure he loves me & I cannot tell him how happy he makes me & how dearly I love him & thank him for all his affection which makes the happiness of my life more & more every day. (*Darwin's Corespondence Project*, Cambridge University, <https://www.darwinproject.ac.uk/letter/DCP-LETT-471.xml>)

Charles Darwin added the following notation to his wife's letter:

> When I am dead, know that many times, I have
> kissed & cryed over this. C. D.

Emma Darwin's liberal oppositions to the socio-cultural patriarchy of the times didn't, go as far as they might, however. When their daughter's beloved pet cat was found to have mauled one of the pigeons Darwin used to test his theories on selective breeding, Emma and Charles Darwin saw no betrayal of familial relations by ordering that the child's much-loved pet be killed. Charles and Emma's daughter, even as an older adult, never got over what, to her, had been an act of parental treachery (Sarah Perry, 'Charles Darwin: Victorian Mythmaker, by A N Wilson', *The Observer*, 2 September 2017, p. 72).

Those taking part in the 2002 BBC poll to decide who was the greatest Briton voted for the British prime minister who in 1937, inspired by Darwin's hypothesising, declared:

> I do not admit that a great wrong has been done to the Red Indians of America or the black people of Australia by the fact that a stronger race, a higher grade race, to put it that way, has come in and taken their place.

This UK prime minister also advocated incarcerating the mentally and ill and 'tramps and wastrels' in labour camps where they'd be forcibly sterilised. He believed that unemployed people were intellectual and moral degenerates and that such degeneracy, along with the 'steady restriction of the thrifty energetic and superior stocks', constituted a 'national race danger which is impossible to exaggerate'. Against Gandhi and Indian independence, he also declared, 'I hate the Indians. They are a beastly people with a beastly religion.'

Bio-doc films about the great and good typically hide more than they reveal. The two recent bio-doc films on the politician mentioned above don't mention that he 'favoured fascism as a bulwark against communism', and became 'anti-fascist only when Germany threatened Britain and its colonial empire' (Callum A. Scott, 'What Darkest Hour doesn't tell you about Winston Churchill', *The Morning Star*, 12 January 2018; see also: <http://winstonchurchill.org/publications/finest-hour/finest-hour-152/leading-churchill-myths-churchills-campaign-against-the-feeble-minded-was-deliberately-omitted-by-his-biographers/>).

From the 1930s, the modern technology of microscopy, and nowadays x-ray lasers, have enabled scientists to observe living biological matter at increasingly higher resolutions. Cell and molecular biologists, biochemists and geneticists have also long been able to witness the interacting components of the living cell, the building block of all plant, animal, and human life.

Modern scientists can now testify that cells operate at exact, perfectly coordinated, profoundly and irreducibly complex levels of self-assembly. Cells do not have cellular antecedents; no cell has any component without which the cell can perform its function; nor is there one jot of competitiveness within or between cells. After specific cells have done their job, stunningly intricate processes of self-programmed biochemical events lead to cell changes then cell death, apoptosis.

In children between the ages of 8 and 14, approximately 20 billion to 30 billion cells die each day. In the average adult, apoptosis causes between 50 and 70 billion cells to die each day.

> In contrast to necrosis, which is a form of traumatic cell death that results from acute cellular injury, apoptosis is a highly regulated and controlled process that confers advantages during an organism's lifecycle. For example, the separation of fingers and toes in a developing human embryo occurs because cells between the digits undergo apoptosis. Unlike necrosis, apoptosis produces cell fragments called apoptotic bodies that phagocytic cells are able to engulf and quickly remove before the contents of the cell can spill out onto surrounding cells and cause damage to the neighboring cells. ('Apoptosis', Wikipedia)

The explanatory metaphor employed by scientists for both the fathomable and unfathomable interactions of cellular mechanisms is along the lines that all the inter-related mechanics of modern cities, combined with all the expertise involved in the production of today's technology, the intricate processes of nanotechnology included, are primitive compared to the staggeringly precise and cryptic biological processes of the living cell.

As for intra-organ cell development, all are dependent upon such multifarious levels of cooperatively proficient processes as are unlikely ever to be fully penetrable. The minutely coordinated biological events of the intricate workings of the cell and of intra-organ cell functioning, again all operate at astounding levels of cooperation with not a jot of competition in sight. There is nothing in cell biology that fits Darwin's red in tooth and claw, survival of the fittest evolutionary hypothesising.[40]

With each discovery in cell and molecular biology, biochemistry and genetics, the prior assumptions of those scientists who relied upon the Darwinian paradigm are regularly overturned. For instance, the limited number of differences in the genetic makeup of all the diverse biological species is now known to be precisely the percentage of variance that renders each species as astonishingly unique as one from another they are.

The seemingly redundant biological entities that continued to exist, inexplicably according to the known science of the day, and were thus presumed to have once been related to supposed processes that humans must have once shared with their animal ancestors, are nowadays known instead to be newly discovered crucial aspects of human biology. Further, the old presumption of previously inexplicable gene processes thought to be an accumulation of outmoded genetic junk has been overturned by the modern discoveries that reveal the actual genetic functions of those genes previously labelled as extraneous 'junk'.

Moreover, the assumption that mutations are random also has much to answer for. In their effects, mutations can be neutral, helpful or harmful. Mutations can be useful in helping species adapt to their environment, but mutations don't alter species. Moreover, despite Darwin building his hypothesis on notions of changes in mutations over aeons of time, mutations don't occur at the rate nor in the ways required by the Darwinian hypothesis of inter-species evolution.

The cell mutations most often occurring are because of environmental stress on cells from the likes of radiation, chemicals, smoke and pollution. When it comes to congenital disabilities, there are different causes, such as incorrect genetic information, chromosomal problems, infections suffered by the mother during pregnancy or the mother's exposure to medicines, chemicals or other substances during pregnancy. Many of the causes of birth defects remain unknown. The genetic mutations that do occur are not, therefore, interchangeable with the notions related to 'evolution'. Australian geneticist Michael Denton states that the ongoing discoveries of modern science render the Darwinian hypothesis illogical and unreal:

> the genetic programmes of higher organisms, consisting of something close to a thousand million bits of information, equivalent to the sequence of letters in a small library of one thousand volumes, containing in encoded form countless thousands of intricate algorithms controlling, specifying and ordering the growth and development of billions and billions of cells into the form of a complex organism, were composed by a purely random process is simply an affront to reason.

Many scientists declare there is enough evidence to scientifically prove there can be no such thing as inter-species evolution; that each species has instead a specifically unique body plan; and that it is only through those unique body plans that environmentally driven adaptations can take place (Michael Denton, 'Biology of the Baroque', YouTube, February 2016).

Those who are 'educated' and socio-culturally persuaded into accepting pseudo-scientific and socio-culturally engineered concepts find it next to impossible to escape the mind-bending metaphoric paradigms of what is, in fact, misinformation. Consequently, the likes of the unproven Darwinian evolutionary hypothesis gain hegemonic precedence to become a dominating narrative.

Though a very great deal more is now known about the genetics of plant, animal and human biology, substantial though that new knowledge is, it remains infinitesimal compared to all that is unknown. Though a good deal is now also known about the human brain, including the inseparable neurobiological connections between brain and body, such knowledge remains minuscule to all that remains unknown about the brain, mind, and consciousness. Fundamental as consciousness is to existence, its origins are unknowable, and the testimonies of those who have experienced the likes of consciousness of past lives, remote viewing, and out-of-body experiences are discounted in materialistic capitalist culture.

Though meticulous modern scientific study has moved the Darwinian goalposts by a conceptual universe or two, Darwinian gameplay notwithstanding, there is no scientific research, historical or contemporary, that comes anywhere near settling the issue of the existence, or non-existence, of a creator. Nor is there any evidence that can prove the intents, or purposelessness, of the actions of any intelligent designer of life – should there be one.

The Darwinian evolutionary hypothesis suits capitalist, fascist and pseudo-socialist worldviews, though doubtless there are also greater forces at play than the defective hypotheses and ideologies that infuse the horrendous paroxysms of war. Socialists also fell for 'scientific' Darwinism as the perfect foil against the hold that organised religion had, and has, on people's consciousness. Some of today's Marxists, though many fewer than previously, continue to assume inevitable future socialism supported by a politico-economic-socio-cultural law that exists only in the imagination. It's an erroneous view that sidelines the utter necessity of citizen activists coming together in great numbers and working in solidarity to replace the capitalist political economy with democratic socialism.

There are crucial distinctions to be made between Lenin, Stalin, Trotsky, Hitler, Mao Zedong, Churchill and Pol Pot – all of whom were adherents of the Darwinian theory of evolution. Marx sent Darwin a signed copy of *Das Kapital*, and Engels in his funeral speech for Marx declared that 'Just as Darwin discovered the law of the development of organic life, so Marx discovered the law of the development of human history'.

Stalin, from a Russian Orthodox Christian background, abandoned Christianity for survival-of-the-fittest Darwinian atheism. Trotsky, from a Jewish background, was an admirer of Darwin's theory and the social Darwinism that inevitably went with it:

> The idea of evolution and determinism – that is, the idea of a gradual development conditioned by the character of the material world – took possession of me completely. Darwin stood for me like a mighty doorkeeper at the entrance to the temple of the universe. I was intoxicated with his minute, precise, conscientious and at the

same time powerful, thought. (Max Eastman, *Leon Trotsky: The Portrait of a Youth*, New York: Greenberg Inc., 1925)

Lenin, an enthusiastic reader of both Darwin and Marx, when referring to the Soviet population, often used the phrase 'fewer, but better'. Long before becoming the head of the Russian communist government from 1917 to 1922, in his political pamphlet published in 1902, *What is to be Done?*, Lenin set out his distrust of the proletariat, declaring that workers, interested mainly in their pay packet, did not understand the wider tenets of revolutionary socialism. Faced with counter-revolutionary divisionism and all manner of political intrigues, interference from foreign powers, oppositions from internal factions, Lenin's answer to those roiling seas of external and internal troubles was vanguardism: the Soviets, the local and regional councils supposed to have been run by the workers, peasants, soldiers, would be run instead by a vanguard of professional revolutionary government apparatchiks who would carry out the decrees of central government's supposedly well-informed ruling politico-technocratic elite. According to Lenin, that governing elite 'must of necessity be not too extensive and as secret as possible'.

Focusing on the industrialisation of the Russian economy, the system of vanguardism may have succeeded in turning the Soviet Union into a world industrial power. It also bred the opposite of socialism and communism: infighting and political purges; a yes-man job promotion bureaucracy; and all too little freedom of speech and thought. To 'save the revolution', Stalin and Trotsky were also architects of the 'Red Terror' of political purges, State thuggery, military execution, and murder. Lenin built on the Tsarist practice of exiling prisoners to corrective labour camps, with around 30,000 such camps eventually in operation across the Soviet Union, many built under Stalinist totalitarian rule.

Trotsky, as though blameless for the horrors of the 'Red Terror', blamed the ruling communist party for what he saw as its amateur economic planning, harangued Stalin for suppressing democracy and for not pursuing the international struggle for world revolution. Stalin had Trotsky removed from the Politburo and sent into internal exile, banishing him from the Soviet Union in 1928. Still fearing Trotsky's influence on the Soviet Communist Party from exile in Mexico, in 1940 Stalin had Trotsky assassinated.

The 1932–3 Soviet famine that caused the deaths of an estimated 8 million people is attributed to Communist Party mismanagement of agriculture, their collectivisation of the farms of the more well-off Kulaks, designed to rid the Soviet Union of the Kulaks as a class, severe droughts and the deaths of agricultural workers.

Those suspected of opposition to the diktats of the ruling communist party faced show trials, internal exile to distant provinces, imprisonment in labour camps. The surveillance of the population carried out by the ubiquitous secret police was augmented by testimony from people's family, friends and neighbours and those with a grudge against the accused. Of those imprisoned in those 'corrective labour camps' of the GULAG, the Russian acronym for the Chief Directive of Corrective Labour, and used as slave labour for forestry, construction, road building, etc. 1.6 million people died of overwork, hunger, sometimes murder.

To achieve rapid industrialisation, the communist principles of collaborative worker democracy were summarily dismissed and replaced by a pitiless work ethic, rewards given to those who worked produced the most to meet the targets set by what was, in effect, the State capitalist government. Soviet industrialisation played a great part in winning the war against fascism. Soviet-style communism also provided the social goods of education, healthcare, housing, greater equality between men and women and significant improvements in standards of living for millions of people. Soviet modern industrialisation and the provision of those social goods, and a belief in the principles of socialism and communism led many Western socialists to revere Soviet communism.

Meanwhile, the capitalist powers, dreading the degeneration of capitalist hegemony, fought tooth and nail against any forms of socialism and communism. Chapter 4's section on Hitler's fascism details his belief in the Darwinian concept of superior races. According to Hitler, Germans had the right to command and control what the Nazis believed were inferior races and nations.

***

China, a country riven by Western interference, and a long period of social unrest and civil war, chose communism over capitalism. Mao Zedong, chairman of the Chinese Communist Party from 1949 until his death in

1976, ruling according to his interpretation of Marxist-Leninist practices, sought to shift the Chinese agrarian-based economy massively towards industrialisation. The Chinese Communist Party's ambitious national economic plans initiated from the top down were also fraught with tragic errors that contributed to the greatest famine in history, the deaths of 45 million people between 1958 and 1962. In 1957 Mao Zedong described Chinese socialism in Darwinian terms: 'Socialism, in the ideological struggle, now enjoys all the conditions to triumph as the fittest.' From 1966, the Chinese communist leadership initiated 10 years of what it called the 'cultural revolution', much of it based the personality cult of Maoism and used to repress, denounce, persecute and 're-educate' those who protested against government policy.

***

As a student in France after WWII, Cambodian Pol Pot found the intellectual demands of Marxist analyses of economic political and socio-cultural conditions difficult to follow, becoming an enthusiast for Stalinistic strongman State communism instead.

In its war against communist North Vietnam, the US also conducted secret carpet-bombing raids on Cambodia and Laos. The goal being to stop the spread of communism in Southeast Asia, the US dropped 2.7 million tons of bombs on Cambodia, the firepower equivalent to five Hiroshimas. Whole villages obliterated, millions of people displaced and killed, farms and crops ruined. Massive bombing of Cambodia by the US led to the Cambodian power vacuum, social unrest and the civil war that served as a recruiting ground for Pol Pot's nationalist Khmer Rouge army. In 1975, Pol Pot's Khmer Rouge army won the civil war, Pol Pot becoming the leader of a Cambodian 'communist' government that lasted until 1979. Pol Pot's goal was to rid Cambodia of all outside influence, create an agrarian peasant utopia and, in an appeal to the by-gone era of the ancient Royal Khmer civilisation, restore the country to the supposed greatness of the Khmer empire. 1975 was 'Year Zero' for Pol Pot, the Khmer Rouge army and the peasant cadres, the start of a four-year genocide to 'purify' Cambodian society.

Pol Pot's nationalist-communist government regarded upper, middle-class and educated individuals, racial and ethnic minorities as the enemy. Anyone with an education, scientists, engineers, doctors, journalists, etc., plus the racial and ethnic minorities, young children, the old and the sick were rounded up imprisoned, with many shot and killed. Machinery was trashed, books were burned, money was banned, sport, art, music was forbidden, and there was to be no such thing as love or individual freedom, people being told who they were to marry instead. The cities were emptied of their citizens, the population forced to work as slave labour, with hundreds of thousands of people, including civil servants in government ministries, ordered to work on the likes of massive irrigation projects, to the point that there were no longer enough agricultural workers to grow rice, the staple food of Cambodia.

In the four years of the Khmer Rouge totalitarian dictatorship, hundreds of thousands of people were tortured, brainwashed, forced to confess to being enemies of what the psychopatholigical Pol Pot called his 'organisation'. People were taken from all over Cambodia to the Khmer Rouge killing fields to be murdered.

In a population of around 8 million, it is estimated that the Khmer Rouge killed around 700,000 people outright and that around 1.2 million died of overwork, ill-treatment and starvation.

During the US carpet bombing of Cambodia and Laos, the fact that American servicemen were also sacrificed to the secret US war generally went unreported in the Western mass media:

> More Americans died in Laos than in Cambodia, but it was the bombing of Cambodia that sparked protests including at Kent State University in Ohio in May 1970, where four students were killed by the national guard. ('They just kept coming – America's secret war in Laos', *The Economist*, 21 January 2017)

Those protests by US campaigners contributed to eventually bringing those US wars in South East Asia to an end.

Western governments and their aid agencies refused to recognise the new Cambodian government. It was left to war-ravaged, impoverished Vietnam to supply food aid to the starving Cambodian population.

After the North Vietnamese troops defeated the Khmer Rouge army, Pol Pot went into exile in Thailand. The Khmer Rouge commanders involved in the deaths of those 2 million Cambodians went free. They died of old age. Asked near the end of his life if he regretted the genocide he'd perpetrated against the Cambodian people, Pol Pot replied that even amongst his own cohorts there were many enemies that had to be killed. To his mind, he had acted for the sake of the Cambodian people. He had no regrets. In November 2018, the two last elderly remaining Khmer Rouge commanders were found guilty and jailed for genocide.

Of the various YouTube videos addressing the horrors of Pol Pot's genocide, one that also contextualises the history of the ruthless global geopolitics of the times is John Pilger's 1979 documentary for Independent Television, ITV, *Year Zero: The Silent Death of Cambodia*. Following that broadcast, $45 million was raised, in small donations, to help the Cambodian people, almost £4 million of that amount raised by schoolchildren in the UK.

The US foreign secretary who carried out the US president's orders to secretly bomb Laos and Cambodia was awarded the Nobel Peace Prize. That US president was later found guilty by a bipartisan government committee of illegally bugging the offices of the opposition party to find out about the party's election strategies. The president had also amassed an illegal slush fund to pay for his re-election campaign. About to be indicted for these criminal acts, a legal agreement secured his resignation from the presidency instead.

The range and depths to which the Darwinian evolutionary hypothesis and its political, economic and socio-cultural consequences are woven into everyday consciousness is also evidenced by the likes of the Columbine High School, Colorado, USA, shootings of 20 April 1999 when two teenage students shot and killed 12 fellow students, one teacher, and injured 23 other people, before shooting themselves dead. Socio-culturally normalised behaviours of condescension and marginalisation had for years been directed at the two students who bitterly resented being at the bottom of the rigid social hierarchy of that middle-class school cohort of around 1,700 students.

Parents, teachers, fellow students, the police and doctors all played a part in flouting the duty of care that all members of a community ought to have towards one another. For example, the 18-year-old killer told his doctor the anti-depressants he'd prescribed were inducing thoughts of self-harm and injuring others. The doctor prescribed the same pill under a different brand name.

The two teenagers were also avid fans of the 1994 entertainment blockbuster *Natural Born Killers*, a murder-as-entertainment film billed as a black comedy, featuring a young couple with backgrounds of childhood trauma and oppression who by going on a killing spree achieve mass-media fame and social acknowledgement. The film, implicated in copycat murders, was named by *Entertainment Weekly* magazine in 2006 as the eighth most controversial film in US history. Translated from English into 17 other languages, with subtitles for the hearing impaired, the DVD comes with the extra content of the blow-by-blow account by the writer/director on how the movie was made. It's readily available from Amazon, gift-wrapped, next-day delivery.

The multitude of articles and interviews conducted on the Columbine high school shootings almost never mention that the two teenagers were firm believers in Darwin's theory of evolution, the 18-year-old writing in his journal that, through their pre-planned massacre, he and his fellow killer would be kicking 'natural selection up a few notches'. The two teenagers presumed themselves superior to those they wanted to kill – and didn't believe their own lives worth living. Shooting and killing his fellow students before turning his gun on himself, the T-shirt worn by one of the killers had printed across it in red the words, 'Natural Selection'.

The opinion that the two teenaged murderers had been maleducated into believing a simplistic version of evolutionary theory dismisses the socio-cultural, psychological, emotional, and intellectual effects of Darwinian pseudo-science and the 'social' Darwinism that goes with it. Mass shootings in US schools are commonplace, and US teenagers campaigning to get the government to legislate against lax gun law have staged some of the biggest protests in US history. US politicians, blaming not the guns but mental illness amongst the shooters, refuse to make the connections between the sociopathy of US gun ownership, disinformation, maleducation, media manipulations, the routine presentation of horror, perversion and murder as everyday entertainment.

Darwinism continues to function as one of the daily dabs of socio-cultural glue that helps reinforce dominating socio-cultural orthodoxies. For example, Darwin's graven image appears as an imprimatur on the reverse side of the current Bank of England £10 note. On the front of that banknote, and all UK banknotes and coins, is the image of the carrier of another long-outdated politico-socio-cultural narrative, a British Queen as head of a purported UK democracy.

The tightly curated landscape of the UK capitalist political economy is taking a turn for the better, thanks to the work of modern historians like David Olusoga. In the BBC Two 2015 documentary, *Britain's Forgotten Slave Owners*, he traces the UK's many slave owners directly to the villages towns and city streets the length and breadth of Britain. Upon the abolition of slavery, the UK's 46,000 upper and middle-class slave owners sought – and were granted – government compensation, taxpayers' money, for the loss of property, that is, for no longer being able to legally use other human beings as their instruments of capitalist, slave-based profiteering. How many of today's school children know that these UK slave-owners owners used some of their ill-gotten gains to employ an army of UK domestic servants? How many schoolchildren know about the depths of today's modern slavery, people-trafficking and child labour; that worldwide there are 25 million people trapped in forced labour, that 71% of the victims of modern slavery are women and girls? How many UK youngsters understand the intergenerational nature of social class; that if you are a descendant of one of those past British slave owners you are likely to be well-off, whereas if you are a descendant of a family of domestic servants, you are likely to be poor?

David Olusoga's motive for unearthing the buried history of Britain's tens of thousands of slave owners, as well as the history of the people who opposed slavery, is not to induce either intergenerational guilt or self-righteousness. David Olusoga, his father black, his mother white, his childhood home on a council estate attacked by National Front fascists, concludes instead that the pervasive lack of knowledge and understanding about UK and world history, inclusive of knowledge about the perpetual resistance of people in the UK and elsewhere against the powers of domination, force and division, constitutes a severe impediment to progressive politico-economic and socio-cultural relations.

Millions of people want their governments to work nationally and internationally to establish and maintain the political economy that provides for the human rights of all, as set out in Article 25 of the UN Declaration of Human Rights:

> Everyone has the right to a standard of living adequate for the health and well-being of himself and of his family, including food, clothing, housing and medical care and necessary social services, and the right to security in the event of unemployment, sickness, disability, widowhood, old age or other lack of livelihood in circumstances beyond his control.
>
> Motherhood and childhood are entitled to special care and assistance. All Children, whether born in or out of wedlock, shall enjoy the same social protection.

Here's some good news: believing that all people have a right to make a living and provide for their families as best they can, UK primary school pupils and their parents have for decades now been protesting against government deportations of their immigrant neighbours. Glaswegian working-class families, themselves living in economically precarious conditions in council tower blocks, hide their immigrant neighbours from the police deportation squads.

This chapter has reviewed how defective pseudo-scientific hypotheses are used to buttress sociopathic and psychopathic rule; how the modern science of microscopy and genetics have shifted the goalposts in our knowledge of plant, animal and human biology; how the newly unburied knowledge of empire and slavery enables the tracing of the anonymous 'investors' in empire who lived 'ordinary' lives in UK towns and villages – and honours those ordinary working-class people who on the grounds of equal human rights and responsibilities try to protect their their immigrant neighbours.

CHAPTER 15

Politics of Ego and Entitlement

Amongst its ranks of public servants and parliamentarians, the UK has its share of scrupulously honest, trustworthy, hard-working MPs who do their best for the common good. However, the evidence is that they're not in the majority. The Daily Telegraph newspaper revealed in 2009 that across the political parties 60% of UK parliamentarians, MPs, prime ministers, deputy prime ministers, chancellors, cabinet ministers, backbenchers, routinely made expenses claims to which they were not entitled. Their claims ranged from mortgage payments to luxury bath fittings, the cleaning of a duck house on a country estate, claims for packets of biscuits, postage stamps and for the wreaths politicians lay at war memorials on Remembrance Sunday.

Some top politicians used expense claims money to seed real estate portfolios that within a few years were worth millions. Many politicians declared that they had submitted their expenses according to normal custom and practice. Few ordinary citizens would regard it as normal for taxpayers to shell out for others to buy themselves luxury furnishings, pay for decorators to do up their houses, pay for their TV and internet services, for scatter cushions and tin openers, etc. ('List of expenses claims in the United Kingdom parliamentary expenses scandal', Wikipedia).

Should they so wish, MPs are permitted to dole out the jobs of being their secretaries, administrators and advisors positions, paid for by the taxpayers, to their nearest and dearest. A former Labour Minister for Schools, later a Home Secretary, appointed her husband as her £40,000 a year 'adviser', and also ran up expenses claims in the thousands of pounds – inclusive of paying for pornographic films for said husband adviser. Losing her seat to the Conservatives in 2010, she was then employed as chair of an NHS Hospitals Trust, and hired by a right-wing political lobbying outfit to give clients advice on how to win government contracts.

Investigative journalists have filmed ministers selling their in-the-know services to businesses and lobbyists. UK politicians have also taken bribes to raise parliamentary questions in the vested interests of those paying for particular questions to be discussed by the UK government.

The political figures involved in such behaviours continue to be rolled out on TV as worthy socio-political brand names to comment on issues of public concern. In presenting their plausible hypocritical 'front', these pundits seemingly operate on a continuum from being either narcissistically deluded players, useful dupes, or knowing frontmen for more distal powers. TV viewers who happen to recall the past crimes and misdemeanours of these politicians also begin to spot the 'tells' of deceit: the false smiles, narcissistic expressions of self-belief, the lack of self-reflection, the absence of reasonable doubt or honest apology.

***

That bastion of the UK establishment, the Church of England, having hundreds of years ago ditched religious laws against usury, is one of the highest earning investment bodies in the UK, 'earning' around a 17% return on its approximately £7 billion of accumulated wealth. Its investment fund criteria are that it will not invest in companies that make more than 3% of their profits from activities the church regards as immoral. Such criteria haven't prevented the Church of England from investing in businesses making profits from producing components for the armaments industry, investing in the gambling 'industry' and in pay-day loan companies. The head of the Church of England, the Archbishop of Canterbury, having spoken out against payday loan firms was embarrassed to find the Church of England had invested in a highly lucrative payday loan firm big enough to be listed on the stock market, firms specialising in predatory short-term payday loans that charge the poor a 'poverty premium' of obscene amounts of interest. One of those loan companies, set up in 2006 and operating in several countries, was legally allowed to charge over 5,000% interest until public protests caused the government to legislate to cut such pay-day loan rates. In August 2018, because of claims filed against it by claims agencies operating on behalf of ripped-off debtors, the UK sector of this loan company declared bankruptcy. However, the loan company is legally allowed to sell its debt portfolio to the highest bidder, the new owner of the debt still legally allowed to collect 1,500% interest on those loans. The archbishop had also declared that internet giants like Amazon shouldn't be allowed to get away with not paying taxes and that zero hours contract should be abolished – only for it then to be revealed that the Church of England invests in Amazon and that church cleaners are on zero-hour contracts.

The Archbishop of Canterbury, was educated at a private primary school, attended a private boys' boarding school, Eton, has a degree from Cambridge University, is a governor on the governing boards of private schools, previously worked in the oil industry, and as archbishop is also a member of the Lords Spiritual in the House of Lords. Having sat on the Parliamentary Commission on Standards in Banking, the archbishop declared that those bankers whose activities contributed to the 2008 financial crisis should not face prosecution since that would be like subjecting them to a 'lynch mob'. He also postulates that since the banks were operating under legally allowable banking regulations, he might have acted similarly.

In hopes of halting the decline in church congregations, the archbishop promotes a Church of England evangelism that focuses on whatever church practices are most popular with the churchgoers. Pointing out that the church has extensive real estate and significant amounts of capital that have to be professionally managed, the archbishop called for bankers and management consultants to manage the church's recruitment procedures, resulting in a 32% increase in the recruitment of the men who want to become Church of England pastors. Challenged about the morality of the church using bankers as consultants, the archbishop responded that the church provides social glue that helps hold society together, inclusive of pastoral care and food banks.

The archbishop has spoken out against the high prices charged by the energy firms. He has apologised for the failure of the church to sack a bishop later jailed for paedophilia. Little more has been heard from the archbishop about the immorality of the payday loan companies; about investments in firms manufacturing the components for armaments designed to kill; about giant corporations not paying their taxes, or about zero-hours contracts.

The archbishop also declares that he enjoys the religious practice of glossolalia, speaking in tongues ('Justin Welby', Wikipedia).

***

The world of gambling is no longer characterised by punters calculating the outcome of a horse race and having the occasional gambling 'flutter'. Operating in the UK and globally, betting firms are big enough to be listed on the stock exchange. On every UK high street, there are now several betting shops, 55% of the UK population gambling regularly in those betting shops and online. In 2016, the UK gambling 'industry' was worth £13.8 billion, much of that money coming from the Fixed Odds Betting Terminal gambling machines in the betting shops. The UK government rakes in £2.3 billion a year in gaming tax duties. MPs charged with scrutinising and stopping the social damage gambling causes have been recipients of donations from those with vested interests in the gaming business. If UK local authorities refuse planning permission for the opening of another betting shop, the gambling firms cite the lack of legal proof that gambling causes social harms of indebtedness, impoverishment, homelessness, broken relationships, social isolation, etc. – and open another shop anyway.

Gambling is highest in areas of unemployment; about 32% of gambling is done online, with millions of young people hooked on online betting. Of the estimated 2.6 million problem gamblers, 450,000 are young people under 17 years of age, Gambling firms reluctantly donate about 0.1% of their profits, around £13 million, to the bodies set up as charitable organisations to help problem gamblers, but since there is no statutory levy, many firms donate less than 0.1%.

In February 2017, one of the most prominent gambling businesses was fined £6.2 million for not safeguarding at-risk gamblers, and for making £1.2 million from money laundering. That fine by the Gambling Commission was regarded by many as quid pro quo against tighter government regulation (Mark Duell, 'Betting firm William Hill is fined £6.2m for breaking anti-money laundering and social responsibility rules', *Daily Mail*, 2 February 2018).

Instead of revealing it as one of the most ruthless commercial rentier rackets in existence, the corporate–government–media nexus depicts gambling as socio-cultural 'fun' and touts that it's not the job of government to legislate to deprive individuals of their right to engage in gambling should they wish to do so.

In November 2018, a conservative MP resigned her post as Minister for Sport and Civil Society after government announced there would be a six-month delay in restricting the betting on the Fixed Odds Betting Terminal machines, known as the 'crack cocaine' of betting, to £2, a delay worth £1.6 billion to the gambling 'industry'.

That one of the biggest gambling firms in the world is a family-owned global online gambling business with an annual operating profit of £682 million says a good deal about the politics of capitalist entitlement (Rupert Neate, 'Bet365 founder paid herself an "obscene" £265m in 2017', *The Guardian*, 21 November 2018).

The following references are worth checking out:

1. <http://www.theguardian.com/news/datablog/2014/jan/08/uks-gambling-habits-whats-really-happening>.
2. <http://www.independent.co.uk/news/uk/politics/revealed-how-the-betting-industry-keeps-mps-onside-8488393>.
3. <http://www.theguardian.com/society/2016/aug/19/britains-newest-gambling-addiction-charity-funded-industrys-gala-bet365-paddy-power>.

***

Originally set up as charities to educate clever but poor boys, the UK's 'public' boarding school system was soon taken over by the wealthy who used the 'public' schools to educate their offspring. Psychohistorian Nick Duffell In his 2014 book *Wounded Leaders – British Elitism and the Entitlement Illusion* makes a fairly convincing case that many UK politicians sent off at a young age to boys' boarding schools have been damaged by a school culture that isolated them by gender, race and social class. Living in an atmosphere of superiority and bullying where they can't entertain doubt, can't apologise, it's only when faced with antagonisms that pose significant threats to their worldview of ego and entitlement that they can change their minds.

James VI of Scotland, who became King James I of the United Kingdom after the death of Queen Elizabeth I, was born into a royal court of intrigue, bigotry and murder, and a society of domination, misogyny and witch burning. Separated as a baby from his mother, Mary Queen of Scots, by the Scottish elite who ruled in his name until he became of age, he later refused to act to save his mother from execution.

In a kingdom divided by Roman Catholicism and Protestantism, James I ordered the production of the King James version of the Bible, proselytising loyalty to God, King and Country through the mass media of the day, the Church. Another of his mechanisms of control was to impose the system of Scottish lairdism that forbade the speaking of Gaelic and forced the Scottish elite to send their 9-year-old sons off to English boarding schools (Alistair McIntosh, *Soil & Soul, People Versus Corporate Power*, London: Autumn Press, 2004).

The British boarding school system, propagandising itself as morally and culturally superior, produced the viceroys, governors-general, military men and administrators for the British imperialism responsible for the slaughter of millions of people on the continents of the 'new world'.

In some of its British colonies, colonial administrators instituted the boys' boarding school system to assimilate and 'educate' the colonised elites, whose job it then was to impose obedience to British rule on the indigenous populations.

The spectacle of domination held in the likes of castles, palaces, royal ceremonies exhibiting wealth, power and splendour; in the spectacular robes and accoutrements of the bishopric; in fabulous homes, jewellery, yachts, sports cars and so on, commandeer, distort and divert attention. So too do the codes and rituals of the legal system: the statues of the blindfolded upholder of justice; the judges' robes, caps, wigs, gavels and on-high podium in the courtroom; the questions and answers allowed and disallowed. Imagine instead a legal system that brought miscreants to court for wielding unjust economic, political and socio-cultural powers over others, where politicians and generals are tried for the needless killing they authorised.

Though abolishing the 'independent' schools, including for the sake of the pupils who attend them, is not the single answer to the politics of ego and entitlement, it's a clear step along the way.

The politics of ego and entitlement, occurring too frequently to be considered aberrant behaviour in an otherwise benevolent political system governing in the best interests of the majority, has instead been built into UK government–banking–corporate–communications processes as rigidly as the reinforcing rods inside concrete.

Governance by the elite also depends upon a myriad of democratic deficits at local, national and international levels. The UK's unelected House of Lords has approximately 800 lords and ladies compared to 650 members of parliament. Of the 650 MPs, 33% have been privately educated, and 18% went to selective State grammar schools. In the UK population of 32 million males to 33 million females, there are still only 208 female members of parliament compared to 442 males. Of the MPs in the socialist-leaning opposition party, 45% are women, compared to 21% in the right-wing governing party.

Candidates standing to become MPs may never have lived in the constituency they seek to represent and are often parachuted in from afar instead. Nine out of 10 MPs are university educated, with more than 25% graduating from Oxford or Cambridge (George Arnett, 'Elitism in Britain – breakdown by profession', *The Guardian*, 28 August 2014).

The House of Commons does not keep a record of MPs wealth, so it was left to the Daily Mail newspaper to reveal that in the last coalition government of Conservatives and Liberal Democrats of its 29 cabinet members 23 were millionaires. Some cabinet members are also multi-millionaires.

Many of today's parliamentarians regard political office less as a vocation and more as a career path, the opposite of men like Keir Hardie (1856–1915) who was put to work at the age of 7, became a coal miner, subsequently a full-time trade union organiser, and the first Labour Party MP. Hardie was also a lay preacher; a temperance campaigner; a supporter of votes for women; supported home rule for Scotland; self-rule for India; and called for an end to racial segregation in South Africa ('Keir Hardie', Wikipedia).

The intrinsic human drive against the powers of force and domination led to serfs setting fire to the barns full of the feudalist landowners' grain; mutinies on ships; slave rebellions; sabotage of factory looms; resistances to colonial powers; strikes by organised labour; struggles against proxy dictators. Opposition to domination led to the feminist movement, the US civil rights movement, inner-city riots, today's flash mobbing against the capitalist retail chains, the campaigns against austerity, etc.

The name of the Yellow Vest Movement stems from the legal requirement that all French motorists carry high-visibility yellow vests in their vehicles. Wearing the vests identifies the campaigners as opposers of government policies, initially of the purportedly anti-pollution and climate crisis tax on fuel that put the disproportionate onus on the millions of ordinary people dependent on their cars to make a living and manage their daily lives. Decades of government slashing of budgets resulting in poor schools, hospitals, the closure of maternity centres and post offices, poor public transport, etc., also meant people had to travel further to gain access to essential services. The Yellow Vests, with no hope of any general strike by the weakened trade union movement, brought commerce to a grinding halt across the length and breadth of France by the simple measure of blockading roundabouts, highways, toll booths, petrol stations and fuel depots. The French government climbed down immediately on the fuel tax hike and promised to increase wages and pensions, the increase to be funded, however, by general taxation, not by higher corporate and wealth tax.

Non-hierarchical and non-sectarian, the Yellow Vest Movement incorporates middle-class and working-class citizens, anarchists, socialists, pensioners, right-wing anti-immigrant agitators and the 'white van man' of self-employed plumbers, electricians, etc. The movement now demands a re-engineering of the tax and banking system; an end to homelessness; 40% increase in the minimum wage; a hike in pensions and social benefits; mass hirings in the State sector to restore public services; new homes; smaller banks; educational reform; a legal system free and accessible to all; the banning of sectorial lobbyists; ban on planned obsolescence of products and plastic bottles; limiting the power of pharmaceutical companies; no to GM foods, to carcinogenic pesticides and mass-mono-crop agriculture; France to pull out of NATO and leave the EU; prevention of immigration; halting of French neo-colonialism in French-speaking Africa; a national constitutional assembly with citizen participation in the establishment of a national constitution (Nawal Sayed, 'SEE Lists Yellow Vest's Demands to End protests in France', *SEE News*, 9 April 2019). The movement also demands frequent referenda, the aim being for voters to govern more directly in place of the politicians who side with the elite. The movement also intends to run candidates in local and national elections. The emergence of the 2018/19 weekly protests by the French Yellow Vests less than a year and a half into the centre-right French presidency of 2017 shows how quickly the rule of the 1% elite can be challenged.

The hope is that the Yellow Vest Movement signifies the beginnings of authentic democratic socialism by the 99%, and won't become a rejigging of the 'yellow socialism' of capitalist political centrism that leaves 'Fortress Europe' to carry on with its 'business as usual' exploitation of populations at home and abroad.

CHAPTER 16

Housing in the UK

In twenty-first-century Britain, fewer people live in fast disappearing social housing, and many people live in overcrowded conditions in poorly maintained rented accommodation. The choice for young families is to pay exorbitant rents or try to get a mortgage, usually raising the deposit with the assistance of the 'Bank of Mum and Dad'. However, since young mortgagees' wages don't keep up with inflation, they have little in the way of savings, and the squeeze on jobs puts them in a precarious position, financial security remains elusive.

The lack of adequate housing in Britain has a long history. The conscription of 2.5 million men into the WWI's armed forces revealed that due to having to live in overcrowded lodgings without indoor sanitation, and lack of adequate nutrition, many working-class men were in poor health and unfit for combat.

The only accommodation available to workers migrating to jobs in the armaments factories, was in the slums, the landlords charging the incoming tenants higher rents, then hiking the rents of all the other tenants.

Union membership in the armaments factories burgeoned, the workers went on strike for better wages, and women began to mount rent strikes.[41] The factory workers were awarded better wages, and the rent strikes led to the government's Rent Restriction Act, which froze rents to 1914 levels.

Such ameliorations did nothing to temper the anger of the millions who lost loved ones to the industrialised slaughter of WWI. To help stave off social unrest, the government embarked on a programme of house building, propagandised as 'homes fit for heroes' (Trevor Yorke, 'Homes Fit for Heroes: The History of UK Housing', Property Investments UK, 19 December 2018). The funds for building were raised by various means, the Greater London Council of the 1920s raising £4 million by selling housing bonds, for example. The bonds offered 6% interest and were bought by the well-off.

During the post-WWI economic boom, employment rose, and so did the tax base. The 1930 Housing Act gave local councils the green light to demolish slum housing and build new homes. Living conditions in general improved, until the worldwide economic Great Depression of the 1930s brought back mass unemployment. Like today, if a man refused work, he was likely to be blacklisted from future employment.

At the docks looking for a job, an engineer managed to get work on a WWII merchant cargo ship. Though travelling in convey with battleships, those cargo ships were in constant danger of being torpedoed, so it was life and death work. The engineer's wife later told a reporter that the men on those cargo ships had been too patriotic to refuse to sail, her husband contradicting her with the facts:

> Every one of us there had been intimidated by the reality or the fear of long-term unemployment. The fact is, you couldn't have fought that war if people hadn't all first been cowed by the Depression of the 1930s. ('1930s Revisited: We'd been cowed by the Depression; that's why we could fight the war', *The Guardian*, 4 March 2017)

The aerial bombardments of the UK's major cities during WWII pulverised much of Britain's inner-city housing, so housing was again on the political agenda. The post-WWII building boom in social housing meant slum tenements were replaced by council-owned apartment blocks, and in many cases by council houses with gardens. The post-WWII house building boom also included the construction of private homes for the burgeoning post-war middle-class salariat.

The post-WWII building of private homes at affordable prices and government investment in social housing, along with public ownership of public services, formed part of the political consensus of the times. From the 1980s onwards, government incrementally undid that consensus, selling off public services, divesting government of its responsibilities for social housing, loosening banking rules to favour banks and their shareholders, and attempting to shift policy towards supporting a homeowner democracy.

The 1980 Housing Act gave council tenants the right to buy their council accommodation at 20% below market value (Andy Beckett, 'The right to buy: the housing crisis that Thatcher built', *The Guardian*, 25 August 2015). Under RTB, about 1.5 million of the council housing stock was sold off, a move designed to persuade ex-social housing tenants that they owed political loyalty to the Conservative government. Government also enacted legislation that made the interest charges on mortgages tax deductible. It was also certainly in the interests of the banking sector to lend steady wage earners 25-year interest-bearing mortgages on cost-discounted properties with higher collateral value than the mortgage amounts loaned.

Tenants who bought their council accommodation had within a few years acquired enough equity to allow them to sell up and move into the private real estate market, another bonus for the bankers.

RTB regulation prohibited local councils from using money from RTB sales to build replacement social housing and prevented councils from raising local taxes to do so. Today, local councils invest their surplus in the rentier hotel business instead, getting a 10% return which councils now use to offset the central government's budget cuts to the local councils.

For young mortgagees seeking to get onto the property ladder, buying ex-council housing in generally run-down areas was not an attractive proposition. They were also in danger of having to contribute to the costs of any major works carried out on council estates. Though individuals did buy ex-council properties, it was private landlords who subsequently bought up swathes of ex-council housing, adding ex-council housing to their rental property portfolios.

In 1989, the Local Government and Housing Act incentivised councils to hand over management of their remaining council housing stock to housing associations. Housing associations pay their executives higher salaries than the prime minister, charge higher social housing rents, and can choose whether to use their accumulated income to build more social housing.[42]

The Welfare Reform Act of 2012 targeted council and housing association tenants who after their grown-up children had left home ended up with a spare bedroom or two for which they now had to pay an increased rent, known as 'the bedroom tax', or move to smaller council accommodation. Government's purported intention was to free up the shrinking supply of social housing so that council homes could then be rented to struggling young families – except there weren't enough smaller council flats for the older tenants, nor enough the larger accommodation needed by young families.

Today's homeless families are housed in privately owned housing or high-cost bed and breakfast accommodation, the rents paid for by the taxpayers. In October 2018, a local council's perceptions of its duty to house the homeless led it to provide a vulnerable teenager with mental health problems with a tent ('Why did the council "house" me in a tent?', BBC News, 30 October 2018).

Aiming again to tempt social housing tenants into home ownership, the 2016 Housing and Planning Act extended the right to buy to housing association tenants. The 2016 Act cuts social housing tenancy down to 10 years; obliges social landlords to charge higher rents to families earning over £31,000 per year; requires councils to charge council tenants increased rents in high-value inner-city areas; forces councils to sell off any council housing that becomes vacant. The Act also requires private landlords to do what they should be doing anyway: adhere to current electrical safety standards and register the tenants' deposits.

The occasional front-page spectacle of the demolition of tower-block social housing backgrounds UK government policies of disinvestment in social housing. Moreover, many of the tower blocks were pre-fabricated in European factories using cheap material. The factory-produced outer concrete walls were often not slotted and bolted into place properly, causing damp to permeate the internal walls, making it next to impossible to repair the buildings so that demolition was the only choice. Once the council-owned tower blocks were demolished, the land was likely to be sold off to property developers who would then build luxury apartment blocks that were then sold off to foreign buyers, not as homes but as landbanking assets. To this day, despite the UK housing crisis, landbanking remains a well-sanctioned legal practice.

Though international buyers are currently less interested in owning such UK properties, even as the apartments in many newly built blocks lie empty, local authority planning permission for building more of them continues to be granted.

Since the 2008 financial crash, the banks have set interest rates low helping to create a speculative housing market bubble that has led in turn to a shortage in the availability of affordable accommodation for sale or rent.

The government legislates to put a cap on housing benefit for low-income families but fails to legislate to prevent private landlords charging unaffordable rents, leading to increased homelessness, particularly amongst jobless young men and women reduced to sleeping in shop doorways where they are at risk of abuse and violence.

Private construction companies won't build unless they can sell houses at current high prices. Those prices are determined by up to a 250-fold increase in land values the minute planning permission to build is granted. Hiked land values translate into 70% of the price of a home. Those lucky enough to own their own homes pay an average of 12% of their income on accommodation, for renters its 36% (George Monbiot, 'Want to tackle inequality? Our land laws have to change first', *The Guardian*, 4 June 2019). Until the government sets limits on land prices or hikes taxes on land, builds more social housing at affordable rents, caps the amount private landlords are allowed to charge, and prevents bankers from creating interest-bearing debt from nothing, the UK's housing crisis will continue.

The Labour Party's June 2019 *Land for the Many* report states that should it come to power, the Party will introduce a land tax and other measures to tackle the housing crisis, and it also pledges to preserve and expand green spaces and parks for public use. Meanwhile, homeowners fear a tax on their gardens.

CHAPTER 17

Grenfell

Of the 120 flats of the Grenfell Tower block, only about 17 had been purchased by tenants under the right to buy. The intention of the owners of Grenfell Tower block, the London Royal Borough of Kensington and Chelsea, was to keep the 1974 inner-city block as social housing. Amongst the reasons for refurbishing it was to make it more cosmetically in keeping with the surrounding high-value real estate.

Investigative report recommendations made in previous accident reports on fires and gas explosions in tower blocks had generally been ignored by government ministers, local councils and property management companies. Fire risk tests dating back to 2011 revealed that the outer panels of the like procured to cover the exterior of the Grenfell Tower block were highly flammable, gave off toxic smoke, including cyanide from the insulation inside the plastic panels, and the regulation was that because of the high risk of fire spreading quickly from panel to panel, such panelling was not to be used as cladding on tower blocks.

There is no effective UK legislation to prevent UK property management companies from charging high fees for poor buildings management that leads in turn to poor maintenance practices and defective major works contracts. In the competitive tendering process for awarding contracts, local councils are required to consider both quality and price. The RBKC, one of the wealthiest local authorities on the planet, considered mainly price. RBKC also approved the watered down recommendations of the highly paid private fire risk assessor, a former Fire Brigade employee, praising his willingness 'to challenge the Fire Brigade … if he considered their requirements to be excessive' (Luke Barratt, 'Fire risk assessor for Grenfell Tower revealed', *Inside Housing*, 26 June 2017). The fire risk assessor had received £244,318 over seven years from RBKC.

Run as a not-for-profit private limited company, the executives of the Tenant Management Organisation were highly paid. The TMO is also paid for managing another 10,000 residential properties for the RBKC.

It is a common bureaucratic practice that one sector of an organisation considers its job done once it signs parts of a project into the purview of another department. With no management system mechanisms requiring regular cross-department compliance with legislation, regulation and standards, neither the directors of the RBKC, its planning department staff, nor the TMO queried the suppliers proffering the wrong type of cheaper flammable cladding. It was also later found that refurbishment workers had installed some of the cladding upside down.

With the TMO and the Council acting as little more than a letterbox for inspectors, suppliers and contractors, any safety concerns were not followed up – even though no less than 16 in-name-only, toothless 'inspections' were carried out on the Grenfell works. In a farce of paper-shuffling between the TMO, the Council, the suppliers and the contractors, statutory legal and commercial contract responsibilities were disregarded. It was left to Grenfell residents through their Residents' Association to bring the dangerous standards of works to the attention of the Council and TMO – except that their concerns were routinely ignored. The Residents' Association repeatedly told the TMO and RBKC of the incompetent installation of electrics that caused power surges to domestic electrical equipment; fire alarms that couldn't be heard; fire doors to the flats installed incorrectly; lack of emergency lighting and sprinkler systems, etc. Residents feared their concerns would only be registered after the treacherously managed works caused a fatal accident.

On the night of 14 June 2017, the defective cladding installed during the refurbishing caught fire, engulfing the building in flames within 15 minutes. The fire is thought to have been started by a faulty fridge catching fire inside a flat, the flames quickly spreading to the exterior cladding. The architect who had approved the cladding had also designed the works in such a way as to increase the risk of fire spreading from the outside cladding to the inside of the individual flats. Most of the 72 trapped victims were likely to have been poisoned to death by cyanide fumes before their bodies were burnt to ash.

'Value engineering' is the euphemism for manufactures using the cheapest materials possible in the production of white goods, refrigerators, dishwashers, tumble dryers, etc. Since the follow-up procedures for recall of faulty products by the manufactures is next to non-existent, millions of faulty appliances at risk of catching fire remain in flats and houses. Information released under the Freedom of Information Act reveals that the inferior materials used in tumble dryers cause up to 10 fires a day in UK houses and flats (Harry Wallop, 'Is our hunger for cheap white goods turning our homes into death traps?', *The Morning Star*, 1 December 2017; visit <http://www.rospa.com/lets-talk-about/2017/june/white-goods-safety/> and <https://www.gov.uk/government/publications/household-appliances-recalled-due-to-fire-risk>).

The Fire Brigade responded swiftly to the Grenfell 999 calls. The firefighters had poor-quality radio equipment and oxygen masks and the only suitable extension ladder in an area full of high-rise buildings was at a fire station miles away, and the Fire Brigade had not been trained to cope with such a swiftly spreading fire. If the Fire Brigade possessed the Council/TMO list noting which vulnerable, disabled and elderly tenants resided in which flat was, it was, in any case, 15 years out of date.

Blame for those 72 deaths must not be heaped on the men and women firefighters who risked their lives to rescue survivors. The Fire Brigade's 'stay-put' policy is that tenants stay in their flats until the Fire Brigade rescues them, the policy established long before the government's slashing of safety regulations and the cutting of Fire Brigade budgets. The stay-put policy contributed to the deaths of those who obeyed the order to stay in their flats, but the real responsibility for those 72 deaths lies with the local and national government slashing of legislation designed to protect the public. Blame also lies with the RBKC and TMO executives who disregarded the health safety regulation that remained, and with profiteering suppliers and contractors who ignored health and safety aspects of contract law that prevents the sale of products that put lives at risk.

When challenged about RBKC's dismissal of residents' warnings about substandard works, the Leader of the Council said he'd do his best to correct to the councils 'perceived' inadequacies. When survivors protested that the Council was continuing to take rents from the survivors' current accounts, the council spokeswoman responded that this was only a 'tiny thing'. In the eyes of the Council spokespersons, RBKC's routine breaches of safety regulations appeared to have been regarded as motes in the eyes of the misguided tenants, and it was assumed that deducting monies from tenants' bank accounts was a minor inconvenience to the survivors, the majority of whom were poor and working-class people.

The RBKC is the richest local council in Europe, had reserves of £274 million and had given council tax rebates to borough residents (Vickie Oliphant, 'Kensington Council gave richest £100 rebate – but cut corners on tower-block safety', *Daily Express*, 20 June 2017). From its reserves, RBKC had also had paid £5 million to build Opera Holland Park, a venue for the entertainment of wealthy Londoners. It wasn't a lack of money that was responsible for the Grenfell atrocity; it was the hoarding of it.

There was no post-fire local or government emergency aid for the survivors who had lost everything to the fire, many having escaped in their night clothes. It was local people, community and faith organisations instead who provided survivors with emergency aid, collecting and distributing donated clothing, food, water and provided the money for the survivors to buy baby-milk, nappies, sanitary pads, and the cash for survivors to top up their mobile phone credit so they could try to find out what had happened to relatives and friends, the authorities having failed to compile a list of those taken to the different hospitals.

The subsequent revelations of central and local governments' abandonment of their duties of care in the aftermath and then the daily breaking news about decades of government slashing health and safety legislation designed to protect the public shocked the nation. The routine negligence intrinsic to the avoidable tragedy of Grenfell led many ordinary citizens to think that perhaps their naive confidence and trust in the State's 'rule of law' had been something of a mug's game.

There are 20,000 long-term vacant properties across London, 1,300 in the Royal Borough of Kensington and Chelsea. Buckingham Palace, the residence of the Queen, is located in the borough right next door, Westminster. In a newspaper cartoon, the Queen is asked if she wouldn't mind offering some of the 775 rooms in her palace as temporary accommodation to the 230 survivors – no reply forthcoming.

Months later in November 2017, only 20 of the 196 Grenfell households had been rehoused, the rest remaining parked in hotel bedrooms and bed and breakfast accommodation, fearing that when eventually rehoused, they'd be dispersed far away from family and friends.

Compare that with the £2.4 million of taxpayers' money spent on the 2018–19 refurbishing of a property owned by the royal family to house the newly married royal couple, Harry and Meghan, as revealed by the anti-monarchy group Republic (Bill McLoughlin, 'Meghan and Harry's Frogmore refurb an "abuse of public money" as group attacks scandal', *Daily Express* newspaper, 27 June 2019). Republic also reveals that the cost to the public purse of maintaining the royal family for the financial year 2018–19 is £67 million.

Subsequent fire testing of the cladding used on many of the UK's thousands of 1970s–80s council tower blocks revealed that all over the country tower blocks failed to meet basic cladding standards.

Flammable cladding still covers hundreds of buildings, private and public, from hotels to hospitals to schools. Some of that cladding had to be urgently taken down at public cost. Many of the freehold owners of buildings with dangerous cladding refuse to pay for its removal, claiming it's the responsibility of the leasehold owners of the flats to pay for it instead. With no other recourse in law, lessees who had bought their flats face unpayable bills for the removal of flammable cladding. Unable to come up with the funds to remove the flammable cladding and unable to sell devalued flats, lessees are stuck in a dangerous limbo-land, some residents' associations organising fire spotting duties amongst tenants to raise the alarm in case of fire.

A year after Grenfell, the government had failed to ban the manufacture, sale and use of such cladding. The government is now organising a special fund of several million pounds to remove the most dangerous cladding, but there is no legislation to change freeholder-leaseholder status that would force the leaseholders to be responsible for the safety of their buildings.

Many people who have recently bought private housing inclusive of flats were misled into believing the property was freehold when it was leasehold. Properties on leaseholds normally sell for less, especially as the years left on the lease decline. A holdover from feudal property law, the purchaser of leasehold property and her/his beneficiaries may 'own' the property only for a designated period, for example, from 190 to 900 years. Should the leaseholders want to extend their lease, they must pay hefty additional amounts to the leaseholder to do so. They also must pay yearly 'ground rent' to the freeholder, with many of those freeholders increasing the annual ground rent charges.

Environmental activist and investigative reporter George Monbiot believed the public inquiry into the Grenfell catastrophe would be set up with narrowly ineffective terms of reference:

> An inquiry that honours the dead would investigate the wider causes of this crime. It would examine a governing ideology that sees torching public protections as a sacred duty. (George Monbiot, 'The Grenfell inquiry will be a stitch up. Here's why', *The Guardian*, 5 July 2017)

Notwithstanding the codes of ethics – though not the law – that the voices of disaster survivors ought to be heard, the Grenfell survivor groups had to campaign hard to get the public inquiry to include their testimony of what happened that night. The Grenfell Action Group resolved that the inquiry must not be restricted to the usual 'lessons to be learned' format. The action groups want the inquiry to be able to recommend that people responsible for dereliction of their legal duties to uphold the building regulations and contract legislation that did exist face charges in court.

In his appearance at the inquiry, Hisam Choucair, who lost six family members to the fire, testified that the Grenfell tragedy was not an accidental confluence of unforeseen circumstances, but was a man-made atrocity.

Survivors complained of the 'Grenfell cough', but Public Health England and the Royal Borough of Kensington and Chelsea reported that after the fire the air quality in the area was at acceptable levels. Approximately a year and a half after the fire, preliminary research by a professor of fire chemistry at the University of Central Lancashire, appointed by the Grenfell Inquiry as an expert witness, found hydrogen cyanide and carcinogenic toxins in the ground up to a mile away from the tower ('Soil tests around Grenfell Tower reveal "huge concentrations of toxins"', *The Independent*, 13 October 2018). The health implications for survivors, residents and workers in the area have yet to be determined.

The Grenfell atrocity is to many an act of social murder as defined by Engels over 174 years ago in *The Condition of the Working-class in England in 1844* (Panther Press, 1976). Local and national government officials, the executives of the Tenant Management Organisation, profiteering businessmen, the negligent fire risk assessor and the toothless inspectors, careless workers and uncaring office staff, all have a hand in the deaths of the 72 people killed, a hand also in the grief of the families and friends of those people who were burnt to death and the life-long trauma of those who survived the blaze.

In 2017, Arconic, the manufacturer of the cladding used by Rydon construction company in the refurbishment of the Grenfell Tower, made revenues of £10.3 billion. Nevertheless, shareholders are now bringing a US class action against the manufacturing company's board of directors alleging that Arconic 'made false and/or misleading statements and/or failed to disclose' that Arconic 'knowingly or recklessly' supplied its highly flammable Reynobond polyethylene (PE) cladding panels for use in highrise buildings. The shareholders allege that 'a 'precipitous decline' in the company's share prices after the Grenfell fire lost them money. The lawsuit claims that Arconic also provided 'an inaccurate prospectus for a £1.3 billion share issue in 2014'. Investors are suing Arconic and the banks involved in underwriting the share issue. The banks are Royal Bank of Scotland's US operations, Morgan Stanley, Credit Suisse, Citigroup, Goldman Sachs, JP Morgan, BNP Paribas, Mitsubishi UFJ and RBC Capital Markets (Jasper Jolly, 'Sorrell and RBS named in suit against Grenfell cladding maker', *The Guardian*, 20 December 2018).

Groups of wealthy investors can afford to bring legal action. The Grenfell fire merits a public inquiry, not UK legal action by local councils against the firms making the flammable cladding. In June 2016, the Grenfell survivors' group mounted lawsuits in the US against Arconic and Celotex who make the cladding and against Whirlpool, the parent company of the Hotpoint fridge that went on fire and is thought to have started the fire. Whirlpool states that tests show the model was safe. Arconic and Celotex will rebut the case on technical legal grounds.

Environmentalist and campaigner George Monbiot went on to report that even as the tower blazed, the government-backed organisation Red

Tape Initiative, convened its pre-arranged meeting on the further slashing of regulation it considers unnecessary 'red tape' that hinders their business and profits. The members of the Red Tape Initiative hail from the typical establishment network of the likes of Tory ex-newspaper editors; chairmen of right-wing think tanks; corporate chief executives; government ministers; a childhood friend of the former Tory chancellor married to a wealthy financier who owns properties in London, France and Switzerland. The Red Tape Initiative also includes token representation from trade union and non-governmental organisations, their voices well outnumbered. Monbiot states that in seeking to dismantle legislation meant to protect the public, the Red Tape Initiative is 'one of many such schemes set up in recent decades by Conservatives and New Labour.'

> This assault on public protections is just one element of the compound disasters that neoliberalism – promoted by opaquely funded groups such as Policy Exchange – has imposed on Britain since 1979. Its central purpose is not just to empower corporations and the very rich, but actively to disempower everyone else, through austerity, outsourcing and privatisation. (George Monbiot, 'The Grenfell inquiry will be a stitch up. Here's why', *The Guardian*, 5 July 2017)

Amongst the lessons of Grenfell, it surely must now be clear that all citizens have a responsibility to hold national and local governments to account, and to ensure that legislation designed to protect the public is reinstated, developed, kept to the fore, and rigorously enforced.

CHAPTER 18

Charities and Foreign Aid

Workers employed by the homeless charity Shelter were shaken to discover that the chairman of the UK company that sold the faulty cladding for Grenfell was a member of Shelter's Board of Directors. Having received donations from the company, Shelter then agreed the cladding company could display Shelter's logo on the company's promotional materials, thus helping to market dangerous cladding (Patrick Butler and Dawn Foster, 'Shelter under microscope over partnerships with construction industry', *The Guardian*, 27 June 2017).

The role of charities and foreign aid in helping support the global capitalist political economy is covertly reflected in the September 2016 report of a multi-million-pound international UK-based charity Oxfam, entitled 'How to Close Great Britain's Great Divide: The Business of Tackling Inequality', a six-page factoid dependent on highly selective statistics. Charities may make recommendations but must refrain from addressing the politico-economic causes of the poverty they presume to address. To step over the line puts their tax-free charitable status at risk.

All to the good, the charity's report calls for:

- improved cooperation between governments to prevent tax dodging that costs poor countries at least $100 billion every year;
- government action to encourage companies to act for the benefit of their workforces and wider society as well as their executives and shareholders;
- taxes on wealth to generate funds for healthcare, education and job creation;
- action to tackle the barriers that hold back women including lack of educational opportunities and the burden of unpaid care work.

The above statements are predicated on:

> A more human economy where *markets* – a vital engine for prosperity – are better managed in order to ensure no one is left out or denied basic rights such as decent work, healthcare and education. (Italics mine)

The Report's other recommendations for solving inequality are: that businesses should pay the Living Wage; include workers on their executive boards; corporations should cut executive salaries from around 120–150 plus times that of the ordinary worker down to 20 times; that government should legislate to prevent tax evasion; should stop transfer of profits to tax havens; and should incentivise those receiving social benefit payments to improve their skills so they can get better-paid jobs, thus reducing the costs of social welfare.

Though you'd almost hardly notice, the report's recommendations to close the UK inequality divide are predicated on the operations of a 'fairer' capitalist 'free-market' economy, the contradiction in terms seemingly going unnoticed. The report is also silent on the revolving door between UK political office, banking, finance and the corporatocracy; makes no mention of the monopoly that the government-banking-corporate nexus has over the UK's politico-economic life; contains no phrase about the governmental policy of the 'charitisation' of UK public services.

Charitistion is the attempt by the government to use unpaid volunteers to do the work of public services workers, the likes of, for instance, two female Spanish students training in Spain to become teachers coming to the UK, getting low-paid jobs and being engaged as part-time unpaid volunteers to replace a female Arabic, French, and Spanish-speaking UK local authority Teaching Assistant. The Spanish-speaking volunteers were engaged as teaching volunteers to support GCSE pupils learning Spanish and French – except the Spanish-speaking volunteers didn't speak French.

The philanthropy team of a charity providing information on dementia is calling for donations to provide their 'Side by Side' services of unpaid volunteers to accompany a dementia sufferer for an hour a week, on a walk in the park, an outing to a museum, a visit to a dementia café. There is no doubt that those unpaid volunteers will do what they can to support the dementia sufferer and provide that one hour a week relief for the dementia sufferers' regular carers. What those volunteers can't do is meet the 24/7 primary healthcare needs of dementia sufferers who are unable to look after themselves safely. Despite parliamentary inquiries, these patient's legal entitlements to NHS 24/7 Continuing Health Care costs are routinely denied (House of Commons Committee of Public Accounts, *NHS Continuing Healthcare Funding*, Thirteenth Report of Session 2017–19, 10 January 2018).

In its subsequent 16 January 2017 Report, the charity notes that eight white males now own as much of the world's wealth as half of the world's population of 3.6 billion people. Oxfam postulates that a primary reason for UK citizens voting in June 2016 to leave the European Union was that voters didn't trust either UK or EU politicians to address exponentially increasing inequalities. Oxfam welcomes the newly appointed prime minister's declarations of collecting more corporation tax. No mention is made that said prime minister is a beneficiary of private schooling; has a degree from Oxford University; had a former career in banking; and as Home Office minister was responsible for slashing police force budgets and promoting the UK's 'hostile environment' against the Caribbean *Windrush* generation who migrated to Britain to help rebuild the post-WWII economy, a UK policy of State hostility towards Caribbean immigrants, a policy that had been inbuilt from the very beginning (David Olusoga, *The Unwanted; The Secret Windrush Files*, BBC Two 24 June 2019).

Though not of the same order as corporatism, but of the same system, UK charitable organisations are big business. Britain alone has 168,000 registered British charities with a turnover of approximately £74 billion a year. Around 10% of that money goes on administration, inclusive of high salaries for the executives running the charities.

Ordinary people donate a higher percentage of their income to charitable causes than do the wealthy, and make those donations without expecting any return. Donations from corporate philanthrocapitalists enable them to gain politico-economic leverage over the institutions of the receiving countries. Donations made by philanthrocapitalists also enable them to reduce their income-tax bills.

In the above-mentioned charity's Report, there is next to no mention of the business model of well-paid executives to low-paid and no-paid volunteers. Nor is anything said about the steady flow of wages to an army of Western Non-Government Organisation workers.

Sexual Abuse and Exploitation (SEA) is all the more shocking when uncovered in the organisations people trust to have high moral standards, for example, churches, mosques, synagogues, private schools, sporting organisations and charities. Shortly after the above charity's 2017 Report had been written, news broke that some of the charity's workers had paid for prostitutes to come to their lodgings at the villa owned by the charity. Also revealed was that other charity workers in impoverished Third World countries had committed acts of sexual exploitation and abuse (SEA). SEA classically occurs when males exercise power over women and underage girls and boys. The charities whose workers committed SEA knew of those crimes, failed to make them public and allowed the perpetrators to move on unhindered to employment with other charities.

Besides getting donations from the public, major charities are also provided with taxpayer-funded government grants. After the sexual abuse and exploitation scandal, there were calls for the government to withhold its £31.7 million per year grant to the above-mentioned major charity and for the EU to withhold its £29 million (Dulcie Lee, 'How much government aid does a charity like Oxfam actually get?', *New Statesman*, 4 February 2018).

In charities where staff were found to have committed SEA, celebrities were also considering withdrawing their sponsorship. Ultimately, the scandal had less effect on the government grants, more on donations from a distrusting public (Alice Sharman, 'European Commission resumes awarding grants to Oxfam', Civil Society Media Ltd, London, 11 June 2018).

The public is generally unaware that some elements of some Western NGOs also act for the 'Deep State' of the transnational elite, using aspects of Western and local NGO structures as a Trojan horse to help underwrite the vested interests of the wealthy in influencing local and national government (The Corbett Report, 'NGOs Are the Deep States Trojan Horses', Opensource Intelligence Report, YouTube, 21 May 2018).

***

The public is rightly concerned their charitable donations and public foreign aid (FA) don't end up in the hands of charlatans. There seems to be a general notion, however, that donations, corporate philanthrocapitalism and FA aid budgets function as reparations of sorts for past colonialist exploitation of the Third World countries, an opinion indicative of the gap in public understanding of how a large proportion funding ends up back in the pockets of Western corporations supplying the 'charitable' goods and services to poor countries.

The UK spends 0.07% of its Gross National Income, around £12 billion, on foreign aid. About 40% of that £12 billion goes to organisations such as the United Nations to fund disaster relief. The remaining 60% goes directly to the developing countries to support education, healthcare, water and sanitation projects, etc. Through the government foreign aid budget, therefore, taxpayers' money is also going to charities. Since much foreign aid money had previously found its way into the pockets of the corrupt rulers of impoverished countries, FA money goes now instead to non-government organisations (NGOs) so that the uses of FA can be better monitored and controlled.

It's not a no-strings gift from the wealthier nations that is in operation, however, but 'reverse aid'. As with charitable donations, a considerable proportion of FA money goes to wages for the army of Western NGOs who work on various education, health and other programmes. FA money also goes to Western corporations providing the goods for those services. As for the bank loans to Third World governments, those governments pay hefty interests on those loans. The result is that far more money flows out of those countries into the West:

> In 2012, the last year of recorded data, developing countries received a total of $1.3tn, including all aid, investment, and income from abroad. But that same year some $3.3tn flowed out of them. In other words, developing countries sent $2tn more to the rest of the world than they received. If we look at all years since 1980, these net outflows add up to an eye-popping total of $16.3tn – that's how much money has been drained out of the global south over the past few decades. (Jason Hickel, 'Aid in reverse: how poor countries develop rich countries', *The Guardian*, 4 January 2017)

Of the money from the Third World countries that goes to the rich nations, $4.2 trillion went on loan interest payments to the private Western banks, that is, to pay the employees and provide unearned income to the shareholders of those banks.

The upshot is that charitable and foreign aid money plays a significant part in keeping poor countries in their economic place within the global capitalist system.

Given the decline of public services in Western countries, many citizens of First World countries want their governments to halt foreign aid. Third World countries also want to be free of the reverse aid business model of charity, Foreign Aid, bank loan and investments. The system is such, however, that abrupt removal of FA money is likely to hurt the millions of people who depend on it to mitigate the impoverishments of their everyday lives.

It should also be noted that the great majority of charity workers are honest, decent people doing their best to try to help others.

There can be little doubt, however, that the government-corporate-charity-philanthrocapitalist nexus currently in operation needs to be transformed and that the populations of poor countries can't continue to be forced to funnel reverse aid into the West.

As in the case of the homeless charity, Shelter, it's not uncommon either for charitable organisations to polish their image while ripping off consumers. The law firm promoted by a well-known charity as a trustworthy company offering expert advice to the elderly was found to have inserted itself as 'crooks in suits' executors into last wills and testaments, charging hefty fees for acquiring probate and discharging the wills.

Claiming that from past donations that a charity had reasonable expectations of being named as a beneficiary, charities have also taken families to court. Some will-making firms now take the precaution of advising testators not to name charities in their will but insert a general clause stating that decisions about where the charitable pecuniary gifts are to go will be at the discretion of the testator's executor.

To ensure public confidence in the work of charities, government needs to legislate to ensure separation of the charitable world and commercial world. Regulations on charitable donations and Foreign Aid money need to be such that Third World populations have more say on the best uses of that funding. The gagging clauses that in return for tax-free charity status bans charities from mentioning the politico-economic causes of impoverishments and other problems need to be abolished. The Annual Reports of charities concerned with attempting to diminish disadvantages and other problems must include comprehensive politico-economic analyses of the causes of those privations and difficulties. No charity would then be allowed get away with pontificating over selective factoids that hardly scratch the surface of the harm caused by the reverse aid exploitations that donors, volunteers and aid workers do their level best to ameliorate.

CHAPTER 19

Educational Apartheid

The UK population of approximately 66,797 million, includes 5.3 million in Scotland, 3.1 million in Wales, and 1.8 million in Northern Ireland. The vast majority of the UK's children, around 8 million, 93 percent, attend UK around 30,262 State funded schools. There are around 2,408 private fee paying schools in the UK. In England, approximately 583,000, 7%, of the child population go to the private fee paying schools; around 4.1% in Scotland, fewer in Wales and very few in Northern Ireland. Private school pupils go on to the top universities and get the top jobs.

State education costs around £5,500 a year per child. Annual fees per child at private schools range from £15,000 to £35,000. Private schools are incorporated as charities, pay no tax on their considerable income derived from school fees, high-value alumni donations, educational consultancy fees, hiring out well-appointed premises for events and conferences.

Not all private schools are equally well funded, and some are also poorly managed. That said, the majority of private schools provide what wealthy parents pay for, providing their offspring with the sort of education and insider politico-economic knowledge and socio-cultural networking that almost guarantees a lifetime of socio-economic advantage.

Research shows that at ratios higher than one teacher to 15–18 pupils, the teacher doesn't have time to attend to each pupil, to differentiate learning materials and pedagogy to match to pupil's levels of learning development, with each child's attainment declining as a consequence.

The top private schools enjoy a teacher-pupil ratio of 1:9. In State schools, the ratio is 1:30, higher than that in some primary schools.

Government slashing of State school budgets means that in some State schools subjects like music and drama are being dropped, and parents are being asked to contribute from £12 to £50 a month to the school budgets. By contrast, a top private school provides its pupils with:

sixteen rugby pitches, two floodlit AstroTurf pitches, a state-of-the-art sports hall, twenty-two hard tennis courts, twelve cricket pitches, an athletics track, two lacrosse pitches and six netball courts, a shooting range, a nationally acclaimed nine-hole golf course, six art studios ... its own theatre, its own TV crew ... a professional recording studio for aspiring musicians.[43]

Fees at this school, (co-educational, day and boarding, as it happens) are around £35,000 per pupil per annum. The average annual salary in the UK is £27,500. The headmaster of the above-mentioned wealthy private school, regarded as a chief executive running a business enterprise, is paid an annual salary of around £170,000.

To match-fund the budget of the average private school, the State school budget would have to be increased threefold, sixfold to match that of the top private schools.

The charity status of private schools means they don't pay taxes on their considerable earnings, don't pay VAT on their purchases, receive 80% exemption on the business tax rates. Successive governments have also continued to provide the wealthiest families with other valuable tax breaks. The business rate exemption alone means the sector will save £522.3 million over the next five years, money that would have gone to the cash-strapped local authorities instead.

A recent ex-headmaster of the above mentioned wealthy private school, privately educated and with an Oxford University degree in Philosophy, Politics and Economics, plus a doctorate in Economics, is now a university chancellor and adds to his high salary from the firms publishing the biographies he writes about British politicians, his books generally regarded as hagiographies. During his headship of the aforementioned private school, he jacked up the school's public examination performance and introduced classes in 'leadership', and in 'happiness and well-being', these an antidote, perhaps, to an education that delivered all too much of the opposite. This headmaster, also a member of well-connected educational lobbying groups, advocates that State schools be allowed to raise investment capital and be run for profit, is a patron of the project to promote literacy in State primary schools via the teaching of Latin (see the Iris Project).

This socio-politically paid-up member of the UK establishment is regularly trundled out in the British media as an expert on education, with little mention being made of the politico-economic and socio-cultural educational ideology in which his educational 'expertise' is rooted.

The private schools are likely to be affiliated with a religion, usually Church of England or Roman Catholic. The term 'faith school' applies to the 28% of State primary schools and the 18% of State secondary schools that cater for 1.9 million pupils in State-funded faith schools. State-funded faith schools are required to teach the national curriculum. The private schools are not required to do so. Many citizens contend that private schools should not enjoy tax-free charity status, that all State schools should be secular, with the general taxpayer not forced to pay for schools affiliated with religions.

Would a newly elected progressive government put a stop to well-heeled parents of private school pupils paying several years of private school fees in advance, with the lump sums then being invested in the stock market by the schools funding managers? Will wealthy parents continue to be allowed to declare those lump sum advance payments of school fees as liabilities on their tax returns? Indeed, will they be able to continue to cut their income tax obligations, while at the same time 'earning' dividends on the lump sum invested (Richard Garner, 'Private school fees scheme allows wealthy parents to save thousands of pounds in tax', *The Independent*, 2 February 2014)?

The UK's privately funded independent school system ensures the intergenerational educational, political and economic privileging of the UK's politico-economic elite. State-funded education aims to produce a sufficiently educated and compliant middle-class of middle managers and administrators; a literate and numerate working class; an acquiescent reserve army of the unemployed. Though the mass manufacturing jobs on which the aims of State schooling are premised no longer exist, the goals of State schooling remain the same.

During WWII, around 50% of UK city children were evacuated to the countryside, and many urban State schools were closed as a consequence. Conscription of male teachers into the armed services also meant there was a teacher shortage, and those city schools that did remain open were often overcrowded.

Poor education, bad housing, missing fathers, unsupported mothers, no recreational facilities, and gangster films were some of the factors contributing to the increasing juvenile delinquency, with the government then recognising that education is a common good that can't be left to chance.

Before the end of WWII, several local education authorities had already created large comprehensive secondary schools that combined grammar, secondary modern and technical education. Later, through Circular 10/65, the Secretary of State for Education abolished the grammar schools, establishing comprehensive education as national policy. ('Circular 10/65', Wikipedia). Grammar schools in politically conservative areas managed to retain their State grammar school status. Other State grammar schools opted to become private schools instead. About 164 State grammar schools remain, most of them in England, a few in Northern Ireland, none in Scotland or Wales.

The nominally non-selective State comprehensive schools organise children according to their perceived worth to the capitalist political economy, streaming the pupil intake into 'ability' sets, then setting pupils inside the streamed classrooms according to further suppositions of their ability.

Disaffected pupils end up being expelled, and often before that expulsion can be quarantined in sin bin isolation booths where they're prevented from interacting with other pupils.

Teachers can't beat the impositions of a system that could be seen as a type of child abuse that's become largely acceptable as practicable, as the 'way things are'.

The State education reforms of 1944 and 1965 brought significant changes. At the secondary school level, the merging of academic, ordinary and technical education meant that the new comprehensive school buildings were built to provide a greater range of facilities, from science labs, art rooms, woodwork and metal workshops to indoor spaces for dance, drama, sport. Accommodating larger numbers of pupils and teachers, comprehensive inner-city schools could have 1,000 to 1,500 pupils, with 60 plus teachers.

Class sizes were to be no more than 30 pupils per teacher and teachers' pay and conditions of service improved. From 1962 to 1998, the government policy of education as a common good was translated into government paying maintenance grants to middle and working-class university students. For those 36 years, those grants provided chances of upward social mobility for increasing numbers of young people.

Head teachers and deputies usually came up through the teaching ranks, classroom teacher to head of department. School managers, from the head teacher to deputies and senior teachers, also had teaching timetables, which kept managers in touch with the chalkface. The local education authority was responsible for ensuring there were enough school places for the local population; for calculating the formula for each school's funding; organising central services to schools, for example, supply teachers; advisory and inspection services; speech therapy and educational psychology, etc. Children with moderate learning difficulties were taught in mainstream schools. Disabled children and children with severe behavioural difficulties were taught in inter-borough State-funded special schools.

At both primary and secondary level, the mixed abilities of the pupil intake led to developments in mixed-ability educational theory and practice, discursive and collaborative learning, and child-centred pedagogies that took the differing learning needs of individual children into account.

Always on the lookout for means to improve educational outcomes, LEAs might promote specific teaching methods in their schools. For instance, in the teaching of literacy some LEAs implemented 'look and say' word recognition, a feasible means of teaching literacy if the word meanings are within the socio-culturally understandings of the learners. However, as a 'one-size-fits-all' method, the 'look and say' method often proved more hindrance than help. Had classroom teachers been allowed to conduct teachers' action-research on the method first, the life-long negative consequences for the literacy development of many pupils could have been avoided.

The first clause in the UK government-corporate-media narrative rebutting any increased funding for State education is that, in this the fifth largest economy in the world, there's no money. The next clause is that State school failure has nothing to do with inadequate funding. Blame for the comparatively poor outcomes of State education vis-a-vis the private school sector is instead laid at the door of incompetent local education authorities; bungling head teachers; inadequate teachers; feckless parents; and deficient children.

Today's government educational 'reform' has been the academisation of State schools. Academisation has done nothing to alter the 1:30 pupil–teacher ratio; the inadequacies of a one-size-fits-all curriculum; top-down transmission teaching pedagogies; lack of opportunity for teachers' action-research; and there's no time allowed for the pupils to pursue autonomous education. Parents, stuck with an offer they couldn't refuse, were left to hope that, as promised, these reforms would make things better for their children.

***

Historically and currently, migration, inward and outward, figures large in the lives of the majority of UK citizens. To escape run-down post-WWII Britain, significant numbers of UK citizens emigrated to Canada, Australia, New Zealand. The British Nationality Act of 1948 gave Commonwealth citizens the right to settle in the UK, their labour required to help rebuild the post-war UK economy, the immigrants coming mainly from the Indian subcontinent and the Caribbean, some West Indian men returning to Britain after having served in the UK British Army, Royal Navy and Royal Air Force during WWII. For many of those ex-forces immigrants, the reason for having joined the mother country's fight WWII fight against fascism was the fear that Mussolini's invasion of Abyssinia (Ethiopia) would bring in a new era of global slavery.

For the UK, adjusting economically, politically and socio-culturally to the end of empire, big changes were in store. Inner-city primary and secondary school classrooms quickly became multi-lingual, multi-ethnic and multi-racial. To devise new teaching methods for what was, in effect, an educational emergency, UK teachers, local education authorities, university education departments devised new teaching methods for the new times. Josie Levine (1936–96), a university lecturer specialising in multi-lingual, multi-cultural and equal opportunities education, encapsulates in her phrase 'creative disruption', the efforts of classroom teachers to do the necessary.

> Multi-lingual classrooms, although not alone in acting as prompts to pedagogical development, have obviously been *the* significant site for the development of an equal opportunities education. Such classrooms were perceived by many teachers as threatening, but for others the existence of such dynamic classrooms provided the

creative disruption to the educational status quo which allowed them to take the practical and theoretical steps necessary for establishing egalitarian frames of reference in the support of learning.[44]

Commonly, the teaching of language and literacy to monolingual English-speaking primary school pupils had been – and still is – reliant on the reading of fiction. The outsize fiction books on the classroom reading stand are also used to help teach vocabulary, comprehension, spelling, grammar punctuation, with children also often tasked with writing about which character in the story they liked, and so on.

Whether the immigrant children were literate in their first language or not, teachers realised that the fictional stories in English didn't reflect the children's lived experiences and couldn't meet their urgent language learning needs. That realisation led teachers to recognise the same problem of fictional decontextualisations was also true for many of their indigenous English-speaking mono-lingual pupils who had been 'left behind' in their struggles for language and literacy development. The task was now for teachers to find ways of achieving successful language and literacy development outcomes for both the immigrant and indigenous children:

> We were, at this time, too, focusing on ways that the knowledge and abilities brought to school by monolingual English children could be built on and extended. (Ibid.)

Schools were by now being challenged by parents convinced that teachers were paying more attention to the needs of bilingual pupils. Teachers also had to contend with the educationally conservative attitudes of some immigrant parents and of some immigrant fathers towards the education of their daughters. In a few inner-city primary schools, the solution for dealing with these tensions was to invite the different sets of parents to come into classrooms and see for themselves the education teachers were trying to provide. In those few such primary schools, parents of the indigenous children began to act as the classroom teaching assistants, and bilingual parents served as interpreters for their children – or more commonly, the children did the interpreting for the parents.

One inner-city primary school decided the most practical way of promoting participative language and literacy development for all would be to run a Family Book Scheme. The aim was to create handmade books based on pupils' everyday experiences and family stories that are part of all children's family history. The books would be illustrated by photographs and children's drawings:

> We wanted to give the children every opportunity to enjoy books and to find them relevant to their own experiences. ....The work interested the parents and they encouraged their children. At times they were amazed at the quality of the books their children produced. They were real authors. About eighty books were produced in all. (Ibid.)

Almost all the books were written in English, a few in the languages of the bilingual learners who were already literate in their language.

> Our work had helped us to turn aside from the idea that had come to us as received wisdom, that children who are unable to speak English come to school knowing nothing and are ill-equipped for learning. (Ibid.)

This 'creative disruption', a newfound way of developing children's language and literacy by contextualising the children's knowledge, lived experiences and linguistic abilities, aimed to leave no one behind. The teacher was also no longer in sole charge of learning so that parents, pupils and teachers became instead co-managers of the children's language and literacy development. In the process, the cooperative buzz of collaborative classroom talk became an official classroom pedagogy.

Prior to the introduction of the 1988 National Curriculum, secondary school pupils followed separate syllabi based on purported abilities, with around 20% of secondary school pupils being prepared for the Certificate of Secondary Education Ordinary Level classes (O levels), the other 80% doing the more coursework-based Certificate of Secondary Education classes (CSE). The English CSE syllabus also aimed to help pupils develop their Speaking and Listening skills, each pupil required to give a talk, often based on a hobby, for example, how to take care of a pet, with many a budgie, guinea pig and dog brought into classrooms. To prepare pupils for giving their talk, group and class discussion work would be introduced. Instead of pupils sitting separately in rows, desks were clustered together so that pupil groups could discuss a set topic – although the conversation often centred instead on pupils' everyday concerns, ambitions, fears, gossip, jokes, exploration of ideas, etc. Desks were also put together to form classroom conference tables, though it was usually the teacher who chose the topic and facilitated the discussion.

More generally, however, secondary school English lessons, 'O' Level and CSE relied on the anthologies containing a mix of poetry, essays, articles, extracts from literary fictions and dramas, along with comprehension, grammar and vocabulary exercises. Grammar books were also used to develop vocabulary, spelling, grammar Writing tasks were often set around the subjects in the anthologies, or on topics set by the teacher, pupils tasked with writing essays, poetry, persuasive writing, newspaper articles, creative writing, playwriting, writing for personal development, and so on. A considerable amount of time is also spent on the set books for the English literature part of the final exams, based more on literary appreciation than critical analyses.

Secondary school syllabi for English was, therefore, no more designed to meet the urgent English language learning needs of the bilingual learners or the learning needs of the 'left-behind' mono-lingual pupils than were the language and literacy development methods of the primary schools. Consequently, secondary school teachers also found themselves trying to open up the English curriculum and make it more readily accessible to both bilingual and monolingual pupils.

In the early 1980s, the Inner London Education Authority (ILEA), one of the largest education authorities in the world, responding to conflicting pressures from both the conservative right and the progressive left, set up its Equal Opportunities Unit. In 1983, the ILEA provided all its schools with ILEA-produced Aides Memoires designed to help school management teams and subject departments develop whole school equal opportunities policies regarding race, gender and social class across all curricular and pastoral aspects of the school. The ILEA also appointed inspector/advisors for equal opportunities and multicultural education.

The Aide Memoire on social class was significantly shorter than those on sexism and racism. Race and gender were also generally approached as separate areas of contention. The economic exploitation of the poor and working-class went largely unaddressed in the ILEA's Aides Memoires, as did the effects of socio-economic conditions in relation to gender and race.

How actual social relations between white, black, female, male adults and youngsters played out in their everyday lived experiences was not yet the identifiable 'subject' that would later be kicked into the academicised study of 'intersectionality'.

In almost equal measure, the conservative right and the progressive left criticised mainstream multi-lingual, multi-cultural and equal opportunities education. For the left, so-called equal opportunities and multi-cultural education came nowhere near the right of children to an egalitarian education that would first and foremost have to be resourced at a level to meet the actual educational needs of the poor and working-class majority. Many on the left also judged 'multicultural' and 'equal opportunities education' a liberal fudge that failed to examine how the issues of classism, sexism and racism arose from and intersected with the exploitative capitalist political economy. Such critiques were lambasted by the right as the ravings of the 'loony left'. The conservative right pushed for a purportedly social-class, gender and race-blind education with teaching and learning to be based on an imagined meritocratic 'level playing field' that does not exist.

Meanwhile, the publishing world began catering to the new multi-cultural and equal opportunities' education market, producing children's fiction that focused on the lives of black children and girls. Also putting in an appearance were texts and learning materials revealing the contributions made by non-Caucasian people to civilisation, for example, in mathematics, medicine, the arts, navigation, map-making, uprisings against oppressions, etc.

Though to the teachers caught in the curriculum and pedagogical wars where every small step of classroom democratisation was a victory, the powers of the status quo educational establishment remained dominant, with multi-cultural and equal opportunities education functioning more as an optional add-on to an education that is based on the underlying politico-economic and socio-cultural assumptions of the market-based political economy.

Nonetheless, in a typical inner-city State school classroom with a couple of upper-middle-class and some lower-middle-class pupils, the majority being working-class white, black, ethnic minority girls and boys, levels of acceptance of differences in race and ethnicity were generally high, and firm friendships between pupils were formed. Those friendships were also because white, black and ethnic minority working-class pupils were likely to be next door neighbours living on council estates.

Though teachers did also have to find ways of negotiating the tensions within the wider society that were sometimes played out in the classroom, pupils and teachers were primarily engaged with the business mastering the curriculum and preparing for end-of-school examinations. If at the chalkface pupil relations were generally good, in the sixth-form common room for 16- to 18-year-olds the students tended to congregate in separated social class, gender, racial and ethnic groups.

In an inner-city London comprehensive school of about 1,500 youngsters with a mix of social classes, the majority being from working-class backgrounds, with the usual inner-city contingent of bilingual learners from Africa, the Middle East, the European continent, the Indian subcontinent, Hong Kong and so on, pupils spoke around 40 different languages between them.

Taught separately in a 'sin bin' classroom were about half a dozen disruptive teenage boys who had also been openly recruited by the National Front. Trying to acknowledge their feelings of alienation and their claim to the sin bin classroom being their 'territory', the teacher had acceded to teenagers' request to paint a union jack on the classroom wall. These boys were a magnet for other unemployed former pupils, who entered the school and who were also sometimes joined by former pupils from other schools unofficially all coming into the school to see their mates. This joint group of boys, a total of about eight to 14, caused considerable disruption, roaming the corridors, kicking classroom doors open, etc., to the point that the school management asked the ILEA for help in dealing with them.

However, rather than taking remedial action to treat these boys as pupils who'd been failed by their schools, the response was instead to send in a small squad of a few uniformed security guards, young men not much older than the boys themselves. The task of the security guards was to guard the entrances to the building to prevent the intruders from coming into the school and patrol the interior of the school to stop the sin bin boys from roaming the corridors. The school featured fleetingly in the tabloid newspapers after the presence of the security guards was leaked to the press.

The sin bin boys, confronted by the security guards, started yelling racist insults at a young turban-wearing Sikh security guard, and fisticuffs broke out between the other security guards and the boys. School staff, already shocked at the 'solution' of sending security guards into the school, asked for the guards be withdrawn.

Having got the point that the school and the ILEA wouldn't tolerate their disruptive behaviour, there was a lot less noise from the sin bin boys. In a now calmer school, the staff heaved a collective sigh of relief and got on with business as usual, that is, trying to get their pupils through the various syllabi and preparing their older pupils for the end-of-school public examinations.

The teacher with responsibility for the whole-school, one-hour-a-week lesson in Personal and Social Education got permission from school management and governors for teachers to use Campaign for Homosexual Equality materials to teach against homophobia and about equal rights and inclusiveness.

Around the same time, the teacher with departmental responsibility for developing the English department curriculum for the third year, that is, 14-year-olds, informed by work being done in another inner-city secondary school, compiled a sourcebook on a topic of current concern in the media of the day, South African apartheid. The sourcebook contained photographs, maps, newspaper reports, poetry, short stories, excerpts from novels, biographies and plays and covered a variety of topics: the identity passbooks that determined where people could live; life in the townships; education; culture, etc. The sourcebook could be employed in the conventional English subject teaching manner, using the newspaper reports, fictions, plays and poetry, etc., as a basis for comprehension exercises, grammar, punctuation, vocabulary extension, and so on. The sourcebook provided more contextualisation for the excerpts than is ordinarily available in the anthologies of essays and excerpts from literature and poetry, etc., that are traditionally used in English lessons.

About half of the 12 teachers who taught English, some of whom also taught other curriculum subjects, were reluctant to use what they believed were overtly political materials in their classrooms. A fraught departmental meeting concluded the project could only go ahead if approved by the ILEA'a advisors for multicultural education. One of the advisers tried to help with the project, the other adviser, of mixed race, declared that if he were an English teacher, then for the sake of preserving good relationships with parents and school governors he wouldn't touch the subject of apartheid with a bargepole. The Head of English then announced that there was no money available to print copies of the sourcebook in any case, case closed.

The head teacher, known for having done voluntary work in Sudan, was reluctant to give the total thumbs down to what he regarded as a liberally progressive project. He was also very canny about contradicting anyone who might object to the project, inclusive of the Head of English, who, perhaps paradoxically, had a reputation of being on the political left.

In a final departmental meeting on the matter to which the Inspector for Multicultural Education had been invited, the inspector pointed out that even the tabloid press ran articles critical of apartheid. On the inspector's say-so, the sourcebook of learning materials on apartheid was approved for use in English lessons – for those teachers who might be interested in using it. Around copies 60 copies of the home-made sourcebook were printed and bound at the modest cost of £95, enough for small group work in about six classes.

The tensions involved in getting the go-ahead backgrounded the fact that the project was an optional multi-cultural and equal opportunities flavoured 'add-on' to the syllabus for English – even though the Head of English later hyped the sourcebooks as a sign of the department's liberal progressivism.

The advisory teacher who had supported the project contributed a UNESCO educational factsheet that consisted of two columns of statistics about the number of doctors, teachers, etc., for each of two economically distinct groups in one anonymised country. The content language required to comprehend that factsheet was minimal. So it was decided that the factsheet could be used in a 50-minute ESL/English lesson with two small groups of 14-year-old stage 2–3 and 3–4 bilingual learners, the aim of the lesson being to use the fact sheet to stimulate group discussion work by asking the two groups of learners to which country they thought the factsheet referred. The discussion of one of the two groups would be recorded and transcribed as part of teacher action-research, the aim being to discover whether such discussion-based lessons on a topic of current concern supported language and literacy development – or not. The small group of four pupils whose discussion would be recorded included a Kurdish speaker who was also learning Arabic; a Portuguese speaker, a Hungarian speaker who was also learning Russian, and an Italian speaker who had been in England a matter of months.

It takes considerable time to transcribe any discussion lesson, yet when many months later the pupils were presented with the transcript, they remembered that lesson in remarkable detail. Asked why, their response was that in none of their lessons before or since had a topic of current public concern been a matter for discussion. One pupil added that in his then fifth year at the school, he had never had a discussion-based lesson.

Asked if in English they preferred lessons based on fiction or factual information, they said they preferred real information, because 'You know about the world because you know there is a world and it's true.' Whereas, 'a story is a story', wasn't true and since it was also closed off from real life, there wasn't a lot of real-life point discussing it. Asked how often they would like to have discussion-based lessons, they said once a week, adding that school lessons focused too much on school-type knowledge, that school knowledge and fictions weren't all that useful for thinking about the real world – and that this was all the teachers' fault (Helen Davitt, 'Political and Moral Contexts in English and ESL Teaching', in Josie Levine (ed.), *Developing pedagogies in the multi-lingual classroom*, London: Falmer Press, 1990).

Discussion for learning lessons do go on in State schools, if still too rarely. Nevertheless, viewers of the classroom 'fly-on-the-wall' documentaries can see for themselves that pupils are usually sat in rows and that discussion for learning lessons are not much used – not so easy to do with a teacher-pupil ratio of 1:30 in any case.

Such as they were, those brief moments of the democratisation of curriculum and pedagogy proved too much of a threat for the government to allow them to pass unhindered.

Government's answer was to produce the 1988 English National Curriculum and Key Stage Testing regime, a short history of which is presented in the next chapter.

CHAPTER 20

English National Curriculum and Key Stage Testing

No longer in a position to directly undermine the anti-sexist and anti-racist movements that had gained traction in State schools, the UK educational establishment turned its firepower on anti-homophobic teaching instead.

The now out of print 1983 children's book by Susanne Bosch, a (straight) Danish author, *Jenny Lives with Eric and Martin* portrays the everyday life of a young girl living with her father and his male partner. The author's rationale for writing children's literature on topical issues is:

> The entertainment value has always been important to me, but it seems just as important to give children relevant stories and, in a gentle way, to help them understand themselves and the society they live in. I believe that a good children's book has a built-in tiny bit of wisdom – like the old fairy tales. As mother, father, teacher or author we should give our children stories that give them all the time in the world to remain in, and enjoy, their childhood. But we are also responsible for giving them stories that gently open their minds and prepare them for meeting the world as adults – a world in which adults are no longer available to solve the children's problems with a hug and a kiss.
>
> For what it's worth, I don't personally think homosexuality (or any other subject) should be aggressively promoted in schools, but I do think it should be talked about in an informative, unsensational, way. One way of doing that is by making books like mine available to children in schools and libraries – as is done in Denmark – and by letting teachers and parents be prepared to answer questions without unnecessary drama. (*'Jenny, Eric, Martin ... and me*, Susanne Bosche', *The Guardian*, 31 January 2000)

Not available in schools, the book was discovered in an Inner London Education Authority teachers' centre. The government and media pundits immediately pounced on the liberal ILEA as being agents for the promotion of homosexual propaganda, which is said to have led to the infamous Clause 28 amendment in the 1986 Local Government Act:

> A local authority shall not: (a) Intentionally promote homosexuality or publish material with the intention of promoting homosexuality; (b) promote the teaching in any maintained school of the acceptability of homosexuality as a pretended family relationship.

Since contravening Clause 28 didn't constitute a criminal offence, no one was prosecuted under it. However, as a piece of political intimidation, its effects were dire. Teachers, straight and gay, using the Campaign for Homosexual Equality teaching materials immediately stopped doing so; support for lesbian and gay student groups was withdrawn; and, in dread of public scandal and in fear of their jobs, head teachers, school managers and classroom teachers turned a blind eye and a deaf ear and on homophobic bullying, hate speech, jokes and name-calling. It took 15 years of political activism by anti-bullying and gay rights campaigners to get the government to repeal Clause 28.

As far as gender identity is concerned, considerable progress has been made, but with teachers largely untrained in equal opportunities education, the verbal and physical abuse of gay and lesbian pupils can go unchallenged. In a now more tolerant society, gender-based bullying still goes on, and epithets such as 'poof', 'batty boy', 'lezzie', and worse, continue to be heard in today's school playgrounds.

The immense amount of work that went into the establishment of the 1988 National Curriculum for England wasn't premised on comprehensive public discussion of what mass State education in a changing world should be. The keynote message was that for the UK to succeed in the fiercely competitive economic world, and for children to improve their life chances, there was – and is – no alternative to the NC Programmes of Study and its Key Stage Standard Attainment Tests at the ages of 7,11,14. From ages of 14 to 16, pupils follow the Key Stage 4 NC Programmes of Study in preparation for their end-of-school General Certificate of Secondary Education (GCSEs), with the study of the core curriculum of English, Maths and Science mandatory.

Many costly conferences and in-service training sessions were held up and down the country, their purpose being to firmly embed the National Curriculum in every school in England, the training sessions often led by teacher colleagues seconded on higher pay to do the job. In attendance were head teachers, school management teams, heads of department and, sometimes, classroom teachers – parents and pupils conspicuous by their absence.

Prior to the implementation of the NC, cross-curricular humanities projects based on the history, geography, technology, art and culture of a particular time and place had been established, the projects devised to extend children's literacy and learning through cross-curricular, empathetic study of the lives of the people of a particular historical era, for example, Vikings, Romans, Tudors, and so on. These humanities projects commonly employed progressive pedagogies of mixed-ability teaching, child-centred learning, collaborative study, discussion for learning. Some projects were of excellent quality, others less so. Implementation of the NC Programmes of Study and the Key Stage Tests regime meant that schools abandoned those cross-curricular projects.

With its compartmentalised Programmes of Study for each subject, the NC can support depth-of-study. It can also induce a lack of enthusiasm for learning, disinterest and boredom. Though not obliged to teach the NC, and unconcerned about the NC's social class, race and gender-blindness, some of the private schools initially adopted the NC as a handy curricular template – before dropping it as too constraining and as setting the educational bar too low.

Pupils' performance in the Key Stage Tests took precedence over teacher assessments of overall development of individual pupils, and NC learning outcomes were codified in the academic rubrics of being able to 'explain', 'recall', 'investigate', 'reflect', 'differentiate'. Laudable aims as those are, they leave less room for the acquisition and expression of knowledge through empathetic human understanding.

Long lasting recall and deeper understandings are more likely to be achieved when the study of topics and their cross-curricular connections are pursued by the curious learner, the child's innate curiosity sparked by what the child wants to know, and by teachers, parents, carers helping the child build on what the child already knows and can do. Teachers know that collaborative and cross-curricular learning is an efficient and enjoyable method and they do what they can to provide such opportunities within the NC POS, though the margins for doing so are limited.

Nowadays, the NC is designed as broad curriculum subject frameworks. The intention is to allow teachers to develop lesson content to meet the learning needs of the specific groups of children in their particular classrooms. However, the main drivers of education in UK State primary and secondary schools are the NC POS, the Key Stage Tests, the end-of-school examinations, and that overarching lever of control, the school league tables based on the performance of individual schools in the Key State Tests and end-of-school exams. The regional examinations boards which used to run the final examinations procedures have transmuted from being charitable organisations to being billion-pound businesses (Holly Watt and Claire Newell, 'Exam boards: Edexcel went from charity to £1bn business', *The Telegraph*, 9 December 2011).

None of this is to say there should be no compulsory areas of study and no formal assessment of learning. On the contrary. It is to say there should be more parental–teacher–pupil input in deciding what those compulsory areas of learning should be; that the development of pupils' self-esteem and confidence in themselves as learners should be paramount; and that there must always be room for self-chosen autonomous learning.

The ILEA, established by the Labour government in 1965, had become one of the most progressive education authorities in any comparable Western democracy and had a well-earned reputation for innovations in mixed-ability teaching, child-centred education, and collaborative study. Two years after the introduction of the NC, the right-wing government abolished the ILEA, and responsibility for State education in the capital was, in classic divide-and-rule manner, allocated to the 12 separate inner London boroughs.

A Conservative candidate for the 2016 London mayoral elections stated that in abolishing the ILEA, his party had been guilty of 'throwing out the baby with the bathwater', and that 'some of the politics that we shouted down were in fact incredibly progressive', adding, somewhat illogically, that the ILEA 'was just before its time'. The Head of Education in the National Union of Teachers said that the ILEA had had a 'strategic approach to education', inclusive of the establishment of its teachers' centres across the capital, adding that, 'Nothing like that exists now … all sorts of things were made available for teachers, some of which will never be replaced or matched.'[45]

The Local Management of Schools (LMS) section of the 1988 Education Reform Act that saw the imposition of the NC also incentivised schools to cut themselves adrift from the local education authorities. School governors and head teachers choosing MS would get their funding directly from and were responsible to central government, bypassing the local education authority. (For a comprehensive account of this period, see Derek Gillard's *Education in England: a brief history*, <http://www.educationengland.org.uk/history>.)

This shift in the control of schools from local democratic to central government control was in line with the recommendations of the free-market think tanks such as the Institute of Economic Affairs (IEA) that advocated abandoning the post-WWII socio-economic consensus, recommending that government devise policies to divest itself of responsibility for the public services by selling those services to private companies, the marketisation of services to schools included. Affiliated to other right-wing think tanks, worldwide, the IEA, which does not publish where its £1.5 million annual funding comes from, continues to influence UK government policy.

The implementation of the LMS of Schools and the NC was accompanied by a steady stream 'how to' memoranda for head teachers, school managers and classroom teachers, with glossy teacher instruction booklets for each subject and stage of the NC. A teacher at a conference on education niftily illustrated how teachers were drowning in NC directives, paperwork and curriculum documents, by approaching the lectern pushing a delivery trolley stacked high with those National Curriculum documents and directives. Those curricular documents were also systematically deskilling classroom teachers at the chalkface. NC paperwork also imposed ludicrously repetitive teacher tasks, for example, translating curriculum learning objectives from the NC documents onto teachers' lesson plans and into pupil's progress reports, with teacher assessment largely confined to the goals of the NC and its Key State Tests as set down in teachers' lesson plans. Teachers ticked boxes to confirm whether or not those NC and Key Stage Test goals had been attained, and if not had to show how subsequent lesson plans would ensure that those NC and Key Stage Test goals would be achieved.

Each school's 'value added' is calculated on the extent to which it improves its Key Stage Test results from one stage to the next, or not, and on its final examination results, and parents and the public judge the success or failure of each school according to how its results compare with other schools. Test and exam results are decontextualised from the long-known key indicators of educational attainment: parental education, employment, income.

GCSE grades A to C are achieved by 67% of State secondary school pupils compared to 96% of private school pupils. Private schools gain five times more A* grades than State schools. Much of the State school pupils' A* grades are achieved because parents who can afford it hire private tutors. New cheaper tutoring businesses have now also sprung up beside supermarkets and elsewhere, a type of pay-as-you-go educational top-up service.

The NC tests and mark schemes for primary school Key Stage 1 and 2 change each year, with the total marks that pupils need to pass each year's tests announced annually by Ofsted, the Office for Standards in Education. Primary schools are obliged to meet the government target of 65% of Key Stage 2 pupils reaching the required levels in reading, writing, maths. In secondary schools, 40% of pupils must achieve grades A to C in their GCSE public examination results, inclusive of their exam results in English and Maths.

In both primary and secondary State schools, NC results improve, stall, fluctuate. Comparisons between schools from one year to next don't take account of cuts to school budget; changes in subject teaching expertise; rising pupil-teacher ratios; changes in the rates of pupil educational needs; rates of bilingualism, special educational needs, etc.

State Schools that don't meet the previously mentioned 'floor level' percentages of basic educational outcomes trigger inspections by Ofsted. The inspected schools deemed by Ofsted to be failing risk closure or takeover by academy school chains. Teachers can lose their jobs, and pupils can be stuck with the reputation of being slow learners.

To avoid the considerable dangers of being seen as a failing school, State secondary schools will use their internal data monitoring systems to trigger increased teaching assistant support for particular groups, for example, to move pupils expected to get a D grade up to C – often by taking those extra support hours away from already inadequate teaching assistant hours elsewhere. Meanwhile, those pupils projected to get either below or above C grade, unsupported by teaching assistants or other forms of backup, are left to get on with lessons as best they can.

For almost three decades now, 'teaching to the test' has become the norm, with pupils in English State schools amongst the most tested in the developed world, the schools described as exam factories.[46] There are many contributing factors to states of mental ill-health in young people: insecurities about the self; feelings of isolation; emotional, mental, physical and sexual abuse; bullying, cyber-bullying; inability to see a future; a myriad of other anxieties, for example, over body shape, looks, fashion; stress and anxieties about school, tests and examinations. Not to be excluded amongst those reasons for mental ill-health is the fact that UK children are now obliged to take approximately 70 formal tests and examinations during their school lives – not to mention the mock tests and exams in preparation for the 'real thing'.[47] Rather than enjoying their school lives, too many youngsters suffer from the stress of having to keep their noses to the educational grindstone; of studying a curriculum that's not of their choosing; having to take a barrage of Key Stage in the separate subjects of that curriculum.

Studies now show that 60% of UK youngsters are frequently in states of anxiety and stress about the NC and its Key Stage Tests regime. There are reports of young children feeling sick and being in tears because they perceive themselves as educational failures. Of the 1,300 youngsters completing the Childline charity's exam stress survey, 96% felt anxiety about exams, with 59% feeling under pressure from their parents and teachers to excel in those exams.[48]

Around 1 million UK children between the ages of 5 and 15, more boys than girls, are now experiencing mental health problems likely to lead to increased levels of mental ill-health in adulthood. To cope with that stress, some youngsters have taken to smoking, alcohol, drugs and self-harming. Suicides in young people below the age of 18 are now a worldwide phenomenon; in the UK the number of under-18s who committed suicide during the year 2014 to 2015 was 66.[49]

Young people in today's education systems are living under threat of the tsunami of testing and examinations based on the deceptive presumptions of a non-existent meritocracy, an imaginary 'level playing field' that does not exist.

UK sociologist Michael Young (1915–2002) used the term meritocracy as a derogatory description of the UK socio-political-cultural structures and processes through which the UK's elite politico-cultural class reproduces itself according to a narrow set of self-serving goals and interests.[50]

Mr Young senior seems to have been unable to pass those observations on to his son. Mr Young junior is a proponent of schools operating outside of local democratic control. The new 'free' school, that is, 'freed' from local democratic control, with which Mr Young junior was associated, depends on donations of thousands of pounds from wealthy parents. Since the outcomes in that school were not as hoped for, the trust's plans for setting up another were shelved.

The January 2018 revelations of Mr Young junior's sexist and racist remarks made on social media and of his attendance at a meeting hosted by a London university where the topic on the agenda was eugenics led to his withdrawal from his appointment to the new Office for Students. Though he was rapped on the knuckles by UK media, the PM had refused to back calls for Mr Young to step down from his new job, perhaps an indication that government isn't concerned about a eugenicist stance amongst its protégés, or a sign of there being little to choose from in government's pool of appointees for the top jobs (Josh White, 'The Existence of Toby Young', *Souciant*, 5 January 2018).

State school budget cuts, the job losses, teacher shortages, larger classes, professional deskilling, excessive paperwork, and performance pay mean the State school teaching profession is under enormous stress. Performance pay can require, for example, that a music teacher demonstrate an 80% improvement in the achievements of the 500 pupils he teaches for one period a week. Unsurprisingly, 30% of teachers leave the profession after five years in the job.[51]

In any democratic society, the first stage in improving its institutional structures is having knowledge and understanding of the purposes, qualities and outcomes of those structures. The issue here is not that schools are not to be held accountable to parents, pupils and the public for the quality of teaching and learning going on in schools – on the contrary. The point is that all children have a right to an education that meets their learning needs; doesn't harm their mental well-being; helps them achieve individual and socially accountable educational goals, and respects their innate desire for fairness for themselves and others. Those imposing educational regimes that fail to uphold those non-negotiable basic educational rights must be held equally accountable, whether government ministers, local education authority executives, governors, academy trustees, headteachers and school managers.

CHAPTER 21

Pre-privatisation of State Schools

Scotland has a population of 5.3 million, Wales 3.1 million, Northern Ireland 1.8 million. England, the most populous part of the UK, has a population of 55.8 million. This chapter will review the 'reform' of the 'academisation' of English State schools instituted by central government over the past 18 years or so. The academisation policy is that management of the existing State primary and secondary schools is taken over by Academy Trusts sponsored by businesses, universities, faith groups and voluntary groups. Sponsor groups are also allowed to set up new 'free' schools, free from local authority control. Funded by the government, academy and free school trusts are answerable to central government through eight English regional authorities. Academy Trusts can run chains of academy schools, and some multi-chain Trusts also have strategic oversight of new 'free' schools. The sponsors of the academies and free schools get extra government funding for each of their schools, and the Trusts running the schools may also provide extra funding from the Trust's own private resources. The Trusts are allowed to alter teachers' pay and conditions and are free to hire unqualified teachers. Approximately a quarter of English State Primary schools, 4,363 primary schools were academised as of 2017, and 2,075 of England's 3,381 State secondary schools.

As long as schools deliver a broad and balanced curriculum inclusive of English, maths, science and religious education, academy and free schools don't have to implement the whole of English National Curriculum. However, since academy and free' school pupils must take the NC Key stage tests in the subjects of the NC that they do teach, in practice most academy and free schools follow most of the National Curriculum. That there has been little deviation from the NC is also because curricular and pedagogical innovation is a risky business requiring educational research, development, design, monitoring and evaluation of proposed changes in curricula and pedagogies.

The academisation project is the equivalent of US State 'charter' school reforms of the last 25 years or so, under which US State governments are legislatively allowed to confer 'Charter' status on schools which takes Charter schools outside the democratic control of public district schools. Conferring Charter status was also a response to the failures of underfunded run-down State schools. Charter schools, like the English academised schools, are run by charities and business sponsors outside local school district control.

US Charter schools and UK academised schools are likely to be managed under the tenets of the School Effectiveness Movement. SEM claims that regardless of the socio-economic background of the pupil intake, the combination of optimum business-type school management leadership, high pupil expectations, teacher performance monitoring systems and performance pay, and the use of data-driven tracking procedures to monitor each child's curricular progress results in improved educational outcomes. SEM aims to get the greatest number of pupils to achieve the schools pre-set curricular goals. The data systems used to track pupils' progress triggers systematised intervention procedures for pupils not achieving curricular targets.

US research on charter and academy school 'reform' shows little difference in educational outcomes between charter schools and State district schools. Results in charter schools are also often below those of schools operating within local School District control – a fact known about before the UK government instituted its programme of academisation. So too was the fact that the managers of some US Charter schools have been found guilty of corruption and criminal misuse of funds.

UK research mirrors that of the US, with the same mixed results in educational outcomes for academy schools compared to local education authority State local district schools, and a similar heritage of financial mismanagement in both the charter and academised schools.

In the UK, all English State schools, academy and free schools must submit to school inspections by the purportedly independent government agency, the Office for Standards in Education (Ofsted). However, rather than acting as a politically independent external agency, Ofsted has been working more or less hand-in-glove with the governmental policy of the academisation of State schools.

A government project initially set up to improve educational outcomes in low-performing inner-city State schools, the UK government's reform of the academisation of existing State schools in England and the setting-up of new schools free of local democratic control started in the early 2000s. It then quickly became government policy to coerce State schools into academisation. The rebranding of the State schools as 'academies' is meant to signify educational outcomes comparable to the selective State grammar schools and the private schools, both often called academies.

Existing State schools, including those that had opted out of local authority oversight under the Local Management of Schools section of the 1988 Education Act, were monetarily incentivised to acquire 'academy' status. Academy trustees were also permitted to set up 'free' schools even in areas where no new school is needed. The new school skews the pupil intake of nearby local authority schools, which in turn affects the funding of nearby local authority schools.

A recent Secretary of State for Education and Minister for Women and Equalities, privately educated, with a law degree from Oxford, previously a corporate lawyer specialising in mergers and acquisitions, highly literate in the narratives of her class, and continuing with her predecessor's enthusiasm for the academisation of State schools, openly declared that she saw businesses being allowed to run schools for profit. A long political game with a clear goal, academisation also leads to increased standardisation and control of the curriculum which leads to increased use of standardised educational technologies and reduction in the biggest expense of State schooling, teaching jobs.

Though unlike the State grammar and private schools, academy and free schools cannot legally select their pupils, they do so by using diverse means. By selecting pupils on purported ability, some academy schools are in contravention of their statutory duties on racial equality. Some academy schools have also been found to be excluding pupils for poor behaviour at a higher exclusion rate than local authority-run schools. As of July 2018, the rate of pupil exclusions in some academy schools exceeded 20%.

Pupils expected to do poorly in their GCSE final examinations also began to be taken off the school roll, a practice also discovered in State grammar and local education authority schools. Some State grammar schools have also been found to be off-rolling A level students, 17-year-old students predicted not to do well in their final A level exams at 18. At the end of the first year of the two-year A-level courses, those pupils were chucked out of school. Some academy school managers were found to be doing the same. Like all State schools, academy schools have been subject to central government school budget cuts. Since some academy schools can no longer find the funds to support disaffected pupils, some of those pupils have also been off-rolled.

The further twist in the tale of a State grammar school ordered by the court to desist from illegal off-rolling of pupils is that the school was in the process of setting up a company intending to market educational products and services, manuals, school management services, edu-tech materials, etc. – based on the school's reputation for obtaining top-grade educational outcomes (David Pegg, 'St Olave's head caught up in school trademark ownership row', *The Guardian*, 5 September 2016).

Some academy schools have also been found to be imposing religious beliefs and promoting sexism and homophobia. The Chair of Governors of an academy school also prohibited staff from using any textbook that referred to contraception.[52]

Despite their efforts to socially engineer their pupil intake and the school's exam cohort, when the government abolished the less challenging courses that still attracted GCSE qualifications, the exam pass rates of some such academy schools declined.

Funded by taxpayers, academised and free schools pose no financial risk to the groups of parents, religious organisations, businesses and voluntary organisations running them as tax-free charities. The same can't be said of the financial hazards these schools pose to the taxpayer, hazards not publicised by government. Over the last decade and a half, It's largely been due to the efforts of parents' groups and investigative journalists that the fiscal incompetence and dodgy behaviour of some of these academy schools have been revealed.

Some academy schools have had to be bailed out by the Department of Education, firstly to the tune of £11 million, then an additional £8 million over another three years, that is, a burden of an extra £19 million on UK taxpayers.⁵³ Some academies have paid out thousands of pounds of taxpayers money to the individual board members of the academy trusts to provide various services to the schools. For example, a head teacher paid a friend £50,000 to run a one-day training course; and an academy trust pays its US parent company, Mosaica Education, approximately £100,000 a year to use its patented curriculum. Over three years, another academy trust that runs 80 schools paid nearly £500,000 to private businesses owned by its trustees and executives for services that ranged from project management to Human Resources consultancy.⁵⁴

The largest academy chain in the UK seeks to become a for-profit organisation. One of the largest chains of academy schools aims to outsource all non-teaching posts in its 77 schools, from librarians to caretakers – a move characteristic of the pre-privatisation of public services.⁵⁵

In some academy schools, staffrooms have been closed, the space used for offices or classrooms instead, with the result that the teachers no longer have a central meeting space in which to discuss issues of concern. The laws on trade union collective agreements, convoluted at best, are essentially weak. Teacher trade unionists, already overburdened with teaching jobs at the chalkface, are put at serious disadvantage in attempting to protect teachers' employment rights from being undermined by the academy trusts.

Education barrister David Wolfe comments that the Secretary of State for Education's Academies Bill, undemocratically drawn up in haste and rushed through parliament, renders parents and teachers powerless and allows the academy trust governorship to 'steal' the school:

> It is hard to escape the conclusion that this bill is undemocratic. What this does is remove the public process. ... You are handing power to the governors to steal the school ... and parents and teachers will be powerless to stop them.⁵⁶

The government has also supported the altering of the two-year secondary State school GCSE public examination courses, doing away with coursework and imposing end-of-school public examinations instead. The examination grading system has also been rejigged so that from 2017, the old seven alphabetic grades will become nine numerical grades (not counting U for ungraded). For students to be awarded the top 7, 8, 9 grades, close academic study is required. Rejigging the exam grading system favours the chances of the top 20% of State school students gaining access to higher education, and thus, to the shrinking pool of well-paid employment. Contemporaneously, government takes credit for making the less academic pupils 'employment ready' – the declining pool of jobs for the majority going unmentioned.

In these various ways, government, the State grammar and academised schools have been gaming the education system in favour of the top 20% of State school pupils. Meanwhile, some of the private school sector has been found to be gaming exam results in the private sector by sticking to easier International GCSEs (IGCSEs) which are not tied any specific national exam system (Toby Helm, 'Exam reforms boost private pupils in race for universities', *The Observer*, 29 December 2018).

Because teacher turnover in the academised schools is high, school managers have instructed teachers to prepare standardised lessons that can be taught by whoever steps into the job, which, in turn, reduce the likelihood of teachers making curricular adjustments to match pupils' actual learning needs.

In September 2017 the Office for Standards in Education informed the sponsors of a chain of academy schools that out of its 21 schools, 11 of 14 of its primary and six of its secondary schools were performing at below the national average. The trust running the chain declared that it was unable to deliver the 'rapid improvement our academies need', withdrew their sponsorship, and transferred the reserve funds of the individual schools into the account of the academy chain (Frances Perraudin, 'Furious parents say collapsing academy trust asset-stripped its schools of millions', *The Observer*, 22 October 2017). Due to government education budgets cuts, some academy trusts have also withdrawn their sponsorship from the academised schools, that withdrawal leaving those schools in management limbo. In these various ways, the government's almost 20-year educational 'reform' of the academisation of State schools is failing pupils, teachers, parents, communities.

Instituted in 2011, the Pupil Premium is trumpeted by UK politicians of the left and the right as evidence of their commitment to the education of disadvantaged pupils. This 'extra' Pupil Premium funding currently stands at around £2.5 billion of the education budget of around £97.2 billion, around 14.15% out of total government expenditure of £687 billion.

State-funded schools, local education authority schools, academised and free schools and are invited to apply for a share of this earmarked funding by submitting a detailed case for a project that school managers believe will improve educational outcomes for its economically disadvantaged children, those on free school meals. Schools are also duty-bound to provide outcomes data for any such Pupil Premium–funded project undertaken.

Pupil Premium money has been allocated to schools to fund the likes of peer-to-peer reading schemes; one-to-one tuition for pupils with special educational needs; Saturday schools; after-school activities; extra teaching to show children how to plan and monitor their own learning; home-school schemes to increase parental involvement, and so on. To achieve government targets for reducing truancy and for meeting school attendance rate thresholds, an academy school was awarded Pupil Premium funding to bus its pupils to school.

Before government set up the Pupil Premium, State schools had previously instituted their own schemes to improve pupils' educational outcomes, good practices such as homework clubs; teaching pupils to plan and assess their learning, and so on. Subsequent cuts to the State education budget meant schools then lacked the resources for such schemes, and State schools now have to apply to fund those good practices as special Pupil Premium–funded projects instead. With swinging cuts to school budgets, Pupil Premium money meant to support the most disadvantaged pupils is being used to plug funding gaps, and a fifth of teachers are unaware of their school's aims for Pupil Premium funding.

Her Majesty's Revenue and Customs department fails to collect £34 billion a year in taxes documented as owed; loses £2.7 billion a year through tax avoidance by business; loses an estimated £4.4 billion through the tax evasion of wealthy UK citizens using offshore tax havens to hide their money; and £5 billion per year lost through government's reduction in corporation tax. Government chooses not to make the legislative choices needed to prevent that loss of tax revenue, leaving not a lot of doubt that government chooses to service the wealthy, and not least at the expense of the lives of the working-class majority of the UK State school children.

This chapter has provided credible evidence of government's failed 'reform' of its 'academisation' of State schools – such 'reform' openly declared by some ministers as a pre-privatisation stage for the privatisation of State education. This chapter suggests government halt its academisation 'reform', and stop its cuts to the State education budget, where many more teachers are required, not a demise in their numbers.

CHAPTER 22

Parliamentary Monitoring of State Education

In 2014, the Parliamentary Select Committee (PSC) on Education mounted its Inquiry, *Underachievement in Education by White Working-Class Children*. In his keynote evidence to the PSC, the UK Minister for Schools, a man with a reputation for intellectual acuity, declared:

> many of the problems with low attainment in school are due to factors that are outside the school gate: parental support or lack of support, parental aspirations, poverty in the home environment, poor housing, lack of experience of life.[57]

Privately educated, with a first in Economics from Cambridge University and, like his father before him, having worked as an investment banker, the minister presumed working-class parents and pupils had less experience of life than the minister, his rationale also being that if only poor and working-class children would leave their life experiences, or that of their parents, behind them at the school gates, perennial educational failure could be avoided.

Not long into his previous post as Chief Secretary to the Treasury, the minister had been found guilty of claiming tens of thousands of pounds in parliamentary expenses to which he was not entitled.[58] Though obliged to resign from the Treasury, in a process not atypical of the moral and democratic deficits of UK parliamentary procedures, this MP was soon shoehorned back into the UK cabinet, this time as the Minister for Schools.

The mostly white male MP members of the PSC on Education, highly educated and well-off, appeared to be as unaware as the minister of their own social class bias. Despite some witness testimony to the contrary, the PSC didn't take on board how social class biases in school learning materials, books and pedagogies can contribute to school failure. The social-class, gender and race blindness of the National Curriculum went largely unnoted. Of the effects of the traditional top-down transmission teaching pedagogies, little mention was made. Unrecognised also was the close correlations between the language and culture of home and school that is taken for granted in the private school sector. All in all, the members of the PSC appeared unaware of the import of the hidden curriculum that requires poor and working-class State school pupils to detach themselves from the socio-economic, linguistic and socio-cultural realities of their everyday lives. The PSC gave even shorter shrift to the gap between State school funding at around £5,500 per pupil a year compared to the £15,500 to £35,000 per child in the private school sector.

At the end of their 'inquiry', the PSC concurred overall with the Minister for Schools that inadequate funding for State schools had little or nothing to do with the persistent State school failure of working-class children, white working-class children in particular, and that their school failure was largely caused by defective linguistic skills in the working-class home, particularly crucial 'given the importance of oracy to child development', except the PSC's understanding of oracy wasn't based on knowledge of the socio-biological and socio-cultural nature of language development.

The PSC recommended that further 'research' be carried out into the linguistic failures of poor and working-class parents and into the disconnections between working-class parents and State schools.

Losing his parliamentary seat in the 2015 elections, this ex-schools Minister currently has a job as chief executive of a think tank run as a tax-free charity which, after hiring private consultancy assistance, will help government with the provision of education courses in UK prisons.

Except as a Dario Fo farce, you could hardly make it up, but it's far from make-believe and no comedy that tens of thousands of poor and working-class State school pupils leave school each year semi-literate and largely innumerate.

The great majority of teachers in State schools work themselves into the ground doing all they possibly can for the pupils they teach. They and their pupils have a right to more than the half-baked opinions and judgements of a government minister whose moral integrity and intellectual discernment are in serious question. Pupils, parents and teachers also have a right to far more than the social class prejudices of the members of any Parliamentary Select Committee.

CHAPTER 23

Educational Technology

Allowing ease of access to knowledge on every topic under the sun, Information Technology is a fabulous resource for all learners and teachers. Today's edu-tech encompasses laptops in schools, computer programmes to teach basic literacy and maths, with edu-tech used for all manner of educational tasks, from the submission of homework to the delivery of computerised degree courses online. The digitalisation and computerisation of educational provision also include the jazzy learning applications on mobile phones, gamification and virtual reality platforms.

Edu-tech businesses are set to transform how education is resourced, taught and consumed. The combined worldwide monetary value of IT in education and the training industry is estimated at more than $4 trillion, an 84% increase since 2000.[59] In the UK alone, there are currently over 1,000 edu-tech start-ups of all sizes.

Standardised participative democracy is a contradiction in terms, yet the claims that standardised information technology-based lessons democratise access to education goes largely unexamined. Nor is there much debate as yet on the hazards of edu-tech: control of curricula and subject syllabi, of pedagogy and pupil assessment; of the questions to be asked, the answers permissible.

How and to what extent could edu-tech be the solution for Third World countries where there's an enormous shortage of trained teachers whose wages are poor and who teach in often dilapidated and overcrowded schools that are sometimes called chicken coop schools?

Investors and venture capitalists are currently buying shares in the new edu-tech enterprises now operating in Third World countries, those private businesses and their shareholders set to mine income streams from the hopeful parents of millions of poor children in the Third World.

One such edu-tech company based in the US received its start-up money from well-known US philanthrocapitalists, the World Bank, a world educational publisher, and the UK Department for International Development. The company's unique selling point is its electronic 'academy-in-a box' curriculum for Third World schools.

The edu-tech company pays its teachers poorly, and 80% of the academy-in-a-box teachers are unqualified. The academy-in-a-box digitalised lessons are designed in the USA and transmitted online to a curriculum hub in the receiving country. The lessons for each class are then electronically transmitted each day from the hub to the schools – called academies – and downloaded onto the teachers' IT electronic tablets. The lessons are scripted in their entirety on the teachers' electronic tablets, inclusive of instructions to the teacher about when to pause, when to look up, when to circulate amongst the pupils. The pupils use traditional exercise books and commercially published workbooks in which to do their work.

The government of an African country involved in the scheme, after pressure from the teachers' union, ordered an inspection of the edu-tech schools. The inspection report stated that poor sanitation in the run-down school buildings was putting the health of 12,000 pupils at risk, so the minister for education ordered the schools to be shut down.[60]

The company then attempted to sue the country for loss of profits but lost the case ('Uganda judgement on the closure of Bridge International Academies must signal a move towards fulfilling the right to education in Uganda and other countries', Right to Education Initiative, 10 November 2016).

According to Justice Now:

> The British government is a world leader in using aid money to push privatised education on Africa and Asia. They treat these continents as guinea pigs for a model, which is also being increasingly pushed here – running education for profit rather than need. It's shocking that the aid budget is being used to fuel the profits of education multinationals.[61]

Did they but know about it, most UK citizens would object to the UK DfID using taxpayers' money to back profiteering by 'investors' syphoning up unearned income from edu-tech rentier streams made off the backs of the world's poorest workers and teachers. UK citizens are far more likely to want their taxes to go to non-profitmaking worker-owned educational enterprises, with the income raised by those enterprises going to a living wage for teachers and improving school buildings.

That the West's edu-businesses are instead lining up to rake in millions from the world's poorest countries speaks of neo-colonial control of global education systems (Angelo Gavrielatos, 'The Global battle for the soul of education', *The Morning Star*, 14 April 2017; see also Educational International: <http://www.ei.ie.org>; and Global Response: <http://www.unite4education.org>).

The UN is calling for investors to stop their support for such edu-tech businesses which can also diminish the rights of children as set out in the 1989 UN Convention of the Rights of the Child to an education based on freedom of thought and the right to be listened to.

Each generation always learns anew, and must have the right to an education that enables them to do for themselves what ultimately no one else can do for them: pick their way through the intricacies of ideologies, biased rationales and justifications, learn how to be canny and watch their backs, yet still be able to honour the inborn desire to live in societies based on fairness, freedom and justice.

All young people must have the unencumbered right to an education that equips them to also deal with the downsides of modern information technology, those indicated above, plus cyberbullying; trolling; sexual grooming; extremist radicalisation; technologically niche-marketed consumerism; the uses of IT in voter manipulation and in surveillance capitalism.

Though UK private school pupils have every access to all IT and edu-tech that they could ever need or want, their wealthy parents continue to pay very high fees for an education that most crucially provides the low pupil-teacher ratio vital for individual educational attainment and the elite's great prize of the upper-class consciousness and cohesiveness that defines the UK elite establishment.

***

The UK government's 1985 defeat of the National Union of Miners had the desired knock-on effects on the other trade unions, teacher trade unions included, with job cuts initially targeted at the system's most vulnerable point, supply teachers whose pay was cut from the per diem rate to a wages based on only the number of supply lessons actually taught. Subsequently, supply teaching services were taken over by the costly private agencies. As of 2016, the teacher supply agencies were being paid £1.26 billion from the public purse (Diane Reay, *Miseducation*, Bristol: Policy Press, 2017, p. 182).

Regular classroom teachers had no contractual right to their approximately five hours per week lesson preparation, administrative and marking time, so the next cut was in the ruling by local education authorities and school managers that teachers be called upon to teach the lessons previously covered by the supply teachers. Next came teaching staff 'restructuring', the euphemistic language used to denote further job cuts. It was left to the teaching union representatives to spell out that refusing to work more than their contractual hours and taking strike action didn't automatically mean jobs would be saved, but if teachers failed to act, then jobs would certainly be lost.

Teacher trade union executives looked unfavourably on rank and file motions for strike action, declaring there was little to be gained and fearing strikes would incur negative reaction from the public.

The prospect of teachers taking union action is entangled with feelings of letting pupils and parents down; fear of the monetary cost of strikes, not being able to pay rent, mortgage, bills; being targeted as troublemakers by school managers.

Few in number, those union reps most vocal in opposing job cuts took the brunt of character assassination by school managers, the local education authority, union executives and central government, who labelled those reps 'bolshie' and 'political', with some teacher colleagues calling the reps 'lefties' and 'militants'.

In a large comprehensive school of 100 teachers, about 20 teachers would normally attend union meetings. Attendance at union meetings declined, and teachers also began to avoid conversations about the looming job cuts. In inner-city schools of around a 100 members of staff, teachers would soon count themselves lucky to be able to discuss job cuts, the socio-economics of State school educational provision, children's educational rights, with maybe three or four other colleagues.

Nowadays, instead of dealing with one local education authority, teacher trade unionists must deal with the different academy trusts and with each school's governing board, whose role is controlled by the academy trust managers.

The UK's two main education trade unions amalgamated into the National Education Union In September 2017. With around 500,000 members, it is now the largest teacher trade union in the UK. The NEU aims to train local cohorts of its half a million members to become teacher trade union negotiators and to create teacher trade union links across local authority, academy and free schools.

Challenging bosses, managers and politicians over workers' pay and conditions is always a daunting task. In today's bureaucratised trade union environments, how likely is it that the trade union executives will call upon the teacher workforce to take strike action against the ever-increasing cuts to education budgets? How likely is it that trade union executives will act to protect their own jobs and backs instead? How likely is it that teacher trade unionism will pressure government to legislate to bring an egalitarian UK education system into being? If not teacher trade unions, who else?

Over the last 10 years or so, teacher pay has declined by approximately 15% relative to the rate of inflation. The teachers' unions campaigned for a 6.5% rise; government acceded to 3.5% for some teachers, less for others, with schools having to come up with 1% of the pay award to fund the pay rise, meaning schools would have to fund part the pay rise by cutbacks in school budgets. The teacher trade unions, including the NEU, agreed to that settlement.

Only too well aware of the effects that Key Stage tests have on children, some parents have resorted to keeping their children off school during these tests. Some primary school teachers have refused to administer the Key Stage Tests to 7-year-olds. In September 2017, many teachers considered an official boycott of the Key Stage tests for 7-year-olds. Consequently, the Minister for Education made Key Stage 1 Tests in reading, writing and maths for 7-year-olds optional after 2023, but government has now imposed baseline testing of reception-age children, purportedly as a means of enabling the school to target resources at children needing the most assistance and providing the school with a baseline for its 'value-added' accountability.

The above overview has attempted to outline some of the prevailing characteristics in current State educational provision, job cuts and the place of edu-tech in State education. No doubt many people will disagree with some of that depiction. Nonetheless, the facts presented above must surely also mean the public, parents, teachers, pupils and students, and professional educationists are obliged to get themselves together to put in place the participative organisations and mechanisms that will help them hammer out what an authentically democratised education system entails, and that will ultimately ensure it is robustly and effectively put in place.

Imagine, for instance, a constitutional federation of local businesses, public services of nursery, primary, secondary schools, community centres, mothers' and toddlers' clubs, day care centres for the elderly, funded by government, advised by the best expertise available, governed by neighbourhood and regional democratic assemblies of clients, managers, businesses.

CHAPTER 24

Office for Standards in Education

Funded by the taxpayers, the Office for Standards in Education, Ofsted, a purportedly independent evaluator of the school system, conducts inspections of State schools, colleges, and services for children in England, supposedly without fear or favour.

Head teachers of favoured academies have been given illegal advance notice of school inspection, allowing them to update their marking, record-keeping, lesson plans and whole-school policies. An academy head teacher, admired as a 'superhead', is alleged to have substituted a new teacher with a highly experienced teacher who had never before been to that school so that Ofsted inspectors could observe outstanding lessons being taught. The head teacher of a several Norfolk academy schools, also alleged to have been given prior notice of inspection, was exonerated after the evidence of the advance notice went missing. The then Secretary of State for Education had declared his admiration for this head teacher, declaring that he wished he could clone that particular head teacher 23,000 times so that every school in England could have such a leader. To refute the allegation of advance notice of inspection, Ofsted notched up taxpayer-paid legal fees more than £350,000. Ofsted later had to admit it had received a complaint from a parent about children being briefed on how to behave and work during the upcoming Ofsted inspection.[62]

The above-mentioned Minister for Education, after consulting with 300 head teachers, governors, teachers, parents and educational professionals, also declared that Ofsted's inspection procedures were anything but robust and that a school's performance might just as well be judged by the tossing of a coin.[63] This minister was also accused of packing the Department for Education with Conservative Party donors, inclusive of a sponsor of academy schools who was also a former trustee of the conservative think tank Policy Exchange who had to resign from his post as non-executive director at the Department for Education after it was discovered that he had attended a sleazy charity dinner where sexily attired young women hired to serve the guests and go to guests' bedrooms, were made to sign non-disclosure agreements to prevent them from testifying about the sexually exploitative attitudes and abuse that came from all too many of the all-male attendees (Richard Adams, 'David Meller, the Tory donor "desperate to be part of establishment"', *The Guardian*, 24 January 2018).

In September 2018, teachers in an academy trust that runs 47 schools reported that 10 expert advisory teachers were sent into their school by the trust during an Ofsted school inspection. The same school had previously had to annul its Key State Standard Attainment Test results after being found coaching pupils to pass the SATs (Emma Youie, 'Top Academy Chair Accused of Cheating during Ofsted Inspection', *Huffington Post UK*, 19 September 2018).

***

Probably the most significant damage to Ofsted's reputation occurred during its flawed investigation into a local authority's procedures related to the physical abuse and death of a child at the hands of his grossly maleducated mother, boyfriend, and the boyfriend's brother, adults mired in generations of maleducation, mental and physical abuse and perversions. Kicked out of the ball-court in the reviews of such cases are the political and legislative interventions required to deal with the effects of the psychological and educational abuse suffered in the first place by the perpetrators of such terrible acts. Such acts get shunted instead into the unfathomable category of 'evil', which amounts to the political refusal to acknowledge that such monstrousness is embedded in the fabric of politico-economic and socio-cultural relations of the society that produces them.

When this case became front-page news, the then leader of the opposition (currently an ex-prime minister) pressured the then Secretary of State for Children, Schools and Families (now an ex-UK Chancellor) into ill-thought-out action. During this case, neither of these politicians nor the UK media saw fit to reveal that upwards of 50 UK children a year are killed by their parents, carers, other adults, even by other children.[64]

Rather than ordering a full investigation by the police, social services and medical practitioners in contact with the perpetrators and the child before the child died from injuries his abusers inflicted upon him, the Secretary of State hastily ordered an Ofsted investigation into the case instead. Replete with inaccuracies, the Report was also later found to have been redrafted an inordinate number of times – purportedly on the interventions of the Secretary of State – and had been doctored to wrongfully scapegoat the woman head of children's services in the borough where the abuse and death of the child occurred.

That scapegoated head of child services eventually won her case for wrongful dismissal. Not so, the two women social workers with impossible caseloads who took the brunt of the blame.[65] The appeal court had ruled that the government's sacking of the head of child services was unlawful. The Secretary of State declared that he'd do the same thing again.

In a display of narcissistic adversarial party politics, these two male politicians in the top echelons of UK government, both with University of Oxford first class honours degrees in Philosophy, Politics and Economics, had used this case as a political football to score points against each other.

Tighter child protection procedures have been introduced since the abuse and death of that child. However, the social workers who continue to bear impossible caseloads can only ever do their level their best to try to prevent destructive behaviours by those people most damaged by the politico-economic, socio-cultural and education system that is still a very long way from being based on the cultures of nurture, care, mutual respect and reverence for life.

The Serious Case Review local authorities are obliged to carry out in cases involving the death of a child is likely to have remained back-page news had an investigative journalist not smelled a rat in the prior political-media scrum. What he and his co-researchers then discovered was blame for the child's death had, indeed, been wrongfully heaped on the female head of child services and that, separately and combined, the police, social services and the National Health Service had each and all failed in their duty of care towards the child. Amongst the cover-up tactics unearthed by the journalist was that an NHS Foundation Trust hospital involved in the case had attempted to bribe a woman doctor to keep quiet about the inadequacy and failure of that hospital's child protection procedures. Another woman doctor, originally from Pakistan, had been hounded by the media over the case, was wrongly sacked, became suicidal, and suffered long-term depression.[66]

Neither of these two politicians so spectacularly involved in this case now holds office. The first, who resigned as prime minister after losing the EU referendum vote, is the same PM who refused to testify about his role in the debacle of the Lybian conflict. He is currently appointed as unpaid, high profile head of a well-known charitable organisation; has signed a contract for £800,000 to write a book about his time as PM; makes a considerable income as a speaker for a global guest speaking agency; and has now taken on two paid jobs, working two days a month for US electronic payments firm, First Data Corporation, and works also for a billion-dollar investment initiative between the UK and China to build transport infrastructure of road, rail and ports between China and the nations it trades with. The second politician, the then Minister for School, Children and Families, was defeated in the 2015 general election. Narcissism winning out over talent, he was next seen in a TV dance competition during which he declared that waiting to hear whether the TV audience would vote for him to remain in the contest or vote him off made him feel more tense than waiting to find out if he'd won or lost his constituency seat in the general election. He now makes a living as a university professor of economics and government; is chairman of a UK football club, and regularly appears as a known political personality-brand in various TV shows.[67] His wife, an opposition party MP, lost her bid to become the leader of the opposition party, achieving only 17% of the vote.

Ofsted's research and statistics department provides the government with the overall picture of educational provision in England. The Department collates that data for its evaluation of education in the UK as a whole. Much of Ofsted's information comes from the inspections it carries out on State schools, colleges and child services.[68] To capture the evidence for their inspection reports, Ofsted uses a 30-point lesson observation grid, not that the complexity of what goes on inside classrooms, and all that impinges from outside, can be caught by any such grid. Notwithstanding the £40 million cut from its budget over the last six years, Ofsted claims to be providing a more efficient inspection service. Ofsted's annual report for 2017 includes self-congratulatory notations that Ofsted was cited 14 times by parliamentarians; that the number of speaking engagements by Ofsted staff was 162, and that the aim is to increase those engagements to 325 by 2022. Since only 19% of schools agree that 'Ofsted is a force for improvement in England's schools', the aim is to have 35% of schools agreeing with that statement by 2022.[69]

Ofsted still has a budget of around £140 million. What Ofsted does not do with that budget is to develop, ensure, curate:

- Curricula specifically relevant to children's present circumstances and future educational needs.
- Socio-culturally contextualised learning materials and pedagogies related to children's learning styles, socio-cultural experiences and aspirations.
- Teaching and learning that acknowledges the collaborative and cooperative intelligence between teachers and learners and between learners.
- The rights of all children to critical, political and multi-functional literacy.
- Accurate and comprehensive factual learning materials.
- The publishing of a modern children's literature.

The Ofsted budget could be better used to fund an accountable educational advisory service jointly charged with the other relevant bodies for the provision of comprehensive action plans that effectively address the factors known to be integral to educational attainment: parental access to employment, sufficient income, housing, adult education, and the physical nurture, care and mental wellbeing of each school's cohort of school children.

CHAPTER 25

Battle for Critical, Political and Multi-functional Literacy

An officially high rate of literacy of 99% masks the reality that amongst the UK's working age population, 9 million people have low basic literacy and numeracy; 5 million of them in regular employment; 4 million sometimes in employment with 1 million of those being mostly unemployable. Of the 9 million with low basic literacy and numeracy, 5.2 million are classified as functionally illiterate.

The most developed and high-income countries are the 35 nations of the Organisation for Economic Co-operation and Development (OECD). Amongst the 23 of the most developed nations of the OECD, 16- to 19-year-olds in England have the lowest levels of literacy, coming twenty-second in numeracy (Małgorzata Kuczera, Simon Field and Hendrickje Catriona Windisch, *Building Skills for All: A Review of England*, OECD Skills Studies, 2016).

Poor levels of literacy in England can range from being below that of an average 11-year-old to being illiterate to the extent of not being able to fill out a form unaided.[70] Some functionally illiterate adults will be immigrants who are literate in their first language; their skills in English expected to improve. Around half a million immigrants are expected to continue to have weak basic skills.

Not all, but a majority of the UK's functionally illiterate adults have one factor in common in that they've had 11 years of State education. Moreover, tens of thousands of UK youngsters continue to leave UK State schools each year with not much literacy or numeracy. The OECD reports that the educational attainment of the poor and working-class majority of UK children is, by the age of 6, already behind that of their well-off peers, and recommends the UK government shifts State educational resources towards early-years education.

***

The covers of children's books are in eye-catching primary colours; inside there are pages of attention-grabbing illustrations, and millions of children learn to read on books that are otherwise decontextualised from their lived experiences. One of the ways that parents, carers and teachers meet children's socio-biological, emotional and psychological need to feel nurtured, cared for can be by reading to them, no matter the content of the books. For hundreds of thousands of the UK's poor and working-class children, however, that sense of inclusion is missing, often less in terms of family relations and more in terms of the impoverished and alienating conditions in which so many UK children live. The 2017 report by the Children's Commissioner for England states:

> Millions of children in England are growing up in vulnerable or high-risk environments. The numbers uncovered are only the tip of the iceberg: 670,000 children are growing up in families seen as 'vulnerable', and the actions of 370,000 youngsters put them at risk, with 46,000 of them being gang members. Almost 55,000 children are reported as missing and nearly 160,000 young people are excluded from school. More than 27,000 children live with an adult being treated for drugs or alcohol, and almost 120,000 are homeless or living in temporary accommodation. The numbers of youngsters with long-term health or mental health problems, or who have special educational needs or a disability number 2.3 million. (Peter Walker, 'Children's watchdog says millions at risk', *The Guardian*, 4 July 2017)

That such politico-economic deprivation and socio-cultural oppositions to the hierarchical social relations of the status quo should continue year after year calls into question the adequacy, purposes and intents of the governmental institutions purportedly designed to support the child population. Societies that fail to meet the socio-biological and socio-cultural imperatives of youngsters to be nurtured, cared for, respected and valued also produce in those young people states of lethargy, resignation, confusion, frustration, alienation, aggression and rebellion – attitudes not uncommon in many a classroom.

Should doubts remain about the nature of the books presented to youngsters as a means of developing their literacy and their understanding of the world they inhabit, books which might well constitute, in fact, an element in the alienation of so many youngsters, readers might well lay those doubts to rest by conducting the brief experiment outlined below – it will take a couple of hours.

Go to your local library or bookshop and head for the books for children and young adults. Pick a dozen fictional books, four each for ages 4–7; 8–11; 11–16. Skim through enough of each book to discover the main protagonists, antagonists, themes and conflicts. For each age category, record the titles of the books that have the following characteristics:

1. Books on the climate crisis that show the politico-economic causes of ecocide.
2. Books where the social class of the protagonists is clear.
3. Books that have human characters and settings familiar to the poor and working-class majority of children, in whatever country.
4. Books with strong, independent female characters who are not subservient to males.
5. Books that have non-Caucasian characters.
6. Books that have an identifiable working-class males or females as the main character.
7. Books with working-class characters dealing specifically with social class issues and conflicts.
8. Books clearly showing the socio-economic and socio-cultural contexts relevant to the hopes, desires, and aspirations and goals of the protagonists, and those of the antagonistic forces opposing those goals.
9. Books with characters of differing social class, gender, race, sexualities, and belief systems.
10. Books showing individuals and groups of youngsters dealing with real-life problems; understanding that those difficulties are neither down to bad or good luck nor 'human nature' – and which show characters realising the need for both individual and group efforts in dealing with problems that are politico-economic and socio-cultural by definition.

11. Books that show young people thinking about equal human rights and responsibilities, thinking philosophically and considering matters of human spirituality.

Now pick half a dozen non-fiction books at random. The task here is to find out how many of the non-fiction books depend on factoids, that is, facts divorced from their wider politico-economic-social contexts. Record your results. Check to see how many of the non-fiction books give children information, however briefly, about:

- The climate catastrophe.
- The 2019 Global Pandemic.
- Politico-economic-socio-cultural contexts of whatever the subject of the book.
- Issues of concern to the poor and working-class majority, for example, jobs, wages, housing, education, health.

Now do a quick check of the bookshelves to find fiction and non-fiction that address the topics and themes that you, as the researcher, believe are important for the educational and socio-cultural development of the lives of young people in a modern democracy, making notes on what you find.

Amongst all the wondrously illustrated books on the shelves, if you can find a couple of books that meet one or two of the criteria above, be well pleased.

You might want to consider buying the book that you think most closely matches any of the above criteria. So that you can write to the publishers telling them of that criteria and asking what plans they have for publishing more such books, note down the names and addresses of the publishers that met any of the above criteria – and some that didn't. For the sake of the overworked and underpaid librarian or sales clerk, don't forget to put the books back on the shelves.

Not at issue here are the rights of parents, carers and teachers to try to protect children from what they see as dangers of various media; nor the extent to which books and other media are both capable and incapable of depicting the lived experiences of human beings. Nor is it being argued that children don't gain significant insights from fairy stories, fables and parables or geography and other books skimpy on the facts – or that they do.

Besides all else that books may or may not do for child readers, the point is that today's youngsters have a right to modern children's literature that also contextualises their lived experiences, thoughts, observations, economic and socio-cultural concerns and aspirations for themselves and others.

Milton's 1644 *Areopagitica* presents the case that censorship curtails freedom of thought; that good can be learned by comparison with the bad; and that the reading of books of all kinds can contribute to the human pursuit of truth. Adopting the Miltonian position doesn't mean absolving schools of their obligations to help youngsters develop the skills that allow them to assess the qualities of the books they encounter.

The combination of elementary, analytical, critical, economic and political literacy, multi-functional literacy, is often called critical literacy. Such a literacy literacy allows learners to do more than decipher and produce surface text, it also enables learners to use their innate intelligence to assess the honesty, rhetorics, intents, ideologies and purposes of whatever the medium of communication, speech acts, images, texts.

There is no human being who doesn't make mistakes, and multi-functional literacy doesn't necessarily make coming to judgements and making decisions any easier. What it can do is make the processes through which judgements and decision are made more transparent; can help people discern relevant knowledge from diversionary banalities; conspiracy theories from real treacheries; distinguish between truth tellers, bigots and liars; can help people assess – in themselves and others – false convictions, indecision, firm certainties. Multi-functional literacy can help youngsters get out from under the branding of poor and working-class children as 'feckless'; the unemployed as 'shirkers'. Phrases such as 'enhanced investigation techniques' are no longer allowed as stand-ins for State-sanctioned torture; 'collateral damage' for the casual killing of innocent civilians.

In celebrating the innate intelligence of the autonomous learner, multi-functional literacy also ought to help people become more well-informed and resilient enough to deal with the half-truths, mistakes, errors, doubts and confusions that communications are also heir to.

Course books produced for school syllabi on citizenship and economic understanding can often 'normalise' exploitative capitalist socio-economic relations to the point that the everyday realities of the lives of pupils, parents, teachers are almost nowhere to be seen. The good news is that many UK head teachers, classroom teachers and the youngsters themselves are savvy to the distortions in such materials:

> Head teacher: In every subject you have a curriculum, a scheme of work, laid down by the DFES that prescribes what you should teach to varying degrees of detail ... and ... virtually gives scripts for certain lessons and I think that that is an undue level of prescription and I don't think it's a successful recipe for developing citizenship education any more than its a successful recipe for developing literacy.
>
> Secondary school teacher: talking about the consultancy-produced learning materials for the study of citizenship: I tell you, all I've got is this great big booklet from this organisation, this private organisation that teaches and runs all this ... and it says 'Induction Handbook' and its very nice and all gold covered, and there are all sorts of things that frighten me to death in there.
>
> Summary of pupils' responses: A major gripe was insufficient depth, with no time to really get into something or to discuss and question. Not being presented with alternative points of view, not dealing with contemporary issues and not having global studies as part of a core curriculum.[71]

The critique and refusal of those materials are also indicative of an innate meta-literacy that enables youngsters to spot inauthenticity.

This chapter presented evidence of the need for critical, political and multi-functional literacy. It suggests that the acquisition of such a literacy should begin with socio-culturally contextualised materials that young children are given to learn to read on. Parents, teachers, pupils and anyone concerned with freedom of thought and democracy need to be involved in the battle for that modern twenty-first-century literacy that enables children to read both the 'word' and the 'world'.

CHAPTER 26

Workplace Democracy

The economic principles on which workplace cooperatives in capitalist societies are founded correspond with those formalised in 1844 by the UK co-operative movement in Rochdale, UK. The rationale for worker-owned business cooperatives is that goods and services are produced in an economically viable, socially responsible manner. The prices of goods and services cover the costs of producing them, paying decent wages, making a reasonable profit, holding reserves to develop the business and paying reasonable taxes. Worker-owned enterprises differ from capitalist businesses in that they are not set up to make excessive profits from which to pay very high salaries to Chief Executive Officers and unearned income to shareholders.

Those myopic politicians advocating that worker-owned cooperative be paid less than required to run a sustainable business and used to deliver below-cost pubic services and are promoting an ultimately self-defeating strategy. Worker-owned cooperatives are not a substitute for public services to which everyone who needs that public service needs access. That said, worker-owned cooperatives could help build the low-cost, high-quality housing the UK urgently needs; could help set up local energy grids; install green technologies; produce and sell locally sourced organic foods; provide good-quality social care for the elderly; run nursery education; leisure facilities; community services; maintain parks and civic spaces, etc. – providing governments institute the necessary banking and other legislation that would enable worker-owned enterprises to deliver such services.

One of the most well-known examples of a worker-owned enterprise was set up in the impoverished Basque region of Spain in the aftermath of the Spanish Civil War and WWII. A priest, and five graduates of the technical college he had established to educate students in technology and to promote Roman Catholic values of unity and humanity, set up their worker-owned and operated business, Mondragon. Their first product was paraffin heaters. Mondragon went on to manufacture other domestic and industrial products, managing to develop the expertise to sustain itself as a worker-owned corporation able to operate in competitive world markets. Now the seventh largest corporation in Spain, the Mondragon Cooperative Corporation is a global federation of worker-owned cooperatives headquartered in Spain. Globally, the Mondragon federation of cooperatives has around 100,000 worker-owners; has a global presence as a large-scale manufacturer, from white goods to car parts; owns and operates retail and financial services, including the Mondragon bank. Mondragon also has a university that does its own research and development.

Mondragon workers earn more than the average wage-earner in whatever the host country in which the Mondragon subsidiaries operate. Mondragon cooperatives pay their worker-owner executives and managers no more than six to nine times the wage of its ordinary workers.

Mondragon's worker-owner directors deal with adverse economic conditions by organising job-sharing; the redeployment of workers to other sections of the company; or by providing temporary redundancy pay until new jobs can be generated. Consequently, the enterprises keep their pools of skilled workers; people still have money to spend; the wider economy is less negatively affected by unemployment, and governments still have the workers' taxes from which to pay for public services.[72]

The Cleveland Group of worker-owned cooperatives in Ohio, USA, is based on the Mondragon principles and those of the Democracy Collaborative founded in 2000 at the University of Maryland, USA, as a research centre for democratic renewal. The Cleveland Evergreen Cooperative Group provides services such as industrial-scale laundry cleaning and meals services to hospitals and universities, 'anchor establishments' not likely to up sticks and move away at the expense of local jobs. One of the Cleveland Group of worker-owned business grows vegetables in large-scale hydroponic greenhouses, selling fresh vegetables to local shops and restaurants. The solar group installs solar panels on large buildings, lighting in parking lots, and generates green energy that can be sold to consumers in other districts. Providing secure employment for local workers, the Cleveland cooperatives also make a point of offering stable jobs to previously unemployed drug users.[73] In the UK, the Labour-run city council of Preston follows the Cleveland Group's model of business enterprises anchored to public sector bodies like the university, hospital, and police headquarters which in 2018–19 spent 'four times their budgets in Preston as they did in 2013'. The aim is to bring the local spend up to 40%. The Italian Marcora Law of 1985 gives the State the power to match-fund money raised by viable worker-owned cooperatives demonstrating their ability to take over and run companies in danger of bankruptcy and employee redundancy. The risk factor introduced to ensure workers' determination to set up only viable businesses is that should the enterprise fail, workers are not entitled to unemployment benefit for up to three years.[74]

Worker-owned enterprises are springing up at home and abroad, though the UK lags behind France and Germany. More mainstream media coverage could help support the development of cooperative economics. YouTube videos that show people's experiences of setting up and running worker-owned cooperatives are now available, for example, 'Own the Change: Building Economic Democracy One Worker at a Time' (YouTube, 9 February 2015); 'Why Worker Co-ops Don't Work (Sorta)' (YouTube, August 2016). Modern economists are also managing to influence politicians about the need for government to improve legislation related to worker-owned cooperatives (Andy Beckett, 'The new left economists: how a network of thinkers is transforming capitalism', *The Guardian*, 25 June 2019).

Established from the merger of several of the UK's biggest construction firms, Carillion became one of the UK's major corporate contractors and one of the biggest outsourcing rentier companies of the UK's service industry. Feeding off UK government private-public finance initiative contracts to build motorways, high-speed rail, hospitals, etc., as well as taking on international construction projects, Carillion ended up with 420 public service contracts to provide the likes of school dinners, NHS hospital meals; manage NHS operating theatres; run prisons, etc., using sub-contractors to do so. To pay high salaries and bonuses to its chief executives, pay its board of directors, and pay out unearned income to its battalion of anonymous shareholders, Carillion skimmed the profits off the top of all of its £7 billion worth of contracts. To keep shareholders, banks and government on board, it also systematically cooked its books, declaring profits instead of losses, doing so with the connivance of one of the UK's biggest auditing/consultant firms.

Something on the order 30,000 small and medium business contractors and sub-contractors were involved in the Carillion supply chain, with Carillion bullying many of those companies into accepting contracts with very thin profit margins and also using dodgy business practices like changing the terms of contracts mid-stream and withholding payments from contractors for up to 120 days. Carillion also used the corporation's pension fund of £2.6 billion to finance the business and took out bank loans to pay their sub-contractors.

Though government procedures dictate that businesses running government contracts must be closely supervised by government, the government failed to monitor Carillion. Instead, knowing that Carillion was indebted to the point of having to declare profit warnings, the UK government had continued to act as the procurer of new government contracts. According to *The Times* newspaper, page 45, Business section, June 2018, Carillion is only one of around 27 corporations operating the same government Public Private Finance Initiative outsourcing model – minus the required levels of government supervision.

One honest woman finance executive at Carillion produced a report on the actual state of the corporation, that of the Carillion Ponzi scheme of taking on new contracts to pay off the costs of previous deals. Unable to pay its debts, the banks had no choice but to stop lending to Carillion's PPFI gravy train. Over a billion pounds in the red, the corporation had no money to pay its 19,000 employees, and many of those other 30,000 small businesses had to lay off employees, go out of business and face bankruptcy. After various arrangements were made for other firms to carry on with some of the projects, around 2,333 workers directly employed by Carillion lost their jobs ('How to lose £7 billion pounds', *Dispatches*, Channel 4, 2018).

The UK government also funnelled £148 million of taxpayers' money to rescue what was left of Carillion. Taxpayers forked out around £70 million to pay the private firms of bankruptcy administrators and lawyers to deal with the administrative fallout (National Audit Office, *Investigation into the government's handling of the collapse of Carillion*, 7 June 2018).

Running any enterprise involves taking calculated risks and acting responsibly to diminish as many of the risks as possible. The job of the government is to support businesses in taking on well-calculated risks and to enact legislation that prevents excessive business gambling.

Carillion is a clear paradigm of the white collar financial rackets carried out at the expense of workers and taxpayers, with the knowledge of government ministers, toothless government regulators, collusive corporate boards of directors, duplicitous corporate executives, and corrupt auditor/consultant firms that are paid by the corporations. In the hierarchical fiefdom of the capitalist corporatocracy, there is no place for workplace democracy. Conspicuous by their absence throughout the whole Carillion scam are the voices of workers, small businesses, taxpayers and informed citizens.

Ignoring the race-to-the-bottom processes built into the competitive capitalist system, armchair commentators criticise the likes of Carillion as 'rogue capitalists' acting disgracefully within 'our economy'.

Today's activists want governments to legislate to democratise the workplace, so that workers not only have a voice on corporate boards, but a real say on how corporations are run. Economic activists also want government to support the establishment of viable worker-owned businesses, and, as per the Italian Marcora law, to part-fund viable worker-owned enterprises and for worker-owned cooperatives produce viable plans for taking over failing companies. Had such legislation been in place, the Carillion debacle, and others like it, might never have happened. It is not hard to imagine very different outcomes had government legislation given preference to viable worker-owned enterprises in the granting of government contracts, such legislation also stipulating that such contracts were not to be used in support of privatising public services.

CHAPTER 27

Democratisation of Mass Media

In Gramsci's terms, citizens are obliged to comprehensively evaluate the effects of the ownership and control of media, and the intent to divert the attention of the majority.[75]

The goals of the media-mogul owners of the means of mass communications are to inform, educate, persuade, distract, manipulate and assimilate audiences into the more or less acceptable realms of the more or less status quo. The mass-media barons recruit a high percentage of their media workers, producers, commissioners, news-casters, actors TV show hosts from those who have been privately educated. The result is that TV programmes and films don't stray too far from the permissible media messages funded and influenced by corporate advertising. Publically owned media offers relief from that the profit-making model, yet also pays heed to the ratings underwritten by viewers switching channels if they don't like or are discomfited by what they see and hear.

News anchors are charged with presenting information in a purportedly 'balance of biases' manner. In practice, this means partially assimilating opposing left-wing leaning views before pronouncing more favour of the 'norm' of the conservative neo-liberal right. However, in something of a turn-up for the cooking of the media books, given mainstream media's failure to cap the gush of information on the climate atrocity, the BBC has recently told its programme executives they no longer need to bring on a climate disaster denier in an attempt to 'balance' what is now incontrovertible knowledge. *The Guardian* newspaper style guide has also been changed to allow reporters to substitute phrases such as 'climate change' with the more accurate 'climate emergency', 'global warming' with 'global heating'.

News programmes showing battlefields often begin with the news anchor warning viewers they may find the footage distressing, followed by the cameraman's brief pan of the devastated area that excludes the bodies, injuries, death and gore of war. Nor is there any appeal to viewers, nor anyone in supposedly higher authority, to do all in their power to end the slaughter.

Today's privately owned media news conglomerates also make billions showcasing well-paid TV anchors who, though revealing some of the goings-on of the kakistocracy (rule by thieves) seldom connect the dots of that wrongdoing to the corruption of social relations inherent in the capitalist political economy. That job is left to the indymedia journalists with their smaller audiences.

In the UK population of around 65 million people, there are about 104 billionaires, a handful of them owning and controlling most of the UK media, and having immense influence on UK socio-cultural life, inclusive on the politics of education narratives on what is good and bad in education, who deserves what type of schools and for what purposes. For instance, the government-finance-media nexus continues to mourn the demise of the selective grammar schools as the educational saviour of the economically disadvantaged bright working-class pupils – against all the statistical evidence that grammar schools mainly support the advancement of around 20% of the more middle-class pupils instead.

The owners of the mass media cut good investigative journalism to the bone. Nevertheless, good investigative journalism does also make its way onto mainstream media. Many of today's investigative journalists and documentary filmmakers are also adept at shining the light on people, places, living conditions and issues of public concern in more authentic ways than ever before possible.

Unfortunately, documentaries can also routinely omit the politico-economic and socio-cultural contextualisation in the narratives they present – as do, for instance, the spectacular natural world and animal life documentaries presented by the wealthy, eugenicist TV personality with a 60-year career hosting these wild-life programmes who, before becoming ensconced at the BBC, had considered a career in the oil business ('David Attenborough', Wikipedia).

Supportive of animal rescue, the presenter believes feeding starving human beings is 'barmy', that famines are caused not by maldistribution of the world's bounty, but by 'too many people for far too little land'. The presenter recently hosted Netflix, *Our Planet*, an eight-part wild-life documentary series costing £25 million to make, filmed in 50 countries by more than 600 crew over four years. Unlike those decades of BBC wildlife documentaries, this series adds the message of environmental decay and species extinction. The 92-year-old multi-millionaire presenter then hosted the BBC's belated *Climate Change – the Facts* (see YouTube videos and newspaper articles featuring this broadcaster, for example, George Monbiot, 'David Attenborough has betrayed the living world he loves', *The Guardian*, 7 November 2018).

Mass media also plays to natural human speculation about the inner thoughts, experiences and motivations of others. Through the ever-fascinating portrayal of the desires, relationships, conflicts, resistances, defeats and triumphs of people in real and fictionalised places and times, from myths and legends, historical dramas, soap operas to feature films, draws audiences in. TV audiences can tune in every day of the week to TV soap operas to watch both the familiar and something of the unfolding spectacle of the hidden lives of others – as authored by the TV screenwriters. For many people in an isolating world, those televisual characters can be their only company for days on end.

Soap operas are played out in half-hour slots interspersed by the corporate wallpaper of ads promoting a range of products, from furniture to river cruises, insurance policies to frozen chips. Soap opera storylines are defined by a series of convoluted yet simplistic plotlines typically centering on domestic life, the romance, betrayals, breakups, crime, the occasional murder, and catastrophes of chance outside the control of the characters, a car accident, a fire, etc. The complex motivations of real-life individuals, of real lovers, real parents, real relatives, friends, enemies are comparatively seldom portrayed.

Though audiences may hanker after more of the authentic range of human emotions and psychologies, they also now rely on the fact that the soap opera will show both something of the other and enough of the familiar to allow viewers to remain more or less undisturbed in their emotional, psychological and political comfort zones.

For many, TV soaps can also provide eye-openers, with storylines raising issues such as domestic abuse; gay and inter-racial relationships; the effects of the likes of Alzheimer's disease on the sufferer and his/

her family. Such depictions stop short of portraying the wider politico-economic and socio-psychological aspects of the issues being presented, with little, for example, about the lack of care facilities for those with Alzheimer's; or about the lack of access to therapy for mental illnesses, and so on. Soaps portraying the workplace seldom focus on the realities of low wages, poor conditions of employment, chauvinistic bosses, etc. Such issues are usually reduced to an isolated line or two in tightly constrained scenes.

The more politically progressive TV shows like the TV drama series *Press* provide some of the warts and all mechanisms of the UK newspaper world; the US series *Madam Secretary* shows some of the workings of US governance. Focusing on the individual relationships between the characters, with not much in the way of authentic depiction of the politico-economic structures underpinning the lives of the characters, indeed the lives of millions of real people everywhere.

TV sport, cookery and competition programmes also draw in huge audiences, as do the visually dramatic blockbusters that portray grand-scale conflicts, for example, *Game of Thrones*, James Bond thrillers, and the costume dramas depicting the romances and socio-cultural intrigues of characters in bye-gone eras.

The parables of science fiction can bring understanding and confirmations that all is not well with the world. The drawback is that science fiction frameworks afford little space for the real struggles of real people against the real dystopias of the tangible world.

The publishing business relies on the best-selling genres of romance and erotica, detective stories and murder mysteries, and the world of cinema regularly features exoticas of deprivation, fecklessness, violence and murder, much of it perpetrated against women.

Computer games commonly employ mini-dimensional story arcs of fast-paced fake dangers that require the viewer/player to obliterate the highest possible number of digitalised enemies in the shortest possible time. Without leaving the sofa or computer desk, the pay-off is the adrenalin rush and fabricated feeling of participation. Computer games based on domestic storylines are also generally simplistically decontextualised.

The topics for popular TV 'debate' programmes, sanctioned by the programme commissioners, allow an acceptable range of topics, for example, immigration, unemployment, welfare benefits, tuition fees, whether female transsexuals should be allowed to stand for political office as women, whether God exists or not, etc. Audiences are pre-vetted; the debating panel consists of brand-name pundits; the 'debate' is ring-mastered by middle-class, middle-aged, highly paid, mostly white male TV presenters. Opinions from the audience that stray from the 'balance of biases' coda are briefly allowed but get short shrift. Next week it's all change for the topics, the panel, the invited audience.

Here's some good news. The World Wide Web, publically available since 1993, used daily by populations around the globe is, despite its flaws, a communications game-changer. Forgotten is the fact that it took 40 years of government and university funded communications and information technologists to bring it to fruition. Again despite flaws and misuse, Wikipedia, established in 2001, Facebook in 2004, YouTube in 2005, Wikileaks in 2006, provide millions of people with ready access to information, knowledge, understanding and connection at a scale never before possible.

Modern communications devices like smartphones with inbuilt cameras and audio recording functions are used by brave whistleblowers, care home workers to tech-savvy operators, who risk livelihoods and lives to reveal wrongdoing. Spilling the beans on corporate corruption and revealing the gory details of government war crimes, the whistleblowers also make it less possible for corporations, governments and the military to use deceit, unlawful renditions, torture and murder as their daily tools of choice.

Some more good news: noted below are some of the organisations set up by progressive journalists and which act as significant levers against the dominations of today's mass media:

The International Consortium for Investigative Journalists is now a global network of over 200 investigative journalists from 70 countries who collaborate on in-depth investigative journalism.

The Independent Media Centre, originating in Seattle during the 1999 anti-World Trade Organisation protests, is a global democratic network that enables any journalist with verifiably comprehensive information to publish articles in the public interest.

Founded in 2014, the Intercept is a news organisation originally set up to report the evidence of NASA surveillance operations by whistleblower Edward Snowden.

There are also campaigning organisations agitating for media reform, for example, Media Reform Coalition, founded in 2011.

Such organisations and groups are an important check on the manipulations of the mainstream corporate-government-media nexus whose primary aim is profit through mass distraction, with commissioning editors filling newspapers, magazines, books and TV screens with spectacle on the lives and affairs of celebrities, sports personalities, royalty. Beamed around the world almost daily are 'news' reports about the marriages, births, deaths, extra-marital affairs of the UK royal family, not forgetting the charities the royals support, for example, sports for the disabled, the Prince's Trust charity set up to help disadvantaged young people, and so on.

In a democratic socialist society, TV debates would not be ringmastered by TV presenters fluent in what the media owners will and won't tolerate; they'd be chaired instead by ordinary people. Through democratic canvassing, TV producers would discover what people wanted to know about. Research panels would be chosen from, let's say, a group of secondary school students in Glasgow, call centre employees in Bristol, farmers in Northern Ireland, pensioners in sheltered housing, each group researching one of the chosen topics and presenting their findings to a TV audience, with that audience free to engage, respond and ask the questions they thought relevant.

Feature films earning accolades from the Political Film Society for raising awareness about human rights, peace and democracy are progressive developments. The films usually focus on the heroic tenacity of an individual challenging the forces of power and domination. For instance, based on a true story, the Universal Studios feature film, *Erin Brockovich*, portrays an impoverished working-class woman with two broken marriages, a mother of three children, who manages to pursue a rigorous investigation into a corrupt corporation releasing carcinogenic toxins into the groundwater. Erin Brokovich succeeds in gathering all the hidden evidence and builds an unassailable legal case that eventually forces the corporation to pay some compensation to the families of the dying and already dead. The world needs and depends on the bravery of extraordinary people; it also needs organised groups of people coming together analyse, educate and comprehensively challenge the forces of power and domination.

Cathy Come Home, Ken Loach's 1966 film, fictionalises scrupulously researched cases that show the critical shortage of affordable housing leading to family break-up and mental illness. Loach's 2016 film, *I, Daniel Blake*, also meticulously researched, is an exposé of the UK social benefits system. In employment all his life, a childless, middle-aged widower is diagnosed with a heart condition that makes him unfit to work. In trying to comply with the humiliating processes to which the benefits system subjects him, Daniel Blake does all he can to maintain his self-respect. The staff at the benefits office continue to refuse Daniel Blake the benefits to which he is entitled. He uses up his meagre savings to live on and to help the impoverished young woman and her two children that he meets at the Job Centre. To keep a roof over his head when his savings run out, Daniel Blake sells his furniture. When he discovers that to buy her daughter shoes, the young mother has had no choice but to prostitute herself, he is devastated. Each step in the process of dealing with the 'benefits' system increases the stresses on Daniel Blake's heart, and immediately after the benefits interview that finally admits he is entitled to social security payments, he dies of a heart attack. The ex-government minister responsible for 2010–15 £15 billion in cuts to the UK benefits system claimed that the film showed the system in an unfair light.

Nowadays, many high-quality analytical documentaries chart the deliberately structured politico-economic exploitations – and also point the way to building the alternatives (William Stills, *The Money Masters: How International Bankers Gained Control of America*, 1996; Ross Ashcroft's 2012 *Four Horsemen*; Ken Loach's 2013 Film 4, *Spirit of '45*). Also readily available are many YouTube video interviews showing up-to-the-minute progressive economists detailing how today's politico-economic infrastructure can be re-engineered for the common good. Dr Richard Werner, economics professor and founder/director of the Centre for Banking, Finance and Sustainable Development, is amongst those modern economists showing how banks create money from setting up interest-bearing debt and is among the first modern economists to connect sustainable development with a re-engineered banking and finance system.[76] In the 2011 YouTube 'Free Lunch' videos, Richard Werner analyses the banking system. The videos are clear and concise, and are well worth watching.[77] He advocates the creation of local banks, credit unions and cooperatives. See also the 2014 YouTube video 'Richard Werner on banking and how banks create money'. Probably the best 15 minutes that can be spent getting to grips with the workings of the capitalist banking system is the March 2017 YouTube interview entitled, 'Prof. Werner brilliantly explains how the banking system and financial sector really work'. Richard Werner explains how banks, creating money from nothing, lend it to debtors, mortgagees and speculators, which can produce the asset bubbles, which inevitably burst, causing financial catastrophe across the system. Professor Warner's concept of how quantitative easing could create readily accessible credit for local businesses was used instead by governments to bail out the big banks after the 2008 financial crash. Richard Werner's 2003 book *Princes of the Yen: The Central BankTruth Documentary*, on which the YouTube 2014 documentary of the same name is based, became the number one bestseller in Japan.

For a cogent explication of how the finance-government-media kakistocracy promotes and profits from war, see the documentary, *The Iron Triangle: The Carlyle Group Exposed*.[78]

Also readily available on the internet are the many talks by and interviews of Dr Richard Wolff. See also the YouTube videos at Democracy At Work with his monthly 'Economic Updates'. Professor Wolff advocates democratisation of the workplace, with workers having significant input in the management of businesses, and calls for the establishment of many more viable worker-owned enterprises. An economist who also advocates socialist economics, he reports that after 50 years of public hostility towards socialism, from around 2011 he has received more invitations from universities, radio and TV talk shows to explain socialist economics than he can fulfil. He presents detailed descriptions of the current exploitative practices of capitalism and, with grace and good humour, he presents the alternative economics of democratic socialism. Perhaps most succinct is his lecture entitled 'Noam Chomsky Interviews Richard Wolff on the State of Democracy' (YouTube, November 2016), a video that also reveals something of Richard Wolff annoyance at the lack of knowledge in a privileged and supposedly well-educated audience. (This video is mistitled; Noam Chomsky doesn't appear in it.)

Much needed are the films and documentaries showing the challenges to power by ordinary people. Phil Agland's five-part 2016 Channel 4 docu-series, *China: Between Clouds and Dreams*, three years in the making, in episode 2 shows a group of primary school child environmentalists doing just that.

Unlike in the 1930s, we now have access to a considerable body of knowledge and expertise on economic, political and socio-cultural processes. More people in more societies now know a good deal more about the economic, political and socio-cultural changes required to replace the greed-addicted rule by the powers of force and dominance, that is, by the 1% and their hangers-on.

Nonetheless, it also remains the case that readers and viewers also use mass media as a form of escapism, or can be all too seductively held in emotionally, psychologically and intellectually passive states of spectatorship; prisoners of the book; voyeurs of the image. The fictional story-arcs, settings, characterisation and themes of the publishing industry largely favour the genres of mystery, crime, horror, romance, science fiction, and the much-hyped 'high-brow' and 'well-rounded' literary novels rely on philosophical and existential ambiguities. Readers are skilfully led along a story arc of whatever content the owner-operators of the book industry decide to make available. The following National Book Tokens advertisement indicates how it's done:

> Two paths divergent, you choose the one less travelled. It leads you through The Shire and past Animal Farm. Up ahead you spot a Little House on the Prairie and inside you find three bears – Paddington, Rupert and Gryllis. Back outside the wind blows in the willows and you pass a hitchhiker who offers you a guide to the galaxy. You go down a rabbit hole, find A Passage to India and arrive Out of Africa. On the horizon lies a Brave New World and there, at the end of The Road, you find it. Choosing a book is an adventure in itself. A National Book token is the gift that starts a journey that ends with a book they'll love.

For some people, books and films can be fonts of information and understanding, windows on other worlds. For many others, books and films can also be a source of intimidation, distrust and lack of confidence in their own observations and conclusions. For many, books give access to a treasure trove and are a source of great pleasure. For millions of others, reading is a struggle – and not always because the language is opaque, but because so much of what is published doesn't speak authentically to the real lives of the majority of readers.

In portraying characters caught up in the overwhelming circumstances of their day, Charles Dickens (1812–70) is cited as one of the world's most socio-culturally progressives novelists, offering a view of an otherwise hidden Victorian world. Charles Dickens' primary male characters, valiant individuals battling against all the odds in an exploitative world, are usually eventually rescued from dire circumstances via the interventions of a wise benefactor – or by an unexpected upturn in circumstances. Portraying a vibrant social realism, what Charles Dickens stops short of doing is unearthing and challenging the deeper political-economic realities that underwrite real social relationships.

To keep his audience coming back for more in the serialised publications of his work, Charles Dickens devised cliffhanger endings for each chapter, the last chapter usually ending with the best of outcomes improbable in real life – the protagonist escaping the politico-economic sources of his difficulties to become more upwardly socially mobile, and live happily ever after.

From his childhood experience of being incarcerated with his family in a debtors' prison, Dickens well knew that in contending with an exploitive world, hope and optimism of the will are vital. Dickens attempts to both critique Victorian society, earn himself a handsome living, and preserve optimism of the will. In the eyes of many, however, the fictions of social realism lead readers instead into psycho-social states of the false hope that 'something will turn up.'

Charles Dickens married the daughter of his employer, and though Catherine Dickens would have 10 children and two miscarriages, Charles Dicken's wealth as a well-paid novelist enabled Charles and Catherine to live a celebrity lifestyle. Fascinated by young women, the 46-year-old Charles Dickens began an affair with a 17-year-old actress. Knowing the affair would offend the moral sensibilities of his public, Charles Dickens did his best to keep the liaison secret – and also seems to have rationalised his estrangement from his wife by unsuccessfully trying to commit her to an asylum. A master of vivid characterisation, it's no psychosocial accident that Dicken's portrayal of women falls short of honest socio-political representation.

It's rare to find depictions of how politico-economic and socio-cultural forces can shape emotions, intellect, fears, doubts, personal and political compromises, attitudes and behaviours. Though creating authentic portrayals of characters grappling with interpersonal, politico-economic and socio-cultural realities is no simple matter, if that's what the author sets out to do, it can be done. The most well-known portrayal of socio-political life as it affects people's daily experiences is Robert Tressell's novel *The Ragged Trousered Philanthropists*. Portraying the everyday lives of ordinary workers in Edwardian Britain, painters, decorators, carpenters, Tressell famously depicts how the interrelating politico-economic, psychological, emotional, intellectual, and spiritual realities of the lived experiences of the workers, their families and their bosses all play out in daily life. Tressell also reveals the differing levels of socio-political awareness amongst his characters. The title refers both to the ordinary kindness between working-class characters and the inescapable 'philanthropy' of their labour being used to provide increasing wealth to the already wealthy. Though Tressell also attempts to depict the politico-economic and socio-cultural reasons for the political illiteracy of his protagonists, he also shows a certain contempt for that illiteracy. Continuously in print since it was first published in 1914, Tressell's novel remains a one-off and a must-read for politicians on the left. The canon of secondary school books for the GCSE English literature exams includes Orwell's *Animal Farm*, his 1945 allegorical fable against totalitarianism. Omitted from that canon is Tressell's portrayal of the realities of life in exploitative Edwardian England.

This chapter has dealt with some of the reasons for media illiteracy and indicates an ultimately innate drive for self-taught critical, political, economic and multi-functional literacy that renders today's many TV channels largely unwatchable, and makes the available print diet undigestable for millions. Urgently needed is a new mass media developed by increasingly well-informed and politically progressive audiences and media activists, a media fit for the twenty-first century and beyond.

CHAPTER 28

Education for Democratic Socialism

We teach children to cross the road safely, not to tell lies, to share with friends, be kind to unknown others, follow a set of values, a culture, perhaps a religion. We also daily send children to schools that render them vulnerable to the 24/7 divide-and-rule apartheids and democratic deficits that run through British education, media, economics and politics like lettering through a stick of rock.

Understanding how those economic apartheids and UK democratic deficits are funded by the UK public is the first move in kicking them into the dustbin of history.

The 800 strong unelected UK House of Lords has 150 more politicians than the House of Commons has elected member of parliament voter representatives. Average attendance in the House of Lords is around 480 out of the 800 members. Instead of being paid a salary for the work they do or don't do, the lords and ladies are instead granted £300 a day, plus expenses for those who live outside London. An already well-heeled a lord or lady can be granted £45,000 a year in expenses. The average wage of UK workers is around £27,500, many families living on less.

Though the UK does have honest and hardworking politicians doing their very best for the common good. That they are not in the majority was revealed by the 2009 scandal of 60% of UK MP's claiming expenses to which they were not entitled. Giving credit where credit is due, there are a few UK politicians who do donate a percentage of their salaries to public service. However, since no one appears to have heard of a UK politician who like the 2010–15 ex-president of Uruguay, Jose Mujica, donated 90% of his presidential salary to good causes, it's probably safe to conclude that the UK has no such politician.

Jose Mujica, a Tupamaros Marxist urban guerrilla in his youth, was caught, tried and incarcerated by the military dictatorship, was tortured and spent long periods in solitary confinement during his 13 of imprisonment. Released in an amnesty by a newly elected leftist government, Jose Mujica, a libertarian Marxist whose politico-economic analysis led him to conclude that the competitive capitalist system imposed unnecessary poverty, joined the Uruguayan leftist broad front political party, Frente Amplio, stating that he was longer chasing a utopian future through armed resistance that was irreverent of the lives of people living in the right here and now, declaring himself instead as a politician who was 'neither the apocalypse nor the promised land'. Elected as a Frente Amplio senator, he was the butt of jokes because his vocabulary and pronunciation marked him as a common man. Elected as president, his goal was to maintain viable government while pushing towards the left as much as he could. As president, Jose Mujica continued to live in modest circumstances, choosing to live on the average Uruguayan wage of £485 a month, donating 90% of his presidential salary to charity, most of it in support of single mothers (Giles Frelett, 'Jose Mujica: is this the world's most radical president?', *The Guardian*, 29 September 2014).

There is no substitute for the collective understanding, solidarity and organised activism essential to establishing and maintaining the viable economic, political and socio-culturally robust democratic socialism fit for the twenty-first century and beyond. It's maleducational, therefore, to suggest that education can of itself re-engineer the economic and political intents of the powers of dominance and force.

Over millennia and all across the globe, governments, politicians, philosophers, educationists have pondered the connections between humanity and livelihood, philosophy and society, politics and education.

In the slave-based societies of ancient Greece, the elite employed pedagogues to educate their offspring. An educational outlook common to many African cultures is encapsulated in the Zulu term 'Ubuntu', that 'it takes a village to raise a child.' What ancient Greek and many African cultures have in common, however, is the misogynistic treatment of women.

Jean-Joseph Jacotot (1770–1840), French professor, soldier, polymath, no stranger to transmission teaching, developed the theory of universal emancipatory, or 'panecastic' education as he also called it, which is based on the observation of children teaching themselves to acquire the language of their community, and the phenomena of illiterate parents teaching children to do what the parent cannot – read and write. Jacotot's emancipatory education acknowledges the intrinsic cooperative intelligence between learner and teacher, the phenomenon well known to anybody helping a child with homework about which the helper knows zilch.

Jacotot, living in brutal revolutionary times, had to exile himself from France to a job teaching French literature at the University of Louvain, Belgium. His students didn't speak French, Jacotot didn't speak Flemish. A novel, *Les Adventures de Telemaque*, was so popular across a turbulent Europe that bilingual versions were published ('Les Aventures de Telemaque', Wikipedia). Though set in ancient times, the novel dealt with topics of crucial contemporary concern, for example, denouncing the decadent behaviour of the elites, calling for the abolition of mercantilism, an end to war, the overhaul of government.

Jacotot set his students this task: read the Flemish version of the text; then by comparing the Flemish and French texts students were to teach themselves French, proving they'd done so by writing about the novel in French. Not only did the Flemish-speaking students succeed in their task, they wrote about the novel in such sophisticated French that even Jacotot was amazed.

According to Jacotot, in a tempestuous world where the oppressed could soon become the oppressor, the function of an educator was not to attempt to explicate that mutable world but to help reveal to the learner the existence of his/her innate intelligence through which the learner can interpret and act upon that mutable world for him or herself.[79] Instead of a diktat deciding on the questions, the learner sets his/her own questions, finds the answer, which leads to the next set of questions. According to Jacotot's educational theory and practice, the incremental nature of learning where one answer leads to the next question means that, potentially, everything is, therefore, in everything. According to Jacotot, teachers who act as the explicators halt the learner with the masters' 'bridle' of control, a sure route to intellectual, political, and economic inequality. Jacotot also objected, therefore, to the pedagogy of using individual pupils or groups to mentor other pupils, such as the Lancastrian 'monitoring' system whereby those pupils who most quickly acquired whatever the knowledge being promulgated then explicated that information to the rest. He also objected to prominent social groups explicating concepts to the less educated who then ended up with second-hand ideas, third-rate minds. Nor did he want his educational theory and practice to be used as a cheap method for the likes of training soldiers through such as the narrowly framed flow charts that instructed learners to perform one task then do the next.

Jacotot's principles of emancipatory education can be summarised as follows:

- All human beings are born intelligent.
- Using the cooperative intelligence that exists between teacher and learner, pupils can teach themselves what the teacher does not know.
- Because of the natural synchronicities of knowledge, learners can educate themselves through self-imposed learner curricula.

The Global Education Reform Movement (GERM), backed by capitalist philanthropists and well-meaning celebrities who, knowing little about the global politics of education, unwittingly support test-based standardisation and data-driven models of education that may not be in the best interests of the youngsters they wish to support. GERM, seemingly 'liberal' in its aims, can constrain education within narrowed down curricular frameworks designed to generate the sort of 'human capital' that can be best used and controlled by the global elite.

By comparison, Education International challenges the GERM paradigm by training teachers to collaborate with parents and youngsters so as to provide an education that helps learners think comprehensively about the politico-economic and socio-cultural conditions in the societies they inhabit and about how to organise education in the interests of the majority.

In his YouTube TED talk of 2010, Sugata Mitra presents the evidence of primary age children in India's urban slums and isolated poor villages teaching themselves to operate an untended 'hole-in-the-wall' computer displaying an internet page that graphically illustrated a science topic with accompanying text in English. The children taught themselves a significant amount of the science, and also learned to speak about the topic in an appreciable amount of English.[80] Sugata Mitra's understandable enthusiasm for computer learning overrides, however, consideration of the extent to which the science topic randomly displayed on the computer was relevant to the children's actual education and politico-economic needs

Those who seek to democratise the education system to meet both the needs of the individual and of the majority might well consider the educational theory and practice of Brazilian educationist Paulo Freire (1921–97). Influenced by the Roman Catholic libertarian theology and the students' movements of the times that demanded politico-economic reforms in housing, healthcare, education, etc., Paulo Freire devised his highly successful 1960s adult literacy programmes in Latin America and elsewhere based on his educational theory and practice of education for freedom and critical consciousness.[81]

Born into a middle-class family and trained as a lawyer, Freire became a teacher of Portuguese in Brazilian Secondary schools instead and also taught worker trade unionists about the law, using informal roundtable discussion methods that put the experiences of the workers at the centre of learning.

Subsequently, as a director in the regional educational and social services authority, responsible for education and social programmes from kindergarten upwards, Freire noted that at whatever the age level, the curriculum and the pedagogy used reflected the politico-economic and socio-cultural intents and purposes of the dominating elite. He described the top-down transmission teaching pedagogy endemic to teaching, from primary schools to universities, as 'banking education.' Using anti-dialectic language and linguistic codes detached from the normal vocabulary, experiences, observations and ideas of the learners, the teacher attempts to 'deposit' knowledge as 'educational capital' in the minds of the learner.

> The teacher talks about reality as if it were motionless, static, compartmentalized, and predictable. Or else he expounds on a topic completely alien to the existential experience of the students. His task is to 'fill' the students with the contents of his narration. ... Words are emptied of their concreteness and become a hollow, alienated, and alienating verbosity.[82]

(For more on educational and cultural capital, see also Pierre Bourdieu's 'The Forms of Capital' (1986), in J. Richardson (ed.), *Handbook of Theory and Research for the Sociology of Education*, New York: Greenwood Press, pp. 241–58.)

In a huge country in which most of the rural and urban population was illiterate, the Brazilian government instituted its 1960s adult literacy programmes nationwide to help boost its backward and sluggish economy. Since only those who were literate could vote, the literacy programme was well supported by the then leftist Brazilian government.[83]

Initially, the adult literacy programme employed top-down transmission teaching methods, and relied on the literacy teaching convention of using socio-culturally decontextualized short sentences like 'The cat sat on the mat' and 'The water is in the well' to teach the textual equivalents of vowels and consonants. The literacy acquisition success rate was poor. Paulo Freire also observed that many of the adult learners who did manage to become literate via these methods also tended to background their nascent understandings of socio-political realities.

Discussing with the learners why the teaching methods weren't working, Paulo Freire found out that the top-down transmission teaching methods were depriving the learners of their sense of agency, and that they also found the socio-culturally decontextualised learning materials too removed from their experiences and concerns to be considered useful to them.

Drawing on what the learners had told him, on his experiences in the field of education, in teaching law to trade unionists through roundtable informal discussions, and on his own childhood experiences of becoming literate, Paulo Freire set himself the task of devising the educational theory and practices for a literacy development that would succeed.

The pre-school Paulo's father had taught the child to read and write by drawing in the sand polysyllabic Spanish words already known to the child. Linking the sounds of the words to the written letters and syllables, the boy was then able to draw other words and phrases that were part of his child's universe.

The death of his father when Paulo Freire was in his teens meant that the family became impoverished. Unable to concentrate because of hunger, the teenager had fallen behind at school, and he now also spent much of his time with other poor street kids. Poverty, hunger, and the sudden change in his everyday social relations had rendered formal education immaterial.

Paulo Freire then devised the educational theory and practices for literacy development, which he called 'education for freedom' and for 'critical consciousness. Trying out his socio-contextualised methods with individual learners and small groups of two or three, he noted that some learners could become literate after only a few hours of such teaching and learning.

Paulo Freire's next task was to show the army of student teachers how to use the newly devised methods. Understanding that learners' sense of agency is imperative, Freire asked the student-teachers to talk less and familiarise themselves more with the lives, experiences, observations, ideas, aspirations and language of the learners. The student-teachers were to organise what Paulo Freire described as 'culture circles', where learners and teachers met to discuss topics of everyday interest and concern. The student-teachers were to extrapolate from these discussions what Paulo Freire termed each learner group's 'generative' words, polysyllabic words denoting the experiences, ideas and concerns uppermost in the perceptions of the group. The group's literacy learning materials were based on these generative words. Learning materials also included labelled photos, slides, booklets and drama scripts depicting the everyday activities, concerns and aspirations of the learners. Using group-generated materials also meant that the usual uncertainties and lack of confidence amongst the learners became a thing of the past:

> Generally, in a period of six weeks to two months, we could leave a group of twenty-five persons reading newspapers, writing notes and simple letters, and discussing problems of local and national interest.[84]

Helping 300 sugar cane workers to become literate in just 45 days was another such achievement.

For Freire, authentic critical, political and multi-functional literacy isn't acquired through the technical attainment of the basic skill of decoding and encoding text.

> This teaching cannot be done from the top down, but only from the inside out, by the illiterate himself, with the collaboration of the educator. That is why we searched for a method which would be the instrument of the learner as well as of the educator, and which, in the lucid observation of a young Brazilian sociologist [Celso Beisegel], would identify learning *content* with the learning *process*.[85]

Paulo Freire's conviction that learners must be free to develop their own autonomy led him to split from political activists who wanted to use his teaching methods to spread direct political messages.

Paulo Freire's decision not to use the teaching of literacy as a means of teaching about socialism, did not stem from any belief that anyone's politically naïve, or 'magical' opinions were sacrosanct, but that teaching and learning methods that imposed the teacher's or anyone else's viewpoint ignored the inborn human intelligence of the learner, disrespected the learners' intrinsic sense of agency, and the dialectic imperative that all opinions have to be subject to open and honest critical analyses and debate.

By contrast, the Cuban government's 1961 country-wide literacy campaign that combined respect for learners' innate intelligence and sense of agency and the mutuality of socialist values is remembered by Cuban learners and teachers as one of the most liberating experiences of their lives ('Maestra – mastrathefilm.org. (8 min. version)', directed by Catherine Murphy, YouTube, 2012).

Paulo Freire's theory and practice of education for freedom and conscientisation might be summarised as follows:

1. People are born with innate human intelligence.
2. There is no such thing as a language without thought.
3. To acquire textual literacy, human thought and socio-biologically and socio-culturally acquired language are required.
4. Successful acquisition of textual literacy requires respect for the learner's innate intelligence and sense of agency; engaging the thoughts, lived experiences and observations of the learner; the development of the cooperative intelligence between learner and teachers who are engaged in open, honest debate and critical analyses.
5. The development of critical education for freedom and conscientisation is not a mechanistic skill that can be acquired through politico-economic and socio-culturally decontextualised top-down 'banking' education.
6. Education for freedom and conscientisation can help learners assess what they can do to alter the economic, political and cultural conditions under which they live.

Education for Democratic Socialism

7. Literacy and education are not a substitute for the solidarity and activism required to institute progressive politico-economic-socio-cultural change.

Central to Freirean educational theory and practice is the dialectical relationship between learners, and between teachers and learners. Consequently, though the pedagogy remains the same, lessons for conscientisation, critical and multi-functional literacy can't be applied like a one-size-fits-all sticking plaster.

The US, intent on pursuing its politico-economic interests in Brazil and Latin America, helped organise the 1964 Brazilian fascist military coup. Declaring education for freedom and conscientisation subversive, the new Brazilian military government jailed Paulo Freire as a traitor.

The Bolivian government then granted Paulo Freire political asylum, appointing him as an educational consultant. Two weeks after Paulo Freire arrived in the country, a US-backed coup brought down the Bolivian government.

Paulo Freire subsequently lived in exile in Chile and the USA, worked as an educational consultant in Africa; and for the World Council of Churches in Geneva. In accepting the World Council of Churches appointment, Freire wrote to them to make it clear that:

> You must know that I have taken a decision. My case is the case of the wretched of the earth. You should know that I opted for revolution.

Freire returned to Brazil in 1980 where he supervised adult literacy programmes and later became Secretary of Education for Sao Paulo, a megacity of 11 million people ('Paulo Freire', Wikipedia).

In May 2019, backed by big business and the intent of the US to maintain control in its Latin American 'back yard', the newly installed right-wing president of Brazil declared that in the country's run-down school system, Freirean educational theory and practices wouldn't be tolerated.

There are reasons to applaud the considerable efforts of the UK head teacher who recently mapped Freirean pedagogical methods onto the pre-set, top-down National Curriculum. With such care and attention expended on engaging those pupils in the acquisition of NC curricular knowledge and understanding, many of them will doubtless attain good NC results What that school can't change is that some of its pupils will also end up with the employment blocking grades the system is also designed to generate.

In following the NC Programmes of Study for English, science, mathematics, for instance, and being subject to the key Stage Tests for those Programmes of Study, to what extent will the innateness of the pupils' intelligence and inherent abilities as thinkers, analysers and users of language be revealed to them? Will those pupils be able to become their own explicators? To what extent will they be able to develop conscientisation, critical consciousness and the combined elementary, socio-economic and political literacy young people need to negotiate their way in this world and change their societies for the better? In preparing its pupils for Key Stage Tests and end-of-school exam success, will that school also be able to teach its pupils how to deal with an increasingly jobless world? The considerable work of mapping Freirean pedagogy onto a top-down pre-set curriculum sidetracks the crucial elements of Freirean educational theory and practice for conscientisation. Does it matter? In a world of exponential inequalities and alienating outcomes at home and abroad and the fragmenting capitalist political economy across the globe to the point of planetary unsustainability, it matters a very great deal.

Government, educationists, parents with understandable vested interests in the educational status quo constitute considerable obstacles to educational innovation. Middle-class parents worry that any upset of the educational apple cart could negatively affect their children's relatively privileged position. And there is the dread amongst poor and working-class parents that another ill-thought-out 'reform' could spell more school failure for their children.

It matters very much at this historical juncture for education that parents, teachers, pupils, governors, academy trusts, local education authorities and national government pay emergency attention to the divisively competitive world of educational apartheids, and get down to cases on how they will go about re-engineering the education system to meet the urgent educational needs of today's children, and of those yet to be born.

Education for Democratic Socialism

The UN Convention on the Rights of the Child 2009, clause 109, upholds the rights of all children to be heard:

> Children's participation is indispensable for the creation of a social climate in the classroom, which stimulates cooperation and support for child-centred interactive learning.
>
> There is also: 'a clear legal obligation on States Parties to recognise this right' ... and 'to ensure this right can be fully enjoyed by the child.'

2010 Equality Act also protects people's rights to religion and belief – which need not include faith or worship of a God or gods:

> A belief need not include faith or worship of a god or gods, but it must affect how a person lives their life or perceives the world. For a philosophical belief to be protected under the Act it must: be genuinely held; be a belief and not just an opinion or viewpoint based on the present state of information available; be about a weighty and substantial aspect of human life and behaviour attain a certain level of cogency, seriousness, cohesion and importance, and be worthy of respect in a democratic society, not incompatible with human dignity and not in conflict with fundamental rights of others. For example, Holocaust denial, or the belief in racial superiority are not protected. Beliefs such as humanism, pacifism, vegetarianism and the belief in man-made climate change are all protected.[86]

It is the belief and conviction of significant numbers of people that children have the right to be taught both the standard form of their language and, whenever they need and want to, express themselves and be heard in the language and dialects of their community Consequently, the users of the standard language are obliged to make an effort to understand the community dialects and cultures of others.

It's also a bona fide belief that all children have the right to the critical, political, economic and multi-functional literacy they need to comprehensively understand and negotiate their way in the world they inhabit and be able to help alter that world for the better.

The demand by the student climate crisis protestors that ecocide become part of the State school 'core curriculum' reflects a certain level of comparative incomprehension of the need to re-engineer the whole kit and caboodle of the politico-economic and socio-cultural relations inside the classroom and beyond, and that such re-engineering encompasses curriculum, pedagogy, learning materials, pupil–teacher ratios, socio-educational relations inside and outside the classroom – and leaves space for autonomous education.

The everyday pressures of today's realities are hardly fertile ground for making the switch from the current silo-subject-separated curriculum to an education based on the principles of individual autonomy, the rights of the majority, reverence for all life, equal human rights and responsibilities, and the collective duty of nurture and care that ensures no one becomes a victim or perpetrator of political, economic and socio-psychological abuse. Except that is surely what now needs to be done.

Education for democratic socialism is likely to be built in part on the best of progressive teaching and learning that already exists. This book suggests the best is likely to be the educational theory and practices of Freirean education for freedom and conscientisation – on the proviso that parents and teachers know the reasons why the temptation to employ Freirean pedagogical practices for conventional inegalitarian educational purposes has to be resisted.

In terms of the already existing best practices within the National Curriculum, below are generic goals for the programmes of study in English and science.

English:

- Use discussion for learning.
- Give children ample opportunity to elaborate and explain their understanding and ideas.
- Develop competence in speaking and listening.
- Make presentations to others and participate in debate.

Science:

- Develop scientific knowledge and conceptual understanding through the specific disciplines of biology, chemistry, and physics.
- Develop children's understanding of science through asking and answering scientific questions about the world around them.

Education for Democratic Socialism

- Be equipped with the scientific knowledge required to understand the uses and implications of science, today and for the future.

Pupils understanding of the science of the climate crisis, the politics of classroom participation and discussion for learning could well benefit from using the above programmes of study in a cross-curricular manner; adding learning goals agreed between pupils and teachers; employing Freirean educational theory and practice and ensuring the most dominant voices don't take over; with pupils assessing their progress; and homework involving parents, family and friends. The above cross-curricular and discussion for learning method can also be used across the other subjects.

In meetings with school governors, public consultations, dealings with the media, those who develop, monitor and evaluate Freirean education projects such as the one indicated above will need to develop the socio-political skills required to deal with the prejudices against egalitarian education in first-world contexts.

Evaluators must also be scrupulously honest about any pilot projects that were unsuccessful – and about why. Innovators and evaluators would also have to ensure that the pilot schemes and any wider application of them are not sabotaged by those with a vested interest in their failure.

Though some schools may be more inclined than others to embark on such projects, the rationale and criteria for doing so needs to be democratically determined, supported, monitored and evaluated at community level and in a communal space to which everyone has equal access – such as the local town hall – as a forum from which to design, implement, and monitor any such pilot projects. The criteria for doing so must also include organising structures that ensure the widest possible participation of parents, teachers, pupils, school governors, the local education authority, local businesses, university departments of education, and so on.

In the interests of celebrating learning and improving relationships between school and community, a social occasion for pupils, family and community could well be used to mark the end of a particular period of study and herald the beginning a new one.

Pilot project networks could quickly extrapolate best practices, publish the results so that successful outcomes can quickly be taken up by more networks, with consultations with a national educational body as to how projects and networks can be expanded, monitored and improved.

To sum up, all children have the right to an education which seeks the most effective ways of letting them in on the act of their learning development and that of others. All children also have the right to collaborative talk, discussion and debate at age related levels. All children also have the right to curricula, pedagogies and learning materials – factional and fictional – that don't deliberately obfuscate pupils' identities or the identities of others; don't attempt to colonise their minds; don't hold them in states of passive spectatorship; don't seek to divert them from their individual goals; nor deter them from their democratic rights, responsibilities and politico-economic and socio-cultural aspirations for themselves and the societies they inhabit.

This chapter has presented some broad brushstrokes on the history and politics of educational thought and reviewed the educational theory and practices of Brazilian educator, Paulo Freire. It suggests that Freirean principles and practices have much to offer a new educational system based on the principles of democratic socialism.

The final chapter will consider how the organisations and structures essential to the institution and maintenance of democratic socialism fit for the twenty-first century and beyond might be established.

CHAPTER 29

Into the Future

The 2019 *Sunday Times* Rich List showed that of the 50 top UK political donors, 47 donated to the Conservative Party, none to the Labour Party. It also revealed that donations to the Conservative Party dropped by 46%, from £16.1 million in 2017 to £8.7 million in 2019 ('The Rich List, The definitive guide to wealth', *The Sunday Times*, May 2019).

The UK media, 80% owned by five billionaires, supports the governing Conservative Party that has a membership of 124,000 and governs in coalition with the Northern Irish Democratic Unionist Party. The Conservative Party's primary goal is to manage and maintain the current political-economic system in the interests of those who benefit most from it, and it also does all in its power to persuade the majority of the population that it's in their best interests to vote Conservative.

The good news is that millions of voters now know that the intrinsically unstable and unsustainable capitalist political economy doesn't come from 'God's will', or an inevitably disastrous 'human nature'. Nor do citizens any longer fall for the media-hyped meme that what drives people to oppose and campaign against the system is blind envy and contagious hysteria. The reality is that despite the many deceits and democratic deficits, increasingly well-informed citizens are, in this Age of Information, able to analyse and identify the inbuilt inequalities and threats of a political economy based on competitive exploitation, profiteering , mass surveillance and voter manipulation.

The fakers, slackers, and aspirers entangled in the hegemonic web of false consciousness look the other way at misogyny, racism, sexual abuse and the everyday government–banking–corporate–media complex's backgrounding of the physical material, psychological and socio-cultural oppression and exploitation of the poor and working class majority at home and abroad.

Millions in that majority are prescribed anti-depressants and anti-psychotic drugs for all too often politico-economically induced mental ill health. Meanwhile, the sociopaths and psychopaths of the dominating status quo sink deeper into the ideology that prods them into contemplating the insanity of 'contained' nuclear war in the name of protecting and maintaining their vested global interests.

Here's some good news: since the 2008 global financial crash, a decade of challenges to the dominating forces of the status quo now leads the Labour Party to pledge to promote progressive economic change 'in every town and city'. The party expects to do so through the likes of the creation of a national investment bank and regional development banks that will work to boost the productive economy across the UK. The party has also produced a 17-point legislative plan to crack down on tax avoidance, making it less possible for high net worth individuals and companies to hide their earnings and tax liabilities under the cloak of confidentiality. Legislation would also prevent corporations from getting away with non-payment of taxes, and make it less possible for the wealthy to hoard their wealth in, and invest their money from, tax haven secrecy. Compared to the estimated £100 billion a year lost to dodgy tax avoidance practices by big business, the party expects to initially collect only around £5 billion a year in those lost taxes. The Labour Party also intends to bring corporation tax back up to what it was a few years ago and to increase taxes on the 5% of the population that earns more than £80,000 per annum. What the party would do about the all-pervasive mainstream banking system remains largely unsaid.

To deal with the housing crisis, the party will impose a land tax and other real estate legislation that will also guarantee present and future public green spaces and parks. Not mentioned is how the party will deal with the interest-bearing debt-slavery of loans and mortgages harvested by the mainstream bankers from their money-from-nothing money-tree.

The Labour Party also pledges to put a stop to universities making debtors of students, that debt swelling the coffers of the private universities and lining the pockets of overpaid university chancellors. From the railways to renationalising the private energy companies, the Labour Party also intends to take public services back into public ownership as and when the private contracts for running those services come up for renewal.

Labour also has plans for giving the Bank of England new powers to check that private investments are geared to cutting carbon emissions. Firms listed on the London Stock that fail to do so risk delisting (Phillip Inman, 'Labour would expand scope of Bank's powers to help meet carbon targets', *The Guardian*, 25 June 2019). What Labour would do about the legislation and trade agreements forbidding States to act to prevent profiteering by banks and corporations remains unclear.

Believing education a public good that must not be commodified, the opposition party also pledges to establish a National Education Service to ensure free education from the cradle to the grave, enabling people to 'retrain and upskill' throughout their lifetimes. The party also intends to impose a tax on the fees charged by private schools, the proceeds to go to funding free school meals for all primary school children. It is also committed to funding an extra £160 million of Pupil Premium money that will help pay for the arts subjects cut from the school curriculum and for extracurricular activities. By reducing 'class sizes to less than 30 for all 5, 6, 7-year-olds,' and seeking to extend that reduction in class size 'as resources will allow,' the party pledges to invest in measures 'to close the attainment gap between children from different backgrounds'. State secondary schools are to provide curricula that 'will enable each [child] to find their learning path through a wide choice of courses and qualifications'. There is no mention of abolishing private schools or of getting rid of the practices of the streaming and setting of pupils inside the State schools.

Compared to the vicious capitalist 'austerity' policies, these changes promised by Labour are to be welcomed. Nevertheless, if the Labour Party is proposing only to bring the UK economy back to somewhere near post-WWII public/private business consensus, then the party is by no means as 'revolutionary' as its incensed critics imply.

The leadership of left-leaning parties, trade unionists, politico-economic analysts and activists must press for working-class majority solutions to the daily exploitations of the ruling elite and its cohorts and their apparent goal of continuing to support the terminal decline of the capitalist political economy.

The World Health Organisation May 2019 report, based on 70,000 scientific papers, shows 90% of populations are affected by toxic outdoor air, a bigger killer than tobacco, affecting every cell and organ of the body, the toxins releasing enzymes, acids and inflammatory proteins that affect the brain, kidneys, pancreas, and other organs. Besides causing endemic respiratory illnesses, the toxins can also trigger diseases from Parkinson's to brittle bones (Damian Carrington, 'Air pollution damages "every organ in the body"', *The Guardian*, 18 May 2019). Consequently, the Labour Party's stance might be compared to the campaign for a four-day working week when, according to the report of think tank, Autonomy, based on OECD data on the increases in carbon emissions, a switch to a nine-hour working week is what is needed (Mathew Taylor, 'Much shorter working weeks needed to tackle climate crises – study. UK workers must move to nine-hour week if carbon levels do not change, says think tank', *The Guardian*, 22 May 2019).

Currently underway in a number of the UK's small local authorities, such as in Frome, Somerset, a town of 25,000 people is a type of political localism labelled do-it-yourself 'flatpack democracy'. Rather than the local political party constituency selecting and backing the party political town councillors, an independent panel selects the candidates on the basis of how the candidate proposes to help run the town, such as a plan for supporting employment-boosting local start-up businesses; a local renewable energy co-op; extending green spaces for public use, and so on. While such politico-economic innovations are to be welcomed, because they can only operate within the limited parameters central government allows local democracy, those much-heralded political innovations could end up being little more than bandaids stretched over the gaping wounds of the governing party's chosen austerity legislation, which is in turn driven by the global elite's command and control of the global economic system, a core aim of which is to impose the exponential inequalities and impoverishments systemic to the capitalist political economy. The unwillingness and hesitations of progressive politicians to call a spade a spade and put forward unmistakably democratic socialist solutions is reflective of Gramsci's observation that: 'The crisis consists precisely in the fact that the old is dying and the new cannot be born; in this interregnum, a great variety of morbid symptoms appear.' Progressive leadership means working with the great majority of people who want to live in a world of economic justice and peace. Despite ever viciously cunning manipulation to the contrary, the numbers of people believing in and working towards bringing the world of democratic socialism closer to reality grows by the day.

In the UK there are 12.7 million people who volunteer to work at least once per month for good causes, and around 700,000 volunteers working for 168,000 registered charities. In its churches, mosques, synagogues, gurdwaras, etc., the UK also has millions of people who in offering a spiritual home to their co-religionists also believe they are working towards the common good. Many volunteers and religionists are likely to vote for the left, but their organisations don't give organisational backing to political parties, not least because the gagging laws on charities and churches prevent it – laws that must be changed. Nationally and globally, these gagging laws uphold the political status quo, with the billionaire-owned mass media heaping praise on the corporatist philanthropists who are, first and foremost, socio-economically rapacious.

Considering the Labour Party's socio-economically capitalist 'bridging' policies and its consequently already stretched organising capabilities could it, should it, attempt to politically include all those purporting to work in the name of the common good? Given that the volunteer organisations and the different religious groups also tend to hunker down inside the silo of whatever their group, how positive or disruptive would their participative inclusion be likely to be?

The next question surely must also be that without the inclusion of those millions of well-intentioned people who do their best to work in the interests of others, how transformative can any socialist, environmentalist, libertarian political party ever expect to be?

The Labour Party has around 540,000 members, making it the largest political party in Europe. There are also around six and a quarter million UK trade unionists supporting the Labour Party.

The People's Assembly against Austerity, founded in June 2013 by trade unions, campaign groups, leftist politicians, entertainers and filmmakers, has many thousands of people as core members and has been able to mobilise sizeable numbers on protests that demand – though still too feebly – that government 'abandon its austerity programme', otherwise 'it must be replaced by one that will.'

Momentum, the opposition party's activist group, formed in 2015, has around 40,000 members, making Momentum larger than the Green Party. Other activists groups, from the Stop the War Coalition to Global Justice Now, have a combined total of maybe around a million or so members.

In a UK population of 66.75 million, is the combination of those left-leaning voters enough to help underwrite the fundamental changes now needed?

The good news is that millions more people than ever now know that beyond all the razzle-dazzle and bling of obscene wealth, yachts, fast cars, private jets, and the secretive, anonymous or celebrity lifestyle of the ruling elite and their hangers-on; that despite all the argy-bargy and theatrical chatter of media punditry, it's no longer possible for the ever more naked emperors of threadbare capitalism to hide the deliberate impoverishments of populations at home and abroad nor the ecological ruination of the very planet.

Millions of people also now understand that re-engineering the system means nothing less than an increasingly better-informed population working together to replace the institutions of inbuilt inequality and systemic impoverishments with surely the most rational and attainable alternative of democratic socialism based on reverence for life and on economic justice for all.

The Extinction Rebellion campaigners and the Yellow Vest Movement show how quickly the status quo forces of power and domination can be forced to change, as do the protests of Hong Kong youth, the indigenous populations of Bolivia, the campaigners for economic justice in the Middle East, Africa, India, and in many other places across the globe.

What remains the case, however, is that millions more well-informed UK analysts, activists and voters for democratic socialism are more urgently needed than ever. Nothing less is now required than the building a modern politico-educational home for the 99%, a base from which to do the politico-economic work of replacing the current system of competitive capitalist profiteering and its now endemic rentierism.

That well-organised political home must be capable of invoking the positive participation of the likes of those well-off and once self-centred conservative grandparents who didn't much know or care how the other half lived, but who now understand that the capitalist political economy is set to deprive their grandchildren of a future. That inclusive political base must certainly welcome with open arms the likes of the council tenant shoving the outdated vote-catchers' bumph back out the letterbox, telling the political egoists to fuck off and don't come back till they get their brains fixed.

The criteria for membership in that new political home is commitment to the principles of reverence for life, equal human rights and responsibilities, control of public services and eventual public control of the means of production, finance and communications. The obligations of membership are for participants to contribute in any way they can to the establishment and maintenance of economically viable, politically robust democratic socialism.

Consequently, it is surely also the task of democratic socialists to establish a people's national constitutional assembly which, by definition, can't be instituted, reviewed and altered as deemed fit by any minority socialist vanguard. Based on the continious political participation of citizens in local, regional and national constituency assemblies, a living, breathing people's constitution must be hammered out, legislated for, implemented, maintained and renewed as decided by those people's assemblies. Well organised and always ongoing, the tasks of such assemblies include examining and considering the applicability of the work of the best of modern socialist economists on the finance and banking system; experts on climate change; renewable energy technologists, and so on.

Grander by far in concept and scale than any of the material symbols of politico-economic status and power, the crumbling castles, cathedrals, palaces of old, the modern bling of multiple homes and the world of private jet-set travel, the question is how is that great political shelter to be built?

Millions more people than previously now have enough economic, political and socio-cultural know-how and the communicative means to help them to right the many wrongs.

There is nothing to stop a tenants' association or a parent-teacher group, let's say, from collecting the dosh and organising the hire of a venue to help hammer out the details of what an organised, networked participative, democratic socialist society at local, regional, national and international levels entails – and would look like – and, in the endeavour of constructing that grand new welcoming home, what it asks of its neighbourhood, regional and national populations.

There is no one who isn't capable of contributing in some way to the urgent tasks of the century, from organising a collection to promote the work of progressive organisations, to joining the many campaigns for socio-economic justice. Daunting as it also might be, it may also be a clearer-headed way forward and a relief to engage in, for instance, those previously backgrounded conversations with family, friends and neighbours about the educational, economic, political and socio-cultural work required of citizens in a democratic socialist society. Those conversations must recognise the eventual, and perpetual, resistances exercised by the manipulated, dominated and exploited – against all the odds. The goal of those conversations, discussions, debates is to organise and establish – at both the personal and political level – the collaborative means supportive of the principles of reverence for life, equal human rights and responsibilities, no greed, no sexism, no racism, no war.

The choice is stark: begin with such as that crucial step of talking to family, friends and neighbours about what is entailed in taking the means of production, finance and communications into public ownership – or sit back in states of politico-economic and socio-cultural morbidity and watch the poor get poorer while the rich sink deeper into their wealth addiction at the expense of the earth's plant, animal and human life.

We have now reached this crucial historical juncture when that redundant old question, 'What did you do in the war, daddy?' becomes 'Dad, Mum, sir thingymajig, teacher, computer operator, student, pensioner, business owner, politician for this or that, lady whatsit, doctor, waiter, care worker, professor, rabbi, priest, imam, manager, director, tell us again what you lot did, whether a whisper, shout, group or inter-group protest, to get yourselves unified, and organised enough to take command and control out of the hands of the psychopaths murdering the planet? What did you do to dismantle the interlocking mesh of socio-economic and socio- cultural exploitations? What preparations did you formulate to treat the rampant ills of exclusion, maleducation, and political illiteracy about the *word* and the *world* – always remembering, of course, how each generation must learn anew?' What transparent and accountable, democratic procedures did you invent to treat the common diseases of hierarchy and the sneaky opportunisms of vanguardism? How exactly did you manage to take control out of the hands of the psychopaths killing the planet? Tell us what you lot did that was different from before? C'mon, tell us again, to save the future – what did you lot all *do*?'

CHAPTER 30

Signposts

In their daily struggles for equal human rights, the 99% majority of people use various means, one of which is the parliamentary vote. The vote is also used by the 1% economic elite as one of their means of dividing and ruling the 99%. The set-up is that instead of the majority voting on the policies they've helped hammer out, every five years or so the population is invited to put a cross against the name of one of the candidates putting themselves forward to be parliamentary representatives – except that the candidate's credentials can only be sketchily fathomed. The elections over, the winning political party will enact a reform or two based on their election pledges – while the competitive, exploitative, profiteering capitalist economic system remains firmly in place.

The innate resistance to domination, abuse, and theft of equal human rights and responsibilities is expressed in various ways, from flight to fight. For instance, a third of eligible voters don't vote in national elections; in local elections, it's two thirds. Activists organise and present petitions to the powers that be. Populist agitators systematically exploit them-and-us attitudes, judgements, and behaviours. Struggles against sexual, gender and racial discrimination are endemic. Campaigners mount protests against the likes of the shutting down of a local library. Anti-racist groups go on the march against neo-Nazis white supremacists. There is looting by the economically marginalised; rioting by the totally disaffected; acts of terror by the politically, economically, and socio-culturally excluded. Millions of people march against war.

Nowadays, mass mobilisations are becoming characteristic of the means of resistance employed by the 99%, such as those organised by the French yellow vest movement; the Hong Kong umbrella movement against Chinese law (umbrellas used as a defence against tear gas); the protests in the cities of the Middle East; Africa; India, Latin America, Russia, USA.

Complex in terms of the groups involved and the goals set, the phenomenon heralds the possibility that mass mobilisations of the 99% acting in its own interests against the 1% economic elite becomes the means by which the juggernaut of the planet-destroying capitalist political economy will be replaced by an equal human rights and responsibilities democratic socialism fit for the twenty-first century and beyond. That possibility is closer – through utter necessity – to being more realisable than ever before. However, any endeavours to build any such politico-economic and social-culturally inclusive sanctuary without the continual active participation of the 99%, will be to scratch in the dust. Environmentalists seeking to build movements that aren't also based on the dismantling of the capitalist economy are destined to do little more than doodle in the margins.

The question is how do we get from where we are to where we need to be? A brief review of the current state of politico-economic governance and the socio-cutural lay of the land offers some signposts of what to avoid and where to go instead.

The UK Parliamentary Vote

The Conservative Party is the UK parliamentary political party of the ruling-class elite, the upper middle and upper working class, the goal being to ensure their members get the biggest slices of the capitalist pie. Established in 1900, the Labour Party, created by the trade union and socialist movements of the nineteenth century overtook the Liberal Party as the main UK opposition party. It does what it can to move the capitalist political economy towards socio-economic reforms.

In 1997, running on a platform of appealing to middle-class and upper-working-class voters, the Labour party won the 1997 general election by a landslide. Rebranding the party 'New Labour', the incoming leadership declared that Labour was now 'intensely relaxed about people getting filthy rich' (Jason Lewis, 'Lord Mandelson: secrets of a filthy rich fortune', *The Telegraph*, Investigations Editor, 17 December 2011).

The prevailing causes of the Labour Party defeat in the UK 2010 general election were the falling standards of living in the UK that emanated from the 1980s onwards deindustrialisation of the Global North by the transnational corporations' exploitation of the cheap labour of the Global South. Contemporaneously, in keeping with global banksterism, there was the UK government's legislation to increase the size and economic function of the national and global banking financial sector. Another significant cause of Labour's 2010 defeat was government privatisation of public services, started under the Conservatives and continued under Labour. Then there was the 2003 debacle of the landslide-victory Labour PM having taken the country to war in Iraq under false pretences. Next, there followed the economic and political fallout from the banker-induced 2008 global financial crash. Then came the 2009 exposé of the UK MPs' expenses scandal that revealed that 60% of UK MPs from across the political parties had their fingers in the till.

The UK Freedom of Information Act (FOI), known as the 'almost too good to be true' Act, came into effect in 2005. Based on one of Labour's manifesto election pledges, the Act allowed public access to information held by government departments, providing the info was publicly relevant and its release didn't endanger national security. In compliance with FOI requests by journalists for sight of MP's expenses claims, the government thought it could comply with the Act by releasing the names and dates and blanking out the amounts and reasons for the claims.

The civil service clerks and temps hired through private companies were instructed to copy the redacted claims forms for release to the journalists. The security guards hired to protect the venues where the copying was taking place were soldiers on leave from Afghanistan who were taking temporary private security guard jobs to earn extra money to pay for decent boots and lightweight body armor, not supplied by the army. The clerks copying the claims forms and the soldier/security guards on duty were angered when they realised that the parliamentary expenses system was being used to make claims on taxpayers' money to which MPs were not entitled. They decided to take matters into their own hands. They organised for the 1.5 million claim forms to be copied – unredacted – onto a small external hard drive. They then entrusted a retired and knowledgeable Special Air

Service (SAS) officer to get the information to the most effective press outlet. The result was that national newspaper publication revealed that prime ministers, cabinet ministers, and MPs had used, and were using, the expenses system to pay for that to which they were not entitled, for example, mortgage payments or their constituency homes while claiming rent allowance on London MP accommodation; claiming expenses to refurbish their mortgaged homes and selling them on at a profit, buying another home and claiming mortgage payments on the new home; MPs used the claims system to buy expensive furniture, widescreen TVs, designer cushions and expensive bath fittings, etc. A wealthy Conservative Party grandee claimed money to pay for the cleaning of a floating duck house on his country estate. A Labour cabinet minister claimed £116,000 in unentitled mortgage payments and also claimed for the rental of pornographic films for her husband (see the documentary made 10 years after the exposé, *Expenses: The Scandal That Changed Britain*, BBC Two, 13 April 2019).

In a 650-seat parliament, 326 seats are required to form a majority government. In the 2010 general election, the Conservative Party won 307 seats, Labour 258, with 57 seats going to the Liberal Democrats. The Conservatives formed a coalition government with the Liberal Democratic Party. The Lib Dems then did their infamous U-turn on their pledge to the middle-class voters, aspiring working-class voters and young people and instead complied with Conservative Party policy to triple student university fees. The reputation of the Liberal Democrats as the non-conformist party fighting for the rights of the individual took a nosedive.

To deal, allegedly, with the 2008 banker-induced global financial crash, first the Labour Party, then the Conservatives Party from 2010 onwards legislated to implement national 'belt-tightening' and 'austerity' policies. Workers' rights were diminished, budgets for the remaining public services were slashed, bringing them to their knees; social welfare benefits for the poor, the unemployed, the disabled were cut; there was new legislation against immigrants and those seeking asylum – and so on. The phenomenon, not confined to the UK, was in various measures common across the deindustrialised Global North.

After the 2010 Labour Party defeat, the party elected a new leader, a centrist/slightly leftist politician, dubbed by the mainstream media as

'Red Ed'. In the 2015 general election, Labour lost to an outright win for the Conservatives at 331 seats, Labour 232, Scottish National Party 50, and Lib Dems eight.

In 2014, the rules for electing Labour Party leaders were democratised under 'Red Ed' to one member one vote. Not only Labour MPs and trade unions could vote for the Labour Party leader, ordinary members in the wider party could also now vote. Hundreds of thousands of people paid to join the Labour party, making Labour the largest political party in Europe. In September 2015, a long-serving Labour MP, known for his anti-war, socialist-leaning, internationalist stance, won the Labour Party leadership election by a landslide.

The government–corporate–media complex, aided and abetted by Labour's right/centrist MPs, went into hyper attack mode against the new left-leaning Labour leader. He was depicted as a Marxist ideologue lacking in modern politico-economic expertise, a backer of Irish terrorism, a supporter of the Palestinian cause – who was also against Israel. He was also portrayed as a male chauvinist who didn't do his share of the domestic chores at home.

Context of the 2016 UK National Referendum to Stay in or Leave the EU

Countries seeking to become members of the EU must sign up to EU rules, two of which are the free movement of capital and the free movement of labour within the EU. Voters in the UK's run-down areas blamed the EU for the UK's economic woes. Many especially blamed the consequences of the free movement of labour, that is, immigration from the poorer eastern EU countries, for example, Poland, Latvia, Lithuania, and Romania, for diminished access to public services and social housing.

The UK is a nation of immigrants. Very many people also have family members who have migrated far and wide. With many UK citizens believing, nevertheless, that immigrants were treated better by government than indigenous workers, there was a public mood against more immigration, and many especially didn't want immigration from the Indian sub-continent and Africa.

By contrast, those on the socialist left believe that in the deliberately skewed elitist-run world of competitive, profiteering capitalism, it is inevitable that people will migrate to escape wars, to search for work, look for a decent standard of living. The EU was also regarded by many on the socialist left as the politico-economic global trading hub under the command of the wealthy elite using the EU, 'Fortress Europe', as a means of exploiting the majority populations both within the EU and those outside it, the peoples of the Global South.

The United Kingdom Independence Party's (UKIP) non-stop anti-immigrant rhetoric and anti-EU stance exacerbated Eurosceptic attitudes within the UK to the point that the millionaire Conservative Party leader and his allies called the 2016 national referendum to settle the matter of whether the UK should remain in the EU or leave it.

The campaign message of the major group that wanted the UK to stay in the EU was 'Britain Stronger in Europe'. Billionaire businessmen bankrolled the Vote Leave campaign, and the 2016 referendum Vote Leave campaign manager's primary political message was for UK voters to 'Take Back Control' from the EU.

The majority of MPs from all parties voted for the UK to remain in the EU. For MPs and for the leader of the Conservative Party the shocking result of the referendum vote was that on a turnout of 72.2% of eligible UK voters, 51.9% voted Leave to 48.1% for Remain. The millionaire Conservative prime minister who'd called the referendum made a swift getaway from UK public political life (see Chapter 1, 'Power Force and Social Class', for a brief account of the PM's family use of offshore tax havens to reduce their UK tax liabilities).

Steps Leading to the 2019 UK General Election

After the EU/UK referendum vote for the UK to leave the EU, the Conservative Party's focus was on whatever UK exit deal it could manage to negotiate with the EU. The public was left in the dark about which sectors of UK society would benefit or lose from whatever deal the Conservatives were cooking up, on the grounds that the government's Brexit negotiation stance had to be kept under wraps so as not to weaken the position of the UK's EU negotiators.

A governing party with a slim majority has difficulty getting legislation through parliament. In an attempt to increase their slim majority, the Conservative government called the 2017 general election – only to see their majority decline further. Consequently, the Conservatives entered into a Confidence and Supply Agreement coalition with the 10 Northern Irish Democratic Unionist Party (DUP) MPs. That agreement involved the transfer of £1.5 billion of UK tax funds for the upkeep of a rundown Northern Ireland.

From the time of his election as leader in 2015, the Labour leader did what he could to bring the consequences of Conservative Party austerity policies to the centre of parliamentary politics, for example, that in the fifth richest nation on the planet, nine years of Conservative Party 'austerity' policies had contributed to the early deaths of 130,000 poor and disabled people. The banker-induced mortgage lending bubble had led to unaffordable property prices and soaring rents. The increasingly privatised National Health Service was on its knees. The central government's slashing of local authority budgets led to the crisis in social care for the elderly. Cuts to State school funding meant some schools had to reduce their humanities curriculum, for example, no music, dance or drama. Unable to pay for staff, some schools had to close an hour early each day, or all of Friday afternoons. Youth and community service funding had all but disappeared. Growing numbers of disenfranchised young people saw drug dealing as their economic lifeline, leading to increases in knife crime.

To cut short the long story of the three and a half years' wrangling over a Brexit deal, parliament voted down the Conservative Party's deals with the EU not once, not twice, but three times. The stalemate could only be broken by the installation of a new Conservative Party leader. Duly elected by the party, the new leader had been a key figure in the 2016 referendum Vote Leave campaign. To cut another tortuous story short, the new PM called for a snap general election on 12 December 2019, to which the Labour Party now agreed.

2019 Parliamentary Electioneering

Rich in donations from businesses and high-net-worth individuals, to fund the 2019 general election campaign the Conservative Party raised 26 times more campaign funding than the Labour Party. Conservative Party donations included money from a UK supermarket chain, from the UK's largest independently owned UK travel company; and £1 million from a billionaire theatre producer (Hugo Gye, 'General election 2019: Conservatives raise 26 times as much as Labour from rich donors including Trailfinders and Iceland Boss', iNews, 21 November 2019). Another donation of £1 million came from one of the UK's richest men, founder of one of the UK's largest stockbroking firms. With the expectation of future NHS contracts, donations also came from companies already running privatised sections of the NHS.

The campaign manager who'd organised the winning UK Vote Leave campaign was now paid to run the Conservative Party's 2019 national election campaign. His primary slogan for the Conservative Party was 'Get Brexit Done'.

Businesses routinely use sales data about buying preferences to micro-target their ads at potential customers. Every £1 spent on digital advertising reaches more people than campaign leafleting, so social media micro-targeting is now a favoured vote-catching technique commonly used by political parties across the globe. Campaign managers buy a range of data from the data collectors and sellers, for example, information about voting records in relation to geographical location, social class, income group, age, gender – and, nowadays, information about people's use of social media. Tech-savvy campaign workers feed the data into algorithmic computer programs that analyse the data. The outcomes are then used to produce campaign materials and social media posts designed to appeal to the political niche demographic to which the voter, the swing voter in particular, belongs.

The Conservative Party's highly paid 2019 campaign manager, who'd also run the 2016 Vote Leave EU/UK referendum campaign, had also previously acted as key advisor to the Conservative Party's cabinet Minister for Education. That minister was so reviled by teachers and parents that in July 2014, the Conservative government had to sack him and replace him with his deputy – who could be relied upon to continue with the same Conservative Party policy of the pre-privatisation 'academisation' of State schools.

In 2013, the wealthy, privately educated, top university graduate, key advisor to the sacked minister had self-published his 237-page essay on what he calls 'Odyssean' education, omitting world-class, evidenced-based educational theories and practices (e.g. Jacotot, Vygotsky, Freire) on how children, and adults, acquire knowledge through their innate human intelligence functioning within the socio-cultural imperative of their learning environment, which involves the operation of the joint intelligence of the child and parents, carers, siblings, peer group, teacher, etc.

No one is responsible for the social-cultural group into which they are born. There are millions of stories of people using their innate human intelligence to bravely escape the socio-cultural bonds that seek to dominate them. This isn't so in the case of the above-mentioned author of 'Odyssean' education who centred his thoughts on education around his favoured philosophers, mathematicians, scientists, war strategists and geneticists. Consequently, his 'essay' echoes the age-old ruling-class mantra that genetics trumps education. It's a stance that forever dodges the question of why the 1% elite work so assiduously in their own vested interests to manipulate and appropriate the innate human intelligence of the majority (see Dr Terry Wrigley, 'Bad Science, Worse Politics', *Socialist Review*, Issue 385, November 2013, for a succinct and scholarly dismantling of the essayist's rationale). Dr Wrigley's conclusion is that:

> Cummings's 240-page rant is about much more than IQ. It is wide-ranging and incoherent, but the connecting threads are key. It regards inequality as inevitable. It shows a deep anxiety about the state of the world economy: the solution lies in finding an elite of geniuses who can save it. The world is in crisis but the solution offered is no more rational than the crude sci-fi plots of films like *Ender's Game* – the search for a boy genius to stop the aliens.

Some insight into the mind and character of the essayist can be found in the videos of his appearance before the April 2016 Parliamentary

Treasury Select Committee that sought answers to questions about the economic and financial costs and benefits of UK's membership of the EU ('Andre Tyrie grills Dom Cummings about NHS Leaflets', YouTube, 20 April 2016; and 'Dominic Cummings FIERY Brexit row over EU membership costs', aired on YouTube, 7 January 2019). If you've got time, have look at the video of the Treasury Select Committee Hearing ('Dominic Cummings April 2016 parts 1 & 2', YouTube, 30 August 2019).

Five billionaires own over 80% of UK mainstream media ('Which 5 People Own the UK Mainstream Media?' INFO Truth, YouTube, 8 January 2015). Spooked by the 2015 election of the new Labour leader who said he'd never press the nuclear button, would scrap the UK's Trident nuclear submarine system, would negotiate the UK's exit from NATO, the mainstream media moguls went into super-psyops mode against the left-leaning Labour leader. No less than 40 stories germinated by the military establishment and UK intelligence services claimed the Labour leader was a threat to UK security. A military source also declared that if the Labour leader became prime minister, British soldiers would mutiny – and it was likely that a UK military coup would ensue. The US Secretary of State declared in a secret recording leaked to the US Press that should the UK Labour leader survive the media onslaught being waged against him, the US would step in to stop him becoming prime minister ('Abbey Martin and Lowkey: A Deeper Look at the UK Election', Empire Files, YouTube, 23 December 2019).

During the five weeks of the 2019 election campaign, the Conservative Party's upper-middle-class millionaire candidate for prime minister travelled up and down the country, often kitted out in workers' garb, to appear in well-choreographed, non-interview photo opportunities during which he repeated over and over again the slogan 'Get Brexit Done'. On the last day of campaigning some polls showed a narrowing of the Conservative's lead, so in an effort to escape what threatened to be a real live interview, the candidate for prime minister, acting that day as Yorkshire dairy worker, chose instead to disappear into a fridge (Heather Stewart and Aamna Mohdin, 'Boris Johnson "hides in a fridge" to avoid Piers Morgan interview', *The Guardian*, 11 December 2019).

In the four years prior to the general election campaign and repeatedly during it, the Labour leader continued to be the object of derision in the mainstream mass media. After 27 Palestinians had been killed in April 2018 during disturbances on the Israeli/Palestinian border, on the grounds that the actions of the Israeli army had been 'illegal and inhumane', the Labour leader had called for a review of UK arms sales to Israel. He continued to be depicted as an out-of-touch Marxist ideologue and was denigrated at every opportunity. For example, he was belittled for not singing the national anthem at a St Paul's Cathedral war memorial service, scorned for not bowing low enough at the War Remembrance Day ceremony at the Cenotaph.

Before and during the 2019 election campaign, the Labour leader was accused almost daily by UK media of being an anti-Semite. In the three years after he became leader of the Labour Party, there were over 5,000 news stories and articles in the national press alone accusing the Labour leader and the Labour Party of anti-Semitism. Compared to the 164 articles in the UK press about Islamophobia in the Conservative Party, there were 1,500 articles that focused on the 0.1% of Labour Party members who had been accused of anti-Semitism. . The UK's chief rabbi, a supporter of the Conservative Party, doubtless in dread at the thought of an unarmed Israeli State, warned Jewish people against the election of a Labour government.

In the autumn of 2019, Pluto Press, a major UK academic publisher, published the Glasgow Media Group's *Bad News For Labour, Anti-Semitism, The Party & Public Belief.* The book is based on media analyses by various academics, and it also provides a timeline of the media smear campaign against the Labour leader. It also shows how the Labour Party dealt ineptly with the propaganda smear campaign. The book also sets out parameters of how the media ought to conduct transparently honest debate about the difference between anti-Semitism and legitimate criticism of the State of Israel. Staff at the bookstore due to hold the book launch in September 2019 were subjected to abuse and threats, causing the launch to be cancelled (see Mohamed Maazi, 'Waterstones shuts down book launch exposing the antisemitism witch hunt against the left', *The Canary*, 24 September 2019). Nor did the book appear in the review sections of the UK mainstream media that normally flag up academic studies published by major UK publishing firms. The UK media anti-Semitic smear campaign was also likely to have terrorised many traumatised UK Jews into believing that a

Labour Party in power would legislate against free speech, support neo-Nazi scapegoating of Jews, and give backing to physical attacks, thuggery and the murder of Jewish people.

Non-profit fact-checking organisations examined Facebook's advertising library for the ads posted by the three main political parties during the same four-day period early in the 2019 election campaign. The fact checkers found that of the 6,749 ads posted by the Conservative Party, 5,000 contained misleading claims that the Tories would build 40 new hospitals. The fact checkers also and found 500 ads that claimed the Conservative Party would create 50,000 new jobs for nurses. Neither claim was deliverable during the next five-year parliament. In the same analysis period, there were no misleading claims by the Labour Party (see Faye Brown, 'Investigation finds 88% of Tory ads misleading compared to 0% for Labour', Metro, 10 December 2019). The 2019 general election campaign has been branded the 'dirtiest on record', with misinformation and lies 'sanctioned from the top'.

The broadcasting conventions of the adversarial political TV interview also functions as a 'normalised' form of political abuse. The interviewee is asked to respond to the seemingly neutral interviewer's questions/accusations, which are taken from elsewhere in the media. In answering accusations about alleged anti-Semitism and lack of patriotism, the Labour leader would attempt to clarify his position: that no form of racism is acceptable; that anybody in the party found guilty of anti-Semitic and other forms of racism will be expelled; that he was not anti-security, he was anti-war; that in attending memorial services he chose to honour the dead of all sides by what he called respectful silence. The interviewer would frequently move on without comment to the next accusation, leaving the Labour leader's responses to be perceived not as clarifying explanations, more as limp apologies for the Labour leader's alleged sins.

Honouring the death of soldiers assuages some of the agony of losing sons, siblings, fathers, comrades to war. It is then, however, taken as consensual, as routinely portrayed in books, films, art, TV reports from war zones, flag-draped coffins in body repatriation ceremonies, that through a willingness to sacrifice their lives for family and nation, soldiers achieve that pinnacle of loyalty and devotion against which every other form of patriotism is debased. For instance, the courage of conscientious objectors in standing up against the killing other human beings is not only airbrushed but almost scrubbed out of history.

In the symbiotic embrace of adversarial interviewing, no time is allowed for comprehensive discussion, no space is permitted for analyses of the socio-cultural presumptions in which the adversarial interview is entrenched. No mention is made, for instance, of the multiple reasons why people opt for employment in the armed forces. A left-leaning, anti-war politician attempting to unbind himself – and his audience – from that interwoven web of socio-cultural bondage is bound to incur the same levels of outrage as the Russian Pussy Riot feminists sacrilegiously whooping it up in Moscow's Cathedral of Christ the Saviour. Though not subject to arrest and jail, as were the heretical feminists, the socialist-leaning politician's would-be-Houdini-act would instantly become the next media story against him.

The decline of mass trade union membership; the closure of community centres; working men's clubs that are nowadays solace to a few pensioners; voter alienation in a digitally isolating world, etc., all mean there are fewer places where significant numbers of people can engage in the back-and-forth grassroots discussions about what's what – and what they might do about it. These are amongst the factors that help create a sense of democratic stalemate – which is right up the street of the powers that be.

The continuous participation of the 99% majority in political life involves continual analyses, education and organisation by that 99% majority class at local, national and international level. The UK does not have a written constitution. The argument against, is that a written constitution may render governments inflexible in dealing with complex situations. The arguments for a written constitution, hammered out by the participative engagement of all citizens, alterable by the recommendations of the country's permanent constitutional assembly and ratified by the population, makes clear the rights and responsibilities of all citizens. Is it not the case that any written constitution in support of democratic socialism fit for the twenty-first century and beyond has to be based on the values of reverence for life and equal human rights and responsibilities and must surely also take full account of the responsibility of UK governance both towards its own citizens and towards the intergovernmental action needed to halt the climate catastrophe? In the age of climate catastrophe, would such a constitution not also have to take into account both proportional representation between countries and the proportional representation of the popuations within countries, from managing director to manual worker, rich rentier to refugee, the once uber-rich to the unemployed?

Party Political Pledges

Though the 2019 Labour Manifesto had gone through more stages of consultation than manifestos before, it still wasn't subject to inclusive, discursive doorstop discussion – never mind input – from the grassroots. Worked out in consultation with progressive economists and designed at executive party level, the 2019 Labour manifesto was one of the most socio-economically progressive manifestos in decades – though not as revolutionary as its irate critics implied. Delivered to constituency offices, local party officers didn't have the wherewithal to publicise that manifesto effectively. Organising political campaigns is a hard slog, and not many ordinary working-class voters have the time, or are not minded to give time, to doing the work that needs doing. By contrast, the 1% elite is expert at servicing their politico-economic chumocracy network, including at closed-shop constituency-level. In what stands in for the concept of socialism, the constituency practices of left-leaning political parties are by no means as social as they need to become. As for those 40,000 Labour Momentum activists, they were more or less told what they could and couldn't say to local voters about the issues the manifesto attempted to address – and any other sorts of political discussion were ruled out of bounds.

The Labour Party declared in its 2019 Manifesto that on gaining power the party would negotiate a new Brexit deal within three months, and within six months put the deal to another national referendum – alongside an option for the UK to remain in the EU.

The result of the 2019 general election was 13.9 million votes to the conservatives, 10.3 million to Labour, 365 parliamentary seats to Conservatives, 203 to Labour. Of the 60 seats lost by Labour since the 2017 election, 56 were in deindustrialised towns and conurbations that for decades had been politically neglected by Labour MPs elected from those safe Labour seats. The voters in those seats had also voted in the 2016 referendum for the UK to leave the EU. The Labour Manifesto contained well thought out yet not believable pledges of a reformist economic 'fix'. It also contained what many voters believed was the crucial fudge of holding a second referendum to remain in the EU. This was like a red rag to a bull to those Labour voters who in the 2016 Referendum had voted to leave the EU. Fifty-two of those previously red Labour seats now turned Conservative blue.

Rob Griffiths, general secretary of the Communist Party of Britain (CPB) puts the reasons for Labour's defeat like this: 'much of the Labour left ceased analysing, exposing and criticising the EU in class terms as the anti-socialist alliance of capitalist states that it is' ('The way forward? Organise, organise and organise', *The Morning Star*, 1 February 2020). Let it be clear that he CPB had also advised people to vote Labour as their best bet.

The new Conservative government, having been pushed by the left and by public opinion, now has to come up with the goods as promised in its manifesto. In particular, it will have to act to assuage the demands of those ex-Labour voters whose votes, depending on your point of view, were lent, stolen, or squandered to the Conservative Party. The government Office for Budget Responsibility forecast is of weak UK economic growth over the next five years of the incoming parliament. Known about long before the election, that forecast of weak economic growth is the Conservative Party's first obstacle in fulfilling those election pledges. By-the-by, the party's promise to middle-class voters to reduce their income taxes is also likely to be undeliverable, unless the government cuts spending elsewhere – except the government can't politically afford to cut public services further (Richard Partington, 'Boris Johnson's tax cut plans face squeeze as public finances worsen', *The Guardian*, Economics Correspondent, 16 December 2019).

The Conservative Party appears to believe that imminent UK economic recovery is to be found in 'free-market' deals that hark back to Britain's imperialist past. Their current narrative is that of an exceptional

Brexit Britain, rich in science and technology; advantaged by politico-economic links with its former colonies, and enjoying a 'special' relationship with the world's largest economy, the US. The belief is that this Brexit Britain is also still in firm possession of historically proven abilities of arranging asymmetrical global trade deals for the benefit of its wealthy elite, with trickle-down economics providing a living for the rest of the population. It's a narcissistic elitist narrative that is deaf to the reality that in today's multi-polar global economy, the unipolar politics of Western trade protectionism has just about had its day.

The date set by the UN Intergovernmental Panel on Climate Change (IPCC) for the net-zero carbon emissions required to prevent irretrievable climate catastrophe was 2050. In the 2016 Paris Agreement, nations signed up to that date. In October 2018, the IPCC had to revise that date down from 2050 to 2030 (Matt McGrath, 'Final call to save the world from "climate catastrophe"', BBC News, Environmental correspondent, Incheon, South Korea, 8 October 2018). At the meeting to consider the scientific evidence, shocked and grief-stricken politicians and scientists were seen to be in tears.

The reasons the 2050 date is now untenable, and the 2030 date perhaps unachievable, are that corporate and shareholder investments in the fossil fuel industries are not declining but soaring. In the last four years alone, 33 of the world's major banks have poured £1.9 trillion into fossil fuel production (Greta Thunberg et al., 'At Davos we will tell world leaders to abandon the fossil fuel industry', *The Guardian*, 10 January 2020). Of that funding, £25 billion came from UK banks, Royal Bank of Scotland, Barclays, HSBC, Standard Chartered Bank (Luke Barratt, 'Revealed: UK banks' £25 billion support for global coal', Greenpeace Unearthed, 5 December 2019). The International Monetary Fund (IMF) estimates that in a variety of ways governments also subsidise the fossil fuel industry at a rate of $10 million a minute, $5.2 trillion a year (Umair Irfan, 'Fossil fuels are underpriced by a whopping $5.2 trillion', Vox, 17 May 2019). Despite growing knowledge, and experience of severe weather events, droughts, fires, floods, of the consequences of the cascading effects of climate disaster, with each tipping point causing the next, the gap widens between scientific evidence and the willingness of the politicians, the wealthy elite, corporate CEOs, and shareholders to act to prevent the coming climate catastrophe.

To reach net-zero carbon emissions in the UK, the Conservative Government has stuck with the old date of 2050. Labour's fudged date of 2040 isn't much better. It has also been disclosed that the new UK PM doesn't fully understand the geopolitical and economic implications of the science of climate catastrophe (Joe Murphy, 'Boris Johnson admits he 'doesn't get' climate change, says sacked No 10 adviser', MSN news, 4 February 2020).

If the government and political parties don't fully comprehend the geopolitical economics of the climate catastrophe, what hope is there of UK trade agreements – never mind a written constitution – that factor in the global politico-economics of gross climate injustice and impoverishments? Does the Conservative government intend to seek intergovernmental legislation to bring the banking, finance and the government subsidy systems under control? Will the new government legislate to ensure that investment and employment flows into the production of renewable and alternative energy – with the concomitant democratisation of corporations and people's workplaces? Where are the headlines about trade deals designed to prevent conflict and chaos? How about trade deals that do even the minimum, like protecting food safety standards? What news is there of comprehensive global trade agreements to help goverments, nationally and internationally, to transition away from the global agri-businesses and meat industries that add daily to the global greenhouse gas emissions cooking the planet (*Apocalypse Cow: How Meat Killed the Planet*, Channel 4, 8 January 2020)? The stark reality is that British trade deals that seek to evade the intergovernmental commitment needed to establish the transformational economics vital to protecting the planet and the life upon it will turn to ash before the ink is dry.

Through the upper-class chumocracy network, the current UK PM, educated at a boys' private boarding school, a graduate of a top UK university, his ambition from childhood to be 'king of the world', was slotted into lucrative positions in UK mainstream media institutions. He became a journalist for a leading conservative newspaper, was sacked for making up quotes; became editor at another top UK Tory newspaper; then editor of the *Spectator* magazine, the current affairs magazine that aligns with the Conservative Party's worldview. Networked into positions as an MP, he later became Mayor of London. Apart from the pursuit of a vanity project or two, he was known in that mayoral office, as the 'do nothing' mayor. He pledged to totally eradicate rough sleeping by 2012; it doubled under his leadership. He promised to reduce transport fares, they increased by 4.7% (Kyrsty Major, 'Why are we so surprised that Boris Johnson lied when he's been sacked for lying twice before?', *The Independent*, 27 June 2016). One of Johnson's vanity project was to build a garden bridge over the Thames, a concept presented to him by a family friend who'd known him from childhood, a successful actress/comedienne whose celebrity cache is also boosted by being networked into celebrity sponsorship of various charities – and whose associate won the contract to build the said garden bridge. With increasingly estimated costs of £200 million, construction was to be funded by private money, with gift-aid tax reductions, charitable donations and taxpayers' money. The completed bridge was also intended to become a lucrative venue for those staging public events upon it. Pushed to cancel the project as unnecessary and wasteful, the incoming mayor did so. The planning of the bridge had already cost £53 million, £43 million of that being taxpayers' money that would have been far better spent on fixing dilapidated roads and infrastructure in London's run-down boroughs, some of those boroughs being the most impoverished in the country.

'Run-it-up-the-flagpole-and-see-who'll-bung-us-the-dosh' projects often arise from the said-with-a-jokey-smile, abusive ruling-class addiction to wealth and supremacy, in this case by second-tier frontmen and women. From a wealthy family of the old British Raj, the actress/comedienne friend of the once mayor of London, now PM of the UK, owns a mansion; maintains a collection of cars; has a net worth of $16.5 million; and has been granted the Order of the British Empire by the queen ('Joanna Lumley Net Worth 2019', NetWorthPortal, 13 January 2019). Now in her seventies, the TV celebrity-name-brand continues to appear in celebrity-led TV travelogues featuring exotic locations (Desiree Baptiste, 'Joanna Lumley's India: is her show guilty of airbrushing history?', *The Guardian*, 19 July 2017).

People are generally well aware of the domination, abuse, and theft built into UK socio-economic relations. The majority of people are necessarily preoccupied with looking after their families, looking out for friends, trying to get by, watching their backs. Millions of people are are almost unavoidably less likely to be concerned about the degree to which economic domination, abuse of consciousness, and the stealing of their emotions are deftly woven into the fabric of the UK institutions that control the information, education, entertainment and communication systems that the public must interact with daily. Some of those institutional mechanisms are deliberately designed to conceal the inevitable consequences of the capitalist political economy, and those in control of those institutions also well understand the inherent actuality of people's joint intelligence means that truths cannot ever be totally contained. That's a major reason why the communications systems, owned and operated by a handful of media moguls and publishing corporations, routinely present the public with jigsawed pieces of those uncontainable truths. Take, for instance, just two pieces of high production values TV drama documentaries, the 27 December 2018 *Brexit: The Uncivil War* and the 19 December 2019 *The Cure*. *Brexit: The Uncivil War* is about modern electioneering's use of micro-targeting on social media platforms. The storyline of *The Cure*, based on investigations by a female journalist, is rehashed by a highly skilled TV writer and, using top-knotch UK actors, is produced by Channel 4. *The Cure* focuses on the scandal of patients dying from ill-treatment and neglect on the understaffed wards of an NHS hospital run by a semi-privatised NHS hospital trust. Both such 'stand-alone' docu-dramas, indeed much factual reporting and fictionalised drama, routinely omit, background, and sideline the overarching politico-economic contexts in which those docu-dramas are thoroughly embedded, that is, the politico-economic context of the exponentially profiteering capitalist political economy that permits the theft of the world's wealth so that eight men now own more than the total assets of half the people on the planet, 3.6 billion people (Oxfam, 'Press Release', January 2017). The media owner-operators are also in command and control of when programming will be aired. For example, *The Cure* was not broadcast until after the 12 December 2019 general elections. Had it been broadcast contemporaneously with the news leaked by the Labour

Party about UK government officials meeting with US lobbyists to discuss Brexit deals for US pharmaceutical companies to supply the NHS with more expensive medicines, more voters might have been more able to put the jigsawed pieces of truth together and think twice about which party they'd vote for.

Another telling instance of such decontextualisation of particles of truth is in the likes of, for instance, the 20 December 2019 episode of BBC Radio 4's *Great Lives* series. A celebrated adversarial host/TV interviewer, retired, invited to air his opinions on the Earl of Shaftesbury (1801–1885), declares with broadcast authority that the earl had 'got off his fat arse' and 'got things done' to help the poor. Omitted in that half-hour programme are the following facts: that the earl exploited poorly paid workers to run his estates in Dorset, Hampshire and Yorkshire; that the evangelical Christian earl feared that the patriarchal philanthrocapitalist order to which he belonged was threatened by the socialist demands of workers, as set out in the People's Charter of the times:

> movements dedicated to advancing the political interests of the working classes [were regarded by the earl] as 'the two great demons in morals and politics'. ('A Tory Christian Warrior: The Seventh Earl of Shaftesbury', Official Historian of the Conservative Party, Lord Lexden OBE, July 2015)

Lord Shaftesbury's Lodging Houses Bill called for the registration and inspection of the lodgings of the poor, for example, two 10-foot rooms with six beds for 32 lodgers, male, female, children, places of 'dirt, confusion and obscenity'. Minus an adequate budget for registration and inspection, and with little effect on grossly exploitaive landlordism, the bill was heralded as 'The best law that was ever passed by an English Parliament' by the country's feted writer of fiction then living the celebrity lifestyle in the capital, Charles Dickens.

Dickens' *A Christmas Carol* appears like clockwork on UK Christmas TV. The reader is sustained by the writer's satarising of the Victorian business class, and by the sentimental portrayal of the major characters. The novelist, knowing what sells, contributes significantly to the notion that the causes of domination, abuse and exploitation reside in the moral or immoral character of the individual boss. The fact is that billions of people, readers included, daily exercise that vital individual moralilty. By cutting those moral choices adrift from the politico-economic and social-cultural fabric in which those choices are contextualised, i.e. in the inbuilt effects of structures of the capitalist political economy, is to steal the readers' emotions, abuse their intellect, by telling less than half the story. That 'normalised' less-than-half-the-story formulaic template is apparent 24/7 in every communication aiming to render audience into states of trusting spectatorship, from the history books to newspapers, magazines, popular novels, comics, video games, the bardology of lit-er-a-ture, films, TV, radio, etc.

Today, enough comprehensively contextualised examples of fictions and factions now exist to prove it is eminently possible to produce satisfying and sustaining politico-economic and psycho-emotionally contextualised works. The job of the public is to demand much more of it.

CHAPTER 31

Pandemic Politics

The Basics

The 'Spanish Flu' pandemic of 1918, the second wave being deadlier than the first infected 500 million people worldwide, a third of the world population at that time, and killed an estimated 50 million people across the globe. The epidemiological and socio-economic analyses of that pandemic led to the expansion of national public health authorities and the establishment of the World Health Organization. These bodies set out the basic procedures for dealing with any pandemic: governments must have Standard Operating Procedures permanently in place; mount the earliest possible public health campaigns; legislate to prevent public gatherings; ensure compliance with social distancing and self-isolation measures; have sufficient stockpiles of personal protective equipment (PPE) for health workers (Dr Larry Brilliant, 'My Wish: Help Me Stop Pandemics', *TED Talk*, February, 2006).

Compared to governmental armaments' budgets, for fighter jets, nuclear subs, predatory drones, bombs and bullets, the cost of stockpiling and distributing PPE is minuscule.

Difficult to do, the ultimate solution to controlling pandemics is to discover and produce a vaccine. Governments must then make the vaccine available to all who need it, wherever they live. The old Human Immuno Deficiency Virus (HIV) surfaced again in the 1980s. In the thirty years of all the efforts since then to come up with a vaccine, no vaccine has yet been discovered. Borderless and bulletproof, deadly viruses do not discriminate. The politicians in command and control, unfortunately, all too often do.

The UK may have had cases of COVID-19 as early as late December 2019. By late January 2020, UK COVID-19 infections had reached recognisably pandemic proportions.

Having won the contest for the leadership of the Conservative Party, the UK prime minister had also gone on to win the December 2019 general election with an increased majority. The prime minister was busy with celebratory balls and parties, sorting out his new cabinet, and attending to personal matters, finalising his divorce settlement, getting engaged to his pregnant girlfriend, going on a Caribbean holiday, paid for by a wealthy Conservative Party supporter. His political attention was fixed on his election pledge to 'Get Brexit Done', and on his declaration that Britain would leave the EU by 31 January 2020, with the transition period ending in December 2020.

In a speech on 3 February 2020, the UK prime minister, using his characteristically flamboyant vocabulary, declared that the economic lockdowns and social isolation measures put in place by other governments to try to keep the pandemic under control amounted to little more than 'bizarre autarkic rhetoric'. The prime minister then proceeded instead to paint a picture of Brexit Britain as an economic Superman with special powers to organise a bonanza of trade deals that would soon place the UK in the sunny uplands of unrivalled prosperity.

The prime minister spent days at a government country residence, apparently not thinking that it was vital for him, as the country's political leader, to attend important government pandemic meetings. His 'do-nothing' stance provoked the then Labour leader to call him a part-time prime minister.

In early March, mingling with equally ill-informed sports fans, the prime minister made celebrity type appearances at crowd events, a rugby match and the Cheltenham horse races. As later evidenced by the data, a spike of COVID-19 deaths occurred in the surrounding areas where those crowd events took place.

A later BBC Radio 4 programme about the prime minister's brash attendances at those crowd events included audio clips of UK epidemiologists who stated, in polite middle-class terms, that by attending crowd events the prime minister had acted 'recklessly' (BBC Radio 4, 'Game Changer: How the UK Played during Coronavirus', 26 May 2020, 8 p.m.; see Chapter 15, *The Politics of Ego and Entitlement*).

Some days later, the prime minister, his unelected chief advisor, selected cabinet ministers, and the Chief Executive of the NHS, joined by spokesmen from big-tech corporations, Google, Facebook, Amazon, Apple, Microsoft, Deliveroo, Uber and Babylon met to discuss the government's official pandemic policy (Gian Volpicelli, 'Inside Dominic Cummings Coronavirus Meeting with Big Tech', *Wired*, 12 March 2020; Tom Coburg, 'Johnson's Coronavirus Chaos Criticised by UK Doctors Demanding Greater Transparency', *The Canary*, 15 March 2020).

To combat the pandemic, the UK Conservative government had opted for a eugenicist, survival-of-the-fittest herd-immunity policy. The government based this pandemic policy on the purportedly scientific advice that anti-body immunity amongst those who recovered from COVID-19 would deprive the virus of human hosts and stop it from spreading – at an estimated cost of a quarter to half a million lives, wrongly assumed to be confined to the elderly.

Epidemiologists, scientists, doctors, non-partisan public health officials, political activists, independent journalists, and members of an increasingly well-informed and outraged public eventually managed to get the scientific critique of the government's herd immunity notion across to much of the Press. The UK government continued, nonetheless, to refuse to put crucial physical distancing measures in place.

Alarmed at the UK government's refusal to put social distancing and self-isolation measures in place, which would involve shutting down sectors of its economy, the French government declared it would have to stop all transport to and from the UK. The UK cannot feed its population; a high percentage of its food imports has to come through the French ports; the Conservative Brexit government had to quickly change tack; and towards the end of March 2020, UK physical distancing and self-isolation measures became legally enforceable.

Successive UK governments had over the last fifty or so years withdrawn funding from the network of local and regional public health authorities that had been set up from 1946 onwards to work in conjunction with the NHS. Consequently, the much reduced capacities of UK public health authorities meant they were not capable of organising or overseeing the production of the blood tests to detect the virus in carriers so that the carriers could be quarantined. Nor were the public health authorities capable of mounting the necessary tracking and tracing measures (Paul Hunter, 'Why the UK Failed to Get Coronavirus Testing Up to Speed', *The Guardian*, 1 April 2020).

The EU Commission had invited the UK to join their efforts to procure PPE; the UK government claimed firstly it had not received the email invitation; then declined to attend the EU 25 March 2020 meeting convened for national health officials of the EU nations to spell out their PPE needs to the EU Commission. The UK government also declined offers by UK manufacturers to supply PPE, opting instead to sign contracts with factories abroad. UK manufacturers of PPE then had to export their stocks of PPE to Germany, Spain, Italy (Bill Gardner, 'Exclusive: Millions of Pieces of PPE Are Being Shipped from Britain Despite NHS Shortages', *The Telegraph*, 21 April 2020).

NHS medical staff and care home workers had to resort to making PPE from bin bags and buying dust masks and safety goggles from do-it-yourself stores. Later, volunteers up and down the country would make the surgical suits also needed by hospital staff.

The government had exempted the NHS from paying Value Added Tax on PPE. However, care home owners had to continue to pay VAT. Moreover, the price gougers, cybercriminals and scammers were by now forcing care home owners to pay 400 per cent more for PPE (Jill Rennie, 'Covid-19: Care Homes Forced to Pay VAT on PPE, but NHS Is Exempt', *carehome.co.uk*, 14 April 2020).

The ventilators which were needed to help severely ill COVID-19 patients to breathe were in short supply. Instead of providing the already existing small UK ventilator manufacturers with government funds to expand their manufacturing capacity, the government commissioned the big companies producing the likes of vacuum cleaners to retool and make ventilators – but retooling takes time. The health minister's premature declaration that ventilators would be available 'within days' was wrong.

Doctors were also learning as they went along about how to treat COVID-19 patients with severe respiratory and lung impairments. Ventilator Intubation is of itself an invasive procedure and those put on ventilators are the very ill whose chances of survival are already poor. The reality was that rather than 'following the science' as the government claimed, government's ventilator procurement procedures lagged behind up-to-date medical knowledge and understanding (Bob Davies, 'The Inside Story of the UK's NHS Coronavirus Ventilator Challenge', *The Guardian*, 4 May 2020).

Care Homes

Local government had once been responsible for much of UK care home provision. After government privatisation of public services, running a care home became a lucrative business based on charging high fees and employing untrained, low-paid workers. Families and care home whistleblowers later revealed that low staffing levels, poor facilities and inadequately trained workers led to dangerous levels of care, indeed to the deaths of some care home residents, so those homes were forced to close down. Some of the care homes that remained open and later revealed to be providing low levels of care, and that were either unwilling or unable to improve their facilities, staffing levels and training also closed down, declaring bankruptcy.

Prior to COVID-19, many elderly hospital patients, unable to afford nursing-home or care home fees, or pay for social care in their own homes, got stuck in NHS hospitals. The Conservative government now ordered the opening up of closed down care homes to take in these elderly 'bedblockers' and free up NHS beds for COVID-19 patients. The government also ordered the many care homes that were still in operation to take in elderly patients with COVID-19. The care homes were told to obtain Do Not Attempt To Resuscitate agreements from patients or families.

Care home workers, who had almost no access to PPE, were not tested to determine whether they had the virus, or had developed anti-bodies. The result was that care home workers became a source of the virus and helped spread COVID-19 to the outside community.

Doctors were by now issuing the death certificates for care home residents after only phone consultations with the care homes. Many frail, elderly and dementia care home patients who had died were designated not as dying from the virus but because of their underlying medical conditions.

After it had become apparent that care homes had also become a source of contagion, family visits had to be stopped. Relatives and the care homes sounded the alarm on the high rates of COVID-19 care home deaths. Only after public pressure about those high rates of deaths in the care homes, did the government include those care home deaths in the government's COVID-19 death rate statistics.

Needing to work to support their families, many uninfected, low-paid, skilled care home workers moved into the residential care homes to look after the elderly patients, and to protect their own families at home. Some care home workers even took to living in camper vans and tents in the care home grounds.

In March 2016, the government had stopped funding the bursaries for trainee nurses, which led to a reduction in the numbers of nurses. In March 2020. The government announced that it had ordered army engineers and commissioned private companies to turn conference and exhibition centres into huge field hospitals. The government assigned socio-cultural virtue to itself by naming these field centres as 'Nightingale' hospitals. However, in part because the many elderly COVID-19 patients had been shifted into the care home sector, and because there were not enough trained nurses to staff the new field hospitals, the field hospitals were barely used.

Risk Factors

Globally, those most at risk from the COVID-19 pandemic were the elderly; the poor black women of the global South: white and black working-class men and women living in the most crowded types of housing; those employed in the most crowded work environments, for example, the Third World garment industry; prison inmates and wardens; workers in meat-packing, food processing plants and warehouse distribution centres. Many of the workers employed in those workplaces were low-paid immigrants. Amongst those with the very poorest chances of survival, were the tens of thousands of people stuck in overcrowded and unsanitary conditions in the world's refugee camps

The US, the UK and Brazil had the highest rates of COVID-19 deaths. At the time of writing, early June 2020, reports of the effects of the pandemic on the rest of the world, for example, in Latin America, Africa, India, and countries with the most pockets of overcrowding, deprivation and poor health care systems came as snippets of information. The enormous public market in Mexico City rife with COVID-19 could not be shut down because millions of people depended on it as the source of their food. In India and elsewhere, the millions of people earning pennies a day had to continue to put themselves at risk of infection and death to earn those pennies to try to survive and feed their families. There could be no doubt that the poor populations of the countries of the global South would suffer the highest rates of COVD-19 deaths.

In the affluent West, those who lived in spacious houses with gardens, had sufficient income and were able to work by computer from home were much less affected by the lockdown than those who were unable to work from home, lived in bedsits in dilapidated accommodation, or lived with their families in pokey flats.

Public Volition

COVID-19 economic lockdowns and border closures had been quickly put in place by many other countries. Travel restrictions and the decisions of millions of people who could still travel but decided not to do so meant the airline, luxury cruise, and holiday businesses were amongst the first to close down. Social distancing and self-isolation at home also meant that shops, pubs, hotels, businesses, GP surgeries, universities, cinemas, gyms etcetera, also closed. The local authorities closed the State schools, keeping enough capacity to allow the children of key workers to continue to attend school – otherwise, there was no one to look after their children.

Doctors and nurses in the private sector were asked to work for the NHS. The NHS also recruited 20,000 retired nurses and doctors to come back to work. Across the country, people volunteered to do the shopping and collect medicines for the isolated elderly; taxi drivers gave free lifts to take NHS workers to and from work; the Royal Voluntary Service called for volunteers to help the NHS, and 750,000 people signed up within days. The RVS did not have the resources, however, to match volunteers to where they might be needed.

Hospital surgical operations, procedures and medical treatments deemed 'non-essential' were cancelled. People were also fearful that if they attended hospital accident and emergency departments, they were in danger of contracting COVID-19. Consequently, the non-COVID-19 death rate went up by around 20 per cent.

Panicked supermarket customers had cleared supermarket shelves. Pasta, toilet paper, hand sanitisers and alcoholic drink disappeared within hours. The government declared that supermarkets, banks, post offices, newsagents, and – interestingly – off-licenses were to remain open as essential service providers. Supermarkets quickly restocked and introduced pre-opening shopping times for medical staff and the elderly.

No longer able to go to pubs, cafes and restaurants, the millions of people in lockdown ate their meals at home and ordered most of their other purchases online. The profits of supermarkets and online businesses went up by 20 per cent. The stock market went down, then rose, driven largely by the online global internet giants like Amazon and Netflix. At any news of a possible easing up of the economic lockdown, stock market activities increased overall. The share prices of the medical diagnostics, bioengineering and pharmaceutical businesses that stood to gain from pandemic medicines shot up. Fossil fuel production dropped, and the share prices of fossil fuel corporations fell. In the UK, crime went down, including rape. Rates of internet pornography consumption and the ordering sex toys online went up. Isolation at home caused rates of domestic violence to go up. Online book sales burgeoned, BBC News of 26 March 2020 reporting that Waterstones online sales rose by 400 per cent, with children's book sales increasing by 243 per cent.

Pandemic Fiscal Stimulus Packages

Governments around the world that could do so, introduced fiscal stimulus packages to try to mitigate the effects of pandemic economics. The UK prime minister, some of his cabinet, industry leaders, bankers and trade union officials met to decide what the UK stimulus package would be.

From a middle-to-ruling class family, privately schooled, a Politics, Philosophy, and Economics graduate of Oxford University, an ex-banker, married to the daughter of a billionaire, an ex-director of his father-in-law's hedge fund, a UK MP for only five years; appointed to the UK cabinet only five weeks previously, the UK chancellor, a firm supporter of the Brexit prime minister, made his first budget speech in the UK parliament on 11 March 2020. The speech was a bravura performance of the type commonly delivered by head boy of the most expensive private schools, where the wealthy send their offspring to learn the tricks of the politico-economic divide-and-rule trade. The chancellor's budget speech was approved by the prime minister, who nodded and smiled his approval from the front bench. However, chancellor's announcements fell far short of what political bosses required. Rebriefed by his seniors, banks and industry, the chancellor later pronounced that, certainly, he'd do 'whatever it takes' to save the UK economy, except that 'In spite of what are unprecedented measures in scale and scope, I can't stand here and say I can save every single job, protect every single business or indeed every single charity' (Darren Boyle, 'Chancellor Rishi Sunak Warns Ministers 'Can NOT Save Every UK Job' as World Trade Organisations Says Coronavirus Will Spark the Worst Global Recession in Our Life Times', *MailOnline*, 8 April 2020). Most people already knew that well enough; what most people wanted above all was to be treated fairly. However, the concept of equitable treatment had little space in the psyche of the Conservative Party and its chancellor.

The big-ticket items in the revised (u-turn) UK budget announcements were that the government would make £330 billion in bank loan guarantees available to businesses; through a wages furlough scheme, governments would pay 80 per cent the wage bill to those businesses putting valued workers on standby (up to £2,500 a month per worker). Banks would provide a three month mortgage holiday for mortgagees and buy-to-let landlords, though with no stoppage of the banks' accrual of mortgage interest from their money-from-nothing money trees (Chapter 7, *Bank Racketeering*).

For the already unemployed or the homeless there was no provision and nothing for the five million self-employed – until public outrage forced the government to make some provision for the self-employed based on proof of past taxable income. Those with no money at all were told to apply for Universal Credit (UC) social welfare benefits. Designed to refuse and downgrade benefits, the UC system was such that desperate claimants were stuck in an interminably long queue for the funds they desperately needed to live on in the right here and now.

Had the government been ideologically capable of treating people equitably, it could have provided a living wage for all.

Instead, the government fiscal stimulus package left out millions of people, as if they did not matter.

As for the wealthy being required to donate a portion of their income to help others who had nothing, the fiscal package said not a word.

Brought up and educated to function as the technocrats and governmental representatives of the ruling class, the likes of the UK prime minister, his sidekick young chancellor, from a wealthy Asian background, and the middle-to-upper-class wealthy cabinet members of the UK Conservative government were not capable of devising economic coronavirus emergency solutions outside the box of the mindset, attitudes and behaviours of the ruling-class elite and their devotees. Owning the means of production, that elite does what it can to prevent others from setting up rival businesses; shapes its finance system to hinder lending to worker-owned-and-operated enterprises; and has designed its communication system to disseminate the well-modulated messages that pronounce the capitalist political economy as the best of all possible worlds.

A handful of the world's billionaires donated small slivers of their billions to various COVID-19 emergency causes, from bio-lab research to community food distribution centres (Hayley C. Cuccinello, 'Billionaire Tracker: Actions the World's Wealthiest Are Taking in Response to the Coronavirus Pandemic', *Forbes*, 17 March 2020).

For millions of people, it is counterintuitive to believe the reality that while philanthrocapitalists are making their tax-deductible donations, they are also continuously extracting their profiteering billions from workers and consumers.

Mass Media Culture in the Time of COVID-19

Millions of people stuck at home in self-isolation depended on television for company and entertainment, though the old storylines and themes were even more irrelevant than before. Millions of people knew that they lived on the verge of the biggest global economic depression ever known. Nonetheless, commercial TV advertising continued non-stop. Left with little choice but to try to read between the lines, millions of people also took comfort in that avalanche of non-stop ads on the televisions in their living rooms, as if those ads were a sign of a return to a post-pandemic 'normality', as though, indeed, the dominating, exploitative, abusive pre-pandemic capitalist economy constituted 'normal' human behaviour.

The good news is that millions of people now have the means to more rigorously investigate the truths and imports of the ruling-class elites and the policies of the governments that they largely control. Moreover, the world also has that small key cohort of investigative journalists who, despite the attempts of the government-corporate-media matrix to shut them up to the point of jail and murder, continue to put themselves at risk to unearth the facts behind the manipulations of the mainstream mass media. The fundamental competitiveness of the capitalist system is such that, upon occasion, mainstream media outlets will even compete to publish such reports, which will often firstly appear on independent media.

Some mass media outlets use the format of the well-known TV presenter who focuses on incidences of shambolic government policy and the contradictory statements made by hapless politicians. Solutions to the problems highlighted are seldom presented, and anything resembling measured analyses of the politico-economic system over which the government and the politicians preside is nowhere to be seen or heard. Instead, the show helps herd audiences into the usual divide-and-conquer camps: one for those who champion the TV presenter's diatribes; one for those who could not disagree more.

Even though the COVID-19 pandemic had changed the socio-economic world beyond recognition, there was next to no comprehensive TV discussions or debates between economists on what a post-pandemic political economy could become; nothing about how a fair banking and investment system could be instituted; nothing about a people's quantitative easing; nothing about how to get out from under surveillance capitalism.

On the contrary, the habitual mass media 'balance of biases' TV discussion and debate formats that permit just enough steam to escape to keep the lid on continued as usual. BBC One's *Question Time*, 19 March 2020 (repeated 22 March) gives some indication of how it is done. The topic for this episode was the government's handling of the COVID-19 pandemic so far.

The reduced host panel consisted of the recently appointed female presenter, the two obligatory political representatives of the Conservative and Labour parties, joined on this occasion by a trade union executive and two middle-class members of the public. In the interests of social distancing, they were all sat well apart. The presenter and the panel members responded to video statements from a junior doctor, a nurse, and a student, and a few online questions were also read out by the presenter. The comments made the host panel members that government actions had been inadequate tended to be muted by the panellist's almost identical remarks that the government was doing the best it could in extraordinary circumstances.

Having to deal with horrendous death rates and the massive ruptures of a closed-down economy is undoubtedly a dreadful situation for any government to have to deal with. However, the 'we're all in this together doing the best we can' statements coming from various TV commentators also act as a barrier to comprehensive discussion, and, therefore, to full and frank consideration of whatever the topic happens to be.

Instead, the 'we're all in this together' media messages function to turn the political opposition into the loyal opposition. Those who protest become the conscientious objectors and can expect to be scapegoated as being downright disloyal and thoroughly unpatriotic.

In many countries, the practice of 'clapping-for-carers' had become a social phenomenon. On the evening of 26 March 2020, millions of people in the UK in self-isolation opened their windows and doors to clap their hands, bang pots and pans, whistle and cheer to show their thanks to the National Health Service workers who put themselves at risk daily to help others.

On behalf of thirty-nine corporate clients, that is, producers of beauty cream, house paint, razors, instant coffee etcetera, to the providers of various financial services, a major UK TV channel instantly hijacked that meagre moment of community and produced an ad of the corporate workers clapping for carers. The TV producers labelled their broadcasting of that ad as a 'takeover' of a TV commercial break (Charlie Spargo, 'Channel 4 Stage Ad Takeover in Partnership with 39 Advertisers', *Prolific London*, 27 March 2020). The channel's Director of Sales declared:

> Feeling connected to each other and being part of a shared national 'moment' has never felt more important and we are incredibly proud to be able to play our part in showing appreciation for the fantastic NHS. What better way to do this than by joining forces with our advertisers who have responded, at lightning speed, to create this moving commercial break.

Given the sophisticatedly coercive pervasiveness of modern mass media and the publishing world in people's lives, it becomes akin to a political act to ask of whatever the communication: what does this broadcast, this TV 'debate', this newspaper, book, film, video, computer game, radio programme, celebrity image, piece of art, etcetera *do* – and *not* do? *Who* is it aimed at, and *why?* What are its purposes and intents? Where is the evidence for and against? How do these messages achieve their objectives? In what ways *don't* they achieve those aims – and why? If these images, broadcasts and messages do not support the livelihoods, well-being and equal socio-cultural rights and responsibilities of the majority of the population, then who and what is it that is being sustained and supported?

The Basics of Democratic Socialism

Democratic socialists aim to act on collaboratively well-informed judgements based on the principles and practices of reverence for life, equal human rights and responsibilities. Democratic socialist leadership must always be considerate of human feelings – and must still expose the ill-conceived emotionalism of populist demagoguery.

Understandable as it may be to feel pity for the hapless politicians of hierarchic, democratically deficient parliamentarianism, the consequences of their egocentric politics of domination and abuse are unforgivable.

The unpreparedness of so-called 'democratic' governments, of their dereliction of the basic duty to safeguard populations, is often characterised as 'nobody-is-perfect' cock-ups by clueless politicians. However, the dire circumstances with which governments must deal with are seldom unpredictable or unprecedented.

For example, competitive capitalist boom-and-bust is so common that it is accepted as theory in the textbooks of capitalist economics. The 2008 global financial crash, the disastrous climate catastrophe, and the global pandemic, all were predicted by analysts and scientists decades before they happened.

That the politicians in command and control were, and are, dismissive, secretive and untransparent, indeed unaccountable, in their handling of whatever the ensuing disaster. It then becomes the job of political analysts to unearth the hidden facts. For instance, the uncertain outcomes of First World War, compounded by the 1918 Spanish Flu pandemic, led military commanders to convince governments to order the Press to cover up the fact that military camps and troopships had become sources of pandemic contagion. That some of those soldiers would assuredly die on those troopships was of far less importance to commanders and their governments than having enough soldiers to send to the war front.

Governments are pressed to meet the democratic demands of their populations, and the same governments are focused on creating – at the same time – the politico-economic conditions for their ruling-class elites to exponentially accumulate more wealth. Their success in doing so is evidenced by the fact that by 2017, eight men owned more than the total assets of half the people on the planet, 3.6 billion people.

Previous chapters show some of the means by which governments maintain the conditions for the economic elites to hold onto and increase their wealth, and indicate how governance based on the principles of democratic socialism differs radically from the adversarial habits of parliamentary democracies. The few paragraphs below re-iterate one or two of those key differences.

The UK prime minister thanked immigrant nurses for saving his life after he was hospitalised with COVID-19. The same prime minister then continued with finalising the government's points-based immigration legislation designed to curtail the entry of poorly paid immigrants to the UK. Mid-pandemic, the Conservative government was also focused on negotiating trade deals with the European Union and elsewhere. Those trade deals would also be designed to be largely in the interests of the accumulation of wealth by the economic elites. Those trade deals would also pay lip service only to the crucial connections between the climate catastrophe and the continued climate abuses carried out in the name of the 'growth' of the UK capitalist economy.

The April 2020 contest for the new leader of the Labour Party saw hopes of the socialist left dashed by the election of an ex-lawyer, 'safe pair of hands' leader. He had been elected as a Labour Party MP in 2015 after his acceptance in 2014 of a knighthood for his 'services to the law and the criminal justice system'. Dubbed 'born to be mild', the new Labour leader declared his mission was to unite the divided Labour Party, while not 'oversteering' to the right. Criticisms of the Conservative government's glaring policy errors was not all that difficult. For example, the government continued to impose an NHS surcharge on the entry visas of immigrant workers, inclusive of NHS workers, and also charged immigrants working for the NHS treatment they might need. The prime minister had to make a u-turn. Nevertheless, the Conservative government's major fiscal package, criticised by many on the left, was more or less uncensored by the new Labour leader.

If there were ever to be a radical grassroots democratic socialist structure through which the poor and working-class majority could mobilise over anything resembling significant alterations in the embedded dominations and exploitations of the capitalist political economy, they would have to build it themselves. That grassroots, from-the-ground-up democratic socialist structure would have to be based on nothing less than the collaborative participation of the majority though the likes of interdependent democratic socialist commissions on, for instance, housing, health, social, and child care; employment, business, and economic well-being; biology, consciousness and socio-psychological health; education, culture, media and communications; neighbourhood, domestic and international relations, and so on.

While democratic socialist governance must protect itself against anti-socialist oppositions, it must also find ways of engaging the pro-capitalist groups, whether those intent on supporting the capitalist political economy or those groups of grossly maleducated young white men caught up in the dead ends of anti-socialist racism and fascism.

Above all, democratic socialists must know the difference between whatever they can muster at particular points in time and the goal of building nothing less than open, transparent, participative democratic socialism.

The Imperatives of Trade

The exchange of goods and services is an interdependent act, whether at the level of farm and village, factories or at the level of nations or groups of nations. Moreover, agri-business, manufacturing, the exchange of services and the development of technology are all intrinsically inseparable from the natural world. In the better world of the fair-exchange-no-robbery trading of goods and services, one group's expenditure becomes the reasonable income of the other.

Given the interdependent, ecological nature of economic exchange, it is not possible to exercise the principles, practices of democratic socialism in one location or country only. Nevertheless, it is entirely possible to demand that governments democratise existing workplaces and support the setting up of economically viable worker-owned businesses and worker-owned and operated corporations such as the Spanish transnational Mondragon Corporation (Chapter 26, *Workplace Democracy*).

Though today's modern politico-economic monopolies and trade agreements are backed ultimately by militarism and war, the economic textbooks used worldwide continue, nevertheless, to spread the deluded abstractions of an imaginary 'free market' based on supposed economic 'laws' of supply-and-demand (Chapter 14, *Sociopathy of Defective Hypothesis*).

Big Pharma provides a paradigmatic example of the capitalist trade monopolies. The brand names of the big pharmaceutical corporations that produce most of today's medicines are well known; the origins and costs of the ingredients of those pharmaceuticals are one of today's best-kept trade secrets. From countries around the world, transnational pharmaceutical corporations buy up the medicinal raw materials for pennies, add various other chemicals and preserving agents and sell the finished product for an arm and a leg.

Many of the raw pharmaceutical ingredients come from poor countries, or what were once poor countries, such as China and India. In these now dominant and emerging economies, the rise of a capitalist middle class, urban development, and the investment 'opportunities' these economies present to the world's asset managers, investors and shareholders, means that these countries may now be considered wealthy – except that the vast majority of their populations are still amongst the poorest in the world (David Lazurus, 'Column: Where Do Prescription Drugs Come From? Good Luck Answering That Question', *The Los Angeles Times*, 15 May 2018).

Reverse Aid

The history books of the capitalist oriented education systems are likely to obscure how today's one per cent economic elite acquired dominance and profiteering wealth and continue to pass it on to the next ruling-class generation. Often omitted is the fact that European monarchs conferred corporate status on the groups of businessmen exploiters who established the likes of the Royal African Company set up in the 1660s to engage in the global slave trade, part of the profits to go to the Crown. The history books are likely to print perhaps half a page of the illustrations from old engravings that show how slaves were cram-packed into the slave ships to maximise profits, that half-page often followed by several pages in praise of the parliamentary abolitionists of a couple of hundred years later.

Today's global trade agreements, written in secret behind closed doors, continue to favour today's exploitative and abusive ruling class economic elite through their ownership of today's modern corporations. Those transnational corporations exploit the peoples and raw materials of the global South, that is, appropriate the crude oil of those countries that have little or no control over their own oil industry, use their cheap labour and hoover up their raw materials, minerals, precious metals, medicinal ingredients, agricultural products at low prices, etcetera.

Modern ruling-class domination and exploitation also lie in the perpetual rentierism of today's corporate monarchs, the giant internet firms. Too often forgotten is the fact that governments funded by public taxes first invented the communications and systems technologies on which they are based. Economic activists make the case that to lower costs for their internet services and pay back profits into the public purse, these giant corporations, often using international capitalist law to avoid and evade paying taxes, must be brought into public ownership, the profits used to build hospitals, schools, community centres etcetera.

The continuity of ruling-class dominance and exploitation also lies in the disinvestments in the productive economy and world trade that are made by some of those corporations. The remunerations of the corporate chief executive officers and the unearned income of shareholders now depend on corporate high-risk gambling in the financial markets instead

The economic injustice perpetrated by the ruling-class economic elite also lies in the imposition of 'reverse aid' on the countries of the global South. These ex-colonies, now economically neo-colonised, are forced to pay out more to the economies of the global North than they receive in bank loans, inward investment payment for their raw materials, foreign aid and charitable donations combined.

In 2012, the poor countries of the global South received a total of £1.3 trillion from the countries of the global North but paid out £3.3 trillion to the financial institutions of the governments of the global North. Much of that outflow lies in bank loan interest paid by Third World countries to the Western banks for bank loans. That outflow also includes the 'capital flight', whereby the corrupt 1 per cent wealthy elite of those poor Third World countries, businessmen and women, and politicians, also exploit their populations by siphoning up profits, then using the money to buy up legally untouchable real estate property and business assets in the West. They also use their profits to make global investments through the world's sixty offshore tax havens and the onshore tax havens of the likes of the City of London, Delaware in the USA and other US cities.

The employees of the many Non-Governmental Organisations (NGOs) do good work in trying to help the poor in those Third World countries, often putting themselves at risk in dangerous situations to do so. However, some NGO employees are involved in sexual abuse and exploitation. And, at the behest of some of the NGOs employing them, some NGO workers are also engaged in political interference against the governments of the host countries. It should not go unnoted either that the many thousands of the world's NGO employees, whose wages are paid from the donations given to charitable organisations and from foreign governmental aid, are part of an employment process that also keeps them off the books of the social welfare systems of the global North (Jason Hickel, 'Aid in Reverse: How Poor Countries Develop Rich Countries', *The Guardian*, 14 January 2017; Chapter 18, *Charities and Foreign Aid*).

To get rid of these perennially exploitative practices requires nothing less than that the controlling economic structures of the global capitalist system waste no time instituting fair-exchange-no-robbery trade and investment agreements, anti-corruption banking regulations, international legislation and contract law designed to prevent the likes of reverse aid and capital flight. Instead, the International Monetary Fund and the World Bank proposed merely that the banks of the global North offer 'debt repayment holidays' to the governments of the global South. The presumption was that bank loan interest payment 'holidays' would allow the deliberately impoverished countries to use several years' worth of bank loan interest payments to pay instead for helping to build their infrastructure, roads, sanitation systems, schools etcetera. Bank loan interest payment 'holidays' do not, however, stop the actual accrual of bank interest; do nothing to reduce the national debt; do nothing at all to prevent corporate profiteering; have no effect on corruption and capital flight; and do not even touch the corrupt operations of the offshore and onshore tax havens. Consequently, as far as the Third World Countries are concerned, indeed as far as the goal of achieving anything resembling global economic justice, bank loan interest repayment holidays are about as effective as applying a Band-Aid to metastasising economic cancer.

The United Nations Conference on Trade and Development has most recently declared that to avoid further chaos, disaster and starvation for billions of people in Third World countries, the Northern governments and banks ought to provide urgent and ongoing assistance to these impoverished countries, particularly given the further economic disasters experienced by the poorest countries during the COVID-19 pandemic. Little mention is made of the fair-exchange-no-robbery trade agreements urgently needed, nor, indeed, the compensatory packages to which the countries of the global South are entitled (United Nations Conference on Trade and Development Update Report, 'The Covid-19 Shock to Developing Countries: Towards a "Whatever It Takes" Programme for the Two-Thirds of the World's Population Left Behind', March 2020).

Fair-exchange-no-robbery investment and trade agreements would provide more jobs for the workers of the North, and the corresponding development in the South would provide employment for the workers of the South.

Instead, of the forty most highly indebted 'reverse aid' countries of the global South, the populations of thirty-nine of them are at risk of mass starvation. Mass starvation means more chaos, conflict, and millions of people migrating across the globe in search of survival.

Centuries of ruling-class control over the very narratives of the global economic elite's 500 years of global slavery and the colonisation and neo-colonisation of the countries of the global South have yet to become part of the collective human consciousness. The daily dominations, exploitations and abuses of the poor and working-class majority, of whatever gender, race and sex, by that same ruling-class economic elite and their devotees have also yet to become a significant enough part of the divided-and-conquered consciousness of the 99 per cent majority.

The good news is that populations are beginning to realise how the introduction of non-animal eco-farming and the rewilding of deteriorated land and soil is linked to the regeneration of the atmosphere and the recreation of watercourses. Rewilding and eco-farming must now become key elements of the modern economics of the new era – if the sixth mass extinction is to be avoided, that is, if the catastrophic loss of ecological biodiversity and the resultant climate catastrophe is to be avoided (Vandana Shiva, 'We Must Fight Back Against the 1 Percent to Stop the Sixth Mass Extinction', *Democracy Now*, 22 February 2019; Chapter 3, *Usurious Banking and the Great Depression*). This also means the phasing out of the markets across the world where wild animals and dogs are butchered and eaten. It also means changing consumption patterns of Western populations still hooked on the socio-cultural notion that if animals are treated humanely while alive, it's OK to gas, slaughter and butcher them for human consumption (BBC Three, 'Veganville' Documentary, 2 January 2020).

Populations also know that they cannot allow the drive towards green energy to merge into green capitalism and that the use of consumables such as wood chips and biofuels instead of fossil fuels is not the answer (Michael Moore & Jeff Gibbs, 'Planet of the Humans', *YouTube*, 4 May 2020).

Nevertheless, if the processes of autonomous self-education and the increases in public understanding grows day by day, it is also daily evident that the owners of the means of mass production, finance, and communications continue 24/7 to maintain their tight grip on levers of power. One of the means of holding onto those powers is to engage in every diversionary trick in the book to obstruct the crucial development of the emerging collective public consciousness.

Show and Tell

The UK National Curriculum states that for children to develop their knowledge and understanding of the world, from the age of 7, they must read widely across fiction and nonfiction.

Much of today's literature for young children continues to be based on animal characters talking about, purportedly, matters of fairly universal human concern. There are also plenty of factual books on science, geography, music, art, etcetera. Fictional books for older primary and secondary school youngsters are likely to focus on de-classed single issues of concern to teenagers, for example, self-esteem, family problems, sexual identity, life in a children's home, etcetera. Whatever the issue being examined, it is usually largely authorially snipped off from the socio-economic and socio-cultural contexts in which those 'single' issues are likely to arise. The same is true of the factual books. The result is that children's books and media routinely divert the attention of children and young people away from understanding the socio-economic and socio-cultural matrix under which billions of children and their parents must live. Moreover, the output of just one of today's book publishing, audio-visual media-producing, theme park building conglomerates is translated into 40 languages and sold to 170 countries (Mark Sweeney, 'Entertainment One Takes Control of Peppa Pig Creator in £140m Deal', *The Guardian*, 30 September 2015).

To accept the claim that the publishing and media conglomerates have no commercial choice but to meet public demand by following set-in-stone socio-cultural practices is to ignore the reality that these fat cat conglomerates are also responsible for maintaining and prolonging that demand.

Fortunately, today's mobilisations by young people against the refusals of governments to act to cut the use of fossil fuels quickly enough to prevent the global climate disaster have also led to the production of books and audio-visual media about the climate catastrophe. Unfortunately, most of these materials attribute the climate calamity to an undifferentiated 'we': everyone is equally to blame; no banks or corporations; no battalions of shareholders; no dominating economic class; no colluding governments; no set of politicians are to be held accountable.

Though few in number and under publicised, there are, nevertheless, now enough works of libertarian socialist fiction and nonfiction, including for children, in existence to prove that the routine practice of the production of books and media that set out to divert attention away from socialist thought, speech, feelings and social relations is by no means a guiltless practice

Undoubtedly, to scare the wits out of children by focusing relentlessly on the harsh truths of life is unconscionable. To prevent youngsters from knowing about the in-built structures of the competitive, profiteering capitalist political economy of the societies they inhabit is, however, to insult and distort their inborn intelligence. It is also to deprive youngsters of their right to examine the underlying political, economic and socio-cultural structures of their everyday world, and to consider how those structures are to be changed for the good of all.

Consequently, it surely becomes one of the tasks of socialist and religious leaders who purport to care about economic justice and the intellectual and spiritual freedom of the individual, to demand a modern children's literature and media relevant to the lives and well-being of the vast majority of the world's children at home and abroad who live in conditions of gross economic injustice and who do not enjoy intellectual and spiritual freedoms.

The resultant production of new books, audio-visual media, comics, magazines, computer games needs to be as readily available as the fairytales, fables, myths and legends and the politico-economically decontextualised and de-classed fictions and factual books that continue to be churned out in industrial proportions for today's children.

Instead, in age-related, child-centred language, the new children's literature could show, for instance, how when people across the globe took swift pandemic action for the sake of their families, friends and others stayed at home in self-isolation and stopped using cars and aeroplanes, the massive decline in the use of fossil fuels cleaned up the earth's near atmosphere, land, rivers and seas in a matter of weeks.

Were the public to demand a new literature, there would be every good reason to produce the picture books and videos that reveal the day-to-day consequences of wealth hoarding by the elite one per cent; the results of corporate disinvestment; of the grossly asymmetrical global trade deals; of the abuse of low-waged-labour; of the global capitalist politico-economic structures that by demanding reverse aid from the countries of the global South consign two-thirds of the world's population to unnecessary impoverishment and early deaths. The new modern literature also needs to show what is to be done so that all children can live in decent conditions and can look forward to fulfilling their full human potential.

At the risk of repetition, were the public to demand it, there would be no reason either not to produce the books and audio-visual media that could show how charitable donations and 'reverse' foreign aid does not alter those exploitative relationships, but, on the contrary, helps to keep the abusive capitalist political economy irredeemably in place instead.

Of the earth's seventeen rare earth elements, sixteen of them, plus cobalt, are needed to manufacture a smartphone. Because the cheapest place to mine cobalt is in the Democratic Republic of the Congo (DRC), 60 per cent of the world's cobalt is extracted from the DRCs vast open-pit mines and the smaller 'artisanal' mines that are worked by impoverished labourers, including women and children. The adult workers are paid a pittance a day, and around 35,000 to 40,000 child-labourers, some as young as 6 years old, earn a mere 50 pence for a hard day's labour.

Open-pit mining destroys enormous swathes of land and natural habitats; mine tailings containing mercury and arsenic are dumped into the rivers; the poisoned water supply causes muscular and respiratory illnesses. Through grossly asymmetrical trade deals; indebtedness to the banks of the global North; and 'capital flight' from the DRC, the country does not have sufficient funds to develop its water and sanitation works, which means that the low-paid miners and child slave-labourers of the Congo do not have clean water to drink (Sidharth Kara, 'Is Your Phone Tainted by the Misery of the 35,000 Children in Congo's Mines?' *The Guardian*, Modern Day Slavery Focus, Global Development, 12 October 2018).

Most UK seven-year-olds own a smartphone. Were parents, teachers, professional educationists and the public to demand it, picture-books and audio-visual materials could easily show the stark differences between the daily lives of those UK 7-year-olds and the child slave-labourers of the Congo.

The point being made here is not to ban forthwith the publishing of all children's books with animal characters, or the de-classed single-issue fictions disembedded from the politico-economic contexts in which those 'single' issues are likely to arise. Nor that the factual books on, for instance, the growing of exotic agricultural products for export that fail to reveal the reality of land-grabs and low-waged labour should be removed from the bookshelves of school libraries.

Nor is it being argued that there ought to be an embargo on children's animated cartoon films, which, with their eye-candy colours, special effects and archetypical characters speaking a chirpy mix of street language and magical moralisms, are designed more to beguile than to enlighten.

The contention is simply that all children, rich and poor, male and female, black and white, the religious and not so religious, have a right to know, and an obligation to learn about, the toxic brutalities of the capitalist political economy that have such materially damaging and soul-destroying effects on the lives of billions of young people around the globe.

Young people, indeed people in general, also have the right to know about the alternative politico-economic knowledge and understandings that are geared to uprooting the capitalist ideology and replacing it with a fair-exchange-no-robbery political economy.

People also have the right to counter the diversionary arguments that profiteering economic exploitation and abuse provides employment. Consequently, poor and working-class children, in particular, have the right to the age-related, child-centred narratives that can provide them with the clues and concepts they need to detect the livelihood-wrecking ulterior motives of the likes of the big bad wolves of Wall Street; the employment and public services slashing practices of the tax-evading abusers of the offshore and onshore tax havens – and about the collusions of the governments that support those corrupt activities.

The good news is that the majority of today's populations now understand what indigenous groups have always known: the physical ecology of the planet cannot be ignored.

Populations now also know they cannot allow abusive consumerism to continue; that local and national economies must instead become as sustainably independent as possible; that those social classes and countries that appropriate the highest incomes and wealth of the world for themselves must contribute far more and consume only their fair share.

Were parents, teachers, the professional educators in the university departments, the public and the youngsters themselves to demand it, a new literature and media could become – and perhaps soon enough – the keystone narratives that portray the motivations and actions of all those who work incessantly to ensure that decent, fair-exchange-no-robbery economic exchanges and social relations take precedence.

That sense of fair treatment and justice resides in the everyday exchanges between all those who do all they can to ensure that family members, friends and neighbours survive, thrive and feel free to fulfil their human potential – and the same innate sense of justice also helps drive the protests, campaigns and mobilisations for equal human rights and responsibilities in which increasing numbers of people also take part.

Moreover, parents, relatives, teachers, carers and young people already possess the knowledge, understanding and skills to become the producers of the millions of the oral, written, audio-visual stories of the socio-biological imperatives of everyday socialisms. These are the stories that describe ordinary people living in familiar surroundings and speaking in everyday language; the depictions of the unique yet recognisable personalities possessed by all human beings; the plots, themes and characterisations that enable audiences to honour the emotional power and intelligence held in such narratives; the stories that also allow the reader to revel in the humour of recognition that can also come with richly authentic representations. These are the stories and narratives that emanate from the everyday socialisms that arise from the in-built moral compass possessed by the vast majority of people – which the forces of exploitation constantly seek to distort and deform (Family Book Scheme in Chapter 19, *Educational Apartheid*).

UK Pandemic Message Shifts from 'Stay at Home' to 'Stay Alert'

Prior to the UK government putting legally enforceable social distancing measures in place on 23 March 2020, the UK COVID-19 pandemic infection rate had been doubling every three to four days. Had those social distancing measures been put in place even one week earlier, a leading UK epidemiologist calculated that the lives of 25,000 people who had died from COVID-19 could have been saved.

The economic lockdown and physical distancing had succeeded in reducing the COVID-19 infection and death rate. However, by the end of May, there were still 8000 new infections a day in England and the independent body of scientists that advises the government, the Scientific Advisory Group for Emergencies (Sage), warned the government against lifting the economic lockdowns too soon. Doing so would be likely to cause a second spike in infections and deaths, making a re-imposition of economic lockdown necessary (Sarah Bosley, 'COVID-19 Spreading Too Fast to Lift Lockdown in England – Sage Advises', *The Guardian*, 29 May 2020).

The graphics used by the government in the daily TV updates were not as reliable as they needed to be. In early June 2020, the government had reported a COVID-19 death rate of 40,000, a figure that was 10,000 fewer than the 50,000 recorded by the government's Office for National Statistics. These sorts of discrepancies meant that much of the public did not believe the government's pandemic figures, or believe that some of the government's guidelines and pandemic announcements could be fully trusted.

The mindset of UK government politicians, and, apparently, of the new Labour Party leadership appeared to be nowhere near considering pandemic economics as the opportunity to make massive alterations to the structures of the political economy, that is, to do all that a government can do to save lives *and* to move away from unsustainable capitalist economic growth towards an economically viable, robust and sustainable fair-exchange-no-robbery economy at home and abroad

Millions of people were desperate to get out of lockdown and get back to work to earn a living – if they could – and the drive of government was to get the economy as back to 'normal' as possible.

Less than two months after the lockdown of 23 March 2020, the Conservative government's first move in attempting to open up the UK economy was on 10 May 2020 when it changed its public health message from 'Stay at Home' to 'Stay Alert'. The strategy was firstly to open up the State primary schools to free up parents to get back to work. The British Medical Association first warned against the dangers of opening up the primary schools too soon, then backtracked and changed its mind.

Though there were different rates of infection and deaths in the various local government authorities, the government announced that for Reception age, Year 1 and Year 6 children, by employing social distancing measures in classrooms, corridors and playgrounds, all State primary schools in England would open on 1 June 2020. To those who questioned what would happen when a child, parent, grandparent, teacher, ancillary worker caught the virus, the answers were of the 'we'll cross that bridge when we come to it' variety. The majority of parents and teachers decided to take matters into their own hands instead, and nearly all the State primary schools in England stayed shut on 1 June 2020.

In the US, the gun-toting minority of the devotees of the National Rifle Association, nearly all of them poor and working-class white men desperate to earn a living, claimed that the freedoms guaranteed by the US Constitution and Bill of Rights were being sacrificed to economic lockdowns. They took to the streets to campaign for the opening up of workplaces. Their actions were right up the street of the US president who from day one of the pandemic had argued against economic lockdowns. In campaigning for the lifting of the lockdowns, these supporters of the president appeared to be interpreting 'freedom' as the right to go back to low-paid work, gather in social groups, sit in a bar, eat in a restaurant, go to the hairdressers.

In the UK, the opening up of UK workplaces and non-essential retail outlets depended largely upon people using public transport. Transport union leaders had first talked the talk of keeping pubic transport within the lockdown orbit, until, enticed by government investment for the London transport network, a major transport union then approved the government's back-to-work policy (Jean Shaol, 'UK Government Ties Transport for London Bailout to "Back to Work" Drive', *World Socialist Web Site*, 16 May 2020).

Every worker should join a union, at the very least to lend their weight to a potentially unified majority of workers. However, notwithstanding the existential pressures of the moment, the minute the rank and file abdicates responsibility in favour of allowing union bureaucrats to 'negotiate' with the bosses, then whatever reform the union bureaucracy 'wins' is almost guaranteed to become the longer-term loss for the trade union movement as a whole.

The next stage in the government's strategy was to permit the opening of garden centres, stately homes, car showrooms, hairdressers, hotels, B&Bs

and caravan parks etcetera, providing social distancing measures were put in place. Sports events, football, horse racing, car racing, etcetera, with audience participation by video, would also be allowed to take place. UK pubs and restaurants that put social distancing measures in place could later also be opened, even though infection and death rates had risen in countries that had allowed restaurants and nightclubs to resume business. Close proximity venues such as indoor gyms, swimming pools, spas and casinos were to remain closed.

There is no doubt that working out the possibilities of lifting economic lockdowns is an enormous logistical challenge. Governments caught up in those logistics, inclusive of reducing social distancing from two metres to one metre, appeared, however, to be sidelining their primary duty of care to secure the lives of the population and prevent a second spike in pandemic deaths, which would lead to further economic lockdowns.

Opening up economies also depends on having a viable test, trace and isolate mechanism in place. The contacts of any anyone testing positive for the virus need to be traced so that quarantining can take place. In early June the UK government's commissioning of major commercial firms to institute and manage a much belated national system of testing and tracking was met with distrust and alarm – not least because one of these firms had a record of failing to deliver on previous government-commissioned public service contracts (Lamiat Sabin, Parliamentary Reporter, 'Fury over Serco Plan to Exploit Test and Trace', *The Morning' Star*, 6 June 2020).

The Ongoing Battles

If history tells us that it is through the constant oppositions and struggles of the poor and working-class majority that progress in human rights and responsibilities is made, history also tells us that the one-step-forward-two-steps-backwards reforms achieved do not radically alter the profiteering capitalist political economy. History also shows, however, that despite the enormous obstacles arrayed against them, the organised struggles and mobilisations of poor and working-class people against domination and abuse does not stop.

It is sometimes said that knowledge is not invented, it already exists and only waits instead for human beings to use their inborn intelligence, individually and jointly with others, to come up with all that they need to know. In a brutally abusive and spiritually demeaning world, however, millions of people forsake their innate human intelligence to seek instead uncertain shelter in the 'come-to-us' hierarchical organisations, the religions, trade unions, political parties, etcetera that promise various forms of 'exceptionalism'. All of those hierarchical organisations are intolerant of autonomous thought, and all practice their specific rituals of exclusion.

In the years before the COVID-19 struck, however, significant numbers of an increasingly autonomously well-informed poor and working-class majority had been able to conclude, for instance, that the 'exceptionalism' of the capitalist political economy had hit the buffers.

More people were also joining and working in more organisations that were increasingly mobilising for greater equal human rights and responsibilities.

In India and Africa, millions of women, joined by men, mobilised against endemic sexual exploitation and rape, and also against authoritarian domination, profiteering, abuse and impoverishments.

In Europe, the yellow vest movement mounted weekly demonstrations against the 'democratic' authoritarianism of the French government. In the UK, the campaigning against what many deemed the social murder of the Grenfell fire continued. UK activist groups also campaigned against the effects of the ten years of government austerity policies. Campaign groups also opposed the government's policies designed to further impoverish the UK's working poor and to make it increasingly difficult to try to claim the social welfare benefits needed by more and more people.

And so on.

Nonetheless, local and global protests, campaigns and mobilisations had failed, so far, to reach the tipping point where change appeared to be truly on the cards. Such a move would mean, for instance, that US voters would no longer opt to be led by a corrupt billionaire US president; in Europe, Latin America and elsewhere, populist right-wing governments would no longer be electable; in the UK, half the population would no longer allow themselves to be persuaded to elect a political party headed by a prime minister who once believed in an imaginary EU/UK customs border down the middle of the Irish sea.

Though for the last seventy-five years or so new legal rights for women, black people and the disenfranchised poor and working-class have been continuously fought for and won, over the last fifty years or so, the owners of the means of production, finance and communications, and the governments that work to support them, have systematically downgraded the public services, health care, social housing, educational provision, employment rights, etcetera. Governments have also continuously worked to keep those in command and control on top, locally and globally. For instance, mid-pandemic, in the early months of 2020, mercenaries were sent by groups backed by the US government to kidnap the elected president of Venezuela. The US government also imposed economic sanctions on the people and government of war-exhausted Syria. A joint project by the US government and a giant private corporation sent two civilian astronauts into space, a precursor to space tourism, even to the colonisation of Mars. That same private space travel corporation also sold contracts to the US government to enable the US government to use the corporation's private launch facilities to deliver payloads related to 'national security', a euphemism for cyber warfare – or worse. Definitely not done was the funding of down-to-earth infrastructure projects to ensure that, for instance, the poor children of the Congo have clean water to drink.

And so on.

This sort of 'business as usual' command and control continues also in the UK. For example, in the two years after the UK Grenfell fire disaster, 56,000 people have no choice but to continue to live in fear in buildings still covered in the type of flammable cladding that caused the Grenfell fire to spread in minutes and kill seventy-two people. The UK Department Work and Pensions continues to withhold 'benefits' from those who cannot live without them. Furthermore, after the DWP's routine denial of claims submitted by the disabled, their desperate appeals claims accompanied by copiously detailed medical evidence are now shoved to the back of the interminably long queue newly created by the millions of people suddenly unemployed by the pandemic of COVID-19. On the international level, the UK government continues with its pursuit of global trade deals designed to advantage the UK and the transnational corporate owners of the means of production, finance and communications. The UK armaments export trade continues to make big profits.

And so on.

In the US on 1 May 2020, led by the Black Lives Matter movement, groups of unemployed and low-paid US workers mobilised against the US government's policies to lift the COVID-19 economic lockdowns and to drive the poor and working-class majority back to precarious work in unsafe workplaces. The campaign slogans were such as 'No Work, No Shopping, No Rent'. In other countries across the globe, similar May Day demonstrations also took place

On 28 May 2020 in Minneapolis, Minnesota, USA, four routinely maleducated armed white police officers detained an unarmed poor black man. The most senior of those policemen knelt on the black man's neck for eight minutes and forty-six seconds until George Floyd was dead. Caught on surveillance cameras and by the public on multiple mobile phones, the video clip of that police murder went viral around the world. Led again by the Black Lives Matter movement, tens of thousands of protestors – black and white – ignoring the police and National Guard curfews (and too often also ignoring pandemic social distancing) took to the streets across seventy-five US cities to demonstrate against the continual police killing of black people. Campaign slogans read 'Abolish the Police', 'No Justice, No Peace'.

In Washington DC, riot-geared policemen used tear gas, flash grenades and 'non-lethal projectiles' against campaigners to clear the way for the US president to walk over to a church vandalised the night before so that he could be photographed standing outside the church holding a bible aloft in his hand.

The protests over George Floyd's murder, and against the systemic global racist exploitation and abuse the murder signified, spread to Canada, the UK, Germany, France, Spain, Australia, South Korea, Belgium. In the UK city of Bristol, built like so many other cities on the proceeds of the global slave trade, today's modern Bristol protestors, multi-racial groups of young black and white people, had toppled the statue of slave trader

Edward Colston from its plinth, rolled the statue through the streets and shoved it into the waters of Bristol harbour. The UK prime minister and his home secretary declared the actions of the Bristol protestors as thuggery by lawless mobs.

In the US, TV pundits decried George Floyd's murder as a consequence of lousy police training combined with the unfortunate election of a 'bad apple' racist president. Several US mayors and governors ordered their police forces to stop using violent means when making arrests. Millions of people believed that the wife of the black, 'I Have a Drone' ex-president would be an excellent candidate to replace the current US president at the next election. That her ex-president husband had dropped more bombs on the world than his predecessor, and that drug-crime, police violence and the killing of black people on US streets increased during his tenure were not so much forgotten facts but information not generally known by the majority of the US public in the first place.

The embedded profiteering domination and abuses of the capitalist politico-economic system will not be altered by banning police from using chokeholds when arresting and carting the systemically criminalised off to jail – nor by replacing a corrupt, narcissistic, racist, sociopathic president with a somewhat more empathetic personality.

On 13 June 2020, groups of young, white UK neo-fascist men travelled to London's Trafalgar Square with the intent of attacking those who were campaigning against the murder of George Floyd, and all that it signified in local and global terms.

On that same day, in the city of Atlanta, Georgia, USA, the birthplace of Martin Luther King Jr, another armed white policeman shot another unarmed black man dead.

There can be little doubt that amongst enormous questions of the current era is whether the poor and working-class majority, black and white, can and will develop the strategic means necessary, locally and globally, to unify itself soon enough for long enough to undertake the tremendous collaborative mobilisation and daily organisational work required to uproot the political economy of brutally exploitative capitalism, and – *at the same time* – establish instead the robustly viable politico-economic structures founded on nothing less than the democratic socialist principles and practices of reverence for life, equal human rights and responsibilities for all.

Notes

1. 'About BIS, Overview,' Bank of International Settlements (1930–present), Basel, Switzerland, <http://www.bis.org/about/>.
2. Yuri Rubtsov, 'History of World War II: Nazi Germany was financed by the Federal Reserve and the Bank of England', Centre for Research on Globalisation, 2018 (<http://www.globalresearch.org>).
3. 'International Bankers Famous Quotes on Banking (1694–2009)', Conspiracy Analyst.org.
4. 'The Great Depression', Wikipedia, 2019; 'Hooverville', Wikipedia, 2019.
5. 'Women in Nazi Germany', History Documentary Films, YouTube, 18 October 2015.
6. 'Conscientious Objection in Britain, 1914–1945', Peace Pledge Union, <http://www.ppu.org.uk>.
7. James Meek, 'Sale of the century: the privatisation scam', *The Guardian*, 22 August 2014.
8. Peter Latham, *The State and Local Government: Towards a New Basis for 'Local Democracy' and the Defeat of Big Business Control*, London: Manifesto Press, 2011.
9. 'Five richest families in the UK worth more than the poorest 20% in society', *The Telegraph*, 17 March 2014.
10. Gen. Wesley Clark, *Winning Modern Wars*, New York: Perseus Books, 2003, p. 130.
11. Richard Norton Taylor, 'Afghanistan war has cost Britain more than £37bn, new book claims', *The Guardian*, 30 May 2013.
12. *We Are the Many*, dir. Amir Amirani, documentary DVD, Universal Pictures, August 2016.
13. Chris Ames and Jamie Doward, 'Revealed: Chilcot inquiry set up "to avoid blame"', *The Observer*, 20 November 2016, p. 21.
14. 'Protests against intervention in Iraq 2002–03', Wikipedia, 2019.
15. Seamus Milne, 'If the Libyan war was about saving lives, it was a catastrophic failure', The Guardian, 26 October 2011.
16. Ian Sinclair, 'No, the intervention in Libya wasn't a success', Stop the War Coalition, 24 June 2016.

17   Rob Merrick, 'David Cameron "ultimately responsible" for Libya collapse and the rise of ISIS, Commons report concludes', *The Independent*, 24 September 2016.
18   Anne Marie Hemanstine, 'Examples of Petrochemicals and Petroleum products', *ThoughtCo*, 23 December 2018.
19   Tom Philpott, 'No, GMOs Didn't Create India's Farmer Suicide Problem, But …', *Mother Jones*, 30 September 2015.
20   Andrew Singer, 'In Breast Implants Scandal, Where Was Dow Corning's Concern for Women?', *Ethikos*, Corporate Conduct Quarterly, June 1994.
21   'London 2012: Dow chemical deal is fine by me, says David Cameron', *The Guardian*, 12 March 2012; and 'London 2012: How does Dow Chemical gain from Olympics?', BBC News, 23 January 2012.
22   John Simkin, 'The 1888 London Matchgirls Strike', *Spartacus Educational*, 2017.
23   Tariq Modood, *Essays on Secularism and Multiculturalism*, London: Rowman & Littlefield, May 2019.
24   Geraldine Bedell, 'Coming out of the Dark Ages', *The Guardian*, 24 June 2007.
25   Adrian Smith, 'The Lucas Plan: what can it tell us about democratising society today?', *The Guardian*, 22 January 2014.
26   Bethan Bell and Shabnam Mahmood, 'Grunwick dispute: What did the "strikers in saris" achieve?', BBC News, 10 September 2016.
27   Seamus Milne, 'During the miners' strike, Thatcher's secret state was the real enemy within', *The Guardian*, 3 October 2014.
28   Donald Macintyre, 'How the miners' strike of 1984–85 changed Britain forever', *New Statesman*, American Edition, 16 June 2014.
29   David Conn, 'Hillsborough disaster: deadly mistakes and lies that lasted decades', *The Guardian*, 26 April 2016.
30   Sam Volpe, '"She is a martyr":25 years on, Joy Gardner's mother is still fighting for justice after death in custody', *Ham & High*, 26 July 2018.
31   'Murder of Stephen Lawrence, 1993', Wikipedia, 2019.
32   Mark Townsend, 'No convictions over 500 black and Asian deaths in custody', *The Guardian*, 21 March 2015.
33   'Innateness Hypothesis', Wikipedia, 2019.
34   Sarah Cassidy, 'Feminism to be dropped from A-level politics syllabus', *Independent*, 19 November 2015.
35   Kelsey McEachern, 'Vygotsky's Socio-cultural Theory', YouTube, October 2016.
36   Jeremy Sawyer, 'Vygotsky's revolutionary theory of psychological development', *Internationalist Socialist Review*, Issue 93, Summer 2014.
37   M. O. Grady, 'The Origins of Children's Literature', *British Library Newsletter*, 2014.
38   'Real books beat reading schemes', BBC Three News, 19 January 2002.

39 Jack Zipes, 'Breaking the Disney Spell', Academia.edu, 1995.
40 Prof. Michael Behe, *Darwin's Black Box: The Biochemical Challenge to Evolution*, New York: Touchtone Press, 1998.
41 *Domestic Impact of World War One – Society and Culture*, BBC Bitesize History.
42 Ross Clark, 'Why housing associations are the true villains of the property crisis', *The Spectator*, 25 July 2015.
43 John Smyth, Terry Wrigley and Melissa Benn, *Living on the Edge, Rethinking Poverty, Class and School*, New York: Peter Lang, 2013, Chapter 7, 'Neoliberal School Reform: Blaming Teachers, Blaming Schools', p. 141.
44 Josie Levine (ed.), *Developing Pedagogies in the Multi-lingual Classroom*, London: Falmer Press, 1990.
45 William Stewart, 'Why "Ultra-looney" ILEA Was Actually Ahead of its Time', *Times Educational Supplement*, 3 April 2015.
46 Merryn Hutchings, *The impact of accountability measures on children and young people*, Report Commissioned by the National Union of Teachers, 4 April 2015 (<http://www.teachers.org.uk/files/exam-factories.pdf>).
47 Ellie Concannon-Gay, *Does Education Fail Young People?* Unpublished A-Level sociology project, September 2016.
48 'Exam stress overwhelming for thousands of children', NSPCC, 12 May 2017.
49 C. Rodway *et al.*, 'Suicide in children and young people in England: a consecutive case series', *The Lancet Psychiatry*, 3 August 2016.
50 Michael Young, 'Down with meritocracy', *The Guardian*, 29 June 2001.
51 L. Lightfoot, 'Nearly half of England's teachers plan to leave in next five years', *The Guardian*, 24 October 2016.
52 'What Does the Academies Act 2010 mean for State Education?', Anti-academies Alliance, <http://antiacademies.org.uk>.
53 John Dickens, 'Government's £8m academy and free school bail-out', *Schools Week*, 9 May 2016.
54 Oliver Wright, 'Academies Criticised Over Payments to Board Members', *Independent*, 17 September 2014.
55 Daniel Boffey, 'Academy Chain Accused of "Privatisation by stealth" Over Plan to Outsource Jobs', *The Guardian*, 20 September 2014.
56 Jessica Shepherd, 'Academies bill is anti-democratic, lawyers warn', *The Guardian*, 6 June 2010.
57 *Underachievement in Education by White Working Class Children*, House of Commons, Parliamentary Select Committee on Education Report, June 2014.
58 Holly Watt, 'David Laws suspended over pages of expenses claims', *The Telegraph*, 12 May 2011.
59 'EdTech comes of age', Media Planet, Future of Technology, 2017.

60 James Tweedie, 'Kenya will crack down on Gate's filthy shack schools', *The Morning Star*, 7 December 2016.
61 'UK aid money linked to chain of private schools in Uganda closed down by High Court', Global Justice Now, 7 November 2016.
62 Warwick Mansell and Louis Goddard, 'Ofsted admits complaint about school's prior knowledge of inspections', *The Guardian*, 9 September 2014.
63 Padraig Flanagan, 'Ofsted inspections: "you'd be better off flipping a coin"', *The Telegraph*, 7 November 2015.
64 Robert Watson and Nigel Hawkes, 'How many children are murdered in Britain every year', *Straight Statistics*, 23 September 2010.
65 Patrick Butler, 'Sharon Shoesmith wins appeal against sacking over Baby P tragedy', *The Guardian*, 24 May 2011.
66 *Baby P: The Untold Story*, BBC One, 27 October 2014.
67 Rowena Mason, 'What is David Cameron doing now?', *The Guardian*, 29 December 2017. Mikey Smith, 'What is Ed Balls doing now? Life after parliament for the self-tweeting ex-MP', *The Mirror*, 29 April 2016.
68 'About Us', Ofsted, Gov., UK.
69 *Office for Standards in Education, Children's Services and Skills*, Annual Report and Accounts, 2017–18.
70 'Adult Literacy', National Literacy Trust, 2017.
71 Lynn Davis, Clive Harber and Hiromi Yamashita, *Global Citizenship: The Needs of Teachers and Learners*, Centre for International Educational Research (CIER), University of Birmingham, Report for Department for International Development, Key Findings, September 2014.
72 'Understanding the Mondragon Worker Cooperative Corporation', YouTube, April 2014.
73 'Evergreen Cooperatives', YouTube, March 2014.
74 'The Marcora Law – Multiplying the employees' stakes', Wikipreneurship, 25 September 2015.
75 'Gramsci and Hegemony', Power Cube: Understanding Power for Social Change.
76 Richard A. Werner, Professor of Banking and Finance, Linacre College, University of Oxford, <https:/professsorwerner.org/blog/>.
77 Richard A. Werner, The Free Lunch Videos & BlogSpot, 2011–19.
78 'The Iron Triangle – The Carlyle Group Exposed', based on a book by Dan Briody (Hoboken, NJ: J. Wiley, 2004), YouTube, May 2012.
79 Jacques Rancière, *The Ignorant School Master*, see Introduction by Kristin Ross, 'The Practice of Equality', Stanford, CA: Stanford University Press, 1991.
80 Sugata Mitra, 'Kids can teach themselves', TED Talk at LIFT, 2007, *Paulo Freire (1921–1997) Prospects: The Quarterly Review of Comparative Education* (Paris:

UNESCO, International Bureau of Education). Heinz Peter Gerhard 1993 (<http://www.ibe.unesco.org/sites/default/files/Freire.PDF>).
81 Paulo Freire, *Education for Critical Consciousness*, London: Continuum Books, 2012.
82 Paulo Freire, *Pedagogy of the Oppressed*, London: Penguin Education, 1972, Chapter 2, p. 45.
83 Maria M. Velho, *Literacy in Brazil: For What Purposes?* Working Papers in Educational Linguistics, 1991 (<https://repository.upenn.edu/cgi/viewcontent.cgi?article=1068&context=wpel>).
84 Paulo Freire, *Education for Critical Consciousness*, London: Continuum Books, 2012, p. 50, note 16.
85 Ibid., p. 43.
86 *UK 2010 Equality Act, 2010*. <http://www.equalityhumanrights.com/sites/default/files/religion-or-belief-guide-to-the-law.pdf>.

Bibliography

Achcar, Gilbert (2017). 'Morbid Symptoms. What did Gramsci mean and how does it apply to our time?', *International Socialist Review*, Issue 108, May 2019.
Adams, Richard (2018). 'David Meller, the Tory donor "desperate to be part of establishment"', *The Guardian*, 24 January.
Agland, Phil (2016). *China: Between Clouds and Dreams*, Channel 4 docu-series, available on YouTube, November.
Al Jazeera (2013) *The Secret of the Seven Sisters*, 4 of 4: 'A Time for Lies', YouTube, 26 April.
Ames, Chris, and Jamie Doward (2016). 'Revealed: Chilcot Inquiry set up "to avoid blame"', *The Observer*, 20 November, p. 21.
Amirani, Amir (2016). *We Are the Many*, documentary DVD, We Are the Many Productions, Universal Studios.
Anti-academies Alliance (2010). *What does the Academies Act 2010 mean for State education?* <http://antiacademies.org.uk/>.
'Antonio Gramsci (1891–1937)', Wikipedia, 2019.
'Antonio Gramsci', Wikiquote, as cited in Davidson (1977), *Antonio Gramsci: Towards an Intellectual Biography*, London: Merlin Press.
'Apoptosis', Wikipedia, 2019.
Arnett, George (2014). 'Elitism Britain – breakdown by profession', *The Guardian*, 18 August.
Ashcroft, Ross (2012). *Four Horsemen*, Motherlode Productions, UK, 14 March.
Associated Press (2019). 'Jury orders Monsanto to pay £2billion in weed killer cancer case', *PBS Newshour*, 13 May.
Bank of International Settlements (1930–present), Basel, Switzerland, 'About BIS, Overview', http://www.bis.org/about/index.htm.
Baptiste, Desiree (2017). 'Joanna Lumley's India: is her show guilty of airbrushing history?' *The Guardian*, 19 July.
Barratt, Luke (2017). 'Fire risk assessor for Grenfell Tower Revealed', *Inside Housing*, 26 June.
Barratt, Luke (2019). 'Revealed: UK banks' £25 billion support for global coal', *Greenpeace Unearthed*, 5 December.
Bartosch, Jo (2017). 'It isn't the stigma that is killing sex workers', *The Morning Star*, 6 September.

BBC Bitesize History, *Society and Culture: Domestic Impact of World War One Rent Strikes (Revision 4)*.
BBC Films and BFI (2016). *I, Daniel Blake*, dir. Ken Loach, Sixteen Films, Why Not & Wild Bunch Productions, 21 October.
BBC Four (2015). *The Secret Lives of 4 and 5 Year Olds*, February.
BBC Four (2018). 'Poisoning America: The Devil We Know', *Storyville*, November.
BBC News (2016). 'EU referendum: the results in maps and charts', 4 June.
BBC News (2018). 'Final call to save the word from 'climate catastrophe'', Matt McGrath, Environmental correspondent, Incheon, South Korea 8 October.
BBC News (2018). 'Why did the council "house" me in a tent?', 30 October.
BBC News Education (2002). 'Real Books Beat Reading Schemes', 19 January.
BBC One (1966). *Cathy Come Home*, The Wednesday Play, Ken Loach film, 16 November.
BBC One (2011). *Poor Kids*, three-part documentary, June.
BBC One (2014). *Baby P: The Untold Story*, 27 October.
BBC One (2017). 'Damian Green and John McDonnell on costing manifestos', *Andrew Marr Show*, YouTube video, 2 May 2017 (at 28:47 minutes).
BBC One (2019). 'Climate Change – The Facts', 18 April.
BBC One (2020) *Question Time*, 19 March 2020.
BBC Radio 4 (2017). *Where Are All the Working-Class Writers?*, November.
BBC Radio 4 (2020) 'Game changer: how the UK played during coronavirus, 26 May 2020, 8 pm.
BBC Radio 4 Great Lives Series 50 (2019). 'Jeremy Paxman Nominates Lord Shaftesbury', 20 December.
BCC Two (2015). *Britain's Forgotten Slave Owners*, dir. David Olusoga.
BBC Two (2018). *No More boys and Girls: Can Our Kids go Gender Free?*, dir. Dr Javid Abdelmoneim.
BBC Two (2019). 'The Scandal That Changed Britain', 13 April.
BBC Two (2019). *The Unwanted: The Secret Windrush Files*, dir. David Olusoga, 24 June 2014.
BBC Three (2020) 'Veganville' documentary, 2 January 2020.
Beckett, Andy (2015). 'The right to buy: the housing crisis that Thatcher built', *The Guardian*, 25 August.
Beckett, Andy (2019). 'The new left economists: how a network of thinkers is transforming capitalism', *The Guardian*, 25 June.
Bedell, Geraldine (2007). 'Coming out of the Dark Ages', *The Guardian*, 24 June.
Behe, Michael (1998). *The Biochemical Challenge to Evolution*, New York: Touchstone Press.
Bell, Bethan, and Shabnam Mahmood (2016). 'Grunwick dispute: what did the "strikers in saris" achieve?', BBC News, 10 September.

Bernays, Edward (1928). *Propaganda*, New York: Ig Publishing, 2005.
Bernays, Edward (2012). *Selling War*, YouTube, November.
Beyond Extinction Economics (BEE) network (2018). 'Awkward questions about diversity', Letter to *The Guardian*, 15 March.
Bilek, Jennifer (2018). 'Who are the Rich White Men Institutionalizing Transgender Ideology?', *The Federalist*, 20 February.
Boffey, Daniel (2014). 'Academy chain accused of 'privatisation by stealth' over plans to outsource jobs', *The Guardian*, 20 September.
The Borgen Project, *Malthusianism: Theories on Poverty and Aid.*
Bosche, Susanne (2000). 'Jenny, Eric, Martin ... and me', *The Guardian*, 31 January.
Bosley, Sarah (2020) 'COVID-19 spreading too fast to lift lockdown in England - Sage advises', *The Guardian* Health Editor, 29 May 2020.
Bourdieu, Pierre (1986). 'The Forms of Capital', in J. Richardson, *Handbook of Theory and Research for the Sociology of Education*, pp. 241–58.
Boyle, Darren (2020) 'Chancellor Rishi Sunak warns ministers "can NOT save every UK job" as World Trade Organisations says coronavirus will spark the worst global recession in our life times', *MailOnline*, 8 April 2020.
Brignell, Victoria (2010). 'The eugenics movement Britain wants to forget', *New Statesman*, 9 December.
Brilliant, Dr Larry (2006) 'My Wish: Help me stop pandemics', *TED talk*, February 2006.
Brooks, Richard (2018). *Bean Counters, The Triumph of the Accountants and How they Broke Capitalism*, London: Atlantic Books.
Brown, Faye (2019). 'Investigation finds 88% of Tory ads misleading compared to 0% for Labour', *Metro*, 10 December.
Butler, Patrick (2011). 'Sharon Shoesmith wins appeal against sacking over Baby P tragedy', *The Guardian*, 24 May.
Butler, Patrick, and Dawn Foster (2017). 'Shelter under microscope over partnerships with construction industry', *The Guardian*, 27 June.
'Campaign for Homosexual Equality', Wikipedia, 2019.
Carrington, Damian (2018). 'What is biodiversity and why does it matter to us?', *The Guardian*, 12 March.
Carrington, Damian (2019). 'Air pollution damages "every organ in the body"', *The Guardian*, 18 May.
Carson, Rachel (1962). *Silent Spring*, London: Penguin Modern Classics, 2000.
Cassidy, Sarah (2015). 'Feminism to be dropped from A-level politics syllabus', *The Independent*, 19 November.
Cavallo, Francesca, and Elena Favelli (2007). 'Sexist stories keep girls down. A new kind of heroine can set them free', *The Guardian*, 13 April.

CBC News (2017) 'If you're addicted to your Smartphone (Marketplace)', 3 November 2017.
Centre for Literacy in Primary Education (CLPE) (2017). *Reflecting Realities within the UK, Survey of Ethnic Representation within UK Children's Literature*.
Chalabi, Mona (2014). 'UK's gambling habit: what's really happening?', *The Guardian*, 8 January.
Channel 4 (2018). 'Brexit: The Uncivil War', drama documentary, 27 December.
Channel 4 (2019). 'The Cure', drama documentary, 19 December.
Channel 4 (2020). 'Apocalypse Cow: How Meat Killed the Planet', 8 January.
'Chomsky on Lenin, Trotsky, Socialism and the Soviet Union', YouTube, undated.
Chulov, Martin (2017). 'How the Saudi Elite became five-star prisoners in the Riyadh Ritz Carlton', *The Guardian*, 6 November.
'Circular 10/65', Wikipedia, 2019.
Clark, Gen. Wesley (2003). *Winning Modern Wars*, New York: Perseus Books, p. 130.
Clark, Ross (2015). 'Why housing associations are the true villains of the property crisis', *The Spectator*, 5 July.
Clarke, Cath (2018). 'Nae Pasaran review – how the Chilean coup was protested in East Kilbride', *The Guardian*, 31 October.
Coburg, Tom (2020) 'Jonson's coronavirus chaos criticised by UK doctors demanding greater transparency', *The Canary*, 15 March 2020.
CommonSpace, Scotland 2018. *'Activist group dumps rotten food in support of Yarls Wood hunger strikers'*, 2 March
Concannon-Gay, Ellie (2016). *Does Education Fail Young People*, Unpublished A-level sociology project, September.
Conn, David (2016). 'Hillsborough disaster: deadly mistakes and lies that lasted decades', *The Guardian*, 26 April.
ConspiracyAnalyst.org.(2019). '1694–2009 International Bankers Famous Quotes on Banking'.
The Corbett Report (2018). 'NGOs Are the Deep State's Trojan Horses', Open Intelligence Report, YouTube, 21 May.
Cuccinello, Hayley C. (2020) 'Billionaire tracker: Actions the world's Wealthiest are taking in response to the coronavirus pandemic', *Forbes*, 17 March 2020.
Curtis, Polly (2011). 'Reality check: how much did the banking crisis cost taxpayers?', *The Guardian* News Blog, 12 September.
Darwin, Charles (1859). *On the Origin of the Species by Means of Natural Selection, or the Preservation of Favoured Races in the Struggle for Life*, Hertfordshire: Wordsworth Classics of World Literature, 1998.
Darwin, Charles (1871). *The Descent of Man*, Hertfordshire: Wordsworth Editions, 2013.

Darwin, Charles (1876). *The Autobiography of Charles Darwin*, pp. 119–21 (<http://www.pbs.org/wgbh/evolution/educators/course/session2/explain_c.html>).
'Darwin, Health', Wikipedia, 2019.
Darwin Correspondence project, Cambridge University.
'David Attenborough', Wikipedia, 2019.
Davies, Bob (2020) 'The inside story of the UK's NHS coronavirus ventilator challenge', *The Guardian*, 4 May 2020.
Davis, Lynn, Clive Harber and Hiromi Yamashita (2014). *Global Citizenship: The Needs of Teachers and Learners*, Key Findings of Report for Department of International Development, Centre for International Education and Research (CIER), School of Education, University of Birmingham.
Davitt, Helen (1990). 'Political and Moral Contexts in English and ESL Teaching', in Josie Levine (ed.), *Bilingual learners and the mainstream curriculum*, London: Falmer Press, 1990.
Defarge, N., J. Spiroux de Vendemois and G.-E. Séralini (2018). *Toxicity of formulas and heavy metals in glysophate-based herbicide and other pesticides*, Elsevier Toxology Reports, Vol. 5, 2018, pp. 156–63.
Denton, Michael (2016). *Biology of the Baroque*, YouTube, February 2016.
Department for Education, National Statistics (2018). *School pupils and their characteristics*, 28 June.
Dickens, Charles (1843). *A Christmas Carol*, Wikipedia, February 2020.
Dickens, John (2016). 'Government's £8m academy and free school bail-out', *Schools Week*, 9 May.
Dore, Jimmy (2016). 'Why Are We in Syria? Shocking Facts Media Doesn't Tell You', YouTube, 26 October.
Duell, Mark (2018). 'Betting firm William Hill is fined £6.2m for breaking anti-money laundering and social responsibility rules', *Daily Mail*, 20 February 2018.
Duff, Carol (2019). 'Chlorpyrifos: Toxic Pesticide Harming Our Environment and Children', Earthjustice, *Veterans Today*, 24 March.
Duffell, Nick (2014). *Wounded Leaders: British Elitism and the Entitlement Illusion*, London: Lone Arrow Press, 7 June.
Eastman, Max (1925). *Leon Trotsky: The Portrait of a Youth*, New York, Greenberg, 1925.
The Economist (2017). 'They Just Kept Coming, America's Secret War in Laos', 21 January 2017.
Educational International: <http://www.ei.ie.org>.
Empire Files (2019). 'Abbey Martin and Lowkey: A Deeper Look at the UK Election', YouTube, 23 December.
Engels, Friedrich (1844). *The Condition of the Working Class in England in 1844*, Panther Press, 1976.
Equality Act UK 2010, see *Religion or belief: a guide to the law*.

Erin Brokovich (2000), Universal Studios, 17 March.
ETC Group (2008). *Who Owns Nature, Corporate Power and the Final Frontier in the Commodification of Life*, Communiqué Number 100, 11 November.
European Parliament Briefing (2016). *TAPI natural gas pipeline project: boosting trade and remedying instability?* 26 November.
Evergreen Cooperatives, YouTube, March 2014.
'Expenses claims list in the United Kingdom parliamentary expenses scandal', Wikipedia, 2019.
Feinstein, Andrew (2011). *Shadow World, Inside the Global Arms Trade*, London: Penguin 2011.
Flanagan, Padraig (2015). 'Ofsted inspections: "you'd be better off flipping coin"', *The Telegraph*, 7 November.
Freire, Paulo (1972). *Pedagogy of the Oppressed*, London: Penguin Education.
Freire, Paulo (1974). *Education for Critical Consciousness*, London: Continuum International Publishing Group, 2012.
'Freire, Paulo (1921–1997)', Wikipedia, 2019.
Frelette, Giles (2014). 'Jose Mujica: is this the world's most radical president?', *The Guardian*, 29 September.
Gallagher, Paul, and David Watts (2013). 'Revealed: How the betting industry keeps MPs onside', *The Independent*, 10 February.
Gardner, Bill (2020) 'Exclusive: Millions of pieces of PPE are being shipped from Britain despite NHS shortages', *The Telegraph*, 21 April 2020.
Garner, Richard (2014). 'Private school fees scheme allows wealthy parents to save thousands of pounds in tax', *The Independent*, 21 February.
Gavrielatos, Angelo (2017). 'The Global battle for the soul of education', *The Morning Star*, 14 April.
'Genie Energy', Wikipedia, 2019.
Gerhard, Heinz-Peter (1993). 'Paulo Freire (1921–1997)', *Prospects: the quarterly review of comparative education* (Paris: UNESCO, International Bureau of Education <http://www.ibe.unesco.org.default/files/Freire.PDF>).
Gibson, Owen (2012). 'London 2012: Dow Chemical deal is fine by me, says David Cameron', *The Guardian*, 12 March.
Gillam, Carey (2017). *Whitewash – The Story of a Weed Killer, Cancer and the Corruption of Science*, Chapter 11, 'Under the Influence', Washington, DC: Island Press, 2017.
Gillard, Derek (2011). 'Education in England: a history of our schools', <http://www.educationengland.org.uk/history>.
Glasgow Media Group (2019). *Bad News for Labour: Antisemitism, the Party and Public Belief*, Greg Philo, Mike Berry, Justin Schlosberg, Antony Lerman and David Miller, *Pluto Press*, September 2019.

Global Response: <http://www.unite4education.org>.
Global Justice Now (2017). 'UK aid money linked to chain of private schools in Uganda closed down by High Court', 7 November 2016.
'Glysophate', Wikipedia, 2019.
Gov.UK National Statistics (2018). 'Schools, Pupils and their Characteristics', January.
Grady, M. O. (2014). 'The origins of Children's Literature', *British Library Newsletter* (<http://www.bl.uk/romantics-and-victorians/articles/the-origins-of-childrens-literature>).
Gramsci, Antonio (2005). *Selections from Prison Notebooks*, London: Lawrence & Wishart.
'Gramsci and Hegemony', *Powercube: Understanding Power for Social Change*.
'The Great Depression (1930s)', Wikipedia, 2019.
'The Green Revolution', Wikipedia, 2019.
'Greenham Common Women's Peace Camp (1981–2000)', Wikipedia, 2019.
Greenpeace International (2018). 'Rantan: the story of dirty palm oil', YouTube, August.
Grierson, Jamie (2016). 'Britain's newest gambling addiction charity funded by betting firms', *The Guardian*, 19 August.
Griffiths, Robert (2020). 'The way forward? Organise, organise and organise', *The Morning Star*, 1 February.
The Guardian newspaper supplements (2017). '1930s Revisited: The Great Depression and the Breakdown of Society. We'd been cowed by the Depression, that's why we could fight the war', 4 March.
Gye, Hugo (2019). 'Conservatives raise 26 times as much as Labour from rich donors including Trailfinders and Iceland Boss', *iNews*, 21 November.
Harrington, Brooke (2016). 'How to hide it – inside the secret world of wealth managers', *The Guardian*, 2 September.
Hazarika, Sanjoy (1984). 'Mother Theresa Carries her Message to Bhopal', *New York Times*, 12 December.
Helm, Toby (2018). 'Exam reforms boost private pupils in race for universities', *The Observer*, 29 December.
Hemanstine, Anne Marie (2018). 'Examples of Petrochemicals and Petroleum products', *ThoughtCo*, 23 December.
Hickel, Jason (2017) 'Aid in reverse: How poor countries develop rich countries', *The Guardian*, 14 January 2017.
Hirschman, Alan (1977). *The Passions and the Interests: Political Arguments for Capitalism before its Triumph*, Princeton, NJ: Princeton University Press.
Hirst, Michael (2012). 'London 2012: How does Dow Chemical gain from Olympics?', BBC News, 2 January.
History Documentary Films, 'Women in Nazi Germany', YouTube, October 2015.
History International (1988). *Economics: Banking with Hitler*, Top Documentary Films.

'Hooverville (1930s)', Wikipedia, 2019.
House of Commons Committee of Public Accounts (2018), *NHS Continuing Healthcare Funding*, Thirteenth Report of Session 2017–19, 10 January.
House of Commons Education Committee Report (2014). *Underachievement in Education by White Working Class Children*, June.
'How to lose £7 billion pounds' (2018), *Dispatches*, Channel 4.
Huffington Post (2017). 'Martin Luther King was a Democratic Socialist'.
Hunter, Paul (2020) 'Why the UK failed to get coronavirus testing up to speed', *The Guardian*, 1 April 2020.
Hutchings, Merryn (2015). 'The impact of accountability measures on children and young people'. June 2015 (<http://www.teachers.org.uk/files/exam-factories.pdf>).
The Independent (2018), 'Soil tests around Grenfell Tower reveal "huge concentrations of toxins"', 13 October.
INFO Truth (2015). 'Which 5 people own the UK mainstream media?', YouTube, 8 January.
Inman, Philip (2019). 'Labour would expand scope of Bank's powers to help meet carbon targets', *The Guardian*, 25 June.
'Innateness Hypothesis', Wikipedia, 2019.
Inside Job – The 2008 Meltdown Was Avoidable (2010), Charles Ferguson (dir. and writer), Sony Pictures Classics.
International Consortium of Investigative Journalists report (2017). *Paradise Papers: The True Stories Behind the Secret Nine Month Investigation*, Vice News video documentary, 2019.
Irfan, Umair (2019). 'Fossil Fuels are underpriced by a whopping $5.2 trillion', *Vox*, 17 May.
The Iris Project, estab. 2006.
The Iron Triangle – The Carlyle Group Exposed, video based on book by Dan Brody, Hoboken, NJ: J. Wiley, 2004, YouTube, May 2012.
Jackson, Sarah (2015). 'The suffragettes weren't just white middle class women throwing stones', *The Guardian*, 12 October.
Jewish Virtual Library, 'Concentration Camps: How Many Camps? (1933–1945)'.
Jolly, Jasper (2018). 'Sorrell and RBS named in suit against Grenfell cladding maker', *The Guardian*, 20 December.
'Justin Welby', Wikipedia, 2019.
Kara, Sidharth (2018) 'Is your phone tainted by the misery of the 35,000 children in Congo's mines?', *The Guardian*, Modern Day Slavery Focus, Global Development, 12 October 2018.
'Keir Hardie (1856–1915)', Wikipedia, 2019.

Kuczera, Małgorzata, Simon Field and Hendrickje Catriona Windisch (2016). *Building Skills for All; A Review of England*, OECD Skills Studies, OECD.
The Labour Party Report (2019), *Land for the Many*, June.
Latham, Peter (2011). *The State and Local Government: Towards a New Basis For Local Democracy and the Defeat of Big Business Control*, London: Manifesto Press, 2011.
Lazarus, David (2018) 'Column: Where do prescription drugs come from? Good luck answering that question', *The Los Angeles Times*, 15 May 2018.
'LeBon, Gustave (1841–1931)', Wikipedia, 2019.
Lee, Dulcie (2018). 'How much government aid does a charity like Oxfam actually get?', *New Statesman*, 14 February.
'Les Adventures de Telemaque', Wikipedia, 2018.
Levine, Josie (ed.) (1990). *Developing Pedagogies in the Multi-lingual Classroom*, London: Falmer Press, 1990.
Lewis, Jason (2011). 'Lord Mandelson: secrets of a filthy rich fortune', *The Telegraph*, Investigations Editor, 17 December.
Lexden, Alistair (2015). 'A Tory Christan Warrior: The Seven the Earl of Shaftesbury', *alistairleaxden.org.uk/news/tory-christian-warrior-seventh-earl-Shaftesbury*, Official Historian of the Conservative Party, July 2015.
'Liberalism', *Encyclopaedia Britannica*.
Lightfoot, L. (2016). 'Nearly half of England's teachers plan to leave in next five years', *The Guardian*, 24 October.
'Literacy with an Attitude', Wikipedia, 2019.
Loach, Ken (2013). *The Spirit of '45*, Film 4, 15 March.
Maazi, Mohamed (2019). 'Waterstones shuts down book launch exposing the anti-semitism witch hunt against the left', *The Canary*, September 2019.
Macdonald, Callum (2007). *The Assassination of Reinhard Heydrich*, Chapters 1 and 2, Edinburgh: Birlinn, 2007.
Macintyre, Donald (2014). 'How the miners' strike of 1984–85 changed Britain for ever', *New Statesman*, American Edition, 16 June.
Made In Dagenham (2010). BBC Films & UK Film Council.
Major, Kyrsty (2016). 'Why are we so surprised that Boris Johnson lied when he's been sacked for lying twice before?' *The Independent*, 27 June.
Mansell, Warwick, and Louis Goddard (2014). 'Ofsted admits complaint about school's prior knowledge of inspections', *The Guardian*, 9 September.
Marcal, Katrine (2015). 'Paid or not, women have always contributed to the wealth of nations', *The Guardian*, 11 October.
'The Marcora law – Multiplying the employees' stakes' (2015), Wikipreneurship.
'Marshall Plan (1948)', Wikipedia, 2019.
Marx, Karl, and Friedrich Engels (1846). 'The German Ideology', Wikipedia, 2019.

Marx, Karl, and Friedrich Engels (1848). *The Communist Manifesto*, Cardiff: Cardiff Books, 2017.
Mason, Rowena (2017). 'What is David Cameron doing now?', *The Guardian*, 29 December.
Maynard, Lily (2019). 'Kool-Aid for Kiddies – teaching little ones about the gender fairy', lilymaynard.com blog, 29 June 2019.
Mazzucato, Mariana (2013). 'Government – investor, risktaker, innovator', TEDTalk, YouTube, 28 October.
Mazzucato, Mariana (2015). *The Entrepreneurial State*, London: Anthem Press.
McCoy, Alfred (2018). 'How the heroin trade explains the US–UK failure in Afghanistan', *The Guardian*, 9 January.
McEachern, Kelsey (2016). 'Vygotsky's Socio-cultural Theory', YouTube, October.
McIntosh, Alistair (2004) *Soil & Soul, People Versus Corporate Power*, London: Autumn Press.
McKenna, Tony (2017). 'Who funds the think tanks?', *New Internationalist*, 10 February.
McLoughlin, Bill (2019). 'Meghan and Harry's Frogmore refurb an "abuse of public money" as group attacks scandal', *Daily Express*, 27 June.
Marriot, Red (2009). 'Schoolkids against the Iraqi War', libcom.org, 8 March.
Media Reform Coalition, estab. 2011, June 2019.
MediaPlanet (2019). 'EdTech comes of Age – Future of Tech', Future of Technology.
Meek, James (2014). 'Sale of the century: the privatisation scam', *The Guardian*, 22 August.
Merrick, Rob (2016). 'David Cameron "ultimately responsible for Libya collapse and the rise of ISIS, Commons" report concludes', *The Independent*, 24 September.
'Military intervention in Libya, 2011', Wikipedia, 2019.
Milne, Seamus (2011). 'If the Libyan war was about saving lives, it was a catastrophic failure', *The Guardian*, 26 October.
Milne, Seamus (2014). 'During the miners' strike, Thatcher's secret state was the real enemy within', *The Guardian*, 3 October.
Mitchell, Neil (2018). 'The Hillsborough of British Business Renegade Inc.', Russia Today TV, April 2018.
Mitra, Sugata (2007). 'Kids can teach themselves', TED Talk at LIFT.
Modood, Tariq (2019). *Essays on Secularism and Multi-culturalism*, London: Rowman & Littlefield International.
Mollagh, Jason (2013). 'Palm oil for the West, Exploitation for Young Workers in Malaysia', *The Atlantic*, 9 April.
'The Moment of Truth' (2014), Auckland New Zealand Town Hall, YouTube, 15 September (starts 22 mins in).

Monbiot, George (2015). 'This flood was not only foretold – it was publicly subsidised', *The Guardian*, 29 December.
Monbiot, George (2017). 'The Grenfell inquiry will be a stitch up. Here's why', *The Guardian*, 5 July.
Monbiot, George (2018). 'David Attenborough has betrayed the living world he loves', *The Guardian*, 7 November.
Monbiot, George (2019). 'Want to tackle inequality? Our land laws have to change first', *The Guardian*, 4 June.
Moore, James (2018). 'RBS to face no action over GRG small business lending scandal as the banks get away with it again', *The Independent*, 31 July.
Moore, Michael, and Jeff Gibbs (2020) 'Planet of the humans', *YouTube*, 4 May 2020.
MSN News (2020). 'Boris Johnson admits he 'doesn't get' climate change, says sacked No 10 adviser', Joe Murphy 4 February.
'Murder of Stephen Lawrence ,1993', Wikipedia, 2019.
Murphy, Catherine (2012). 'Maestra – maestrathefilm.org (8 min. version)', YouTube, 31 August.
National Audit Office (2018). *Investigation into the government's handling of the collapse of Carillion*, 7 June.
National Literacy Trust (2017). *Adult Literacy*.
National Society for the Prevention of Cruelty to Children (2017). 'Exam stress overwhelming for thousands of children', 12 May.
Neate, Rupert (2018). 'Bet365 founder paid herself an "obscene" £265m in 2017', *The Guardian*, 21 November.
Neate, Rupert (2019). 'Outrage as help-to-buy boosts Persimmons profits to £1obn', *The Guardian*, 26 February.
Netflix Original Documentary Series, Silverback Film Production, *Our Planet*, 2019.
NetWorthPortal (2019). 'How Much is Joanna Lumley Worth Now?', (2019).
'New American Century (Complete)' (2013), YouTube, 7 November.
New Internationalist (2008). 'Nuclear weapons – the facts', 2 June.
'Noam Chomsky Interviews Richard Wolf on the State of Democracy' (2016), YouTube, November.
'Occupy Wall Street', Wikipedia, 2019.
Office for Standards in Education (2018). *Children's Services and Skills, Annual Report and Accounts, 2017–18*.
Office for Standards in Education, Ofsted, Gov. UK, 'About Us'.
Oliphant, Vickie (2017). 'Kensington Council gave richest £100 rebate – but cut corners on tower-bock safety', *Daily Express*, 20 June.
Oreskes and Conway (2010). *Merchants of Doubt: How a Handful of Scientists Obscured the Truth on Issues from Tobacco Smoking to Global Warming*, London: Bloomsbury, 2010.

Orwell, George (1945). *Animal Farm*, London: Penguin Modern Classics, 2000.
Osborne, Hilary (2018). 'Virgin awarded almost £2bn of NHS contracts in past five years', *The Guardian*, 5 August.
Oswald, Michael (2012). '97% Owned', positivemoney.org, May.
Oswald, Michael (2014). *The Princes of Yen, Central Bank Truth Documentary*, Queue Politely & Hushush video, 5 November.
Own the Change: Building Economic Democracy One Worker at a Time (2015), YouTube, 9 February.
Oxfam Report (2016). *How to Close Great Britain's Great Divide: The Business of Tackling Inequality*, 13 September.
'Panama Papers (2016)', Wikipedia, 2019.
Partington, Richard (2019). 'Boris Johnson's tax cut plans face squeeze as public finances worsen,' *The Guardian*, Economics Correspondent, 16 December.
Partington, Richard (2019). 'Rising level of corporate debt a risk to global economy – OECD', *The Guardian*, 25 February.
Peace Pledge Union (2019). 'Conscientious Objection in Britain', <http://www.ppu.orguk.coproject/guide>.
Pegg, David (2017). 'St Olave's head caught up in school trademark ownership row', *The Guardian*, 5 September.
Pegg, David, and Holly Watt (2016). 'Leaks reveal Amber Rudd's involvement in Bahamas offshore firms', *The Guardian*, 21 September.
Perraudin, Frances (2017). 'Furious parents say collapsing academy trust asset-stripped its schools of millions', *The Observer*, 22 October.
Pettifor, Anne (2017). 'Bailing out RBS', on *Renegade Inc.*, Russia Today, YouTube, 16 April.
Philpott, Tom (2013). 'No, GMOs didn't create India's farmer Suicide Problem, But ...', *Mother Jones*, 30 September.
Pilger, John (1979). *Year Zero: The Silent Death of Cambodia*, Independent Television documentary, 1979.
Perry, Sarah (2017). 'Charles Darwin: Victorian Mythmaker by A N Wilson, a review', *The Observer*, September.
Pettinger, Tejvan (2017). 'Who owns government debt?', *Economics Help*, 1 November.
Pilger, John (2017). 'Terror in Britain: What Did the Prime Minister Know?', Counterpunch.org, 31 May.
Plokhy, Serhii (2018). *Chernobyl, History of a Tragedy*, London: Allen Lane.
Positivemoney.org (2012). 'How Banks Create Money'.
Positivemoney.org (2014). 'How to Waste £375 Billion'.
Positivemoney.org (2014). 'Poll Results: Only 1 Out of 10 MPs Understand that Banks Create Money', 19 August.
Positivemoney.org (2014). 'Why Are house Prices so High?'

'Project for the New American Century', Wikipedia, 2019.
'Protests against intervention in Iraq, 2002/3', Wikipedia, 2019.
Provost, Clare, and Matt Kennon (2015). 'The obscure legal system that lets corporations sue countries', *The Guardian*, 10 June.
Rancière, Jacques (1991). *The Ignorant Schoolmaster, Five Lessons in Intellectual Emancipation*, Stanford, CA: Stanford University Press, 2016.
Reay, Diane (2017). *Miseducation*, Bristol: Policy Press.
Rennie, Jill (2020) 'Covid-19: Care homes forced to pay VAT on PPE but NHS is exempt', *carehome.co.uk*, 14 April 2020.
'The Rich List – the definitive guide to wealth' (2019), *Sunday Times*, May.
Right to Education Initiative (2016). 'Uganda judgement on the closure of Bridge International Academies must support a move towards fulfilling the right to education in Uganda and other countries', 10 November.
Rodway, C., *et al.* (2016). 'Suicide in children and young people in England: a consecutive case series', *The Lancet Psychiatry*, 3 August.
Rubtsov, Yuri (2018). 'History of World War II: Nazi Germany was financed by the Federal Reserve and the Bank of England', Global Research, Centre for Research on Globalisation, globalreserch.org.
Russia Today TV (2019). 'Branson's health service avoids UK corporation tax while racking up millions in NHS profits', 9 January.
Sabin, Lamiat (2020) 'Fury over Serco plan to exploit test and trace', *The Morning Star*, 6 June 2020.
Saddam Hussein – The Truth (Documentary) (2017), Marathon, A Sunset Press Production, YouTube, 10 April.
Sawyer, Jeremy (2014). 'Vygotsky's revolutionary theory of psychological development', *International Socialist Review*, Issue 93, Summer 2014.
Sayed, Nawal (2019). 'SEE Lists Yellow Vest's Demands to End Protests in France', *SEE News*, 9 April.
Scott, Callum A. (2018). 'What Darkest Hour doesn't tell you about Winston Churchill', *The Morning Star*. 12 January.
Shailer, Kirti, 'Biography of Adam Smith (With His Theories)', online student's blog. <http://www.economicsdiscussion.net/economists/biography-of-adam-smith-with-his-theories-economist/20999>.
Shaol, Jean (2020) 'UK government ties Transport for London bailout to "back to work" drive', *World Socialist Web Site*, 26 May 2020.
Sharman, Alice (2018). 'European Commission resumes awarding grants to Oxfam', Civil Society Media, London, 11 June.
Shepherd, Jessica (2010). 'Academies bill is anti-democratic, lawyers warn', *The Guardian*, June 2010.

Shiva, Vandana (2019) 'We must fight back against the 1 percent to stop the sixth mass extinction', *Democracy Now*, 22 February 2019.
Simkin, John (2017). 'The 1888 London Matchgirls Strike', *Spartacus Educational*.
Sinclair, Ian (2013). 'The march that shook Blair', *Peace News*, London.
Sinclair, Ian (2016). 'No, the intervention in Libya wasn't a success', Stop the War Coalition.
Singer, Andrew (1994). 'In Breast Implants Scandal, Where was Dow Corning's Concern for Women?', *Ethikos, Corporate Conduct Quarterly*.
Singh, Radhika, 'Malthusianism: Theories on Poverty & Aid', The Borgen Project blog (<http://www.borgenproject.org.malthusianism-theories-poverty-aid/>).
'Smedley Butler (1881–1940)', Wikiquote, 2019.
Smith, Adam (1776). *Invisible Hand*, Wiktionary, 2019.
Smith, Adrian (2014). 'The LUCAS Plan: what can it tell us about democratising society today?', *The Guardian*, 22 January.
Smith, Mikey (2016). 'What is Ed Balls doing now? Life after parliament for the self-tweeting ex – MP', *The Mirror*, 29 April.
Smyth, John, and Terry Wrigley (2013). *Living on the Edge, Rethinking Poverty, Class and School*, New York: Peter Lang.
Snyder, Susi, (2018). 'Don't Bank on the Bomb, A Global Report on the Financing of Nuclear Weapons Production', PAX, Netherlands, 2 March.
'Special documentary on France's "gilets jaunes" movement' (2018), euronews (in English), YouTube, 17 December.
'The Spider's Web: Britain's Second Empire' (2018), Documentary, YouTube, 4 September.
Spargo, Charlie (2020) 'Channel 4 stage #ClapForOurCarers ad takeover in partnership with 39 advertisers', *Prolific*, London, 27 March 2020.
Stewart, Heather, and Sarah Butler (2016). 'Damian Green says government's benefit cap is a "real success"', *The Guardian*, 7 November.
Stewart, Heather and Aamna Mohdin (2019). 'Boris Johnson 'hides in a fridge to avoid Piers Morgan interview', *The Guardian*, 11 December.
Stewart, William (2015). 'Why "Ultra-looney" ILEA Was Actually Ahead of its Time', *Times Educational Supplement*, 3 April.
Still, William (1996). *The Money Masters: How International Bankers Gained Control of America*, Still Productions, USA, 31 January.
Sweeney, Mark (2015) 'Entertainment One takes control of Peppa Pig creator in £140m deal', *The Guardian*, 30 September 2015.
Sweeney, Steve (2019). 'Italian dock stike blocks deadly cargo headed for Saudi Arabia', *The Morning Star*, 20 May.
Sutton, Anthony (1925–2002). 'Wall Street Funded the Bolshevik Revolution', YouTube Video, 17 October 2011.

Bibliography

Taylor, Mathew (2019). 'Much shorter working weeks needed to tackle climate crises – study. UK workers must move to nine-hour week if carbon levels do not change, says think tank', *The Guardian*, 22 May.
Taylor, Richard Norton (2013). 'Afghanistan war has cost Britain more than £37bn, new book claims', *The Guardian*, 30 May.
The Telegraph (2014). 'Five richest families in the UK worth more than the poorest 20 % in society', 17 March.
Thunberg, Greta et al. (2020). 'At Davos we will tell world leaders to abandon the fossil fuel industry', *The Guardian*, Opinion page, 10 January.
'Tomlinson, Ian: Death', Wikipedia, 2019.
Torossian, Ronn (2014). 'Hitler's Nazi Germany used an American PR Agency', *The Observer*, 22 December.
Townsend, Mark (2015). 'No convictions over 500 black and Asian deaths in custody', *The Guardian*, 21 March.
Treasury Parliamentary Select Committee Hearings (2016). 'Dominic Cummings April 2016, Parts 1 & 2,' YouTube, 30 August 2019.
Treasury Parliamentary Select Committee Hearings (2016). 'Dominic Cummings April 2016, Parts 1 & 2,' YouTube, 30 August 2019.
Tressell, Robert (1920). *The Ragged Trousered Philanthropists*, Hertfordshire: Wordsworth Classics, 2012.
Tweedie, James (2016). 'Kenya will crack down on Gate's filthy shack schools', *The Morning Star*, 7 December.
Tyrie, Andre (2016). 'Andre Tyrie grills Dom Cummings about NHS Leaflets', YouTube, 20 April.
Tyrie, Andre (2016). 'Andre Tyrie grills Dom Cummings about NHS Leaflets', YouTube, 20 April.
United Nations High Commission for Refugees (2015). *Worldwide displacement hits all-time high as war and persecution increase*, UNHCR Report, 18 June.
Upbin, Bruce (2011). 'The 147 Companies that Control Everything', *Forbes*, 22 October.
'Understanding the Mondragon Worker Cooperative Corporation' (2014), YouTube, April.
United Nations Conference on Trade and Development Update Report (2020), 'The Covid19 shock to developing countries: Towards a "whatever it takes" programme for the two-thirds of the world's population left behind', March 2020.
'Vanessa Beeley Interview – Yellow Vests, Police Violence & the Suppression of a Global Movement' (2019), posted by 'The Last American Vagabond', 28 January, YouTube.
Velo, Maria Montenegro (1991). *Literacy in Brazil: For What Purposes*? Working papers in Educational Linguistics (<https://wpel.gse.upenn.edu/sites/default/ files/ archives/ v7/ v7n1Velho1.pdf\o>).

Verity, Andy, and Jake Morris (2016). 'RBS squeezed struggling businesses to boost profits, leak reveals', *BBC Newsnight*, 10 October.
Volpe, Sam (2018). '"She is a martyr": 25 years on, Joy Gardner's mother is still fighting for justice after death in custody', *Ham & High*, 26 July.
Volpicelli, Gian (2020) 'Inside Dominic Cummings coronavirus meeting with big tech', *Wired*, 12 March 2020.
Vygotsky, Lev (1962). *Thought and Language*.
Vygotsky, Lev (1978). *Mind and Society*.
Walia, Arjun (2016). 'It's Not the Zika Virus – Doctors Link Monsanto Pesticides to Birth Defects', Prepare for Change Network, 16 February.
Walker, Peter (2017). 'Children's watchdog says millions at risk', *The Guardian*, 4 July.
Wallop, Harry (2017). 'Is our hunger for cheap white goods turning our homes into death traps?', *The Morning Star*, 1 December.
Watson, Robert, and Nigel Hawkes (2010). 'How many children are murdered in Britain every year?', *Straight Statistics*, 23 September.
Watt, Holly (2011). 'David Laws suspended over pages of expenses claims', *The Telegraph*, 12 May.
Watt, Holly, and Claire Newell (2011). 'Exam boards: Edexcel went from charity to £1bn business', *The Telegraph*, 9 December.
Werner, Richard (2003). *Princes of the Yen: The Central Bank Truth Documentary*, YouTube, 2014.
Werner, Richard (2011–19). The Free Lunch Videos & BlogSpot.
Werner, Richard (2014). 'Richard Werner On Banking and How Banks Create Money', YouTube, 2017.
Werner, Richard (2015). <https://professorwerner.org/blog/>.
Werner, Richard (2017). 'Prof. Werner brilliantly explains how the banking system and financial sector really work', *Renegade Inc.*, Russia Today, YouTube, 9 March.
White, Josh (2018). 'The Existence of Toby Young', *Souciant*, 5 January.
'White Collar Crime: Mind the Gap' (2017), *Renegade Inc.*, Russia Today TV, presented by Ross Ashcroft, 4 December.
'Why Worker Co-ops Don't Work (Sorta)' (2016), YouTube, August.
Wolff, Professor Richard D. (2020). 'Democracy at Work and Economic Updates', youtube.com/democracyatwrk/videos
World Health Organisation (2017). 'Almost half of all deaths now have a recorded cause, WHO data show', WHO Report, 17 May.
Wright, Oliver (2014). 'Academies criticised over payments to board members', *Independent*, 17 September.
Wrigley, Dr Terry (2013). 'Bad Science, Worse politics', *Socialist Review* (Issue 385) November 20.
'Yellow Socialism (Pierre Biètry 1902)', Wikipedia, 2019.

Bibliography

Yorke, Trevor (2018). 'Homes Fit for Heroes: The History of UK Housing', *Property investments UK*, 19 December.
Young, Michael (2001). 'Down with meritocracy', *The Guardian*, 29 June.
Zaritsky, John (2016). *No Limits, Thalidomide Story, Heinrich Mückter, High-ranking Nazi director Head of Research Grünenthal & Inventor of Thalidomide*, KB Productions Ltd, Canada Media Fund.
Zipes, Jack (1995). 'Breaking the Disney Spell', Academia.edu.

Additional References

Accessed by the World Wide Web, the following organisations provide information not readily available on mainstream media.

9/11 Truth.org.
Campaign Against the Armaments Trade.
Democracy at Work.
Democracy Now.
Educational International.
Extinction Rebellion.
Global Justice Now.
Going Underground with Afshin Rattansi, Russia Today.
The Independent Media Centre.
The Intercept.
The International Consortium for Investigative Journalists.
Index on Censorship
Media Reform Coalition.
Momentum.
The People's Assembly Against Austerity.
The Political Film Society.
Real Media
Ross Ashcroft's *Renegade Inc.* on Russia Today.
Stop the War Coalition.
War on Want.

Subject index

academisation of English State
    schools 180, 201–206
    Acts of Parliament 205
    asset stripping, illegal pupil selection
        and off-rolling 203–205
    imposition of business management
        model of School Effectiveness
        Movement 202
accountancy/consultancy firms cooking
    the books 63
adversarial TV interview
    technique 280–281
agri-business: chemical herbicides, fungi-
    cides, pesticides 67, 69
    farmer suicides 72
    genetically modified seeds 73
    global depletion of aquifer water 25
    glysophate and damage to human
        health 70–71
    green revolution 72
    loss of habitat and biodiversity 6,
        12, 69, 74
    soil degradation and effects on
        human health 71
    study of agribusiness absent from
        school curriculum 71
    terminator seeds 71
    top ten seed corporations control
        67% global seed market 72
    vitamin and mineral depletion in
        crops 70
agriculture, transformation of, eco-
    farming, rewilding 25, 26,
    285, 311

Arconic, manufacturer of fire-spreading
    Grenfell cladding 165
    shareholder lawsuit against banks
        underwriting of Arconic share
        issue 165
armaments trade profiteering 19, 38, 41,
    46, 49, 51, 64, 322
    Church of England investment in
        armament firms 144–145
    cryptocurrencies used to buy
        armaments 82
    trades unions and armaments
        factories 153,
austerity policies 39, 47–48, 53, 57–59,
    66, 78, 98, 150, 166, 263–265,
    272, 320
autonomous education xiv–xv, xviii
    see Gramsci, Antonio
    Age of Information 103
    educational structures mitigate against
        autonomous education xiv
    effects of socio-cultural relations on
        autonomous education inside
        and outside classrooms 257–258

bankers creating money from nothing,
    plus from interest-bearing
    finance 16, 18–19
    Bank of England poll: majority of
        UK MPs don't understand how
        national and global banking
        system works 60
    see *positivemoney.org*
    banking and limited public
        liability 19

early bankers and creation of stock markets 16
financial deregulation 36, 38
funding Hitler and Bolsheviks 20, 41
gold 11, 15, 16, 18,
usury 15, 144
banking system xv, 16, 20, 51, 56, 58–60, 66, 82, 99, 150, 242
battle for multi-functional literacy 117, 221, 227–228, 245, 253–257
Bernays, Edward 30, 101–103
Bhopal Chemical Plant disaster 75–77
  Dow Chemical and manufacturer of pesticides linked to brain underdevelopment in children 76
  Dow Chemical sponsorship of 2012 London Olympics 77
  Dow Corning subsidiary manufactures silicone breast implants causing systemic health problems 76
big technology 67–68, 82–85
  9 countries joint inventory 27,000 nuclear warheads 67
  31 countries with 440 nuclear energy plants 67
  blockchain and cryptocurrency capitalism 82–83
  Chernobyl nuclear plant catastrophe and Fukushima 68
  'end of history' tech revolution detached from reality 85
  Facebook and Google 82, 84, 85, 239, 293
  gadgets and offers that can't be refused 84
  petrochemical technology 69
  technology and inequality 85
  technology no substitute for sociobiological connection 85

tech-savvy activists 85
black civil rights and feminist movements, effects of 26
Black Lives Matter movement 322
Brexit 61, 275–278, 282, 284, 287, 288, 292
British royalty and UK taxpayers 163
  connection with Iraqi dictatorship 44
  media promotion of 240
  tax havens and unearned income 2

capitalism: unimagined possibilities, brutal exploitations 9–11
  mass media promotion of 'free-market' capitalism 7, 37, 111, 141
  social class and Marxist analysis of capitalism xiii–xiv
  trade agreements 7, 15, 50, 87–89, 263, 307–308
Carillion: corporate Ponzi scheme with Public Private Finance Initiative government collusion 232–233
  woman executive reveals the truth 232
charities' annual reports and gagging laws 167
  business model 169
  charitisation of jobs 168
  legislation needed to separate charities and businesses 172
  'reverse aid': 3 times more paid to West by poor countries than received in charitable donations and foreign aid 171
  sexual abuse and exploitation 170
Chilcot Inquiry into UK decision to go to war in Iraq 45
Children's literature 113, 117, 191, 221, 227, 313

Index 351

Chinese State capitalism "with Chinese characteristics" 90
   800 million of 1.4 billion population lifted out of poverty, huge levels of poverty remain 89
   exploitation of labour by male-dominated government-corporate matrix 26, 89–90
   global 'one belt, one road' global economic drive 89
   largest army in the world 90
   Mao Zedong speaks of socialism in Darwinian terms 137
   mass incarceration of Chinese Muslims 89–90
   mass surveillance: data capture used to award "social credit" score to all citizens 83
Chomsky, Noam 41
Church of England speaks against zero hours contracts but employs cleaners on zero hours contracts 145
   archbishop enjoys religious practice of speaking in tongues 146
   one of UK's highest earning investment bodies and has invested in armaments, gambling and pay-day loan firms 144
   privately educated archbishop head of C of E is former oil company executive 145
civil rights struggle and feminist movement, socio-cultural effects 26, 81, 92, 150
climate emergency xvii, 74, 86, 235
   environmental eugenicists 7, 237
   fossil fuels 284–285
   green 'solutions' and profiteering 69
   need to reduce global fossil fuel emissions to net-zero by 2025, UK sets target for 2050 instead xvii
   obfuscation of climate crisis in media and education system 235
   renewable green technologies and new 'green' jobs 69
   UN International Panel on Climate Change and US National Aeronautics and Space Administration 74
cobalt mining and communications technologies 314
colonialism: study of history must include colonialism, neo-colonialism, pervasiveness of sexism, racism and the struggles against domination xv
Conservative and Liberal Party 2020 coalition government 275
Conservative Party leader and prime minister 285–286, 292–293, 305
   London garden bridge 286
   track record as Mayor of London 286
communist Soviet Union totalitarianism 135–136
   Cuban communism and education system 254
COVID-19 292–298
   mass media culture during COVID-19 pandemic 303–304
   small contributions to COVID19 causes by the mega-rich compared to their billions 301

Darwin, Charles: evolutionary hypothesis 124–27
   chauvinism 127
   equating politico-economic inequality with intellectual degeneracy 127, 130
   illnesses 129
   molecular biology overturns Darwinian hypothesis 132–133

pseudo-scientific Darwinian
    thought pervades public
    consciousness 134
  race and women 127
  social-class position 127–128
  social Darwinism and Columbine
    achool shootings 139–141
  views on marriage 128
  wife opposed to theory of
    evolution 129–30
  worth of estate 129
Davitt, Helen 188
defective hypotheses: Darwin, Galton,
    Malthus, Smith 121–142
democracy 28, 92, 136, 211, 228, 233, 264
  democratic deficits 63, 95, 96, 149,
    209, 247, 261
  democratic socialism xv, xvi, xviii, 5,
    22, 75, 84, 86, 101, 106, 134 151,
    242, 248, 258, 260, 265–267, 270,
    281 305, 306
  House of Lords 75, 145, 149, 247
  MPs expenses scam 143, 209, 247,
    271–272
  MPs privately educated: 33%; twice as
    many male as female MPs 149
  need for political solidarity xvi, 53,
    81, 84, 134, 248
  need for regional and national consti-
    tutional assemblies 216, 267
  democratisation versus domination
    in education and communica-
    tions industries 113, 184, 188, 216,
    235–245, 238 , 243
  workplace democracy 229, 233, 242
democratic socialism xv, xvi, xviii, 5,
    22, 75, 84, 86 101, 134, 151, 242,
    247–248, 258, 260, 266–270, 281
    304–306
discussion-based learning 188, 197,
    258–259

bilingual pupils 105, 181–183,
    185, 187
collaborative learning 179, 182, 193,
    221, 260
equal opportunities and multi-
    cultural education 108, 180,
    183–184, 187, 192

educational apartheids 175–189
educational and socio-cultural
    capital 175, 251
university tuition fees 51, 262, 272
educational technology 211–213, 216
  Bridge International, The World
    Bank, global publisher, and
    UK Dept. for International
    Development 212
economists, new school: Mariana
    Mazzacato, Richard Werner,
    Richard D. Wolff 241–243
Engels, Friedrich 124, 165
  equates Darwin's 'discovery' of laws of
    development of organic life with
    Marx's discovery of 'discovery' of
    laws of development of human
    history 134
evolutionary hypothesis and Engels,
    Lenin, Marx, Trotsky, Stalin 130,
    135–137
  Mao Zedong 136–137
  Pol Pot 137–139
English National Curriculum, key
    stage test regime, school league
    tables 191–199
  School Effectiveness Movement 202
eugenicism 7, 29, 101, 125, 198, 236, 293
exclusions: religions, trade unions, polit-
    ical parties 320
Extinction Rebellion xvii–xviii, 39, 266

fascism 27–34
  against trade unionism 30

Index   353

concentration camps 30–31
demagogic frontmen for capitalist
    political economy 28
doctors and nurses killing the disabled and citizens labelled by
    Nazi government as 'useless
    eaters' 29
mass murder of millions of European
    Jews and millions of others 30
propagandising German racial
    supremacy 30
ruling class promotion of fascism as
    bulwark against communism 131
women in Nazi Germany 30
US Ku Klux Klan 31
UK royalty and ruling class embrace
    fascism 31, 130
fare-exchange-no-robbery trade 15, 306,
    309, 310, 315, 317
feudalism, resistance to landlordism 150
    leasehold property a hangover from
        feudal property law 163–164
feminist movement in UK 26, 92, 150
    effects of Match Girls' 1888 strike 91
    upper and middle-class suffragists 91
    working-class suffragettes 91
    women workers at Dagenham strike
        for equal pay 92
foreign aid 171–172, 308, 314
Fortress Europe 151, 274
free market trade deals and monopolies 283, 307–309
free movement of capital and
    labour 47, 273
Freire, Paulo and education for
    conscientisation 251–260
    'banking' education and top-down
        transmission teaching leads to
        failure in country-wide Brazilian
        literacy programme 252
    current Brazilian government wants
        rid of Freirean education 255

director of regional educational and
    social services authority with
    responsibility for differing levels
    and types of education 251
fascist coup: government declares
    Freire's education for freedom
    subversive, jailing Freire as
    traitor 255
success of theory and practice of
    education for freedom and
    conscientisation 253
western educational establishment's
    prejudice against Freirean
    education in First World
    contexts 259
UK school's misuse of Freirean
    education 255–256
French Yellow Vest activists' demands and
    methods xvii, 150–151, 266, 320

general election campaign
    donations UK 276
    use of social media advertising 280
global 2008 financial crash 53, 55–56, 89,
    262, 271, 272, 304
    quantitative easing 51, 57–59,
        242, 302
Gramsci, Antonio xiv, 4–5, 235
    effects of subject-separated silo
        thought and capitalism's
        hard and soft powers on
        consciousness xiv–xv, 5, 38
    theory of organic intellectualism and
        political vanguardism 5, 8, 135
Great Depression of 1930s xvi, 21–26, 154
    US global Marshall Plan to ward off
        communism 35
    US New Deal to ward off socialism
        in US 24
Greenpeace 'opposes' environmental
    damage in Borneo 6–7

capitalist causes of environmental
    damage unmentioned 7
Grenfell: corporate corruption 165
    ignoring residents' warnings about
        dangerous works 160, 161
    lobbyists and politicians of Red Tape
        Initiative meet on day of fire
        to cut more health and safety
        regulations 165–166
    local authority hoarding of
        wealth 162
    negligent fire risk assessor
        and toothless works
        inspections 159–160
    refusal of government to legislate for
        landlords to pay to replace dan-
        gerous cladding 321
    ruling class attitudes towards
        working-class tenants 162
    See Arconic
    social murder 165, 320

herd immunity 293
housing in the UK: post-WW1 pro-
        gramme of house- building to
        help stave off social unrest 153
    housebuilding to replace WW2
        bombed inner-city housing 154
    housing planning permission in-
        creases price of land and
        homes 157
    policy of government to rid itself of
        responsibility for social housing
        and create 'home-owning democ-
        racy' instead 154
    publically owned housing sold off to
        tenants at discount on market
        value 154
    Right to Buy (RTB) legislation pre-
        vents local authorities from
        building replacement social
        housing 155

RTB scheme benefits banks 155
social housing ends up in property
    portfolios of the wealthy 155
subsequent lack of affordable housing
    to buy or rent 157

imperialism 29, 108, 148
International Monetary Fund and The
    World Bank 36–38, 284, 309
    conditions of loans to poor coun-
        tries: privatise public
        services 36

Jacotot, Joseph, educational theory and
    practice 248–250
    task of educators is to help dis-
        close learner's intelligence to
        learner 249
    teacher explication of knowledge
        controls learners and compounds
        inequality 249
    theory of intelligence and acquisition
        of knowledge: 'everything is, in
        everything' 249

Labour Party 2019 Manifesto 51, 282–283
Labour Party defeat in 2010 and 'Red Ed'
    as new leader 273
Labour Party defeat in 2019 national
    elections 283
Labour Party proposals to boost economy
    and fund public services 262
    land tax 157, 262
    no plans to regulate private banking
        system 263
    policies not as revolutionary as
        Labour Party critics imply 263
    private schools and streaming in State
        schools to remain 263
language acquisition 105–108
    children are thinkers and learners
        from birth 106

Index   355

influence of socio-cultural
   biases 113–115
resistance to socio-cultural
   biases 116, 118–119
socio-biological imperatives language
   acquisition and of nurture and
   care xvi, 75, 106, 113,
socio-cultural biases in books and
   images 113–119
leasehold hangover from feudal property
   law 163–164
LeBon, Gustave 101
LGBTQ+ 'choice' to serve in the
   military 81
need for solidarity with other
   freedom movements 81–82
prejudices against LGBTQ+ results
   in separatist sexual politics 80
resistance to socio-cultural gender
   performance roles 80
self-chosen gender identity: switching
   performance roles 80
transphobia, accusations of 81
transsexualism 80–81
legal system 9, 88, 94, 150
Equal Pay Act of 1970 92
Equality Act 2010, includes right to
   religion and belief 257
imagine a legal system where it is
   criminal to practice economic
   injustice 148
Race Relations Act 91
Right to vote 1928 28
Sex Discrimination Act 92
symbols of legal power: blindfolded
   statue of woman holding scalesof
   justice and sword; judges' high
   benches, gowns, wigs, gavels;
   questionsand answers allowed,
   disallowed 148
Levine, Josie 180, 188

literacy development 109–120, 188,
   252–255
innate meta-literacy 228
multi-functional literacy 117, 221,
   223–228, 245, 253–257
reading 111–112, 116–117, 181, 207,
   224, 227, 244, 253
see Vygotsky, Lev
socio-cultural nature of literacy
   development 109–120
local authorities: budgetary and
   legal constraints 36, 37, 146,
   176, 264
central government slashes local authority grants 37
local authorities stripped of local
   democratic powers 37
local government implements central
   government austerity 37
'Red Tape Initiative': corporate
   lobbyists and politicians cutting
   of local and national regulations
   meant to protect public 166

Martin Luther King and socialism 22
Marx, Karl xiii, xiv, xviii, 124
   Marx sends Darwin copy of *Das
      Kapital* 134
mass media giant communications
   corporations 84
accuses Labour Party of
   anti-Semitism 279–280
analytical questions 303–304
Chinese communist surveillance
   system 83, 89
global commercial and governmental
   mass surveillance 97
opposition to surveillance 85, 97–98,
   213, 240
seduces audiences into passive
   spectatorship 243

socio-cultural manipulation 111
Soviet Union 136
UK surveillance equipment sold to Saudi Arabia 51
mass mobilisations 269–270
Mitra, Sugata 250–251
Mujica, Jose 247–248
multi-cultural and equal opportunities education 108, 180, 183–184, 187, 191

Nightingale hospitals 296

offshoring hidden wealth tax havens 1, 2, 3, 66, 86, 168, 207, 274, 309, 310, 315
 £200billion annual tax evasion results in massive underfunding of public services at home and abroad 2
 Britain's Second Empire 1
 British prime minister's family benefits from offshoring 2
 British Royalty 2
 capital flight of wealth from Third World countries 2
 government minister's prior tax haven job 3
 Panama Papers and *Paradise Papers* 2
 private school old-boy-network of tax haven wealth handlers 1
Ofsted, UK's Office for Standards in Education 203, 217–222
 30-point grid for school inspection procedures 220
 botched Ofsted investigation into death of vulnerable child 218–220
 budget and self-congratulation exercises 220–221

government 'reform' of academisation of schools 202–203
 illegal advance notice of school inspections 217–218
 Minister for Schools declares inspection procedures unsound 217
Olusoga, David 141, 169
outsourcing industries Preface xiii, 37, 166, 231–232

pandemic lockdown 293
 COVID-19 and care homes 301–303
 failed test-and-trace system 319
 government's mixed messages 316
 ventilators 294–295
Parliamentary Select Committee inquiry into educational failure of white working-class children 209
 expenses-claims-cheating Minister's keynote speech to PSC 209
 hidden curriculum and funding gap between private and State schools ignored by PSC 210
 social class prejudices of members of PSC 210
paedophilia 95, 145
personal protective equipment (PPE) 294, 295–296
pharmaceutical Industry 77–78, 150, 288, 298, 307
 massive increase in anti-depression drugs correlates with areas of unemployment and consequences of government austerity 78
politico-educational home needed for the 99% 266–267
 criteria for membership 267
politics of ego and entitlement built into UK

Index   357

government- banking- corporate-
   communications matrix 149
pollution of the planet 12, 25, 68, 74, 86,
   89, 133, 150, 264
   nuclear radiation 68, 133
pornography and politicians 143
   cryptocurrency funding production
      of pornography 82
   government minister sacked from
      cabinet for lying about viewing
      pornography on parliamentary
      computer remains a
      UK MP 63
positivemoney.org 39, 53, 55, 57–58, 60
privatisation: gov't sell-off of public services to shareholder-owned businesses through 'public-private
   finance initiatives' 36–38, 166,
   201–208, 232, 271
   high-cost failure of government's
      Public Private Finance
      Initiative 36–37, 232
   Tax-dodging corporation sues
      NHS for not awarding
      contract 79
propaganda 5, 29, 30, 37, 66, 76, 87, 101,
   103, 104
   advertising 7, 78, 235, 238
   cigarette industry 102
   crowd psychology 28–29, 30
   LeBon: eugenicist, misogynist crowd
      psychologist 101–103
   Nazis use crowd psychology
      propaganda 28–29, 30
   Propaganda, by Sigmund Freud's
      cousin, Edward Bernays, founder
      of modern public relations
      industry 102–103
   propaganda and obfuscation of sci-
      ence of climate disaster xvii, 3,
      49, 66, 74–75, 235, 237

propaganda and corporate-
   government-media
   matrix 103–104
prostitution 80
quest for peace 91–100
   9/11 Truth Org. 13, 96
   Campaign Against the Arms
      Trade 95
   Campaign for Nuclear
      Disarmament 95
   Greenham Common women's
      camp 95–96
   Lucas Plan 92–93
   national and global protests against
      Iraq war 44, 45, 116–117
   Occupy Movement: 'We are the
      99%' 96
   Stop-the-War Coalition 96, 266
   War on Want 95
   WW One and Two conscientious
      objectors refusal to kill 32

racism xv, 26, 28, 38, 114–115, 183, 184,
   261, 268
   police racism 94
Reay, Dianne 214
rentierism 11, 60, 84, 146, 155, 212, 231,
   266, 308
reverence for life, equal human rights and
   responsibilities xvi, xviii, 219,
   266, 267, 268, 281, 304, 323
reverse aid 171–173, 307–310 313–314,
Royal Bank of Scotland (RBS) 63, 65, 163
   £36 billion bailout of RBS during
      2008 global financial crash 64
   corrupt banking system feeds geno-
      cidal climate disaster 66
   fraudulent RBS Global Restructuring
      Group (GRG) 63–64
   MPs collective amnesia re complaints
      about RBS fraud 64

opposition shadow Treasury Minister states RBS fraudulent activity 'the largest theft anywhere, ever' 64
RBS investments in cluster munitions and nuclear weapons 65
toothless Financial Conduct Authority (FCA) says case against RBS unwinnable 65

sexism xv, 30, 38, 107 114, 115, 183, 184, 204, 268
sexual abuse and exploitation 82, 95, 170, 197, 218, 261, 309
slavery xv, 10, 20, 26, 30, 31, 91, 104, 122, 136, 138 141, 150, 180, 248, 308, 310, 314, 322
Smith, Adam 121–142
social class xiii, xvii, 1–8, 10, 75, 113, 114–115, 141, 147, 183–185, 193, 209, 210, 225, 276
    middle class xvi, 4, 10, 14, 21, 29, 89, 91, 102, 111, 112, 114, 116, 122, 129, 139, 141, 150, 154, 177, 184, 236, 239, 251, 270, 272, 278, 292, 302, 307
    ruling class xiii–xv, 10, 25, 28, 75, 270, 277, 286, 299–301, 305, 307–308, 310
    working class xiii–xvii, 1, 5, 8, 10, 11, 13, 27, 28, 32, 78, 87, 89, 91 107, 108, 113–117, 123, 142, 150, 153, 162, 184, 185, 208, 209–210, 223, 227, 236, 240, 245, 261, 263, 270, 272, 282, 306, 310, 315, 318, 319–320 321, 322
Spanish flu 293
strikes: 1888 Match Girls' Strike and effects on suffragettes 91
    miners' strike1984–85: politicised millions; defeat used by State to quash modern trade unionism 93–94
    need for trade unionism 318
    strikers in saris 93
    teachers and trade unionism xvii, 205, 214–216
    the few union representatives campaigning against job cuts reviled by school managers, local education authorities and trade union executives 214–215

think tanks 50, 166, 195
trade agreements 7, 35, 50, 87–88, 90, 263, 285, 307–308, 310

UK Independence Party 274
UK MPs' expenses scandal 143, 271
UK national elections of 2019, 274–280
UK parliamentary vote 269, 270
UK referendum to stay or leave the European Union 48, 220, 273–276, 283
USSR: fall of Soviet Union: 'reds under the beds' scare stories replaced by 'war on terror' 96

Vygotsky, Lev 109

Wars for geopolitical dominance over oil, gas and other resources 27, 41–54,
    Africa 52, 61, 89, 151, 185, 213, 266
    Afghanistan 42–43, 46, 50, 59
    Butler, Smedley: war profiteering 19–20
    Cambodia 137–139
    civilian slaughter 24, 27–28, 148, 153, 227

Index

government-military-industrial-corporate-media complex 5, 8, 52, 67, 81, 93, 102
Iraq 41–42, 44, 45, 46, 50, 59, 116–117, 271
Laos 137–139
Libya 42, 45–46, 50, 59
North Korea 33, 52, 59
Project for New American Century 41
refugees 12
social class nature of war: ratio of officer class, soldiers, civilians killed 27, 28
Syria 42, 43, 46, 48, 49, 50, 53, 321
terrorism v, 48, 82, 96
Vietnam 137, 139
Yemen 43
WW1 27–28, 29, 31–32, 127, 153, 154
WW2 11, 19, 21, 25, 28, 32, 35, 38, 52, 53, 78, 154, 169, 177, 178 180, 95, 229, 263
whistle-blowers: emotional, intellectual, moral, psychological choice 2, 97–98
Windrush generation 3, 169
workplace democracy 229–234
   Cleveland Evergreen Cooperative Group, USA 232–233
   Democracy at Work and Economic Update 242
   difference between worker-owned enterprises and capitalist businesses 229
   Italian Marcora Law 231, 233
   Japan 53
   Mondragon Corporation: global worker-owned business 229–230, 307
   myopic politicians advocating worker-owned enterprises provide below-cost public services self-defeating 229
   Preston UK 231
   worker-owned enterprises no substitute for provision of public services 229
written constitution 26, 281, 285